America Right or Wrong

An Anatomy of American Nationalism

ANATOL LIEVEN

UNIVERSITY PRESS

For Misha,
Born August 13, 2003:
Beloved Distraction

OXFORD
UNIVERSITY PRESS

Oxford University Press, Inc., publishes works that
further Oxford University's objective of excellence
in research, scholarship, and education.

Oxford   New York
Auckland   Cape Town   Dar es Salaam   Hong Kong   Karachi
Kuala Lumpur   Madrid   Melbourne   Mexico City   Nairobi
New Delhi   Shanghai   Taipei   Toronto

With offices in
Argentina   Austria   Brazil   Chile   Czech Republic   France   Greece
Guatemala   Hungary   Italy   Japan   Poland   Portugal   Singapore
South Korea   Switzerland   Thailand   Turkey   Ukraine   Vietnam

First published by Oxford University Press, Inc., 2004
198 Madison Avenue, New York, New York 10016
www.oup.com

First issued as an Oxford University Press paperback, 2005
ISBN-13: 978-0-19-530005-5   ISBN-10: 0-19-530005-X

Oxford is a registered trademark of Oxford University Press

The Library of Congress has cataloged the cloth edition as follows:
Lieven, Anatol.
    America right or wrong : an anatomy of American nationalism / by Anatol Lieven.
        p. cm.   Includes bibliographical references and index.
    ISBN-13: 978-0-19-516840-2   ISBN-10: 0-19-516840-2
1. National characteristics, American.
2. Nationalism—United States—History.
3. United States—Politics and government.
4. United States—Foreign relations.
5. United States—Foreign relations—2001–.
6. United States—Foreign relations—Middle East.
7. Middle East—Foreign relations—United States.
8. War on Terrorism, 2001–.
9. Intervention (International law). I. Title.
    E169.1.L53949   2004
    320.54'0973—dc22   2004012968

9 8 7 6 5 4 3 2
Printed in the United States of America on acid-free paper

Contents

Zwei seelen wohnen, ach! in meiner Brust.
(Two souls dwell, alas! within my breast.)

—Johann Wolfgang Goethe, *Faust*, Part I

Preface to the Paperback Edition

Republican victories in the presidential and congressional elections of November 2004, which took place after the publication of the cloth edition of this book in English, amply bear out its main theses. Above all, it was on the strength of a mixture of nationalism and an appeal to conservative religious sentiment that the Bush administration won those elections. Again and again, Republican representatives attacked Senator John Kerry and the Democrats in classically nationalist terms, for alleged weakness, cowardice, failure to defend the nation against its enemies, for allowing foreign views of American behavior any validity and foreigners any influence over American policies. In effect, as argued in this book, the Republican Party of the United States has become the American Nationalist Party.

The Republican Party's success lay in its ability to unite the aggrieved and vengeful nationalism stirred up by the terrorist attacks of 9/11 with other strong elements of the American tradition. Thus the first months of the new Bush administration further demonstrated the power of what I have called the American nationalist thesis, and have analyzed in the second chapter of this book: a widely shared and almost religious belief in the values of the "American Creed;" in America's role as the supreme exemplar of democratic civilization in the world; America's right and ability to spread its values to the rest of the world; and above all, of faith in democracy. George W. Bush, like Ronald Reagan before him, won a second term in part because he and his advisers were able to express and exploit national myths, which are believed in by the great majority of Americans. In doing so the Bush administration not only gained votes itself, but also disabled the Democratic Party, forcing it in several areas of debate to become a paler shadow of the Republicans.

The messianic aspect of American civic nationalism dominated Bush's inaugural address of February 2, 2005. In his words,

> America's vital interests and our deepest beliefs are now one. From the day of our Founding, we have proclaimed that every man and woman on this earth has rights, and dignity, and matchless value, because they bear the image of the Maker of Heaven and earth. Across the generations we have proclaimed the imperative of self-government, because no one is fit to be a master, and

no one deserves to be a slave. Advancing these ideals is the mission that created our Nation. It is the honorable achievement of our fathers. Now it is the urgent requirement of our nation's security, and the calling of our time.

So it is the policy of the United States to seek and support the growth of democratic movements and institutions in every nation and culture, with the ultimate goal of ending tyranny in our world. . . . History has an ebb and flow of justice, but history also has a visible direction, set by liberty and the Author of Liberty.

Since 9/11 and during the 2004 elections, the rhetoric of Bush and many of his followers melded secular messianism with an appeal to the old belief in America as a country chosen by God, and in American power as divinely sanctioned. These themes were played upon incessantly in speeches by Bush and other Republican leaders from 9/11 up to and beyond the elections of 2004. This specifically religious belief in America's character and destiny has roots that predate not only the foundation of the American republic, but the arrival of the first White settlers in North America.

These settlers brought with them from sixteenth- and seventeenth-century England and Scotland a belief in these countries as "God's New Israel", islands of Protestant faith and civilization in a damnable Catholic sea, analogous to the Amelekites and Philistines who besieged ancient Israel. This religiously derived tradition feeds into what I have called the troop of myths attendant on the American Creed, myths of American innocence, goodness, benevolence, and inevitable triumph.

Together, these various elements contribute to a nationalist mixture of singular potency. As the 2004 elections demonstrated, this nationalism helps to exclude many arguments and opinions from public discourse in America, concerning foreign and domestic policy. In the domestic arena, it is extremely difficult to suggest that any aspects of the American system are worse than those of other countries, or that America could learn from other countries. To do so would attract charges of lack of national pride and of "apologizing for America."

Most American values are not bad in and of themselves. On the contrary, as this book repeatedly emphasizes, they are immensely positive, and their example has been and should be of inestimable importance to mankind. But as Louis Hartz and other great U.S. thinkers have emphasized, Americans' absolutist faith in those values and in America as the representative of them risks infusing disputes between America and other nations with a frightening self-righteousness on the American side.

Equally important is the way in which this mixture feeds American solipsism, and a difficulty in understanding or even recognizing the interests and views of other nations. This nationalist mixture which works so well electorally inside America tends to be greeted with incomprehension, alarm, and even contempt by many foreigners (although in some cases, including France, memories of their own historical attitudes should at least diminish the incomprehension). A German newspaper headline responded sardonically to Bush's inaugural address: "Bush Threatens: Even More Freedom!" ("*Bush Droht: Noch Mehr Freiheit*")

This mutual incomprehension is especially strong when it comes to belief in America's mission to spread democracy, and the way in which this was made the centerpiece of the Bush administration's political strategy in the Middle East. To a great many Americans the value of democracy and America's sincerity in wishing to promote it is self-evident. As a result, Americans are too often genuinely incapable of seeing that given both U.S. policies in the region today and in the past, American professions of a desire to spread democracy are hardly believable to many Muslims.

Bush's own extraordinary mixture of the desire to democratize the Arab world and absolute indifference to Arab public opinion was demonstrated by his public reliance for much of his democratizing rhetoric on the hardline Israeli minister (and former Soviet dissident) Natan Sharansky. Sharansky's absolute contempt for Palestinian rights has made him a hated figure among a great many Arabs. However, much more important is the fact that his views and behavior blatantly contradict any real respect for "democracy."

This is a contradiction that affects many Democrats just as thoroughly as it does Republicans. The "liberal hawks" whom I describe in Chapter 2 share to a considerable extent the neo-conservative program in the Middle East, of the expansion of American power and the destruction of rival states coupled with the rhetoric of democracy and progress. And like the neoconservatives, the Democratic hawks' emphasis on the lack of democracy in the Middle East is also a convenient way of ignoring the issue of American responsibility for Israeli policies and America's lack of action in promoting an Israeli-Palestinian settlement.

It is important to stress these elements in American nationalism which are shared by both parties so that the Bush victory of 2004 is not seen in too apocalyptic terms. In fact, when it comes to strategy in the Middle East at least, the policies of a Kerry administration might well not have differed very much from those of the Bush administration in its second term.

This similarity, however, is not only due to the strong elements of common ideology in the main American parties, but also because the more extreme forms of that ideology are usually held in check in both parties by the deep strains of pragmatism and realism in the U.S. political tradition that are described and analyzed in Chapter 5. As I point out, neither the Bush administration nor the U.S. establishment in general can be described as "Napoleonic", in the sense of being driven by the nature of their domestic system to seek wildly for one military victory after another. Nor is this in any sense desired by the great majority of Americans, as the increasingly skeptical response to the dragged-out war in Iraq demonstrates. There are would-be Napoleonic elements among the so-called neoconservatives, but by the Spring of 2005 their influence appeared to be in decline.

The realism which tempers American ideological nationalism was demonstrated between 2001 and 2004 most notably in Bush administration's policy towards China. Even before 9/11, the Bush administration was beginning to turn from what had been an extremely dangerous strategy of confronting and containing China to one of pragmatic and moderate realism, very close to that previously followed by Bill Clinton. Indeed, in the second presidential debate of 2004 Bush was entirely sincere when he pointed out that his administration had (belatedly) adopted a multilateralist approach to the question of North Korea's nuclear program, and had above all relied on China to bring influence to bear on Pyongyang.

A similar realism has colored the Bush administration's policy towards Russia. The administration certainly acted quite strongly to deter Russian pressure on Ukraine and Georgia. Equally, however, it has to date rejected pressure from the U.S. Congress (Democrats as well as Republicans) and from powerful lobbies in Congress to "punish" the Putin administration for undemocratic moves by expelling Russia from the G-8 and other international bodies. Instead, at the Bratislava Summit with Putin in February 2004, Bush sought and achieved pragmatic agreement on a number of practical issues.

The central flaw in the Bush administration's realism is not particular to that administration, but is characteristic of the realist philosophy as a whole. This flaw lies in a certain innate tendency to see the world as characterized by opposition and actual or potential hostility between states, rather than by a potential for cooperation, generated by a common stake in the capitalist world system, and finally, to see this opposition as the most important single element in the international system. This element in the thinking of the U.S. establishment was tremendously fuelled by the Cold War and the military, economic, bureaucratic, and academic structures that it created.

The malign consequences of this are twofold. In the first place, while the realist approach may find ample room for pragmatic cooperation with individual states, it contains a built in bias against thinking of the international system as a whole in terms of cooperation. Second, this approach tends to be utterly blind to threats to the international order and indeed to modern civilization which stem from outside traditional realist categories, global warming being the most notable example. In this sense, contemporary American realism might be compared to that of Metternich and his school—sometimes technically brilliant, but incapable of understanding the new world growing up around them.

In the now centrally important field of the struggle against Islamist terrorism, and of relations with the Muslim world, American realism also finds itself limited, and even to a degree disabled, by the nature of America's relationship with Israel. In the elections of 2004, for reasons analyzed in Chapter 6, Kerry and his team vied with Bush in declaring their unconditional support for Israel, in denouncing Palestinian terrorism, and in demanding that the Palestinians adopt full democracy as a precondition for a peace settlement. As a result, there was in fact no debate on the terms of the U.S.-Israeli alliance in the election campaign of 2004. The Democrats therefore essentially collaborated with the Republicans in denying to the American electorate the ability to consider issues vital to their safety and interests.

In its policy towards the Middle East American fundamentalist Protestantism has its worst effect on U.S. policy because of the widespread belief in apocalyptically-minded sections of Protestantism that Israel has to rule over all the lands given to the Jews by God in the Old Testament if the Christian Messiah is to return. The alliance between the Christian Right and Israeli hardliners has become a serious force in the Republican Party and a serious obstacle to any realistically conceivable Israeli-Palestinian peace.

In general, however, the impact of the Christian Right on U.S. politics should not be described either as in some way unnatural, or as inherently bad. Given the profound religious faith of so many Americans, it is entirely natural that this force should find an outlet in politics. Furthermore, many conservative religious beliefs about society and morality are correct. Much of modern mass culture is indeed repellent, inhuman and evil. Belief in and support for the family does indeed have to be at the heart of any civilized and decent version of society, whether conservative, liberal or socialist.

The danger from conservative religion, today as throughout modern history across much of the world, lies rather in its frequent association with social groups and political forces which react not only against the negative features of modernity but against modernity in general. In the case of the United States these are rooted in declining sections of the White middle classes in the American heartland, whose feelings of alienation and resentment are liable to find partial expression in radically conservative versions of religion. Such socio-economic resentment very frequently finds expression in varieties of national chauvinism, whether directed against internal or external enemies. Religious groups threatened by modern cultural change and social, economic, and ethnic groups threatened by social and economic change are natural allies and are indeed very often one and the same; their suffering and alienation naturally creates a strong capacity for embittered hatred.

This potent and poisonous mixture has too often posed a serious threat to peace abroad and democracy at home. It is a mixture fuelled by the disruptive effects of capitalist change, but because it can be directed against the Left, other alien elements at home, and against national enemies abroad, it has very often also served the interests of capitalist elites and been exploited by them.

This mixture is all too evidently at work in the United States. Of course, it does not characterize the whole country, and it should certainly not be regarded as a conclusive statement of the American identity. Very large numbers of Americans are bitterly opposed to the Christian Right and to its association with chauvinist nationalism. The Bush vote of 51 percent in 2004, on a turnout of 59 percent, is hardly a landslide; it represents after all less than one third of the total electorate. Christian conservatism is therefore not a dominant force in the United States as a whole, and may be in long-term historical decline. It is however politically dominant in the greater South and parts of the Midwest, and this gives it tremendous power within the Republican Party.

All this tends to suggest that the policies followed by the Bush administration, and the political culture which this administration reflects, will play a central part in American relations with the world for many years to come. If—God forbid—America once again suffers a massive terrorist attack, American political culture

may generate tendencies that are truly menacing to American values, American democracy, and American hegemony in the world. But even if no such catastrophe occurs, the particular nature of American nationalism will go on largely defining American policies and attitudes for the foreseeable future.
Washington, D.C., March 2005

Preface

P art of the genesis of this book lies in a conversation at a U.S. Embassy party in May 1989 in Islamabad, Pakistan, where I was then working as a stringer for *The Times* (London), covering both Pakistani affairs and the war in Afghanistan from the side of the mujahideen. The party was in honor of a newly arrived U.S. diplomat, who to the best of my recollection had never worked in Pakistan or any other Muslim country before.

I backed up a colleague, Kathy Gannon of the Associated Press, in criticizing U.S. policy on Afghanistan. We argued that especially now that the Soviet forces had left, the United States' giving massive financial and military aid to Pakistan so that its secret service could help mujahideen groups of its choice was lunacy. The groups in question (we were thinking at the time chiefly of Gulbuddin Hekmatyar, who since the overthrow of the Taliban has emerged as an anti-American warlord) and their Arab allies were not only a serious threat to peace and progress in Afghanistan, they were pathologically anti-Western.

To this the U.S. diplomat replied that because of his access to intelligence sources, his knowledge of Afghanistan was greater than ours (we had both visited Afghanistan repeatedly with the mujahideen, Kathy for much longer and much more often than I; he had never been there). He said that he was confident that the Afghan resistance was going to build a "successful free market democracy" in Afghanistan. When these arguments were demolished, others emerged: that the destruction of the Soviet-backed regime in Kabul was essential to "defeat communism" in the world and that "the Russians did it to us in Vietnam, and we're going to do it to them in Afghanistan." Finally, he declared in exasperation that Kathy and I were "the kind of people who lost us Vietnam."

This diatribe encapsulated many of the features of American nationalism addressed in this book. They include the belief of the national security elite that its access to intelligence makes it supremely wise and well informed—despite repeated and catastrophic evidence to the contrary. The belief in the democratization of Afghanistan by the mujahideen reflected a messianism rooted in the American Creed but was accompanied by a total ignorance of Afghan history, society, tradition or reality in general.

And the stance of this U.S. representative reflected not only ideology, but a profound indifference verging on contempt. To him, the Afghans were really only a tool against the Soviets, and their ultimate fate was unimportant. This belief was later reflected in U.S. policy toward Afghanistan after the fall of the Soviet Union—or rather lack of policy, for the country was simply abandoned to be torn apart by the mujahideen groups which the United States and its Pakistani allies had armed and financed. Incredibly, this indifference has been replicated again after the overthrow of the Taliban, with American attention and aid immediately diverted into preparations for war with Iraq.

Policy toward Afghanistan in the 1980s was cloaked in a sickly and completely unreal idealistic language of democratization and progress, but as this diplomat's words make clear, it was in fact motivated by a totally different and very unidealistic mixture of crude and cynical realism (rolling back Soviet influence) and revenge for American defeat in Vietnam. Finally, Western critics of this policy, even those who had demonstrated both knowledge of and commitment to Afghanistan, were demonized as weaklings and traitors.

The ultimate result of this U.S. approach of course was the rise of the Taliban, their alliance with al Qaeda and the events of September 11, 2001. Coming on top of defeat in Vietnam, this disaster should have been enough to produce a serious examination among the U.S. policy elites not only of past U.S. policies, but of the American political cultures which helped to produce them. In fact, as the genesis and conduct of the Iraq War have demonstrated, large sections of those elites have learned precisely *nothing* from the folly and wickedness of their past conduct. And this failure is above all because they have been blocked from doing so by certain key features of American nationalism, features which are examined in this book.

During the Battle of Jutland in 1916, when three British battle cruisers in succession blew up under German fire, Vice Admiral Sir David Beatty, commanding the Battle Cruiser Squadron, drawled to his chief of staff, "Chadwick, there seems to be something wrong with our bloody ships today," before (apocryphally) giving the order to engage the enemy more closely. As many critics have remarked, Beatty should have added, "And with our bloody system." The Royal Navy failed to analyze what was wrong with its system, and its ships went on sinking unnecessarily. Over the past forty years, the United States has stumbled into one disastrously misconceived military intervention after another, both large (Vietnam, Iraq) and small (Lebanon, Somalia). It is time that more Americans begin to ask themselves just what is wrong with their bloody system.

This book should in no sense be read as an attack either on a reasonable American nationalism or on the war on terrorism in its original form of a struggle against al Qaeda and its allies. As I shall argue throughout this book, American civic nationalism is a central support of American power and influence in the world, and has tremendously positive lessons to offer to humanity. I strongly supported the war in Afghanistan to defeat the Taliban and al Qaeda. Indeed, it was largely due to my knowledge of the extremely precarious state of both post-Taliban Afghanistan and Pakistan that I was so horrified by the decision to spread the war to Iraq. I am no pacifist; I also supported the Falklands War, the Gulf War of 1991 and the military intervention in Bosnia, and I will support such wars again in future. But quite apart from issues of legality and legitimacy, military campaigns have to be backed by an intelligent political strategy. As the history of the U.S. occupation of Iraq in particular demonstrates, the conduct of the war against terrorism looks more like a baroque apotheosis of political stupidity.

The most important target of this book is Americans themselves. I hope that in a small way, this work may do something to influence the policy debate in the United States by revealing some of the underlying myths and historical, cultural and ideological impulses which drive U.S. thinking and U.S. policy. However, this book is being published not only in the United States but in Britain, and it also is being translated into French, Italian, Japanese and Korean. I have therefore had to explain in some detail a number of things about the United States which will be familiar to educated American audiences, and for this I ask pardon.

Many people have generously helped with advice during the writing of this book. It would not have been possible without the unstinting help and support of Natasha Fairweather, of A. P. Watt, who worked tremendously hard to find publishers for a highly controversial manuscript, and was a great source of encouragement and strength in moments of discouragement. Tim Bartlett, of Oxford University Press, Michael Fishwick, of HarperCollins, and Charlotte Cachin-Liebert, of Lattes, have been not only supportive but have given critically important advice on the book's form.

A great debt of gratitude is owed to Michael Lind and Stephen Holmes, who gave me the benefit of their profound insights into the American tradition and encouraged me to persevere with this project. Owen Harries, Andrew Bacevich, Bill Maynes, Tom Hughes, William Pfaff, Norman Birnbaum, Stephen Walt, Michael Kraig, Adam Shatz, Justin Vaisse, Tom Geoghehan, Marina Ottaway, Minxin Pei, Robert Tombs, Andrew Gumbel, Charles King and my brother, D. C. B. Lieven, all very generously took the time to advise me on one or another part of the manuscript. In Chapter 6, concerning the U.S.-Israeli relationship, David Chambers of the Middle East Institute in Washington was of inestimable help, as were Brian Klug, Suzanne Goldenberg, Stephen Beller and James Zogby. Responsibility for the statements and arguments made in the book is of course entirely my own. The faculty and fellow students of Troy State University, Alabama, showed me great kindness and hospitality during my stay there in 1979.

I am extremely thankful to Jessica Mathews, president of the Carnegie Endowment for International Peace, for allowing me to embark on this book, and to my colleagues at the Carnegie Endowment for their help and support. Ann Stecker preserved some remnants of order in my working life. Rashed Chowdhury and

Zhanara Nauruzbayeva worked tremendously hard and diligently on the research. Their intelligence, insights and perspectives were also a great help to me. Amanda Muller helped gather much information on American domestic politics. Special thanks are due to Kathleen Higgs and the staff of the Carnegie Library. Not only were they superbly efficient in procuring books, but they were extremely patient with a combination of bizarre-sounding requests and extreme lateness in returns.

Finally, my gratitude and love go to Sasha, who bore the twin burdens of a new baby and a book-writing husband with her customary grace.

America Right or Wrong

Introduction

At first sight there is something surprising in this strange unrest of so many happy men, restless in the midst of abundance.

—Alexis de Tocqueville[1]

T raumatized by the terrorist attacks of September 11, 2001, Americans very naturally reacted by falling back on old patterns of belief and behavior. Among these patterns has been American nationalism. This nationalism embodies beliefs and principles of great and permanent value for America and the world, but it also contains very great dangers. Aspects of American nationalism imperil both the nation's global leadership and its success in the struggle against Islamist terrorism and revolution.

More than any other factor, it is the nature and extent of this nationalism which at the start of the twenty-first century divides the United States from a largely postnationalist Western Europe. Certain neoconservative and Realist writers have argued that American behavior in the world and American differences with Europe stem simply from the nation's possession of greater power and responsibility. It would be truer to say that this power enables America to do certain things. What it does, and how it reacts to the behavior of others, is dictated by America's political culture, of which different strands of nationalism form a critically important part.

Insofar as American nationalism has become mixed up with a chauvinist version of Israeli nationalism, it also plays an absolutely disastrous role in U.S. relations with the Muslim world and in fueling terrorism. One might say, therefore, that while America keeps a splendid and welcoming house, it also keeps a family of demons in its cellar. Usually kept under certain restraints, these demons were released by 9/11.

America enjoys more global power than any previous state. It dominates the world not only militarily, but also to a great extent culturally and economically, and derives immense national benefits from the current world system. Following the death of communism as an alternative version of modernization, American

1

free market liberal democracy also enjoys ideological hegemony over the world. According to all precedents, therefore, the United States ought to be behaving as a conservative hegemon, defending the existing international order and spreading its values by example. After all, following World War II, the United States itself played the leading part in creating the institutions which between 2001 and 2003 the Bush administration sought to undermine.[2]

Instead, under George W. Bush the nation was drawn toward the role of an unsatisfied and even revolutionary power, kicking to pieces the hill of which it is the king. In particular, many observers saw the idea of preventive war against potential threats (rather than preemptive war against imminent ones) as a decisive shift not only to unilateralism, but to a revolutionary, anti–status quo position in international affairs, a position reminiscent of Wilhelmine Germany before 1914 rather than Victorian Britain.[3]

This book seeks to help explain why a country which after the terrorist attacks of September 11, 2001, had the chance to create a concert of all the world's major states—including Muslim ones—against Islamist revolutionary terrorism chose instead to pursue policies which divided the West, further alienated the Muslim world and exposed America itself to greatly increased danger. The most important reason why this has occurred is the character of American nationalism, which in this book I analyze as a complex, multifaceted set of elements in the nation's political culture.

As a study of political culture and its historical origins, this book is not intended to provide a detailed explanation of particular events or decisions, any more than a study of Russian or German nationalism is intended to set out the immediate reasons why the Tsar or the Kaiser took the steps they did in July and August of 1914. Rather, such studies try to provide the ideological and cultural context which made such decisions possible. In the case of the United States, I hope to help to explain why many Americans reacted as they did to the terrorist attacks of 9/11 and why it was possible for the Bush administration later to extend the war on terrorism to Iraq and retain the support of a majority of Americans. The intellectual, cultural and political traditions examined in this book also provide the background to America's reaction in future if—as seems all too likely—this country once again comes under massive attack.

Nationalism has not been the usual prism through which American behavior has been viewed. Most Americans speak of their attachment to their country as patriotism or, in an extreme form, superpatriotism. Critics of the United States, at home and abroad, tend to focus on what has been called American imperialism. The United States today does harbor important forces which can be called imperialist in their outlook and aims. However, although large in influence, people holding these views are relatively few in number. They are to be found above all in overlapping sections of the intelligentsia and the foreign policy and security establishments, with a particular concentration among the so-called neoconservatives.

Unlike large numbers of Englishmen, Frenchmen and others at the time of their empires, the vast majority of ordinary Americans do not think of themselves as imperialist or as possessing an empire. As the aftermath of the Iraq War seems to be demonstrating, they are also not prepared to make the massive long-term commitments and sacrifices necessary to maintain a direct American empire in the Middle East and elsewhere.

Apart from the effects of modern culture on attitudes to military service and sacrifice, American culture historically has embodied a strong strain of isolationism. This isolationism is, however, a complex phenomenon which should not be understood simply as a desire to withdraw from the world. Rather, American isolationism forms another face of both American chauvinism and American messianism, in the form of a belief in America as a unique city on a hill. As a result, it is closely related to nationalist unilateralism in international affairs, since it forms part of a view that if the United States really has no choice at all but to involve itself with disgusting and inferior foreigners, it must absolutely control the process and must under no circumstances subject itself to foreign control or even advice.

Unlike previous empires, the U.S. national identity and what has been called the American Creed are founded on adherence to democracy. However imperfectly democracy may be practiced at home and hypocritically preached abroad, this democratic faith does set real limits to how far the United States can exert direct rule over other peoples. Therefore, since 1945 the United States has been an indirect empire, resembling more closely the Dutch in the East Indies in the seventeenth and eighteenth centuries than the British in India.

As far as the mass of the American people is concerned, even an indirect American empire is still an empire in denial. In presenting its imperial plans to the American people, the Bush administration has been careful to package them as something else: on one hand, as part of a benevolent strategy of spreading American values of democracy and freedom; on the other, as an essential part of the defense not of an American empire, but of the nation itself.

A great many Americans are not only intensely nationalistic, but bellicose in their response to any perceived attack or slight against the United States: "Don't Tread on Me!" as the rattlesnake on the American revolutionary flag declared. This attitude was summed up by that American nationalist icon, John Wayne, in his last role, as a dying gunfighter in the film *The Shootist*: "I won't be wronged, I won't be insulted, and I won't be laid a hand on. I don't do these things to other people, and I require the same from them."[4]

As an expression of pride, honor and a capacity for self-defense, these are sympathetic and indeed admirable words. However, in this context it is useful to remember an eighteenth-century expression, "to trail one's coat." This phrase means deliberately provoking a quarrel by allowing your coat to trail along the ground, so that another man would step on it, thereby allowing you to challenge him to a duel. One might say that American imperialists trail America's coat across the whole world while most ordinary Americans are not looking and rely on those same Americans to react with "don't tread on me" nationalist fury when the coat is trodden on.

Coupled with an intense national solipsism and ignorance of the outside world among the American public, and with particular American prejudices against the religion of Islam, this bellicose nationalism has allowed a catastrophic extension of the war on terrorism from its original—and legitimate—targets of al Qaeda and the Taliban to embrace the Iraqi Ba'athist regime, anti-Israeli groups in Palestine and Lebanon and quite possibly other countries and forces in future. This reserve of embittered nationalism has also been tapped with regard to a wide range of international proposals which can be portrayed as hurting America or infringing on its national sovereignty, from the International Criminal Court to restrictions on greenhouse gas emissions.

A mixture of American energy interests and the addiction of most Americans to the automobile might well have killed the nation's adherence to the Kyoto Treaty in any case. The treaty's American opponents were however tremendously helped by that section of opinion whose political culture means that they see any international treaty involving sacrifices and commitments by the United States as a plot by hostile and deceitful aliens. Many Americans genuinely believe these ideas to be a matter of self-defense—of their economy, their way of life, their freedoms or their very nation.

This background helps explain tragicomic statistics such as the fact that the majority of Americans believe that their country spends more than 20 percent of its budget on foreign aid and that this figure should be reduced; the true figure is less than 1 percent and is the lowest in the developed world. Evidence like this allows international critics of American hegemony to portray the nation as a purely selfish imperial power, without generosity and without real vision. This pattern is strange, and very sad, when contrasted with the tremendous generosity of many Americans when it comes to domestic and private charity, and brings out the degree to which chauvinist nationalism can undermine even the noblest of impulses.[5]

Under the administration of George W. Bush (Bush Jr.) the United States drove toward empire, but the domestic political fuel fed into the engine was that of a wounded and vengeful nationalism. After 9/11, this sentiment is entirely sincere as far as most Americans are concerned, and it is all the more dangerous for that. In fact, to judge by world history, there is probably no more dangerous element in the entire nationalist mix than a sense of righteous victimhood. In the past this sentiment helped wreck Germany, Serbia and numerous other countries, and it is now in the process of wrecking Israel.

The Two Souls of American Nationalism

Like other nationalisms, American nationalism has many different faces, and this book does not pretend to explore all of them. Rather, it concentrates on what I take to be the two most important elements in the historical culture of American nationalism and the complex relationship between them. Erik Erikson wrote that "every national character is constructed out of polarities."[6] As I shall show, this is certainly true of the United States, which embodies among other things both the most modern *and* the most traditionalist society in the developed world.

The clash between those societies is contributing to the growing political polarization of American society. At the time of this writing, the American people are more sharply and more evenly divided along party lines than at any time in modern history. This political division in turn reflects greater differences in social and cultural attitudes than at any time since the Vietnam War. White evangelical Protestants vote Republican rather than Democrat by a factor of almost two to one, with corresponding effects on the parties' stances on abortion and other moral issues. The gap is almost as great when it comes to nationalism, with 71 percent of Republicans in 2003 describing themselves as "very patriotic" compared to 48 percent of Democrats. This difference reflects in part racial political allegiances, with 65 percent of Whites describing themselves as "very patriotic" in that year to only 38 percent of Blacks. Gaps concerning attitudes to crime and faith in American business are even greater.[7]

It is however not the opposition, but the combination of these different strands which determines the overall nature of the American national identity and largely shapes American attitudes and policies toward the outside world. This combination was demonstrated by the Bush administration, which, as Chapter 5 explores, drew its rhetoric at least from both main strands of American nationalism simultaneously.

The first of these strands in American nationalism is examined in Chapter 2. It stems from what has been called the "American Creed," an idea I also describe as the "American Thesis": the set of great democratic, legal and individualist beliefs and principles on which the American state and constitution is founded. These principles form the foundation of American civic nationalism and also help bind the United States to the wider community of democratic states. They are shared with other democratic societies, but in America they have a special role in holding a disparate nation together. As the term "Creed" implies, they are held with an ideological and almost religious fervor.

The second element forms what I have called the American nationalist "antithesis," and stems above all from ethnoreligious roots. Aspects of this tradition have also been called "Jacksonian nationalism," after President Andrew Jackson (1767–1845), and are explored in Chapters 3 and 4.[8] Because the United States is so large and complex compared to other countries, and has changed so much over time, this nationalist tradition is correspondingly complex.

Rather than the simple, monolithic identity of a Polish or Thai ethnoreligious nationalism, this tradition in the United States forms a diffuse mass of identities and impulses, including nativist sentiments on the part of America's original White population, the particular culture of the White South and the beliefs and agendas of ethnic lobbies. Nonetheless, these nationalist features can often be clearly distinguished from the principles of the American Creed and of American civic nationalism; and although many of their features are specifically American—notably, the role of fundamentalist Protestantism—they are also related to wider patterns of ethnoreligious nationalism in the world.

These strands in American nationalism are usually subordinate to American civic nationalism stemming from the Creed, which dominates official and public political culture. However, they have a natural tendency to rise to the surface in times of crisis and conflict. In the specific case of America's attachment to Israel, ethnoreligious factors have become dominant, with extremely dangerous consequences for the war on terrorism.

The reason why "civic nationalism," rather than "patriotism," is the appropriate name for the dominant strand in American political culture was well summed up in 1983 by one of the fathers of the neoconservative school in the United States, Irving Kristol: "Patriotism springs from love of the nation's past; nationalism arises out of hope for the nation's future, distinctive greatness....The goals of American foreign policy must go well beyond a narrow, too literal definition of 'national security.' It is the national interest of a world power, as this is defined by a sense of national destiny."[9]

In drawing this distinction, Kristol echoed a classic distinction between patriotism and nationalism delineated by Kenneth Minogue, one of the great historians of nationalism. Minogue defined patriotism as essentially conservative, a desire to defend one's country as it actually is; whereas nationalism is a devotion to an ideal, abstract, unrealized notion of one's country, often coupled with a belief in some wider national mission to humanity. In other words, nationalism has always had a certain revolutionary edge to it. In American political culture at the start of the twenty-first century, there is certainly a very strong element of patriotism, of attachment to American institutions and to America in its present form; but as Kristol's words indicate, there is also a revolutionary element, a commitment to a messianic vision of the nation and its role in the world.[10] This aspect of American civic nationalism is examined in Chapter 2.

As the American historian and social critic Richard Hofstadter (1917–1970) wrote, "The most prominent and pervasive failing [of American political culture] is a certain proneness to fits of moral crusading that would be fatal if they were not sooner or later tempered with a measure of apathy and common sense."[11] This pattern has indeed repeated itself in our time, with the aftermath of the Iraq War leading to a new sobriety in American policies and the American public mood. In the meantime, however, the Bush administration's appeal to this crusading and messianic spirit had played a major part in getting the nation into Iraq in the first place.

If Minogue's and Kristol's distinction between patriotism and nationalism is valid, then it must be acknowledged that nationalism, rather than patriotism, is the correct word with which to describe the characteristic national feeling of Americans. And this feature also links the American nationalism of today to the unsatisfied, late-coming nationalisms of Germany, Italy and Russia, rather than to the satisfied and status-quo patriotism of the British. Thus this feature helps explain the strangely unsatisfied, Wilhelmine air of U.S. policy and attitudes at the start of the twenty-first century.

But if one strand of American nationalism is radical because it looks forward to "the nation's future, distinctive greatness," another is radical because it continuously looks backward, to a vanished and idealized national past. This "American antithesis" is a central feature of American radical conservatism: the world of the Republican Right and especially the Christian Right, with their rhetoric of "taking back" America and restoring an older, purer American society. As explored in Chapters 3 and 4, this long-standing tendency in American culture and politics reflects the continuing conservative religiosity of many Americans; however, it also has always been an expression of social, economic, ethnic and above all racial anxieties.

In part, these anxieties stem from the progressive loss of control over society by the "original" White Anglo-Saxon and Scots Irish populations, later joined by others. Connected to these concerns are class anxieties—in the past, the hostility of the small towns and countryside to the new immigrant-populated cities; today, the economic decline of the traditional White working classes. As a result of economic, cultural and demographic change, in America, the supremely victorious nation of the modern age, large numbers of Americans feel defeated. The domestic anxieties which this feeling of defeat generates spill over into attitudes to the outside world, with 64 percent of Americans in 2002 agreeing that "our way of life needs to be protected against foreign influence," compared to 51 percent of British and 53 percent of French. These figures lie between those for Western Europe and those for developing world countries such as India (76 percent)— which is piquant, because the "foreign influence" that Indian and other cultural nationalists in the developing world most fear is, of course, that of the United States.[12]

These fears help give many American nationalists their curiously embittered, mean-spirited and defensive edge, so curiously at variance with America's image and self-image as a land of success, openness, wealth and generosity. Over the years, the hatred generated by this sense of defeat and alienation has been extended to both domestic and foreign enemies.

This too is a very old pattern in different nationalisms worldwide. Historically speaking, in Europe at least, radical conservatism and nationalism have tended to stem from classes and groups in actual or perceived decline as a result of socioeconomic change. One way of looking at American nationalism and the troubled relationship with the contemporary world which the nation dominates is indeed to understand that many Americans are in revolt against the world which America itself has made.

However, except for the extreme fringe among the various "militia" groups, the neo-Nazis and so on, these forces of the American antithesis are not in public revolt against the American Creed and American civic nationalism as such.[13] Most radical nationalist and radical conservative movements elsewhere in the world have in the past at least opposed democracy and demanded authoritarian rule. By contrast, Americans from this tradition generally believe strongly in the American democratic and liberal Creed. However, they also believe—consciously or unconsciously, openly or in private—that it is the product of a specific White Christian American civilization, and that both are threatened by immigration, racial minorities and foreign influence. And I am not saying that they are necessarily wrong; a discussion of this point lies outside the scope of this book. I am only pointing out that people with this belief naturally feel embattled, embittered and defensive as a result of many contemporary trends.[14]

American Protestant fundamentalist groups also do not reject the Creed as such. In terms of their attitude to culture and the intellect, however, their rejection of contemporary America is even deeper, for they reject key aspects of modernity itself. For them modern American mass culture is a form of daily assault on their passionately held values, and their reactionary religious ideology in turn reflects the sense of social, cultural and racial embattlement among their White middle-class constituency. Even as America is marketing the American Dream to the world, at home many Americans feel that they are living in an American nightmare.[15]

America is the home of by far the most deep, widespread and conservative religious belief in the Western world, including a section possessed by wild millenarian hopes, fears and hatreds—and these two phenomena are intimately related. As a Pew Research Center Survey of 2002 demonstrates, at the start of the twenty-first century the United States as a whole is much closer to the developing world in terms of religious belief than to the industrialized countries (although a majority of believers in the United States are not fundamentalist Protestants but Catholics and "mainline," more liberal Protestants). The importance of religion in the contemporary United States continues a pattern evident since the early nineteenth century and remarked by Alexis de Tocqueville in the 1830s, when religious belief among the European populations had been shaken by several decades of the Enlightenment and the French Revolution but American religious belief was fervent and nearly universal.[16]

As of 2002, with 59 percent of respondents declaring that "religion plays a very important role in their lives," the United States lies between Mexico (57 percent) and Turkey (65 percent) but is very far from Canada (30 percent), Italy (27 percent), or Japan (12 percent). In terms of sheer percentage points, it is indeed closer on this scale to Pakistan (91 percent) than to France (12 percent).[17] As of 1990, 69 percent of Americans believed in the personal existence of the Devil, compared to less than half that number of Britons.[18]

When a U.S. senator exclaimed (apocryphally) of the Europeans, "What common values? They don't even go to church!" he was expressing a truth, and this is as true of the U.S. political elites (but not of the cultural or economic ones) as of the population in general. Among the fundamentalist Protestant sections of the United States, there has been a strong historical inclination to a paranoid style, originally directed against Catholics, Freemasons and others, and perpetuated by the Cold War and the communist threat.[19] In our own time, "the recent Evangelical engagement with public life reflects religious and cultural habits that Anglo-American Protestants, both liberal and Evangelical, learned when threatened by Americans of different religious and ethnic backgrounds."[20]

The extreme tension between these fundamentalist religious values and the modern American mass culture which now surrounds them is an important cause of the mood of beleaguered hysteria on the American Right which so bewilders outside observers. Across large areas of America, these religious beliefs in turn form a central part of the identity of the original White American colonist population, above all in the Greater South, or what former First Lady Lady Bird Johnson described simply as "*us*—the simple American stock."[21]

The religious beliefs of large sections of this core population are under constant, daily threat from modern secular culture, above all via the mass media. And perhaps of equal importance in the long term will be the relative decline in recent decades in the real incomes of the American middle classes, where these groups are situated socially. This decline and the wider economic changes which began with the oil shock of 1973 have had the side effect of helping force more and more women to go to work, thereby undermining traditional family structures even among those groups most devoted to them.

The relationship between this traditional White Protestant world on one hand and the forces of American economic, demographic, social and cultural change on the other may be compared to the genesis of a hurricane. A mass of warm, humid air rises from the constantly churning sea of American capitalism to meet a mass of cooler layers of air, and as it rises it sucks in yet more air from the sides, in the form of immigration. The cooler layers are made up of the White middle classes and their small-town and suburban worlds in much of the United States; the old White populations of the Greater South with their specific culture; and the especially frigid strata of old Anglo-Saxon and Scots Irish fundamentalist Protestantism.

The result of this collision is the release of great bolts and explosions of political and cultural electricity. Like a hurricane, the resulting storm system is essentially circular, continually chasing its own tail, and essentially self-supporting, generating its own energy—until, at some unforeseeable point in future, either the boiling seas of economic change cool down or the strata of religious belief and traditional culture dissolve. Among these bolts is hatred, including nationalist hatred.[22]

Externally directed chauvinist hatred must therefore be seen as a byproduct of the same hatred displayed by the American Right at home, notably in their pathological loathing of President Bill Clinton. In Europe, Clinton was generally seen as a version of Tony Blair, a centrist who "modernized" his formerly center-Left party by stealing most of the clothes of the center-Right and adopting a largely right-wing economic agenda. To radical conservatives in America, this was irrelevant. They hated him not for what he *did*, but for what he *is*: the representative of a multiracial, pluralist and modernist culture and cultural elite which they both despise and fear, just as they hate the atheist, decadent, unmanly Western European nations not only for what they do, but for what they are.

In the U.S. context it is also crucial to remember that as in a hurricane or thunderstorm, rather than simply being opposing forces, the two elements which combine to produce this system work together. In a curious paradox, the unrestrained free market capitalism which is threatening the old conservative religious and cultural communities of Protestant America with dissolution is being urged on by the political representatives of those same communities.[23]

This was not always so. In the 1890s and 1900s, this sector of America formed the backbone of the Populist protest against the excesses of American capitalism, and in the 1930s, it voted solidly for Roosevelt's New Deal. Today, however, the religious Right has allied itself solidly with extreme free market forces in the Republican Party—although it is precisely the workings of unrestrained American capitalism which are eroding the world the religious conservatives wish to defend.

The forces of radical capitalism in the United States may come to depend more and more on appeals to radical conservatism and nationalism to win votes and to defend their class interests. As Chapter 1 describes, a number of aspects of the United States resemble the Western Europe of 1904 more closely than they do the rest of the developed world in 2004. Among these aspects is the radical character of American capitalism, as reflected in many of the policies of the Bush administration.[24]

The clash between cultural and social loyalties and the imperatives of capitalist change is an old dilemma for those social and cultural conservatives who at the same time are dedicated to the preservation of free market economics. As the distinguished U.S. political and ethical thinker Garry Wills has noted, "There is nothing less conservative than capitalism, so itchy for the new."[25] Karl Marx wrote of the inexorably shattering effects of capitalism on traditional societies in words which remind us that "globalization" and consequent unending and disruptive change are as old as capitalism itself:

> The bourgeoisie cannot exist without constantly revolutionizing the instruments of production, and thereby the relations of production, and with them the whole relations of society.... All fixed, fast, frozen relations with their train of ancient and venerable prejudices and opinions, are swept away; all new-formed ones become antiquated before they can ossify. All that is solid melts into air, all that is holy is profaned, and man is at last compelled to face with his sober senses his real conditions of life and his relations with his kind...the bourgeoisie has through its exploitation of the world market given a cosmopolitan character to production and consumption in every country. To the great chagrin of Reactionists, it has drawn from under the feet of industry the national ground on which it stood. All old established national industries have been destroyed or are daily being destroyed....[26]

A vital function of myth in political culture is to reconcile such conflicting pressures, or rather to create an appearance of doing so which is sufficiently convincing to the society concerned.[27] Chapter 2 examines how American national and nationalist myths do so in the case of the contemporary United States.

The Threat to American Hegemony

Because of a deep-rooted (and partly justified) belief in American exceptionalism and the decline of the study of history in American academia, Americans are not used to studying their own nationalism in a Western historical context—and it is vitally important that they begin to do so. For surely no sane person, looking at the history of nationalist Europe in the century prior to 1945, would suggest that the United States should voluntarily follow such a path. In particular, American nationalism is beginning to conflict very seriously with any enlightened, viable or even rational version of American imperialism; that is to say, with the interests of the United States as world hegemon and heir to the roles of ancient Rome and China within their respective regions.

Nationalism provides one clue to the difference between the strategy and philosophy of Clinton and those of George W. Bush and to the difference between an American approach which seeks legitimacy for American hegemony and one which makes a public cult of the unrestrained exercise of American will.[28]

A number of highly distinguished American and other observers have, however, seen little basic difference between the international policies of Clinton and Bush. People on the Left view the policies of all U.S. administrations as reflecting above all the enduring dynamics and requirements of an imperial version of American capitalism: the domination of the world by capitalism and the primacy of the United States within the capitalist system.[29] This analysis is indeed partly true, but in emphasizing common goals, left-wing analysts have a tendency to lose sight of certain other highly important factors: the means used to achieve these ends; the difference between intelligent and stupid means; and the extent to which the choice of means is influenced by irrational sentiments which are irrelevant or even contrary to the goals pursued. Of the irrational sentiments which have contributed to wrecking intelligent capitalist strategies—not only today, but for most of modern history—the most important and dangerous is nationalism.

Walter Russell Mead, an American nationalist and no Marxist, sees Bush's globalization of the Monroe Doctrine as a process stretching back to World War II. Andrew Bacevich and Chalmers Johnson, basing their work in part on the analysis of the economic and institutional roots of American imperialism by William Appleman Williams, also see the administrations of Clinton and Bush as characterized by an essential continuity when it comes to the extension of American power.[30]

For them, Bush's Iraq is just Clinton's Kosovo or Haiti on a much larger scale and with greatly increased risks. Clinton after all moved rather quickly to combat Russia's plans to retain a sphere of influence on the territory of the former Soviet Union and was not too scrupulous about the regimes he helped in the process. Clinton preserved the North Atlantic Treaty Organization (NATO) as what was then seen as the essential vehicle of U.S. strategic dominance in Europe and, as Basevich argues, fought the Kosovo war largely to justify NATO's continued existence as this vehicle.

Clinton, however, although dedicated to American hegemony, was not an American chauvinist. His vision of global order involved American hegemonic leadership rather than dictation and a desire to "place America at the center of every network" rather than simply to dictate in every situation. This at least was certainly the perception of his critics on the American Right, one of whose leaders accused Clinton of "moving us incrementally into a network of global organizations."[31]

This desire to exercise American leadership through international institutions is an important strand in American international policy dating back to World War II. It stems in part from a conscious determination not to repeat the U.S. mistake of withdrawal from the world after 1919 and in part from the international needs and perceptions of American capitalism. Thus although partisans of the Bush administration repeatedly described its rhetoric of democratization and humanitarian intervention after 2001 as Wilsonian, such an attribution is quite wrong in historical terms, for President Woodrow Wilson also believed passionately in the creation of international institutions and in exerting U.S. power and influence through those institutions. Clinton, not Bush, therefore was the true Wilsonian of our time.

Moreover, Clinton's version of American hegemonic leadership, although often resented by the leaders of other states, was nonetheless far more acceptable to most than Bush's approach from 2001 to 2003. Clinton's strategy was detested by Russians and others who saw its content as a threat to their geopolitical interests and its democratizing language as arrogant, mendacious and hypocritical. Nonetheless, it was greatly preferred by most world governments to the Bush administration's approach in its first three years of power, since it paid some attention to their interests and, equally important, did not publicly humiliate them before their own populations by demanding ostentatiously servile displays of deference and obedience.[32]

The dominant forces of the Bush administration in 2001–2003 were much more overt imperialists than their predecessors.[33] Moreover, in response to their own sentiments but also to appeal to the American people, they made things worse by packaging imperialism as American nationalism, thereby adopting a number of gratuitously unilateralist measures and approaches. And this was no pose or piece of cynical manipulation of American nationalism. Bush, his leading officials and his intellectual and media supporters are genuinely motivated by nationalism, in a way that Clinton was not; and as nationalists, they are absolutely contemptuous of any global order involving any check whatsoever on American behavior and interests.

The harshly nationalist character of the Bush administration was evident from its coming to power at the start of 2001. A whole set of moves bitterly alienated much of the rest of the world and created a level of hostility to the administration in Europe which contributed greatly to the later rejection of the Iraq War by large majorities in most European countries.[34] As antiterrorism coordinator Richard Clarke remarked presciently in the summer of 2001, "If these guys in this administration are going to want an international coalition to invade Iraq next year, they are sure not making a lot of friends."[35]

The rejection of vital international treaties on arms control seemed motivated by a blind nationalist desire for absolute American freedom of action and increased dangers to the United States from terrorism using weapons of mass destruction. The spirit behind these moves was described by John Bolton, later under secretary of state for arms control and international security, as "Americanism," but nationalism is a simpler description.[36]

However, many Americans seemed to have no great problem with this. As of the winter of 2004, 46 percent of respondents to a poll said that the Bush administration was adequately taking into account the interests and views of U.S. allies, while 18 percent actually said it was too accommodating in this regard. Only 30 percent said that it was too dismissive of allies' concerns. The difference between these beliefs and public perceptions elsewhere was simply staggering, with even 61 percent of British citizens declaring in March 2004 that "the US pays little or no attention to their country's interests in making its foreign policy decisions."[37]

Most damaging of all to U.S. prestige in Europe was the outright rejection of the Kyoto Protocol on greenhouse gas emissions and the abandonment of early attempts by U.S. officials to find a substitute—a decision taken in a way which displayed utter contempt both for the international community and American allies in Europe, but also for moderate sections of Bush's own administration. This indifference to environmental threats will probably also be the strongest criticism leveled at the United States and its hegemony by future generations. The attitude to environmental policy displayed by the Bush administration therefore undermines the United States not only today, but in its role as the new Rome, a civilizational force transcending the current epoch.

For coupled with the growing craze for gas-guzzling sport utility vehicles (SUVs) in the U.S. middle classes, this more than anything else seemed to suggest that Americans are interested in using their power over the planet purely for their own most selfish and shortsighted interests and that talk of wider U.S. responsibilities was utter hypocrisy.[38] The former Energy Secretary Paul O'Neill attributed the White House decision on Kyoto to a feeling of "the base likes this and who the hell knows anyway"—not a sentiment calculated to increase faith in American leadership and decision making elsewhere in the world.[39]

In the vision set out in its new National Security Strategy of 2002 (NSS 2002), embodying the so-called Bush Doctrine, American sovereignty was to remain absolute and unqualified. The sovereignty of other countries, however, was to be heavily qualified by America, and no other country was to be allowed a sphere of influence, even in its own neighborhood. In this conception, "balance of power"— a phrase used repeatedly in the NSS—was a form of Orwellian doublespeak. The clear intention actually was to be so strong that other countries had no choice but to rally to the side of the United States, concentrating all real power and freedom of action in the hands of America.[40]

This approach was basically an attempt to extend a tough, interventionist version of the Monroe Doctrine (the "Roosevelt Corollary" to the Doctrine, laid down by President Theodore Roosevelt) to the entire world.[41] This plan is megalomaniac, completely impracticable (as the occupation of Iraq has shown) and totally unacceptable to most of the world. Because, however, this program was expressed in traditional American nationalist terms of self-defense and the messianic role of the United States in spreading freedom, many Americans found it entirely acceptable and indeed natural.[42]

The accusation against the Bush administration then is that like the European elites before 1914, it has allowed its own national chauvinism and limitless ambition to compromise the security and stability of the world capitalist system of which America is the custodian and greatest beneficiary. In other words, members of the administration have been irresponsible and dangerous not in Marxist terms, but in their own. They have offended against the Capitalist Peace.

This difference is terribly important from the point of view of the stability of the world and of U.S. hegemony in the world. A relatively benign version of American hegemony is by no means unacceptable to many people around the world—both because they often have neighbors whom they fear more than America and because their elites are to an increasing extent integrated into a global capitalist elite whose values are largely defined by those of America. But American imperial power in the service of narrow American (and Israeli) nationalism is a very different matter and is an extremely unstable base for hegemony. It involves power over the world without accepting any responsibility for global problems and the effects of U.S. behavior on other countries—and power without responsibility was defined by Rudyard Kipling as "the prerogative of the harlot throughout the ages."

American nationalism has already played a key role in preventing America from taking advantage of the uniquely beneficent world-historical moment following the fall of communism. As Chapter 5 argues, instead of using this moment to create a "concert of powers" in support of regulated capitalist growth, world stability and the relief of poverty, preventable disease and other social ills, nationalism has helped direct America into a search for new enemies.

Such nationalism may encourage its adherents to cultivate not only specific national hatreds, but also hostility to all ideals, goals, movements, laws and institutions which aim to transcend the nation and speak for the general interests of humankind. This form of nationalism is therefore in direct opposition to the universalist ideals and ambitions of the American Creed—ideals upon which, in the end, rests America's role as a great civilizational empire and heir to Rome and China, and upon which is based America's claim to represent a positive example to the world. These ideals form the core of what Joseph Nye has called "soft power" in its specifically American form.[43]

Even some self-styled American liberals have argued that faced with a monstrous threat, such as that of international terrorism, American intellectuals have no choice but to close ranks in patriotic defense of their countries. The response to this was given in 1928 by Julien Benda in *La Trahison des Clercs* (The Treason of the Intellectuals), in which he described the corruption of European intellectuals by nationalism and, in doing so, warned of still greater catastrophes which were to come: "I shall be told that during the past fifty years…the attitude of foreigners to France was such that the most violent national partiality was forced upon all Frenchmen who wished to safeguard the nation, and that the only true patriots are those who have consented to this fanaticism. I say nothing to the contrary; I only say that the intellectuals who indulged in this fanaticism betrayed their duty, which is precisely to set up a corporation whose sole cult is that of justice and truth."[44]

Nationalism therefore risks undermining precisely those American values which make the nation most admired in the world and which in the end provide both a pillar for its current global power and the assurance that future ages will look back on it as a benign and positive leader of humanity.

The historical evidence of the dangers of unreflecting nationalist sentiments should be all too obvious and are all too relevant to U.S. policy today. Nationalism thrives on irrational hatreds and on the portrayal of other nations or ethnoreligious groups as congenitally, irredeemably wicked and hostile. Yesterday many American nationalists felt this way about Russia. Today, prejudices are likely to be directed against the Arab and Muslim worlds—and to a lesser extent any country that defies American wishes. Hence the astonishing explosion of chauvinism directed against France and Germany in the run-up to the war in Iraq.

In a striking essay, the Lebanese American scholar Fouad Ajami in 2003 unwittingly summed up the central danger of chauvinist American nationalism in imperial guise for the United States and the world, and also placed this nationalism squarely in the context of nationalist and imperialist history. The only specifically American aspect of his approach is Ajami's own non-American origins—and even this would have been entirely normal for great civilizational empires of the past. As Chapter 1 discusses, like America today, these empires did not distinguish between the racial origins of their subjects as long as they served the imperial state and accepted unreservedly the imperial ideology. To take a historical example from the Middle East, Ajami could be seen as a contemporary Arab Josephus working as an imperial propagandist for America's Rome.[45]

Ajami's essay ostensibly concerned anti-Americanism. He dismissed out of hand the evidence of Pew, Gallup and other respected survey organizations which demonstrate that hostility to America mounted greatly as a result of the policies of the Bush administration. Instead, Ajami argued, across the world—not just in the Arab and Muslim worlds, but in Europe, Asia and Latin America too—anti-Americanism is congenital, ingrained and a response to U.S. wealth, success and modernity, which is forcing other countries to change their systems. Ajami suggests that U.S. policies are completely irrelevant to international attitudes to the United States and that the sympathy displayed by France and other countries after 9/11 was completely hypocritical: "To maintain France's sympathy, and that of

15

Le Monde, the United States would have had to turn the other cheek to the murderers of Al Qaeda, spare the Taleban, and engage the Muslim World in some high civilisational dialogue. But who needs high approval ratings in Marseille?"[46]

Ajami's argument was taken up in an even cruder form in an article for *Time* magazine by leading right-wing commentator Charles Krauthammer, entitled simply "To Hell With Sympathy." In this he attacked "the world" and sought to tar his domestic political opponents with the same anti-American brush: "The world apparently likes the US when it is on its knees. From that the Democrats deduce a foreign policy—remain on our knees, humble and supplicant, and enjoy the applause and "support" of the world....The search for logic in anti-Americanism is fruitless. It is in the air the world breathes. Its roots are envy and self-loathing—by peoples who, yearning for modernity but having failed at it, find their one satisfaction in despising modernity's great exemplar. On September 11th, they gave it a rest for one day. Big deal."[47]

Or in the words of Phyllis Schlafly, one of the leaders of the Christian Right, in 1998, concerning Clinton's desire to sign a range of international treaties:

> Global treaties and conferences are a direct threat to every American citizen....The Senate should reject all UN treaties out of hand. Every single one would reduce our rights, freedom and sovereignty. That goes for treaties on the child, women, an international court, the sea, trade, biodiversity, global warming, and heritage sites....
>
> Our Declaration of Independence and Constitution are the fountainhead of the freedom and prosperity Americans enjoy. We Americans have a constitutional republic so unique, so precious, so successful that it would be total folly to put our necks in a yoke with any other nation. St Paul warns us (II Corinthians 6.14): "Be ye not unequally yoked together with unbelievers, for what fellowship hath righteousness with unrighteousness? And what communion hath light with darkness?" The principles of life, liberty and property must not be joined with the principles of genocide, totalitarianism, socialism and religious persecution. We cannot trust agreements or treaties with infidels.[48]

This passage beautifully illustrates both the intertwining of democratic and religious exceptionalism in parts of American society and the deep nationalist isolationism which helps feed nationalist unilateralism. Or as Fox News star Bill O'Reilly put it, explaining the great difference between coverage of the push for war with Iraq in the U.S. media and internationally, "Well, everywhere else in the world lies."[49]

U.S. Defense Secretary Donald Rumsfeld has been described by the *Financial Times* as the "anti-diplomat"; the same charge has been leveled at John Bolton and other members of the Bush administration. Vice President Dick Cheney is said to have a "visceral dislike" of the United Nations. The passages just quoted reveal some of the cultural and ideological origins of this antidiplomacy.

It should hardly be necessary to point out the essential falsity of these arguments. To take only two examples: if criticism of U.S. policy is to be explained only by ingrained "anti-Americanism," how would the writers explain the shift in opinion in Britain between the war in Afghanistan (which public opinion strongly supported) and the war in Iraq? Is British society too supposed to be congenitally anti-American and an example of failed modernity? Or try applying the logic of these arguments to other countries. Many Poles do not much like Russians and probably never will, for old historical reasons. Does this mean that Polish-Russian relations would be unaffected by new Russian policies which Poland saw as contemptuous and hostile? Or how about Greece and Turkey? Or South Korea and Japan?

The whole point of these arguments however is precisely that, like all such nationalist discourses, they are intended to free America from moral responsibility for the consequences of its actions and therefore to free America to do anything. To this end, facts are falsified or ignored (e.g., that France strongly supported the United States in Afghanistan) and usual standards of evidence suspended. Thus reputable opinion polls, used as basic sources of reliable information in every other context, are suddenly declared to be irrelevant—leaving national prejudice and an assumption of national superiority as the only standards of judgment.

Other nations are declared to be irrationally, incorrigibly and unchangingly hostile. This being so, it is obviously pointless to seek compromises with them or to try to accommodate their interests and views. And because they are irrational and barbarous, America is free to dictate to them or even to conquer them for their own good. This was precisely the discourse of nationalists in the leading European states toward each other and lesser breeds before 1914, which helped drag Europe into the great catastrophes of the twentieth century. It was also a central part of the old hideous discourse of anti-Semitism.

Thus it is especially depressing that arguments of this kind in the United States are often linked to very similar ones on behalf of Israel, and intended to absolve Israel of any responsibility for the consequences of its actions—a theme explored in Chapter 6. In the words of Brian Klug: "If Israel is basically the victim of persecution in an anti-semitic world, then it bears no responsibility for the situation in which it finds itself: the object of widespread condemnation....Nothing that the Jewish state does or refrains from doing could produce it or prevent it. All Israel can do, if it really is 'the collective Jew among the nations,' reprising the role of pariah, is fight for its survival, defying the world and keeping it at bay."[50]

What also links this kind of radical nationalist discourse in both America and Israel is that the enemy is seen by its proponents as almost universal. Nationalists in other countries restrict their hostility to a limited number of other nations; indeed, over the years I have seen this accusation of incorrigible and wicked anti-Americanism applied to Russians, Arabs and Chinese as an excuse for America adopting whatever policies it likes toward those peoples. But only in America and Israel perhaps could an influential political writer like Krauthammer declare the world itself to be the mad enemy. And this language did not appear on some back-woods talk show, but in America's leading newsmagazine and one of its foremost foreign policy journals. Nor is Schlafly a minor and irrelevant figure; she and her fellow leaders of the Religious Right wield great influence in the Republican Party.

If such visions spread in the United States, they will be disastrous not only for American interests and American security but for America's soul. Pathological hatred and fear of the outside world will feed the same emotions in American domestic politics, until the nation's moral and cultural greatness lies in ruins and its legacy to the future is also ruined beyond repair. In place of these visions, I would like to see the America of today rediscover some of the lessons that it learned for a while from the Vietnam War—although I hope that it will not have to lose tens of thousands of American lives in the process. These lessons were taught not only by the American Left, but also by profoundly conservative and Realist Americans such as George Kennan and Senator J. William Fulbright.

This book therefore is an analysis of different strands of American nationalism and how they interact; but it also has a moral and political purpose. Calling on the words of Julien Benda, it is an appeal to American intellectuals to do what they have asked of intellectuals in other countries: to recognize and confront their own nationalism and to transcend it in the name of higher universal values. To the American political elites, it is intended as a reminder of the catastrophes into which nationalism and national messianism led other great countries in the past. It is an appeal to return to older American traditions of Realist diplomacy softened by ethics and conscience. According to these traditions, America certainly does not "surrender" to other countries. It does however show a "decent respect" to their views and their vital interests and seeks pragmatic accommodations accordingly.

In his great critique of the impulses which drove America into Vietnam, *The Arrogance of Power*, Fulbright wrote:

> Only a nation at peace with itself, with its transgressions as well as its achievements, is capable of a generous understanding of others....When a nation is very powerful but lacking in self-confidence, it is likely to behave in a manner dangerous to itself and to others. Feeling the need to prove what is obvious to everyone else, it begins to confuse great power with total power and great responsibility with total responsibility: It can admit of no error; it must win every argument, no matter how trivial....Gradually but unmistakably, America is showing signs of that arrogance of power which has afflicted, weakened, and in some cases destroyed great nations in the past. In so doing, we are not living up to our capacity and promise as a civilized example for the world. The measure of our falling short is the measure of the patriot's duty of dissent.[51]

One

An Exceptional Nationalism?

We were long since a great power, we were quite used to it, and it did not make us as happy as we had expected. The feeling that it had not made us more attractive, that our relation to the world had rather worsened than improved, lay, unconfessed, deep in our hearts....War then, and if needs must, war against everybody, to convince everybody and to win. We were bursting with the consciousness that this was Germany's century, that history was holding her hand out over us; that after Spain, France, England, it was our turn to put our stamp on the world and be its leader; that the twentieth century was ours.

—Thomas Mann, *Doctor Faustus*
(on the spirit of August 1914 in Germany)[1]

The terrorist attacks of September 11, 2001, struck a country in which the strength of its nationalism already made it very much the "outlier" in the developed world.[2] Since that time this feature of American political culture has been one of the most important factors in alienating the United States from some of its closest allies in Europe and elsewhere. This nationalism separates the United States from what Europeans have come to think of (in their own Eurocentric way) as central patterns of post-1945 modernity, namely the overcoming of a culture of bellicose nationalism by "modern" civilization and the replacement of nationalist unilateralism with international cooperation. To disagreements over policy, it adds the perception of profound cultural differences.

This general, deeply felt and rather unreflective American nationalism was inflamed by the attacks of 9/11 and then exploited by dominant sectors of the Bush administration for their own purposes: abroad, the expansion of American imperial power; at home, the further consolidation of the power and wealth of what Michael Lind has called the American "overclass."[3]

In a poll from 1999, 72 percent of adult Americans declared that they were proud of their country. In the country with the next highest score, Britain, the figure was 53 percent; in France, it was 35 percent. These figures are of long standing: those of 1999 were very little altered from those observed fifteen years earlier, in the mid-1980s (75 percent, 54 percent and 35 percent respectively). Six in ten

Americans in 2003 believed that "our culture is superior to others," compared—against every stereotype—to only three in ten French people.

American figures, by contrast, have been close to those of parts of the contemporary developing world—or of Europe in the past: in the same poll, 71 percent of Indians, 78 percent of Mexicans and 85 percent of Filipinos expressed a similar strong pride in their countries. What makes this similarity with the United States odd is that among Mexicans and Filipinos at least, this pride usually has been seen as reflecting a certain actual national insecurity and even an inferiority complex.

Very high proportions of American youths also expressed a desire to "do something to serve my country": In 1999, 81 percent, compared to 46 percent in Britain and 55 percent in France—although, of course, as the public response to the aftermath of the Iraq War suggests, for many Americans this may be taken with a pinch of salt when it comes to arduous, long and dangerous service.[4]

Closely related is the very widespread presence in U.S. popular culture of national symbolism and national language. This presence extends from the most obvious symbol—the flag—through the patriotic celebrations and primers to be found at supermarket checkout counters. All of this is far more reminiscent of Europe in 1904 than of European nations in 2004. The endless references to the nation also extend in small and unrecognized ways throughout American life, just as they did in Europe before 1914.

The phrases and symbols of nationalism are used in commercial advertising in ways which were very familiar in Europe of previous generations. This extends from the explicit—paid advertisements from companies congratulating the U.S. armed forces, for example—to the more subtle: an advertisement from Freddie Mac in the *Washington Post*, appealing to first-time homebuyers in the name of "Life, Liberty and the Pursuit of Happiness" and "creating a nation of homeowners."[5]

> Visitors to the United States are frequently impressed by the outward show and symbols of conscious nationalism. Children are taught to salute the flag, and it is flown by private individuals to demonstrate their patriotism. The word "American" is used with a wealth of overtones, so that to describe oneself or a custom or an institution as "American" is to claim a whole set of positive values. The all American boy has become something of a joke, but it is a character which most American parents covet for their sons. Conversely, to be "un-American" is not to be merely foreign or unfamiliar, but dangerous, immoral, subversive and deluded. Fourth of July orations are the classic expressions of American patriotism, but hyperbole is not confined to these rhetorical exercises; and to foreign ears, the discourse of public men seems to be marked to an extraordinary degree by appeals to the special character and destiny of the American people.[6]

William R. Brock wrote this in 1974, but it is no less true a generation later. In my local supermarket I bought *A Celebration of America: Your Helpful Guide to America's*

Greatness, part of the "Better Your Home" series.[7] The children's section of Dalton's Booksellers at Union Station in Washington in the fall of 2003 also contained a "Celebrate America" stand, with books with titles like *American Patriots, God Bless America* and *America's Promise,* a small hagiography of Laura Bush, "America's First Lady," and a *Patriotic Primer* "for reading levels 4–8" by Lynne Cheney, wife of Vice President Dick Cheney. The last stretches from "A is for America, the land that we love" to "Z is the end of the alphabet, but not of America's story. Strong and free, we will continue to be an inspiration to the world."[8]

Just as in Europe in the past, emotional support for the American armed forces (although of course not necessarily for their specific missions) is virtually omnipresent in the mainstream media. *Time* magazine made its "Man of the Year" for 2003 "The American Soldier." *Parade* magazine—syndicated to the *Washington Post* and other papers—regularly carries cover articles on military-patriotic themes. In an absolutely classic image of this kind, its last issue of 2003 carried a cover picture of an avuncular American military medic holding a wounded Iraqi child.

Another issue of *Parade* featured former prisoner of war Jessica Lynch on the cover declaring "The Pledge [of Allegiance] Will Never Be Just Words for Me," just months after most of the details of her capture and recapture as reported by the *Post* had been admitted to be wild patriotic exaggerations.[9] Advice columnists like "Dear Abby" often feature pieces about how readers can support the troops abroad. Very little of this kind of thing now remains even in Britain and France, the most military-minded of the European states, although once such images were omnipresent.[10]

Also entirely characteristic of old Europe are traditional ritual affirmations of American nationhood, like the daily recital of the Pledge of Allegiance in schools and the celebration of Memorial Day in smaller towns. "The sentiment that is continually reaffirmed by these sacred ceremonies is the conviction that America is a nation called to a special destiny by God."[11] Of course, all European nations have their own national rituals and ceremonies. Only rarely, however, are these celebrated as widely or with so much emotional force as in the United States.

In the words of the great Russian-born student of America and editor of *The Nation* Max Lerner (1902–1992): "The cult of the nation as social myth has run as a thread through the whole of American history."[12] Alexis de Tocqueville noticed its strong presence in the 1830s, and traced it to the fact that "democratic institutions generally give men a lofty notion of their country, and of themselves." (In an irritated moment, he also remarked that "it is impossible to conceive of a more troublesome and garrulous patriotism."[13]) At that time, even in France, ordinary country people often still had no real conception of France or French identity and were attached instead to purely local loyalties.[14]

The greater age of American mass nationalism is closely related to other key features of American "exceptionalism." The North American colonies inherited from Britain strong elements of a relatively clear-cut national cultural identity centered on a mixture of the Protestant religion and belief in institutions of law, liberty and representative government.[15] This identity was incarnated both in their own institutions and later in the American Constitution.

The fact that as colonists in a new land Americans were in some sense truly "born equal" has been advanced by many scholars from Tocqueville on as the fundamental difference between the political traditions and cultures of the United States and those of Europe; the United States, lacking a feudal tradition and an aristocracy, escaped also from violent social revolution, socialism and most of the political forms and traditions which stemmed from these movements and collisions.

The result was that under the froth and spume of political clashes lay a remarkably homogenous, continuous, basically unchanging, universally held civic nationalist ideology—"an absolute Americanism as old as the country itself."[16] By the early twentieth century, as Herbert Croly, the first editor of the *New Republic*, wrote in 1909:

> The faith of Americans in their country is religious, if not in its intensity, at any rate in its almost absolute and universal authority. It pervades the air we breathe. As children, we hear it asserted or implied in the conversation of our elders. Every new stage of our educational training provides some additional testimony on its behalf. Newspapers and novelists, orators and playwrights, even if they are little else, are at least loyal preachers of the Truth. The skeptic is not controverted; he is overlooked. It constitutes the kind of faith which is the implication, rather than the object, of thought, and consciously or unconsciously, it enters largely into our personal lives as a formative influence.[17]

The Spirit of 1914 and the Exploitation of Nationalism

Such sentiments were given greatly increased force by the attacks of 9/11, which produced for a while a spirit of national unity and exaltation reminiscent of the warring European states at the outbreak of war in 1914. The political atmosphere recalled the various national versions of the French *Union Sacrée* of that year, when Rupert Brooke rendered thanks to God "Who has matched us with His hour, and caught our youth, and wakened us from sleeping."[18]

In a book entitled *Why We Fight*, and in words echoed at the time by innumerable Americans across the political spectrum, the Catholic conservative William J. Bennett wrote of

> the spontaneous upwelling of national feeling that followed upon September 11, the day of trauma. Quite suddenly, as if in the twinkling of an eye, everything petty, self-absorbed, rancorous, decadent, and hostile in our national life seemed to have been wiped away. Suddenly, our country's flag was everywhere, and stayed everywhere. Suddenly, we had heroes again—and what heroes: policemen and firemen, rescue workers, soldiers and civilian passengers who leapt from their seats to do battle with evil personified.

It was true; for weeks and even months after September 11, partisan political issues seemed to fade in urgency, racial divisions to be set at naught. Cynicism and irony were declared out, simple love of country in....Something in those events, wrote an uplifted Peggy Noonan, "something in the fact that all the different colors and faiths and races were helping each other, were in it together, were mutually dependent and mutually supportive, made you realize: we sealed it that day. We sealed the pact, sealed the promise we made long ago....We are Americans."[19]

In the same spirit, Kaiser Wilhelm II declared in August 1914: "I know no parties, I know only Germans." Or as Ernst Glaeser expressed the mood in Germany then: "At last life had regained an ideal significance. The great virtues of humanity, fidelity, patriotism, readiness to die for an ideal...were triumphing over the trading and shopkeeping spirit....The war would cleanse mankind from all its impurities."[20] Earlier that year Georges Docrocq had written, "To act. No longer to have doubts about my country or my own powers. To act. To serve....No more discussions, no more questioning of myself."[21]

But as memories both of European history after 1914 and Republican behavior after 9/11 suggest, in the mouths of politicians and governments passages like this also contain a very large element of conscious or unconscious falsity, above all when it comes to the supposed suspension of "partisan political issues." The Bush administration and the Republican Party (to which Bennett and Noonan belong) in fact moved with ruthless speed to capitalize on the national emergency to strengthen their domestic political position and push through their domestic agendas.

It is extremely unlikely, for example, that the Republicans would have regained control of the Senate in November 2002, or been able to push through tax cuts which so blatantly favored the wealthy, without the assistance of appeals to the voters on nationalist grounds.[22] Such appeals also gained support for the Iraq War from Americans who were in fact worried by it. In the words of Jill Long Thompson, an ordinary citizen from South Bend, Indiana, before the invasion of Iraq: "I think people are very uneasy about a potential strike [against Iraq] on our part, but we are very patriotic in the Second District, and we will support our president, and we will support our troops."[23]

Republican strategists were often remarkably frank about this. As the *Washington Post* reported before President Bush's State of the Union Address in January 2004: "White House officials said they hoped to use the televised speech, and its audience of more than 60 million, to foster an image of Bush as a wartime leader who stands above the fray of politics—the commander in chief, not a candidate....According to Bush advisers, this is the gist of his speech, which will have solemn passages with an overall tone of optimism: 'We are a nation at war. My bold decisions have made America safer, but we are not yet safe. At home, my administration's policies have made us better and more prosperous. But I am not satisfied, and Congress must pass more of what I have proposed.'"[24]

When Republican propagandists like Bennett wrote of "nonpartisanship" after 9/11, it was therefore very much in the way that German patriotic writers like Thomas Mann during World War I spoke of themselves as "apolitical" and called on their countrymen to be the same.[25] They were not only calling for support for the war effort, or even adherence to a nationalist political program; in many cases, they were also seeking to defend a particular class and domestic political position. The use of nationalism to create a mass constituency for parties based on the landowning, capitalist and professional classes was the classic strategy of endangered elites throughout Europe before 1914.

This political exploitation of nationalism does not necessarily reflect conscious hypocrisy or cynical and cold-blooded manipulation of the public, although these elements certainly have been present. The point is rather that as with their equivalents in the Europe of the past, the nationalist Right in the United States and the dominant forces in the Bush administration absolutely and sincerely identify themselves with their nation, to the point where the presence of any other group in government is seen not as a defeat but as an usurpation, as something profoundly and inherently illegitimate and "un-American." They feel themselves to be as much "America" as the Kaiser and the Junkers felt themselves to be "Germany" and the Tsar and the Russian noble elites to be "Russia."

Imperialism and Nationalism

Closely linked to this identification of elites with their countries has been the exploitation of nationalism for the purposes of imperialism—also seen by elites as a higher national good, which the ignorant masses cannot understand and into which they have to be led, if necessary by deceit. Rudyard Kipling and other imperialists notoriously despised the ordinary people of their countries, with their pathetic ordinary lives and dreams, their banal indifference to imperial visions and their unwillingness to die for such visions.

This is how the Bush administration seemed at heart to view the American people. As a range of observers from historian Andrew Bacevich to humorist Bill Maher have pointed out, from the first days after 9/11 the Bush administration carefully omitted calls for sacrifice from its rhetoric to the American people and indeed urged them to resume normal spending patterns to help the economy: "The primary responsibility of the average citizen for the duration of the emergency remained what it had been in more peaceful times: to be an engine of consumption." Sacrifice was to be restricted to the armed forces.[26]

By early 2004 it had become apparent that the United States lacked both the national will and the national means to fight a long-running guerrilla war in Iraq (even one with very low U.S. casualties by historical standards). The United States would also have great difficulty in fighting more than one major conflict at the same time, as required by U.S. military doctrine, at least if such conflicts involved not only ships and aircraft, but also large ground forces—unless the nation itself is directly attacked once again. More than this: the occupation of Iraq has revealed yet again the lack of appetite of ordinary Americans for direct empire, with all its costs in blood and treasure.[27]

This lack of appetite for wars of empire in the case of Iraq was despite the fact that—without any evidence, but with the encouragement of leading Bush administration officials and the pro-war media, such as Fox News (a right-wing twenty-four-hour TV news channel owned by Rupert Murdoch)—a great many Americans continued to believe that Saddam Hussein had been directly involved in the 9/11 attacks and therefore—that the war with Iraq was a legitimate act of traditional self-defense. In a Harris poll of February 2004, 74 percent of respondents still believed that a link between Iraq and al Qaeda before the war was either certain or likely. A March NBC poll showed 57 percent still believing that Iraq had possessed weapons of mass destruction.[28]

Given this belief in the Iraq–al Qaeda link, it is in some ways remarkable not that support for the war was so strong, but that it was not stronger. After all, if I had been convinced that Saddam Hussein had attacked the United States on 9/11, I would have supported the war in Iraq, just as I supported the war against al Qaeda and the Taliban in Afghanistan; and as in Afghanistan, I would have supported whatever long-term commitment was necessary to secure and stabilize the fruits of victory. Such feelings undoubtedly are true of many other opponents of the Iraq War.

In the 2000 American election campaign, discussions of foreign and security policy were overwhelmingly absent both from the debates and from the concerns of U.S. voters as expressed in opinion polls. Even declared Bush voters polled in September 2000 put foreign and security policy seventh on their list of priorities, with only 6 percent saying the candidate's stand on these issues mattered most to them. Top concerns were taxes and abortion, polling at 22 percent each. Gore voters polled did not mention defense as a priority at all. Neither set of voters mentioned foreign policy as such.[29]

As the *New York Times* commented on Bush's neglect of these issues: "But then, Bush may have decided that too much talk about foreign policy is bad business. He has talked often to friends and acquaintances about his father's loss to Bill Clinton eight years ago, when the elder Bush focused on foreign affairs and the Arkansas neophyte emphasized the economy."[30]

An unwillingness on the part of the masses to make serious sacrifices for empire is not new. Until World War I the British empire was conquered and run very much on the cheap (largely by local native auxiliaries—not unlike the situation for the United States in Afghanistan after 2001), and this was true of the other colonial empires as well. The Royal Navy was of course expensive, but then it doubled as the absolutely necessary defense of the British Isles themselves against invasion or blockade.

Then as now, given the overwhelming superiority of Western firepower and military organization, enormous territories could be conquered at very low cost and risk. When European empires ran into areas which would be truly costly to conquer and hold—the British in Afghanistan, the Italians in Ethiopia—they tended to back off. In the view of the British imperial historian Niall Ferguson, the unprecedentedly heavy British casualties in the Boer War can be seen as beginning the process of British disillusionment with empire.[31]

This absence of a willingness to make sacrifices for empire among the European masses was something of which the general staffs and the conservative establishments of Europe were well aware. Acute students both of Clausewitz and of police reports on the mood of the proletariats, they knew the importance of mass support for any serious war and the limits on how far empire could be used for purposes of mass mobilization. So whenever possible, sensible governments always used volunteer troops and foreign mercenaries, not conscripts, for colonial wars. Today, as a result of the widespread demilitarization of culture in the West, even the use of professional troops has become unpopular, as witness popular discontent in the United States at the rising death toll in Iraq.

The French Foreign Legion was created for this explicit purpose. The British Army was a small volunteer force, but Britain used Indian troops as much as possible for the task of colonial war and policing. When countries did use conscripts in colonial wars, the results were often disastrous both to the campaign itself and to domestic political stability—witness Italy after defeat at Adowa in Ethiopia in 1896, Russia after the Russo-Japanese war of 1904–5 and Spain after the catastrophe of Anual in Morocco in 1921, which in some ways began the historical process leading to the Spanish Civil War.[32]

The U.S. adoption of the "Revolution in Military Affairs" with its emphasis on the development of high technology as a substitute for manpower, coupled with the use of local auxiliaries in Afghanistan and elsewhere, has been seen as a new imperialist version of the British use of "gunboats and Gurkhas" intended to spare its own troops.[33] But as the Iraqi debacle has demonstrated, high technology and local auxiliaries only go so far. In a truly imperial strategy, the use of large numbers of American troops will also be necessary—and this will not be popular at home, unless they can be shown to be fighting not for an empire but for the nation itself.

In Douglas Porch's work on the French conquest of Morocco, the author presents a fascinating description of the various stratagems Marshal Hubert Lyautey and the other French imperialists used to convince a thoroughly skeptical French public to support this adventure, which many regarded as economically pointless and indeed a costly distraction from the need to strengthen France's defenses against the real national threat, Germany. French conscripts did serve to a limited extent in Algeria (legally not a colony but part of France), a tour of duty that was extremely unpopular with French youths. Fear of colonial military service fed on much older hatreds of military service, with all its dangers, hardships and oppressions, especially among peasants, which extended across Europe.[34]

26

The French ultra-nationalist Paul Deroulede declared that in Alsace and Lorraine he had lost two sisters, and all the French colonialists were offering him in return were "twenty black servants."[35] Hence the prominence of the propaganda concerning France's *mission civilisatrice* and the need to create a modern Moroccan state and abolish "barbarism" there; but also of suggestions that because Germany also had designs on Morocco, the wider struggle with Germany required French control of that country.[36]

The central domestic political strategy of capitalist elites in Europe before 1914 was to rely much less on imperialism than on nationalism to rally democratic support as a defense against socialism. And in 1914 the impulse which drove the European masses to support the war and to immolate themselves in it was nationalism, universally expressed in the genuine belief that the homeland itself was in imminent danger of attack.

As Jean-Jacques Becker stresses in the case of France, despite the intense nationalism of much of French culture before World War I, the initial popular response to the crisis of July 1914 was worry and the desire for peace. Only when the German ultimatum appeared as a clear case of aggression against the homeland itself did mass enthusiasm for war develop.[37] Despite all the periodic flare-ups of tension over colonial rivalries, in the decades before 1914, the great European powers never did go to war over a colonial issue (with the exception of Russia and Japan in 1904). One key reason for this was a well-based doubt in the minds of European governments and militaries about the response of the masses to a bloody war which had obviously begun in a squabble between two greedy predators in an unpronounceable African swamp.

The terrorist attacks of September 11, 2001, were a real and atrocious assault on the American homeland. Any U.S. administration—indeed any self-respecting country in the world—would have had to respond by seeking to destroy the perpetrators. The war to destroy the al Qaeda forces in Afghanistan and their Taliban backers was a completely legitimate response to 9/11, as are U.S. actions against al Qaeda and its allies elsewhere in the world. What the Bush administration did, however, was to instill in the American public a fear of much wider threats to the homeland from Iraq, Iran and North Korea—states which had no connection to al Qaeda. By doing so, the administration created a belief that anything America does is essentially defensive and a response to "terrorism." By foisting this belief on the American people, the latter therefore could be mobilized to some extent for imperial war.[38]

But even the Bush administration had to remain within certain limits. The common paradigm of hostility to Muslims, and the inability to distinguish between even radically different Muslim states, traditions and ideologies made it possible to mix up Iraq and al Qaeda in the minds of a majority of Americans; but not even Bush would have gotten away with declaring that the terrorists on 9/11 were really Russians, or Chinese, or North Koreans. For that matter, Bush's first election campaign deliberately concealed his followers' imperial ambitions—as in his remark that the United States should adopt a more "humble" approach to international affairs and that "I am worried about over-committing our military around the world. I would be judicious in its use."[39]

The distinction between imperialism and nationalism is an important one to keep in mind. One key way of understanding the political strategy of the Bush administration since 9/11 is that—like some of its European predecessors—it essentially tried to drive a program of imperial hegemony with the fuel of a wounded but also bewildered and befuddled nationalism.

Spared by History

Like European imperialists of the past, many Americans genuinely see their country's national interests and ambitions as coterminous with goodness, civilization, progress and the interests of all humanity.[40] Communal self-deception among members of a shared political culture, driven by a mixture of ideology and self-interest, is the issue here. Or, in the wonderful phrase of Max Weber, "Man is an animal suspended in webs of significance he himself has spun."[41]

To put it another way: the heightened culture of nationalism in the European countries prior to World War I was in part the product of deliberate strategies of the European elites to combat socialist movements and preserve their dominant positions by mobilizing mass support in the name of nationalism. But the resulting nationalism was a cause for which the sons of these elites, the officer corps of old Europe, sacrificed themselves in uncounted numbers and with sincere faith.[42]

Self-sacrifice is admittedly not a thing for which America's right-wing nationalist elites have shown much appetite; but their discourse has some sinister echoes of that of their European predecessors. This is especially true of two linked obsessions: with cultural and moral decline, and with domestic treachery. Both have very old cultural, racial and religious roots; both were reshaped, strengthened and perpetuated by the Cold War; and both have attained new force as a result of 9/11. Thus, Sean Hannity, the right-wing radio and TV host, links gay marriage somehow with Adolf Hitler as evil threats to the United States and declares, "We have a battle within our country with those that want to tear down the foundation, the Judeo-Christian values that made this country strong."[43]

The Catholic right-winger William Bennett exemplifies this concern with "decadence" as a source of national weakness, with particular focus on the liberal intelligentsia and the universities.[44] Now, it must be said that some of the criticism leveled by these forces at American left-wing academia is justified. Chapter 2 touches on some of the lunatic excesses of academic "political correctness"; and even the veteran radical Richard Rorty has denounced the fact that "we now have, among many American students and teachers, a spectatorial, disgusted, mocking Left rather than a Left which dreams of achieving our country."[45]

Rather than aiming at stimulating an engaged debate on improving the United States and U.S. policy, however, the approach of Bennett and his allies such as

28

Lynne Cheney is clearly intended to shut down debate. It also has some extremely troubling antecedents. Its language about the healthy, patriotic American people as opposed to the deracinated, morally contemptible intellectuals could be taken almost directly from European documents of the past; a German nationalist statement of 1881, for example, spoke of "sinister powers" sapping the religion, morality and patriotism that formed the "ancient, sound foundation of our national character."[46] In the United States this kind of thinking was enormously strengthened by the Cold War, which saw repeated waves of anxiety that the country was becoming too morally and physically soft to compete with the supposedly "purposeful, serious and disciplined" Soviet society.[47]

Republican congressman and former House Speaker Newt Gingrich used to teach a course entitled "Renewing American Civilization" at conservative colleges in Georgia, the tapes of which were distributed to Republican activists. As words to describe political opponents, they suggested "decay, failure, shallow, traitors, pathetic, corrupt, incompetent, sick."[48] And this is indeed the standard language which right-wing media stars use to their immense audiences concerning Democrats, liberal intellectuals and Europeans.

The language of these figures is strongly reminiscent of what George Mosse has called the "rhetoric of anxiety" among nationalists before 1914, focused both on external threats to the nation and on moral, sexual and political subversion from within. Its markedly hysterical tone also is similar to that rhetoric.[49] And these attitudes are not just a matter of a few media squibs. In its anti-intellectualism, anti-elitism, antisecularism and antimodernism, this rhetoric strikes very deep chords among that large minority of Americans who feel deeply alienated from the world in its present shape.

As Mosse's work recalls, closely linked to this traditional nationalist rhetoric of anxiety is one virtually universal aspect of right-wing nationalist language throughout history: its obsession with threats to national virility and with the supposed effeminate weakness of critics at home and abroad: "Americans are from Mars; Europeans are from Venus," in Robert Kagan's famous phrase. More crudely, Europeans are "Euroweenies." Lee Harris, another right-wing nationalist author, sees "Spartan ruthlessness" as the "origin of civilization." Robert Kaplan calls for Americans to recover the "pagan virtues" in warfighting.[50]

In British historian and journalist Timothy Garton Ash's summary of this kind of language about Europe in the United States: "If anti-American Europeans see 'the Americans' as bullying cowboys, anti-European Americans see 'the Europeans' as limp-wristed pansies. The American is a virile, heterosexual male; the European is female, impotent or castrated....The word 'eunuchs' is, I discovered, used in the form 'EUnuchs.'"[51]

Much of this kind of talk could be seen as merely silly, although as Secretary of Defense Donald Rumsfeld's attitudes and language concerning Europe demonstrate, it does have serious consequences in the real world. Of much greater and grimmer significance is right-wing nationalist language about domestic treachery. In America today and in so many other countries in the past, such language has fueled and justified domestic repression; and as some of the behavior of the Bush administration indicates, 9/11 and a war against terrorism with no foreseeable end have once again made these attitudes a matter of real concern.[52]

Some of this language has been directed against Muslim groups within the United States—and indeed it is sometimes justified. Just as much effort, however, has gone to vilifying political and intellectual opponents of the nationalist Right. Ann Coulter's amazing book *Treason* is a sustained attempt to portray liberals—and Democrats, categories which she treats as identical—as traitors to America both in the Cold War and the "war against terrorism." As noted, this accusation is the common stuff of right-wing media stars like Sean Hannity, Bill O'Reilly, Rush Limbaugh and Michael Savage, figures who have huge and appreciative audiences and, at their back, the tremendous power and reach of major U.S. television and radio networks.[53]

In the wake of 9/11, a body headed by Lynne Cheney produced a list of 117 statements by American academics and students which they deemed "morally equivocal," anti-American, or both: for "college and university faculty have been the weak link in America's response to the attack." The statements cited for denunciation ranged from the genuinely wicked and unacceptable, such as "Anyone who can blow up the Pentagon gets my vote" (no. 14), to "We should build bridges and relationships, not simply bombs and walls" (no. 19) and "Ignorance breeds hate" (no. 49).[54]

Influential former officials and respected commentators including Richard Perle, David Frum and Irving Kristol have also made accusations of national treachery a central part of their rhetoric, with Frum denouncing not only liberals, but "unpatriotic" conservatives who opposed the Iraq War, for carrying out "a war against America."[55] Hannity's latest book is entitled *Deliver Us from Evil: Defeating Terrorism, Despotism and Liberalism*.[56] The spirit behind the old, ugly German nationalist insult *Nestbeschmutzer* (someone who dirties his own nest) is much in evidence in America today.

The willingness of large numbers of American politicians and intellectuals to use such language, and America's difference in this regard from Europe and other parts of the developed world, is closely linked to what is also the most important root of American "exceptionalism" in its positive sense: that the United States has been spared the greatest European disasters of the two centuries. It has been "kindly separated by nature and a wide ocean from the exterminating havoc of one quarter of the globe," in President Thomas Jefferson's phrase.[57]

The first, and critical salvation, as Tocqueville noted, was from the French and other European revolutions after 1789 and from the extreme reactions to which they gave rise. Thereafter, of immense importance in distinguishing the United States from the rest of the developed world is that the country avoided the truly searing effects of war and revolution in the twentieth century. Of course, the nation participated in both world wars, the U.S. armed forces fought with magnificent courage and dedication in both, and individual units suffered terrible losses; but overall American casualties in proportion to the U.S. population were very small compared to those of the leading European states, and above all America itself was spared invasion or bombardment.

Too many Europeans and Japanese were tortured, imprisoned or executed for some form of "treason"—or did the torturing and shooting—for this word to be one which people from these countries can use lightly. Too many people were killed, maimed, raped or starved to death in wars for the language of militant, outwardly directed nationalism to be acceptable, not merely in political or intellectual circles but in the vast majority of the populations. Even the least educated European can preserve a family memory of a grandfather killed at Ypres or an uncle maimed at Stalingrad, a home destroyed in Cologne or Warsaw and rapes and forced prostitution from Naples to Berlin and Krasnodar.

Precisely because language like Bennett's was used incessantly by intellectuals and politicians in all the major European states in 1914–15, and again by Germany and Italy between 1939 and 1941, it is very difficult for any European today to write or speak in such terms. This is not just a question of thoughts which may be strongly held in private but which can no longer be publicly expressed, like racism in the United States. It is *psychologically* extremely difficult for educated Europeans even to think in these terms.[58] And this is as true of the European elites as of the populations at large. The European nationalist death ride unleashed in 1914 began by destroying the sons of those elites, and by 1945 it had destroyed their dominance and in many cases their countries as well.

American capitalists, however, like America as a whole, escaped the European catastrophes of the first half of the twentieth century. In this America was very fortunate; but it also means that the United States and its rulers escaped perhaps the most searing lessons the world has ever known in the need to keep social, class, economic and national ambitions, and passions, within certain bounds. The greater radicalism of American capitalism therefore also stems from the nation having been spared the horrible consequences to which such capitalist excesses can contribute; and this form of American capitalism feeds in turn the greater radicalism of the American Right and the culture of American nationalism. This complex of radical attitudes can be seen in the editorial pages of the premier newspaper of American business, the *Wall Street Journal*. For a taste of the difference between the culture and politics of American capitalists, taken as a whole, and those of their European equivalents, one could do no better than to compare those pages with those of the *Journal*'s European equivalents, the *Financial Times* (London), *Frankfuerter Allgemeine* (Frankfurt), *Corriere della Sera* (Milan) and so on. This difference was displayed, for example, in the horrified reaction of leading articles in the *Financial Times* to the Bush tax cuts.

Above all, what is striking in the *Journal*—a paper representing a presumably satisfied and dominant capitalist class—is its writers' capacity for both radicalism and sheer hatred. *Wall Street Journal* editorials treated President Bill Clinton as a cultural alien, a dangerous radical and a national traitor. This treatment resembled that which the *Journal* and much of the capitalist class in general meted out in the 1930s to the "communist" Franklin Delano Roosevelt—a man who probably did more than any other to preserve and extend American capitalism in the world. The explanation for this feral behavior is to be sought partly in the conservative cultural and racial anxieties which will be examined in the next chapter, but equally importantly in the pre-1914–style assumption by American capitalists of their unqualified right to dominate the state and to retain profits.

The particular nature of American capitalism is reflected in the contemporary character of the Republican Party. Like so many party labels around the world, the historic names of the main U.S. political parties have long since lost whatever descriptive value they once possessed. As of 2004, it would not be easy to find a truly descriptive name for the Democrats, given the enormous and curious mixture of class, ethnic, cultural and ideological standpoints which they represent. "Progressive Liberals" would be perhaps the closest, and not very close at that. If, however, one were to seek a name for the Republicans which would situate them accurately in a wider historical and international context, there would be no doubt at all as to what that name should be: the Republicans would be renamed the American Nationalist Party.

This is not just because of the Republicans' external policies and the political culture which underpins them. Rather, the entire contemporary Republican mixture is reminiscent of the classic positions of past conservative nationalist movements in Europe and elsewhere. Abroad, these parties stood for "assertive nationalism" and often supported imperialist policies. At home, they were devoted to defending private property in general and the interests of the upper classes in particular, with a special stress on hereditary wealth. They also portrayed themselves as the defenders of traditional national, religious and family values against the rising tide of cosmopolitan, liberal, socialist and foreign decadence. A danger exists that like their counterparts in Europe before 1914, if the Republicans stick to the radical policies in favor of the wealthy which they adopted under the Bush administration of 2000 to 2004, they will be pushed farther and farther in the direction of radical nationalism as their only remaining way of appealing to the mass of the American population.

Chosen Peoples

Underlying the nationalism not only of the American Right, but of American culture in general, is a belief that America has been specially "chosen" and is therefore, in the words of former Secretary of State Madeleine Albright, the "indispensable nation"—whether chosen by God, by "Destiny," by "History" or simply marked out for greatness and leadership by the supposed possession of the greatest, most successful, oldest and most developed form of democracy. In President Woodrow

Wilson's words, in World War I, "America had the infinite privilege of fulfilling her destiny and saving the world."[59] Albright, like Wilson before her, is a Democrat; and the closeness of her language about America to that of George W. Bush illustrates the widespread and bipartisan nature of this belief in U.S. society.

One reason for the persistence of this belief in America is that in the mid-twentieth century, it was actually true. When the popular evangelist Billy Sunday declared at the outbreak of war with Germany in 1917 that "America is placed in a position where the fate of the world depends largely on our conduct. If we lose our heads, down goes civilization," he was engaging in nationalist hyperbole. In the 1940s and early 1950s, this was no exaggeration.[60]

This sense of America not just as an unfulfilled dream or vision, but also as a country with a national mission, is absolutely central to the American national identity and also forms the core of the nation's faith in its own "exceptionalism."[61] It was inscribed on the Republic's Great Seal at America's birth as a united nation: *Novus Ordo Seclorum*: A New Order for the Ages.

Today this belief does indeed make Americans exceptional in the developed world. In the past, however, this exceptionalism was emphatically not the case: "From time immemorial, nations have conceived of themselves as superior and as endowed with a mission to dominate other peoples or to lead the rest of the world into paths of light." A great many nations throughout history—perhaps even the great majority—have had a sense of themselves as especially "chosen" by God, or destiny, for great and special "tasks," and often have used remarkably similar language to describe this sense of mission.[62] Indeed, some of the most articulate proponents of America's universal mission have been British subjects, repeating very much the same lines that their fathers and grandfathers used to employ about the British empire.[63]

In the words of Herman Melville (1819–1891): "We Americans are the peculiar chosen people—the Israel of our time; we bear the ark of the liberties of the world. God has predestined, mankind expects, great things from our race; and great things we feel in our souls. The rest of the nations must soon be in our rear. We are pioneers of the world; the advance guard, sent on through the wilderness of untried things, to break a path into the New World that is ours."[64]

As the leading religious historian Conrad Cherry writes, "The development of the theme of chosen people in both Germany and the United States between 1880 and 1920 illustrates the protean character of the myth of religious nationalism. It has proven itself able to assume the identity of multiple biblical and non-biblical images without loss of its mythic power." The difference today is, of course, that in Germany this myth was killed off completely (at least in its nationalist form) by the horrors of 1933 to 1945, and to a very considerable degree this was true in the rest of Western Europe as well; in the United States this myth is still very much alive.[65]

The Protestant form of this myth was to be found in sixteenth- and seventeenth-century Holland, Sweden and Britain even before it migrated to the United

States. In John Milton's words of the mid-seventeenth century, "Let England not forget her precedence of teaching nations how to live." As in America, this myth usually involved the explicit identification of the country concerned with biblical Israel. Such Protestant and biblical imagery pervaded British imperial rhetoric, including that of the not very religious (indeed, Masonic) Rudyard Kipling. It always strangely blended themes of christianization, liberation and development with racial superiority and celebration of victorious force.

Present in all the great powers in modern history has also been an American-style sense of themselves as "universal nations," summing up the best in mankind and also embracing the whole of mankind with their universally applicable values. This sense allowed these nations to claim that theirs was a positive nationalism or patriotism, while those of other nations were negative, because they were morally stunted and concerned only with the interests of nations.

Germans before 1914 believed that "Germany may heal the world" with its own particular mixture of legal order, technological progress and spirit of organic, rooted "culture" and "community" (*Gemeinschaft*). German thinkers opposed these values to those of the allegedly decadent, shallow "civilization" and atomized, rootless "society" (*Gesellschaft*) of England, France or the United States and to the "barbarism" of Russia. In the words of Johann Gottlieb Fichte a century earlier, "The German alone...can be a patriot; he alone can for the sake of his nation encompass the whole of mankind; contrasted with him from now on, the patriotism of every other nation must be egoistic, narrow and hostile to the rest of mankind."[66]

Russia too had its own sense of universal mission and nationhood under the tsars, closely linked as in some other nations to religion: the belief in Russia as the heir to the Christian empire of Rome and Constantinople. Konstantin Aksakov wrote that "the Russian people is not a nation, it is a humanity; it only appears to be a people only because it is surrounded by peoples with exclusively national essences, and its humanity is therefore represented as nationality."[67] Dostoyevsky wrote that Russians were "the only God-bearing people on earth, destined to regenerate and save the world." This spirit was later to flow into Soviet communism, which envisaged the Russian language and selected aspects of Russian culture as forming essential building blocks of a new socialist nation which would in turn set a pattern for all humankind.

The most interesting parallel to the American sense of universal national mission is to be found in the history of France. Indeed, to a pragmatic and empirical latter-day British subject, the long-running alienation between the United States and France often resembles two brothers quarrelling over a shared inheritance.[68] Like the American state, the French state too has claimed for most of the past 200 years to represent the heritage of the Enlightenment with regard to liberty, democracy and progress and to have the right to spread these ideals to other nations. This belief dates from the French Revolution, but builds on the older conviction of Royal France in the seventeenth and eighteenth centuries that it was *La Grande Nation*, with a cultural mission to lead Europe. Indeed, the ultimate roots can be traced still farther back, to medieval Catholic and proto-national images of France as "the eldest daughter of the Church."

For many years after the Revolution, France was seen—and not only by the French—as a "glorious mother who is not ours alone and must deliver every nation to liberty."[69] As Thomas Jefferson put it, "Every man has two countries—his own and France"—words that could well be applied, culturally speaking, to much of the world today with reference to the United States.[70] Or in the very American words of General Charles de Gaulle, inscribed on the base of his statue on the Champs Elysees, "There exists an immemorial covenant between the grandeur of France and the freedom of the world."[71] As in the United States, this particular belief also can be made into a domestic political weapon. Thus in January 2004 the former socialist minister Jack Lang, attacking the conservative French government for excessive friendliness to China, declared that "the [French] National Assembly has embodied for two centuries the fight for the rights of man"—a sentiment entirely characteristic of the U.S. Congress and, in both cases, equally surprising to Vietnamese among many others.[72]

De Gaulle shared a long-standing French belief that France was intended by Providence to enjoy "an eminent and exceptional destiny." This belief still exists, albeit to a considerably reduced extent, in the French elites, although as the poll cited at the beginning of this chapter suggests, at the start of the twenty-first century mass nationalism is very much less evident in France than in the United States. According to Edgar Quinet, only France had "the instinct of civilization, the need to take the initiative in a general way to bring about progress in modern society....It is this disinterested though imperious need...which makes French unity, which gives sense to its history and a soul to the country."[73]

Such feelings do still exist to a degree not only in France but in Western Europe more widely, but with a crucial difference from their nature in the contemporary United States. This difference lies in the fact that since World War II, these sentiments have separated themselves from the self-images of particular nations and attached themselves to the "European Project" as a whole, as expressed through the European Union (EU) and its predecessor bodies.

In its overt commitment to spread democracy, human rights and development, the EU resembles the United States to an extent and has taken on some of the former civilizing mission of its former imperial member states. But unlike in the United States, an absolutely central part of this mission is precisely to overcome and transcend nationalism and individual nationalist missions. This was after all the most important reason why the European project was started in the first place: to ensure that there would be no repetition of the catastrophic national conflicts which had wrecked Europe in the past: "Europeans have done something that no one has ever done before: created a zone of peace where war is ruled out, absolutely out. Europeans are convinced that this model is valid for other parts of the world."[74]

France too has sunk in the EU and the European Project the greater part of its old sentiments of *mission civilisatrice* and of its great power ambitions. This has

35

occurred for two reasons: because of sheer weakness and because as far as large-scale unilateral intervention in the non-European world is concerned, these sentiments had in any case been largely bled out by the wars of 1946 to 1954 in Indochina and 1954 to 1963 in Algeria.

Thus the experience of several European countries of the often bloody, chaotic disillusioning process of decolonization and of the failure of democracy and development in many of the former colonies already had provided a considerable immunization against the more optimistic and violent forms of the *mission civilisatrice*. As a result, belief in the possibility and justification of spreading civilization by force of arms is also very much lower in Europe than in the United States, although it has been growing in recent years as a result of the shameful and disastrous European failures to prevent wars and atrocities in the former Yugoslavia between 1991 and 1995. But when it comes to a really strong program of development backed by the presence of force, and without American control, the immediate periphery of the EU in the Balkans is still the limit of European ambitions.

Thesis and Antithesis

There is another way in which France provides some very interesting parallels with a key feature of American nationalism: namely its historical separation into very different and frequently opposed ideological and cultural streams. Because of the political and ideological convulsions which repeatedly gripped France between 1789 and 1958, these different streams have been more clearly defined and radical than in the United States, but in some ways they are rather similar.

Since 1789, France like the United States has possessed what could be called a national ideology or Creed, a civic nationalist thesis about itself which France has presented to its own citizens and to the world—albeit one which, unlike in the United States, was for a long time not shared by all French people even in public. I am speaking of the tradition of the core values of the French Revolution, later incorporated to greater or lesser extents in Bonapartism and the French republics: popular sovereignty (even when expressed through a form of plebiscitary monarchy or other leadership), the "Rights of Man," equality before the law, secularism and the "career open to the talents."[75]

These principles became central to the dominant strand of French nationalism: to France's official sense of universal mission and to a concept of French identity and citizenship at home rooted in loyalty to the French state, not in ethnicity or religion. As a result, France was for a long time the most open society in Europe (except for Russia) when it came to the assimilation of foreigners.[76] Note, however, that this openness was intended to create *assimilation*, not mere tolerance. As in the United States, because aliens *could* become French, they were expected to become French.

France was the first country in Europe by many years to emancipate its Jewish minority, but with the explicit intention, voiced by Napoléon, that they would thereby merge into the mass of the French people. This was a very different approach from that of Britain, for example, which was slower to extend full rights to religious minorities but has also been more tolerant of cultural difference. In recent decades this tension has reappeared with regard to France's Muslim minority, as symbolized by the highly controversial decision in 2003 to ban Muslim girls from wearing headscarves in schools, on the principle of the role of the state education system in preserving the secular and assimilatory values of the republic.[77] French civic nationalism therefore is assimilationist but not pluralist. As we shall see, this is also true of some strains of American civic nationalism.

Like the United States, France has also harbored political tendencies, cultures and ideologies which run clearly counter to this French "thesis." These tendencies were most obviously represented in the long refusal of conservative and Catholic forces in the nineteenth century to accept the French Republic and the values on which it was based. However, as in the United States, continuities of political allegiance are not the central feature of this "antithesis." The last watered-down remnants of French monarchism flowed gently enough into loyalty to de Gaulle's Fifth Republic, and the Catholic Church too has long since made its peace with the republic and democracy. Moreover, for long historical periods, even the French extreme Right has largely merged with the center-Rightist mainstream.

It would therefore be wrong to draw any kind of straight political line between the antirevolutionary royalist Chouans of the Vendée in the 1790s and the National Front of Jean-Marie Le Pen in the early twenty-first century. Indeed, as Hans Rogger has emphasized, because historically and internationally the Right has tended to be composed of communities or movements of sentiment rather than of formal ideology, "differences on the Right are even more pronounced than those on the Left, and it is this which makes it so difficult to generalize about the Right, to arrive at universally valid definitions."[78]

Rather, one can trace certain continuities of sentiment which have taken different political forms in different generations. These tendencies have stressed a French national identity based not on secular ideology but on a more or less closed ethnic cultural identity. For a long time this meant adherence to Catholicism; for several decades beginning in the later nineteenth century and culminating in Vichy, it was anti-Semitic; today it means above all being White, speaking good French and not being a Muslim. It generally has been extremely hostile to the administrative, business and cultural elites of Paris, and indeed to Paris itself, with its multiethnic population and modern culture (even when the leaders and ideologists of this tendency have been Parisian intellectuals).

In America, as Walter Russell Mead of the Council on Foreign Relations has written, "The belief that the essence of American nationality lies in dedication to universal principles is constantly at war with the idea that Americanism belongs exclusively to the American people and must be defended against alien influences rather than shared with mankind."[79]

This belief also has been quintessentially true of France. Like every other tendency of its kind, these traditions in both the United States and France have seen themselves as representing the *pays réel,* the true, authentic, immemorial nation, against the *pays légale* of the administrative and cultural elites—a prejudice endlessly appealed to by right-wing American politicians in their diatribes against Washington.[80] Like its conservative nationalist analogues elsewhere in Europe, this French tendency is strongly hostile in spirit to the EU and to globalization—both of which are seen as projects of the cosmopolitan elites and hostile to the interests of ordinary, "true" French people. The natural home of this tendency in the past was the traditional aristocracy and sections of the petty bourgeoisie and peasantry. Today it embraces many workers, often ex-communist ones.

And just as the roots of France's sense of transnational mission can be seen to originate long before the Revolution, so the roots of this antithetical tendency can be traced back to provincial resistance not only against the Revolution, but against previous attempts at royal centralization, standardization, conscription and taxation. Here too is a parallel with the world of the "antithesis" in the United States.

The strong distrust of "government" characteristic of so many Americans has been generally attributed, following the great American historian Frederick Jackson Turner (1861–1932), to the individualist tradition of the American Frontier; and this is, of course, correct. However, this distrust also embodies elements of the old European peasant fear of state authority, which after all had generally appeared to peasants in old Europe—as in much of the "developing world" to this day—in the form of corrupt tax collectors, savage policemen, brutal conscripting sergeants and looting, raping armies (even those of one's own state), all of them speaking in alien languages or dialects. One way of looking at the violently individualistic and antistatist inhabitants of parts of America is to see them as traditional European peasants who ran away into the forests and mountains to escape the demands of the state. They have just run a bit farther.

These "antithetical" tendencies in France have had a natural tendency to rise to the surface in times of economic depression and when France is defeated, humiliated or felt to be in decline. This occurred after France's defeat by Prussia in 1870–71, and culminated in the Dreyfus case.[81] In 1872 Sully Prudhomme repudiated his former internationalism in verse: "I wrote with Schiller:/'I am a citizen of the world'.../ But I have repented at last /Of my perverted love./From now on my love will be/For my country alone./For those men whom I betrayed/Through love of the human race."[82]

This swing to the antithesis happened again in a much more disastrous way with the mass rally to Marshal Pétain and his Vichy regime after France's defeat in 1940. The last time it threatened or transformed the state up to the present came in the 1950s, with the French defeat in Indochina and quagmire in Algeria. But as the popularity of Le Pen's movement indicates, it is by no means certain that some combination of economic depression, immigration and terrorism could not once again raise French chauvinist authoritarinism to truly dangerous heights in the future.

Today, like other such movements elsewhere in Western Europe, this nationalist tendency in France is profoundly defensive, even to a degree "isolationist." It is focused on defending the "traditional" national culture and ethnicity (that is to say, as in the United States, the established ethnic mixture bequeathed in part by previous generations of immigration) against new immigration, new forms of culture and new economic patterns. This form of nationalism shades over easily into various forms of "skinhead" violence.

But this violence too is both portrayed and felt by its exponents to be a matter not of aggression or expansion but of defense of vital collective interests: using ferocious measures to defend the national core community, jobs, "law and order," and so on against aliens. European skinheads and other extreme chauvinists are not really dreaming of marching off to recover Breslau for Germany or Lwow for Poland. And this lack of old-style irredentism and expansionism reflects not only ideology, international reality and contemporary culture but also prudence and the strong and bitter historical memories which permeate European society. Kicking immigrants on street corners is a less formidable proposition than marching off to fight a war.

At present, it seems unlikely that this French antithesis could come to power, at least for a good many years to come. For an intriguing example of a nationalist antithesis which has succeeded in this, India is a good place to look. There too, as in France and the United States, the Indian state and elites after 1947 put forward a civic nationalist thesis about the country to the Indian public and the world. Unlike in France and the United States, this thesis was fostered under foreign imperial rule, but much of its content was the same: India as a secular democracy—indeed, "the world's largest democracy"—dedicated to progress and human rights, and with equal rights and opportunities for all its citizens. For some three decades after independence, closely associated with this Indian civic Creed was a moderate, nontotalitarian form of socialist economics. Internationally, this economic philosophy was associated with a desire to provide enlightened leadership for the former colonial world in its struggle against Western hegemony and neocolonialism.

This democratic civic nationalism has been associated above all with the name of Jawaharlal Nehru and the Congress Party, which he led (and which at the time of this writing is led by his grandson's widow, who—in a testament to the openness of this tradition—is Italian by birth). However, from the start, even the Congress Party harbored elements of a nationalist antithesis based on an idea of India not as a civic but a religious, cultural and to some extent ethnic community. Outside the Congress Party, much more extreme variants were represented by various Hindu political groups, often tinged with fascistic beliefs and modes of organization. These eventually came together to form the Bharatiya Janata Party, or BJP.

As in the French and in American nationalist antitheses, this nationalist tradition rejects the openness and universalism of the Nehruite civic nationalist Creed in favor of a vision of India as a closed cultural community—in this case, of Hindus. It therefore explicitly or implicitly excludes Muslims, Hindus, Christians and others from the "true" Indian political nation. Unlike other such movements, it has become dedicated to modern economic growth and openness (largely because of its desire to challenge China for the role of Asian great power) and enjoys great support among the Indian diaspora in the United States; but it greatly dislikes the more ostentatiously westernized and secular elites in India itself. Like the antithetical tendencies in France and the United States in the past, it can have a very violent edge in dealing with minorities, which are seen as threatening the interests and control of the "core" community. This violent edge has been demonstrated in a long tradition of bloody communal riots and pogroms.[83]

As with their analogues in the United States, over the years Hindu nationalists have come to take on considerable elements of Indian civic nationalism. These elements include what seems to have become a genuine attachment to basic democratic practice—albeit a specifically Indian kind of *Herrenvolk* (master race) democracy in the form of rule by a dominant religious group rather than a race or ethnicity. This partial merger of civic and religious nationalism was certainly not true at the time of independence. In the decades since, leaders of the BJP have seemingly come to recognize that democracy, or at least constitutionalism, is the only system which can hold a country like India together. They also see India's status as a democracy as an integral part of the Indian national greatness of which they are so proud—and not least Indian superiority to the hated Pakistan and the feared China.

The second resemblance to the United States is the complex relationship between this tradition and ethnicity. The roots of the BJP remain chiefly among the Hindi-speaking Hindus of North India, usually of upper and middle castes. But after some weak attempts to make Hindi the Indian national language—abandoned in the face of stiff resistance from South India—the BJP now seems to have settled on a vision of India based on Hindu nationalism, democracy, economic success and military pride. Neither of the Indian nationalisms therefore is an ethnic one—which just shows how limited the relevance of models of nationalism drawn from the "classic" ethnic nationalisms of central Europe are for the study of much of the rest of the world.

The comparison with India is an interesting one, because it goes to the heart of the similarities and differences between right-wing nationalism in the United States and radical nationalist and radical conservative movements elsewhere, both in the past and today. The central point here relates to the "exceptional" attachment of the American radical Right to democracy—not by any means necessarily "liberal" or "pluralist" democracy, but at least the institutions and forms of democracy rather than dictatorship.

40

From Herrenvolk Democracy to Civilizational Empire

This attachment to democracy and the universalist principles of the American Creed has in turn played a central role in America's ability to transcend its racist past and transform itself from a Herrenvolk democracy, based on rigid and savagely oppressive rules of racial exclusion and superiority, into a great "civilizational empire."

The former European national visions of great missions and callings all had a certain guiding image: that of the Roman empire. This is an image which also has a long history in American thought, and which has spread enormously in U.S. public debate as a result of America's emergence as the world's only superpower.[84] Like China and the early Islamic caliphates, Rome not only united many different ethnicities under one language and culture, its legacy continued to shape the history and character of Europe long after the empire itself passed away. These empires were not just states but whole civilizations, transcending racial and ethnic divisions within their borders and projecting their cultural influence far beyond their frontiers in space and time.

As civilizational empires, they are to be distinguished both from purely military empires like the Mongols and from European seaborne Herrenvolk empires, which while undoubtedly transformative of many cultures and societies, also drew a sharp and ruthless dividing line between the master European races and their dark-skinned subject peoples. The Soviet ambition was also that of a civilizational empire: to create a new kind of civilized man, multiethnic in origin but speaking one language and bound by one culture, which in turn would spread beyond the borders of the Soviet Union to influence all mankind.

On its own territory, the sheer size of the United States, its economic dynamism and its ability to assimilate huge numbers of alien (White) immigrants to its Creed and culture have always given America certain features of such an empire. As Justice Oliver Wendell Holmes declared early in the twentieth century, "We are the Romans of the modern world—the great assimilating people."[85]

Beyond its borders, the tremendous economic success of the United States, and the vitality of its culture, also created an informal version of such a civilizational empire. This was shown in the way in which admiration for the United States helped to undermine belief in communism and the Soviet Union in Russia's younger elites in the late 1980s and early 1990s. In terms of the global reach of its "hard" and "soft" power, of American fleets, American language, American food, American popular culture and American versions of economics, the United States today does indeed match the civilizational empires of the past.

In the past, however, U.S. aspirations to play the role of a civilizational empire were long crippled by racism, a fact recognized by many Americans, even if they would not have talked in imperial terms. The intense, specifically Southern racism of President Woodrow Wilson, for example, deeply compromised his liberal internationalism in the eyes of the Japanese and many other non-White peoples of the world, in his own time and since.[86] As the American theologian, moralist and political thinker Reinhold Niebuhr (1892–1971) wrote in 1943, "Our racial pride is incompatible with our responsibilities in the world community. If we do not succeed in chastening it, we shall fail in our task." Gunnar Myrdal's great work of 1944, *An American Dilemma*, was also motivated in part by anxiety at the way in which racism at home was weakening the American struggle against totalitarianism.[87]

During the early years of the Cold War, recognition of the way in which domestic treatment of Blacks undermined U.S. power and influence in the struggle with communism was a major factor in the decision of U.S. national elites to eliminate the public face of this racism in the 1950s and 1960s.[88] Much earlier, President Abraham Lincoln had warned that slavery weakened America's world democratic mission by exposing the nation to the charge of hypocrisy.[89]

When comparing the contemporary United States to other great civilizations of the past, it is vitally important to make a distinction between racism and cultural prejudice. The Han Chinese harbored the strongest prejudices against "barbarians" both beyond and within their frontiers; but these prejudices ceased when the "barbarians" learned Chinese language and culture, adopted the official Confucian ideology (if they aspired to join the elites), and therefore became Chinese. For a central requirement of civilizational empire is a willingness to replace qualifications for membership based on race and ethnic origin with ones based on language, Creed and culture: something that was formally achieved by the Roman empire with the grant of citizenship to all its free subjects in A.D. 212.

Unlike Blacks, Native Americans, or Chinese in the America of the past (and of course in the other West European seaborne empires), barbarians could always be assimilated by the elites of the great empires of Asia. Hence the fact that so many of the great Russian aristocratic names are of Tartar or Circassian origin: Yussupov, Nabokov, Kochubey, Turgenev. Lenin, of course, was a complete ethnic hodgepodge, but also culturally speaking entirely Russian. The Chinese chief minister who led the revolt of 755 which wrecked the early T'ang dynasty, An Lu-Shan, was a sinified Turk from Central Asia; the greatest T'ang poet, Li Po, was also most probably of Turkic origin.[90]

The principle that "one drop of blood" made you Black, and therefore excluded you—whatever your education, property, military valor, or even beauty—from joining or intermarrying with the dominant people and its ruling class, would have been simply impossible for these states. So too would the elaborate racial codings of Dutch colonial Java, New Orleans, Brazil, or the West Indies (quadroon, octaroon, mulatto and so forth). Such rules would have made the expansion of these empires impossible. (To be fair, of course, the cultural differences between Han Chinese and Miao, or Russians and Bashkirs, were also vastly less than those between White Americans and American Indians or newly enslaved Blacks.)[91]

These civilizational empires accepted into their elites anyone who accepted their culture but retained intense hostility to internal groups—such as the Jews in Russia—who were seen either as rejecting that culture or as infiltrating and subverting it for their own national ends. Like the United States today, these empires were also of course strongly hostile to those external "barbarian" peoples who rejected their culture. Indeed, the entire official identity and ideology of these empires was built largely around the distinctions between themselves and the barbarian "Other."

The public elites of America today conform rather closely to this historical pattern of real racial diversity coupled with intense cultural conformity in certain key areas: worship of the Creed and the official imperial gods. Thus the presenters on CNN, picked for their racial diversity, are in fact diverse only in color of skin. They represent a real breakthrough of equality in terms of outward race, but certainly not in culture or even in any real sense of ethnicity. Their presence is a real celebration of America's civilizational achievement—and is also, consciously or unconsciously, intended to be seen as such.

Tremendously positive changes in this regard have occurred in the United States over the past two generations. A striking example is public attitudes to marriages between Whites and Blacks. In 1963, 64 percent of Americans believed in the maintenance of laws against such marriages, which still existed in many states. In 1998, only 13 percent believed that there should be such laws—even though a rather higher proportion expressed private unease about interracial "dating."[92] Moreover, Republicans and Democrats were both equally committed to the legality of interracial marriage.

Racist attitudes still remain deeply embedded in the White South and in the Republican Party. However, they have also had to become modified and coded, usually expressed through policies which are not ostensibly racist (especially regarding welfare, immigration, crime and the "war on drugs") rather than directly. If they had retained their old crude frankness, then it seems likely that far from helping to make the Republicans from 1968 to 2004 the normal "party of government" in the United States (holding the presidency for twenty-four years to the Democrats' twelve), it would have turned them into pariahs and doomed them to minority status. This fact is demonstrated by the speed with which the Republican Party forced Trent Lott to resign as Senate majority leader in December 2002 after he publicly praised Strom Thurmond's segregationist campaign for president in 1948.[93]

Nor has this transformation been simply the work of liberals. On the contrary, a key role has been played by institutions with great right-wing and nationalist prestige: the military, certain Hollywood directors and actors and some evangelical churches. Even in the White South, there has been a development from prejudice based automatically on color of skin to one based on culture (deeply entwined though these two prejudices are).[94] Starting in the 1990s, some of the leading figures and journals of the Christian Right made what seems to be a sincere effort in this regard, with Ralph Reed apologizing for the past racism of the evangelical churches and *Charisma* and *New Man* magazines both publishing articles on successful interracial marriages.[95] The prominent Black appointments to George W. Bush's administration therefore are by no means just tokenism. They mark a real and very positive change of heart.

In the evangelical religious field, a pioneering role was played by the so-called televangelists, who used the new mass media to appeal to a wider audience than ever before. Starting with the Reverend Billy Graham, several of these figures have made a point not only of reaching out to different races, but of including Blacks and others in their church choirs, where the film and television cameras would be sure to pick them up. Graham in particular has been very supportive of a number of Black causes.[96]

One reason for this shift has been the televangelists' own version of America's move from Herrenvolk democracy to civilizational empire—for although from a deeply southern conservative background in North Carolina, Graham was both passionately devoted to the cause of anticommunism and well aware of the ammunition that American racism gave to communist appeals in the "Third World." His move to a form of bland multiracialism also formed part of a shift on his part away from overt and hard-line fundamentalism and toward a form of bland ecumenism which made him acceptable to Dwight D. Eisenhower and later presidents and turned him into "a sort of informal national chaplain."[97]

Moreover, Graham and many other televangelists have aimed deliberately at audiences in the developing world. In the age of globalization, it is no longer possible to keep a missionary appeal abroad completely separate from behavior at home, especially since within the United States, some Protestant churches have set out to woo Latino immigrants away from Catholicism. The Pentecostals already began to reach out to Blacks in the 1950s and 1960s.[98] They have also made major inroads in Latin America.

In other words, Blacks and others who conform to certain forms of respectable behavior—including patriotism and religious practice—are now regarded even by most conservative nationalist White Americans as part of the American "Folk," in Walter Russell Mead's phrase.[99] Secretary of State (and former General) Colin Powell and National Security Adviser Condoleezza Rice are genuinely accepted as good Americans—although of course only through what Black radicals would call "acting White": in other words, accepting the culture, Creed and gods of the civilizational empire.

Of great importance in this shift have been three other institutions with specific prestige in the South and to a lesser extent the "heartland" more generally: the military, the sports industry and the patriotic and macho strain in Hollywood. Thus in stages beginning in the 1940s, the U.S. military has deliberately turned itself into the most genuinely multiracial of all U.S. institutions, one where Blacks and others can advance to the highest ranks without having accusations of unfair preference thrown at them.[100] Starting with President Harry Truman's decision to desegregate the military in 1948, this development was encouraged by all other presidents, with the conscious intention of strengthening America's civilizational appeal to "colored" peoples tempted by communism.[101]

For the military, this shift has increasingly become a matter of necessity as well as ideology. After the military abandoned conscription in the wake of Vietnam, it became highly dependent on low-income groups for its recruits—among whom the racial minorities are overrepresented. More recently, military service has even become a way for American immigrants (including illegal immigrants) to gain early citizenship—a practice which recalls late imperial Rome.

The military also remains deeply mindful of the bitter racial tensions which split the troops in Vietnam, when (thanks to class bias in the conscription system) an army containing a very high proportion of Blacks was commanded by an officer corps which was overwhelmingly White. During the attempt in 2003 to get the Supreme Court to rule against racial preference in higher education, a key part in getting this move rejected was played by friend of the court briefs filed by senior retired military officers, who argued that the well-being of the armed forces requires a large pool of Black university graduates to provide officer material.

Apart from the actual record of courage, success and self-sacrifice on the part of Blacks and other racial groups in the military, Hollywood's presentation of their efforts always has been of great importance, part of a wider pattern by which Hollywood films with a populist nationalist cultural tinge (westerns, police films, sports) have deliberately sought to include a wider and wider range of Americans and present them as valuable citizens and/or soldiers.

A recurrent theme of director John Ford's work is the integration of old and new Americans (and of former Confederates and Unionists) through military service and settlement and defense of the White frontier. Ford paid particular attention to the Irish—not surprisingly, since his original name was Sean Feeny. By 1956 and *The Searchers*, the slow acceptance by the protagonist (played by that arch-conservative nationalist film icon, John Wayne) of a part-Cherokee relative as a comrade has become a central theme (although only because this character is both culturally completely White and Wayne's ally against the savage Comanche, who are to be fought without mercy). One of Ford's last films, *Sergeant Rutledge* (1960), has as its subject a brave and dedicated Black soldier on the frontier, wrongly accused of the murder of a white girl; a nationalist treatment of the theme of Harper Lee's *To Kill a Mockingbird*, with as its "Creedal" backdrop the U.S. Army rather than the U.S. legal system.[102]

During and after World War II, in particular, Hollywood made a point of stressing the courageous war service of American Jews (e.g., William Wellman's *The Story of GI Joe* [1945], with Robert Mitchum). More generally, American war films—like their Soviet equivalents—turned the multiethnic American unit into a formula, with stock WASP (White Anglo-Saxon Protestant), southern, Irish, Italian, Jewish and other elements.[103]

Over the past decade American television soap operas have begun to play a not wholly dissimilar role in promoting racial mixing, although here the field is that of love—or sex—rather than battle. After some four decades of television in which it was wholly absent, interracial "dating" on TV has become if not common—it is hardly common in society—then at least present (although more between Whites and Latinos and Asians than Whites and Blacks).[104]

Another great patriotic film hero, Clint Eastwood, has made a point in some of his films of making a Black (or, in his great *The Outlaw Josie Wales* [1976], an Indian) into his character's closest friend and helper, not as a "Tonto" caricature, but as a dignified, honorable and intelligent character who provides ironic comments on White society and hypocrisy.[105] Eastwood's *Heartbreak Ridge* (1986) is a very Soviet-style example of the mixed-race platoon genre. Coming from directors and actors whom the South and the Heartland have revered, this approach probably had more effect than the more overt antiracism of directors such as Norman Jewison or Denzel Washington.[106] For if Billy Graham *and* Clint Eastwood both suggest a change in racial attitudes, even the most benighted White American must feel somewhere in his heart that his God too is speaking.

But although this process has been a tremendously valuable and noble one, two troubling features of the new order also require notice. The first is that as in Rome, China or the Abbasid caliphate, a relative absence of racism in the strict sense certainly does not denote an absence of bitter hostility and contempt toward culturally different "barbarians" and religious infidels.

Indeed, a process may have been at work in the United States which could be called the "principle of the Claymore mine." A Claymore is essentially a shaped plastic case packed with explosives and steel balls. The explosion, blocked at the rear and sides, hurls shrapnel in the direction of the enemy. Politicians and even media and business figures who express racist hostility to domestic minorities in public now often pay a very heavy price, even though everyone is well aware that, in private, such attitudes continue to stream through much of White American society.

But as with a Claymore mine, the suppression of feelings at home may have only increased the force with which they are directed against foreigners, who remain a legitimate and publicly accepted target of hatred. The former senior U.S. trade negotiator Clyde Prestowitz has written of contemporary Americans' "implicit belief that every human being is a potential American and that his or her present national or cultural affiliations are an unfortunate but reversible accident"—a very imperial Chinese or Roman attitude.[107] In consequence, however, if others nonetheless refuse to behave like Americans, it means that there must be something seriously wicked and malignant about them. In other words, this new order in the United States is a recipe for tolerance within the nation, not outside it. One good definition of solipsism, after all, is that "someone believes that he is the world."[108]

Max Lerner's words of the 1950s remain true today: "One of the American traits is the recoil from the unfamiliar....This seems the more curious when one remembers that America is itself a 'nation of nations' and contains a multitude of diverse cultural traditions. Yet this fact only serves to increase the bafflement of the Americans abroad: since he has seen people of foreign extraction in his own country abandoning their customs and becoming 'Americanized,' he cannot understand why people of foreign countries should not do the same." [109]

Lerner adds that "there is little real hatred of outsiders in this attitude," but that is only as long as outsiders appear completely nonthreatening—which is certainly not the case after 9/11, as far as many Americans are concerned.

The other drawback of the process of building this new American multiracial civilization has been related to conformism and political correctness. The price has often included not only some tooth-grindingly awful films, as in the sickly politically correct piety of Blacks and Whites working together for a sports victory (for example *Remember the Titans* [2000]), but also some positively Soviet-style rewriting of history, as in Mel Gibson's film *The Patriot* (2000). This film, in accordance with the dictates of the American Creed and the national ideology, presents the South Carolina militia of the American War of Independence as an early home of multicultural American patriotism, racial harmony and mutual respect. As in Soviet films, this is all a deliberate part of building a new American nation; unlike in the Soviet Union, the process is voluntary on the part of the directors.

This tendency to a kind of propaganda version of American history and society can be seen as one aspect of the spontaneous "liberal absolutism" of the American Creed, as described by Hartz and many other observers from the time of Tocqueville down to the present. Today it is partly reflected in the phenomenon of "political correctness" and contributes to the limitations on thought and debate in the United States concerning both the American domestic system and the nation's role in the world.

Two

Thesis: Splendor and Tragedy of the American Creed

Even a good idea can be a little frightening when it is the only idea a man has ever had.

—Louis Hartz[1]

Nations, as individuals, who are completely innocent in their own esteem, are insufferable in their human contacts.

—Reinhold Niebuhr[2]

The American Thesis has also been called the American Creed and the American Ideology. It is the set of propositions about America which the nation presents to itself and to the outside world: "Americans of all national origins, classes, religions, Creeds, and colors, have something in common: a social ethos, a political Creed."[3]

Ralph Waldo Emerson wrote of adherence to American governing principles as a form of religious conversion. This Thesis or Creed, with its attendant national myths, forms the foundation for American civic nationalism and makes the public face of the United States an example of civic nationalism par excellence.[4] In theory, anyone who assents to the American Thesis can become an American, irrespective of language, culture, or national origin, just as anyone could become a Soviet citizen by assenting to communism.[5]

The principles of the American Thesis are also rationalist and universalist ones, held by Americans to be applicable to peoples and societies everywhere and indeed throughout time. In Tocqueville's words, the Americans "are unanimous upon the general principles that ought to rule human society"; and this is no less true at the start of the twenty-first century than it was when Tocqueville made his observation in the 1830s.

Partly in consequence, this set of assumptions is also basically optimistic. It suggests both that the United States has achieved the highest possible form of political system and that this great system can be extended to the rest of humanity.

Centuries before Francis Fukuyama recoined the phrase, a certain belief that America represented the "end of history" was already common in American thought and still more in the American subconscious. "I alone inaugurating largeness, culminating time," as Walt Whitman put it, speaking for his country.[6]

In Richard Hofstadter's words, "It has been our fate as a nation not to have ideologies but to be one."[7] This American Thesis is also, both in belief and in reality, the core foundation of America's "soft power" in the world and of its role as a civilizational empire: the American version of *Romanita*. Both in the past and at present, the American Creed has deeply shaped the conduct of U.S. foreign policy.[8]

The essential elements of the American Creed and American civic nationalism are faith in liberty, constitutionalism, the law, democracy, individualism and cultural and political egalitarianism. They have remained in essence the same through most of American history.[9] They are chiefly rooted in the Enlightenment and are also derived from English traditions: the liberal philosophy of John Locke as well as much older beliefs in the law and in the "rights of freeborn Englishmen."

Economic egalitarianism is definitely not a part of the Creed. On the contrary, it has been closely associated with belief in the absolute superiority of free market capitalism, unlimited economic opportunity and consumerism. These elements are contested by larger numbers of Americans than are its political elements, which are believed in by overwhelming majorities. In recent decades racial tolerance and equality have also come to be seen as essential components of the Creed, and the rights of women are also mentioned—although these too are somewhat contested, in private at least, by considerable numbers of Americans. Informally, an important part of the Creed is also the belief that the United States embodies and exemplifies the only model of successful modernity in general: "Americans see history as a straight line and themselves standing at the cutting edge of it as representatives for all mankind."[10]

At the start of the twenty-first century, the contents of the American Thesis are of course not exceptional to America; most of the beliefs are also held by the other developed democracies, and indeed in public at least by most of the world. American democracy forms part of a subworld of Western democratic states; just as American capitalism, although it has highly specific features, is inextricably entwined with the world capitalist system as a whole.

Two features of the Creed are exceptional: the absolutist passion with which these beliefs are held and the degree to which they are integral to American nationalism. Louis Hartz in the 1950s wrote of the Creed's "compulsive nationalism" and the "fixed, dogmatic liberalism of a liberal way of life."[11] The myths attendant on the Creed include a very widespread belief that the United States is exceptional in its allegiance to democracy and freedom and is therefore exceptionally good. And because America is exceptionally good, it both deserves to be exceptionally powerful and by nature cannot use its power for evil ends. The American Creed is therefore a key foundation of belief in America's innate innocence.[12]

According to Samuel Huntington, "It is possible to speak of a body of political ideas that constitutes 'Americanism' in a sense in which one can never speak of 'Britishism,' 'Frenchism,' 'Germanism,' or 'Japaneseism.' Americanism in this sense is comparable to other ideologies and religions. To reject the central ideas of that doctrine is to be un-American.…This identification of nationality with political Creed or values makes the United States virtually unique."[13]

In fact, as noted in Chapter 1, other states also have embodied their own versions of such a thesis in their own versions of civic nationalism. However, in most of these cases the thesis either has been publicly contested by many people, as in France, or has been, historically speaking, mainly the faith of national or imperial elites, as in imperial China. What is unusual about America is the sheer unanimity of belief in these guiding national principles.

The Canadian sociologist Sacvan Bercovitch has described discovering in America "a hundred sects and factions, each apparently different from the others, yet all celebrating the same mission." This ideological consensus, he said, is invested with "all the moral and emotional appeal of a religious symbol." Discovering it gave him "some of the anthropologist's sense of wonder at the symbol of a tribe."[14] At the start of the twenty-first century, the United States may indeed be the most truly ideological society on the face of the earth.

America is not, of course, the most ideological *state* on earth. A number of other states still claim an infinitely more rigorous, ruthless and extensive right of control over the thoughts of their subjects than the American state ever has, or ever could. In their prime, the communist states made such claims. But even in their prime, these ideologies were resisted by large parts of the populations concerned; and after a few decades, not only most of the intelligentsia but most ordinary people as well lost all genuine belief in them, while continuing to go through the required motions in public. The same became true of theocratic Iran in the course of the 1990s.

Russian and Chinese intellectuals of my acquaintance who came to America in the 1990s after living in this atmosphere of private cynicism toward public ideology often reacted with utter astonishment, and some fear, to the way in which ordinary Americans glorify their country's beliefs, institutions, laws and economic practices in private conversations, not just as a matter of defensive patriotism, but with a sincere belief in their validity for all mankind: "They actually believe all this! No-one is forcing them to say it!"[15] Closely related to this tendency is the sense of national mission: "All nations…have long agreed that they are chosen peoples; the idea of special destiny is as old as nationalism itself. However, no nation in modern history has been quite so consistently dominated as the United States by the belief that it has a particular mission in the world."[16]

Even most American dissidents throughout history have sincerely phrased their protests not as a rejection of the American Creed as such, but rather as a demand that Americans, or American governments, return to a purer form of the Creed or to a more faithful adherence to it. Groups which really step outside the Creed soon find themselves marginalized or even suppressed. The mass of the White population at least simply takes the Creed for granted.

Given the general stereotype of the United States as a new, young and ever-changing country, it is important to note that the antiquity of American institutions is one reason why Americans are so loyal to them. These institutions are older and less changed than those in almost any other state in the world. Since the U.S. Constitution was adopted in 1787, the great majority of states have undergone revolutionary institutional change. Even the British political system has changed far more fundamentally than the American has over these two centuries.

The principles underlying these institutions, and the American Thesis which these institutions embody, are much older still. According to Huntington, "The principal elements of the English constitution were exported to the new world, took root there, and were given new life precisely at the time that they were being abandoned in the home country. They were essentially Tudor and hence significantly medieval in character. ...The institutional framework established in 1787 has, in turn, changed remarkably little in 175 years."[17]

Far from being a "new" or "young" state, America therefore has some claim to be almost the oldest state in the world. It is "the oldest republic, the oldest democracy, the oldest federal system; it has the oldest written constitution and boasts the oldest of genuine political parties."[18]

The origins of these American institutions go back to medieval and, more important, Tudor England, before the rise of centralizing monarchies on the continent of Europe and of centralizing parliamentary government in Britain. Huntington links the continuing belief of Americans in a fundamental, essentially unchanging law to the English medieval tradition: *"nolumus mutare leges Angliae"* (we do not wish to change the laws of England), as the barons declared at Runnymede when they forced King John to accept the Magna Carta: "This old idea of a fundamental law beyond human control was given new authority by identifying it with a written constitution."[19] These then are the ancient beliefs and sentiments which filled the dry, rationalist carapace of the U.S. Constitution.[20]

American civic nationalism has been central both to the assimilation over the centuries of huge numbers of immigrants and to America's eventual transition from Herrenvolk democracy to civilizational empire. As Dr. Martin Luther King Jr. declared at the Lincoln Memorial on August 28, 1963, "I still have a dream. It is a dream deeply rooted in the American dream that one day this nation will rise up and live out the true meaning of its Creed."[21]

Thus the contents of the American Creed are of tremendous importance to America and to humanity. On many occasions throughout history, the Creed has led Americans not just to make sacrifices for their own countrymen and for humanity, but to question their national motives and improve their institutions and behavior. It also helps stand between the United States and certain imperial crimes, and indeed makes the U.S. exercise of direct empire less likely, for it enforces at least a surface respect for democracy and self-determination.

It could be said that the American Thesis, like democracy in India, is also a matter of necessity for the United States. It is essential to preventing the country's immensely disparate and sometimes morally absolutist social, cultural, religious and ethnic groups from flying apart. Creedal civic nationalism and belief in the value of the American Thesis for America and humanity are perhaps the only things on which Pentecostalists in Texas and gays in San Francisco can agree.[22]

The American Creed, and the institutions which it underpins, are indeed the nation's greatest glory and will be its greatest legacy after the United States itself has disappeared. The fruits of American economics may prove ambiguous or even disastrous in the long run; but the principles which have allowed masses of diverse people in an enormous land to live together and prosper without coercion will always have positive lessons to teach.

Restoring Innocence

Despite its great virtues, however, this civic nationalism and the ideological consensus underpinning it carry with them certain grave interlinked dangers. As Reinhold Niebuhr wrote: "Irony consists of apparently fortuitous incongruities in life which are discovered, upon closer examination, to be not merely fortuitous....Our moral perils are not those of conscious malice or the explicit lust for power. They are the perils which can be understood only if we realize the ironic tendency of virtues to turn into vices when too complacently relied on; and of power to become vexatious if the wisdom which directs it is trusted too confidently."[23]

Of these perils, two in particular have been remarked on by American historians and commentators: conformism and messianism. Both are usually somewhat latent and held in check by American traditions of empiricism, pragmatism and open debate.[24] In moments of national shock and trauma, such as 9/11, however, they tend to become active and to do much to shape America's response.

Both these tendencies draw on a set of common myths, so deeply embedded as to operate beneath the level of most American's consciousness. These myths are not, strictly speaking, part of the formal Thesis or Creed, but help give it much of its emotional force. Among other things, these myths affirm the idea of America's innocence.[25] Or as President George W. Bush put it, "I'm amazed that there's such misunderstanding of what our country is about that people would hate us. I'm—like most Americans, I just can't believe it because I know how good we are."[26]

As the Bush administration's National Security Strategy of 2002 has it: "Today, the United States enjoys a position of unparalleled military strength and great economic advantage. In keeping with our heritage and principles, we do not use our strength to press for unilateral advantage. We seek instead to create a balance of power that favors human freedom: conditions in which all nations and societies can choose for themselves the rewards and challenges of political and economic liberty."[27]

This belief in American innocence, of "original sinlessness," is both very old and very powerful.[28] It plays a tremendously important role in strengthening American nationalism and in diminishing the nation's willingness to listen to other countries, viewed in turn as originally sinful. This belief in national sinlessness, like all such beliefs, contributes greatly to America's crowning sin of Pride—the first deadly sin and, in medieval Catholic theology, the one from which all other sins originally stem.

This is in origin a New England Puritan, or "Yankee," myth, stemming from the idea of the settlers as God's elect, born again in the New World and purged of the stews and sins of England and Europe. It was later enthusiastically adopted by grateful refugees from Europe and elsewhere, fleeing persecution or war in their homelands.[29] It received an early European endorsement in 1782 from the French Americanaphile Hector St. Jean de Crevecoeur, who celebrated the American as a "New Man," reborn in a kind of Rousseauan natural state in the wilderness and purged thereby of the European past.[30]

The White South was historically suspicious of this myth, because its inhabitants saw it as responsible for the (in their view) high-minded, high-handed, hypocritical Yankee moralizing which led the North to condemn the South first over slavery, then over Civil Rights. A strong but unacknowledged echo of this historical position can be found in the deep skepticism of the Southern patrician Senator William Fulbright of Arkansas concerning the messianic follies which in his view helped embroil the United States in Vietnam and other unnecessary disputes.[31] This attitude is also reflected in the continuing skepticism of many Southern conservative Republicans concerning "nation building." At the same time, however, the passionate American nationalism of this Southern tradition has also led its bearers over time to identify strongly with the "City on a Hill" image of America as part of their belief in the country's unique greatness and moral supremacy in the world.

As the liberal commentator Richard Cohen wrote in 2003, asking how America could have gone to war with Iraq in the face of all evidence and warnings: "[The Iraq War] was no mere failure of intelligence. This was a failure of character. Why? ... Finally, there was our smugness—the sort of American exceptionalism that so rankles non-Americans. No one better exemplified that than Bush himself."[32]

In 1980 Conor Cruise O'Brien quoted *New York* magazine as lamenting that "we lost our innocence in the Seventies, and, for the first time, a war," and commented:

> The lost war is not hard to identify, but the lost innocence is worthy of respectful and inquisitive wonder. The French lost a war (admittedly not for the first time) in the Sixties, in Algeria, in much the same way and for much the same reasons as those for which the United States, ten years later, lost a war in Indochina. Negative generalizations are usually hazardous, but I offer

confidently the proposition that no Frenchman wrote, and no French peri-
odical published, at the end of the Sixties, any claim that France had lost its
innocence as well as a war during that period....Yet the theme of American
innocence—whether lost, preserved, or to be recaptured—is not a mere mawk-
ish conceit, but represents a powerful and active ferment of meaning that has
worked throughout American history.[33]

An unwillingness or inability among Americans to question the country's
sinlessness feeds a culture of public conformism in the nation, which has been
commented on across the centuries. "In the abstract we celebrate freedom of opinion as part of our patriotic legacy; it is only when some Americans exercise it that
other Americans are shocked.... Intolerance of dissent is a well-noted feature of
the American national character," in Senator Fulbright's words.[34]

This is not true of the United States as a whole, and certainly not of American
academia; but in my experience it certainly is true for dominant sections of the
political, intellectual and media worlds of Washington, DC, and the American
ruling elites. Tocqueville (the most famous European admirer of America, it should
be noted) declared that "I know of no country where there is so little true independence of mind and freedom of discussion as in America....The majority raises
very formidable barriers to the liberty of opinion: within these barriers an author
may write whatever he pleases, but he will repent it if he ever step beyond them."[35]

Like the description of Nicholas I's Russia by Tocqueville's compatriot and contemporary the Marquis de Custine, this could be described as an exaggeration of the
truth. America has, after all, throughout its history produced famous dissidents.
However, their spheres have tended to be rather more limited than in other developed countries. The great dissident wave of the 1960s and early 1970s was to a considerable extent an epiphenomenon which was rejected by the American masses.
Moreover, dissent can be in part identified with certain regional and ethnic traditions in the United States, traditions which do not extend to the mass of the American people as a whole: "For all the lip service given to respect for cultural differences,
Americans seem to lack the resources to think about the relationship between groups
that are culturally, socially or economically quite different."[36]

One source of the immense power of the American Creed and civic nationalism in American society is that they combined both the Enlightenment and the
"Protestantoid" religious strands of the old American tradition, in a way summed
up in Julia Ward Howe's "Battle Hymn of the Republic," with its melding of biblical and liberal imagery. The Kingdom of God became identified with the American Republic.[37]

As "mainline" Protestantism in most of the United States (but not, as we shall see,
in the Greater South) became more liberal and latitudinarian in the course of the
twentieth century, a diffuse form of vaguely Protestantoid "civil religion" also came
to form a central part of this national consensus. This civil religion owed something

to the deism of the republic's founders, who had also emphasized the central importance of religion for the survival of the republic, without stipulating what that religion should be (although they certainly meant some variety of Protestant).

In President Eisenhower's much-quoted words, "Our government makes no
sense unless it is founded on a deeply felt religious faith—and I don't care what it
is."[38] The identification of the positive civic virtue of religion with nationalism
was strengthened still further by the struggle against "atheist communism."[39] This
diffuse, nondenominational Judeo-Christian religious culture became in turn part
of what Will Herberg, Robert Bellah and others have called America's "civil religion," composed of a mixture of the principles of the American Creed with a set
of historical and cultural myths about the nation.[40] This became the essential cultural underpinning of America's current version of civic nationalism.

One social studies textbook for fourth graders (ten-year-olds) entitled *Our
People* sums up aspects of this civil religion, including deliberately targeted national integration: The textbook discussion "opens with a discussion of a major
national ceremony, the inauguration of a president, and a visit to the Lincoln
Memorial and other Washington sites. This presentation is clearly intended to
elicit feelings of membership in a national community. The chapter concludes
with a comment by a fictitious character: 'Yes,' said Maria to Pedro, 'this is a great
country. We are all Americans.'"[41]

The conformism of ideological attitudes reflects in part the self-definition of
the great majority of Americans as "middle class." By now this definition has little
to do with class in the economic sense, but everything to do with being "respectable," which means, above all, sharing a certain set of common values, including
the American Creed and American nationalism.

The legacy of the 1960s and of older radical traditions lives on today in American universities—although these often enough suffer from their own form of liberal conformism. Moreover, it must be noted that these myths are both in their
origin and in their location today principally *White* myths. Blacks and others who
wish to join the establishment must worship these gods of the American
civilizational empire, at least in public; but as Richard Hughes has noted, although
Blacks believe in and have appealed to the American Creed, every one of its attendant myths takes on a highly ironic aspect when viewed from the perspective of
Black or Native American history.[42]

As far as the official and semiofficial world of Washington, DC, is concerned, I
can testify from my own experience to the continuing truth of the following passage from Louis Hartz, one of the greatest students of the American Creed and its
consequences, written in the 1950s:

> When one's ultimate values are accepted wherever one turns, the absolute
> language of self-evidence comes easily enough. This then is the mood of
> America's absolutism: the sober faith that its norms are self-evident. It is one
> of the most powerful absolutisms in the world....It was so sure of itself that it

hardly needed to become articulate, so secure that it could actually support a pragmatism which seemed on the surface to belie it. American pragmatism has always been deceptive because, glacierlike, it has rested on miles of submerged conviction, and the conformitarian ethos which that conviction generates has always been infuriating because it refuses to pay its critics the compliment of an argument.[43]

As a consequence, there is a strong tendency to treat even licensed dissidents essentially as jesters. They ring their bells and even dare on occasions to hit the democratic sovereign over the head with a bladder and tell him that he is a fool. The king laughs loudly and tosses them a bone; but does he listen to them? Often, like King Lear, only when evident facts have given him no choice, and the jester's advice is too late to be of much use to him. And perhaps one should not complain. America is not at present *physically* repressive of dissent, and, after all, it is better to wear a jester's cap than a prisoner's chains, let alone a hangman's noose.

This conformism is nonetheless dangerous both to liberty and to the frank and honest discussion of public issues; especially in time of war, when it is exacerbated by a heightened nationalism. It is particularly alarming when combined with the loyalty and trust which many Americans in time of war instinctively feel toward their president and administration, and which was reflected for many months in the deference paid to the Bush administration by mainstream American media after 9/11.[44]

One consequence of a national discourse based on a rigid ideological consensus is that it gives to certain words the power of what W. H. Auden in 1967 called "black magic"—the power to suspend in audiences a capacity for independent thought: "More deadly than the Idle Word is the use of words as Black Magic....For millions of people today, words like Communism, Capitalism, Imperialism, Peace, Freedom and Democracy have ceased to be words the meaning of which can be inquired into and discussed, and have become right or wrong noises to which the response is as involuntary as a knee reflex."[45]

When President Eisenhower in his Inaugural Address of 1952 declared that "freedom is pitted against slavery; lightness against the dark," he was of course expressing a truth about Stalinist communism, but he was also summoning up a spirit of absolutism in America which he himself later seemed to regret.[46] Indeed, this later repentance from messianism has been true of some of the most famous praise-singers of that messianism, including Herman Melville (in his poem *Clarel*), and Walt Whitman. Reinhold Niebuhr, who coined the phrase "the children of light and the children of darkness" for the battle against totalitarianism during World War II, later became one of the most incisive critics of American arrogance, mythopoeia and self-deception.[47]

It has been widely remarked how the Bush administration's use of the words "terrorism" and "evil" after 9/11 partially shut down the possibility for intelligent discussion of American strategy. But this is no less true of the administration's use of the word "freedom" and its identification of this word both with the United

States and with American policies in the Middle East. The Bush administration composed rhetorical spells drawn from the basic elements of the American ideological consensus; until the situation in postwar Iraq spoiled the magic, these spells allowed them for a while to play the Pied Piper to much of the nation.

Lines written by the historian of the South and political thinker C. Vann Woodward on this subject during the Vietnam War are no less valid today: "The characteristic American adjustment to the current foreign and domestic enigmas that confound our national myths has not been to abandon the myths but to reaffirm them. Solutions are sought along traditional lines....Whatever the differences and enmities that divide advocates and opponents (and they are admittedly formidable), both sides seem predominantly unshaken in their adherence to one or another or all of the common national myths."[48]

It may seem surprising that passages like these should still ring so true decades later, given the horrible lessons which the experience of Vietnam supposedly taught. Like so many of the better literary and cinematic works on Vietnam, director Francis Ford Coppola's *Apocalypse Now* (1979) is among other things a profound questioning of civic nationalist myths about the United States, including its inevitable success, its innocence, its benevolence, and its national mission. And as the film's protagonist, Captain Willard (Martin Sheen), says of his task, "I wanted a mission, and for my sins they gave me one....It was a real choice mission. And when it was over, I'd never want another."[49]

At the time, the vast majority of Americans would have agreed with this conclusion. A quarter of a century later, it sometimes seems almost as if the entire historical episode has been erased from American public memory. In Loren Baritz's bitter words of 1985, in a chapter entitled "The American Lullaby": "Our power, complacency, rigidity and ignorance have kept us from incorporating our Vietnam experience into the way we think about ourselves and the world....For one brief moment, later in the 1970s, it looked as if we had developed some doubts about our international and cultural moorings. It looked as if we might have the nerve and wisdom to be concerned not only about Vietnam, but about ourselves. But there is no need to think unless there is doubt. 'The era of self-doubt is over,' President Reagan assured the West Point cadets. Freed of doubt, we are freed of thought. Many Americans now seem to feel better about themselves."[50]

This initial impression is, however, in part a false one. Some of the bitter lessons of Vietnam have sunk deeply into the American consciousness. In 2003–2004, the bloody and chaotic aftermath of victory in Iraq recalled them to life. In the two years after 9/11, however, they were largely swept away by a tide of myth-based nationalism against which it was very difficult to argue. The period during which the memories of Vietnam were suspended was not very long—but it was long enough to get America into Iraq.[51]

The figure of Ronald Reagan is critical to an understanding of how America dealt with the legacy of Vietnam and the consequences for America today and in future.[52] On one hand, Reagan's external policy demonstrated that he and most of his administration were determined not to get involved in any major conflict, and realized full well how bitterly unpopular a serious war would be with a majority of Americans. The common left-wing image of Reagan as a warmonger is therefore quite wrong.[53]

The Reagan administration conforms to a key feature of the American security elites and military-industrial complex examined in Chapter 5: namely that they tend to be "militarist, but not bellicose." In Reagan's rhetoric, however, the "Great Communicator" was a superb restorer of the founding myths of American nationalism, so badly tarnished by Vietnam; and this was without question because he believed them to the full himself, particularly regarding his belief in American innocence, American beneficence and America as the heartland of human freedom and progress. He held "an innocent and unshakeable belief in the myth of American exceptionalism."[54] In Garry Wills's superb phrase, Reagan was "the demagogue as rabble-soother."[55]

Reagan's mixture proved the perfect one to reassure Americans after the combined traumas of defeat in Vietnam, bitter political divisions at home, the Watergate scandal and the Iranian hostage crisis. But by far the most important ingredient in the mixture was that, in Woodward's words, Reagan "reaffirmed" America's national myths. He also did so in a style which not only calmed but united most Americans. In this Reagan's geniality, his acting skill and his genuine identification with his country and countrymen made him a far more uniting figure than George W. Bush, who represents the same nationalist mixture but in a considerably harsher form.

In his brilliant essay of 1982, "The Care and Repair of Public Myth," William H. McNeill examined classic American myths of superiority and benevolence, and remarked that "no one is likely to reaffirm these discredited notions today, even though public rhetoric often assumes the reality of such myths without expressly saying so. Politicians and journalists really have little choice, since suitably revised national and international myths are conspicuous by their absence."[56]

This passage brings out the full responsibility of Reagan and indeed those who voted for him. After all, they elected him in part precisely because he was so good at restoring their myths about their country, including the belief that Vietnam had been a noble crusade.[57] As a result, while Americans remember in their guts that Vietnam was an unpleasant experience the repetition of which should be avoided, its deeper lessons remained largely unlearned, and in our own time it has proved possible to "reaffirm these discredited notions."

One reason for this was that while the Vietnam War was a dreadful experience for those Americans who fought in it, their numbers were small, and—as mentioned before—unlike European and Asian wars, or for that matter the experience of the Vietnamese, Americans at home were physically unaffected: "for most Americans the tangible consequences of the debacle in Southeast Asia seem inordinately slight."[58] This lack of personal knowledge of war was of course true of Reagan himself, and is true of George W. Bush and all the other men in his administration of 2000 to 2004 who were of military age during the Vietnam War but for some reason failed to serve.

In another way, however, the trauma of Vietnam was if anything too deep to be addressed: nothing less than "the death of the national god" and the national religion of American innocence, goodness and God-given success. Without these beliefs, it was feared by Americans at some deep, semiconscious level, U.S. civic nationalism itself would also wither and die. This fallen national god therefore had to be pieced back together and returned to his pedestal.[59]

It is interesting that both McNeill in his essay and John Hellmann in his fascinating study of American literary and cinematic approaches to Vietnam call for American myths to be reformulated on a new basis, one which is more progressive, honest and morally courageous. Neither, however, suggests trying to do without national myths altogether.[60] Actor/director Clint Eastwood's distinctly post-Vietnam western *The Outlaw Josie Wales* (1976) can also be seen as an attempt to help heal the war's wounds by merging Hollywood western traditions with new cultural and social attitudes to create a more humane, open and multicultural American mythology.[61]

Conformism and Political Correctness: Ignorance Is Myth

Perhaps a society as diverse and as bitterly divided culturally as America, with its diversity continually increased both by immigration and by the creative and destructive surges of capitalist change, cannot in fact live without strong common myths and the strong civic nationalism which depends on them. Thus even as memories of Vietnam were being suppressed, other developments within U.S. society and culture were encouraging a tendency to propagate soft, conflict-free, lowest-common-denominator versions of American nationalist myths and history. These versions have been based on a projection of the contemporary form of the American Creed back into the past.[62]

Curiously enough, Reagan's own style can be seen as related in some ways to a phenomenon which at first sight appears absolutely alien to it: "political correctness" on the part of the academic Left and representatives of racial and ethnic minorities, especially when applied to American schools. In its original form, this was supposed to correct the prejudices, reflected in demeaning and contemptuous language, which for so long humiliated and oppressed a range of minorities in the nation. In this the political correctness movement has largely succeeded, although only in the context of much wider changes in society and culture. And this success is an unequivocal good, if one remembers the revolting racist language of the past and the treatment which it encouraged.

The problem is, however, that the picture presented to schoolchildren as a result tends to conform to nationalist myths about America as an innocent, happy, conflict-free society and to propagate the American Thesis in its purest and most basic form. Thus Frances FitzGerald paints a quite Soviet picture of the photography selection in school textbooks about the United States:

The treatment of European minorities is far more realistic than that of non-European minorities, whose sensibilities the publishers are anxious not to offend. The photographs in the mass-market texts rarely show a non-White person who is brutalized, dirty or even poor—unless the photograph specifically illustrates "pockets of poverty in America."...Most of them are smiling. You can find pictures of Chicano farmworkers, but the workers are always clean and look as if they're enjoying their work. They're always smiling at Cesar Chavez. The Puerto Ricans are smiling and healthy. The Chinese are smiling at healthy-looking vegetable stands. Indeed, everyone is smiling so hard you would think that all non-White people in the United States took happy pills. (The Russians, by contrast, appear to be a somber lot. Their grimness dates from a time in the fifties when a group of right-wing organizations made an enormous fuss about a photograph of smiling Russian children.)...Not only fundamentalists but progressives as well have a strong tendency to think that the schools should present the world, or the country, as an ideal construct. The censorship of schoolbooks is simply the negative face of the demand that the books portray the world as a utopia of the eternal present.[63]

Diane Ravitch describes how an American history textbook by Gary B. Nash, a historian of impeccable progressive credentials, was attacked by left-wing and minority representatives in the late 1980s, accused of being "anti-black, anti-Semitic, anti-Muslim, anti-American Indian, anti-gay and anti-Christian."[64]

A few years later, in the mid-1990s, Professor Nash and colleagues came under savage attack from the nationalist Right—with Lynne Cheney again playing a leading role—for their work in drawing up proposals for a new set of National History Standards for teaching in classrooms which allegedly ignored America's heroes, cast doubts on American myths and undermined American patriotism. The groups responsible for the attacks were largely the same as those which in 1994–95 had forced the Smithsonian Institution in Washington, DC, to abandon an exhibition showing the effects of the atomic bombing of Hiroshima and compelled the director of the Air and Space Museum to resign.[65]

This tendency toward a bland patriotic picture of America—of "authorless crimes and sideless conflicts," in FitzGerald's words—is of long standing.[66] Her portrait of smiling America was first published in 1979, but a British journalist, Andrew Gumbel, recorded similar feelings in 2003 when his son first went to school in California. His article is worth quoting at some length, as the appalled reaction of a politically centrist citizen of a vital English-speaking ally of the United States to behavior which most Americans take for granted:

> Even after five years in the United States, I continue to be surprised by the omnipresence of patriotic conformism....With my son's education at stake, I can't help pondering the link between what is fed to children as young as six and what American adults end up knowing or understanding about the wider world. There is much that is admirable in the unique brand of idealism that

drives American society, with its unshakeable belief in the constitutional principles of freedom and limitless opportunity. Too often, though, the idealism
becomes a smokescreen concealing the uglier realities of the United States and
the way in which it throws its economic, political and military weight around
the globe. Children are recruited from the very start of their school careers to
believe in a project one might call Team America, whose oft-repeated mantra
is: we're the good guys, we always strive to do the right thing, we live in the
greatest country in the world. No other point of view, no other cultural mindset,
is ever seriously contemplated....

The manipulation of education is more subtle and, arguably, more insidi-
ous than it was 50 years ago at the height of the Cold War and the great Red
Scare. Then, the battle for hearts and minds was about the straightforward
exclusion of certain books and topics in pursuit of a political agenda. ... These
days, the issue is no longer banning books, even if that still goes on in parts of
the heartland dominated by the Christian right, but rather systemic conformism. It used to be that an inspiring teacher could overcome the shortcomings
of bland textbooks and blinkered administrative madness. But with the cur-
riculum now much more closely defined and homogenized ... [teachers] are
effectively forced into complicity with the textbook pretence that every historical struggle has now been settled and can be summarized in a few sooth-
ing lines of near-meaningless analytical blancmange.[67]

Gumbel quotes a song from his son's elementary school class:

America, I love you!
From all sorts of places,
They welcomed all the races
To settle on their shore...
To give them protection
By popular election,
A set of laws they chose.
They're your laws and my laws,
For your cause and my cause
That's why this country rose.[68]

These words would cause any historically aware Blacks or American Indians to
grind their teeth—but, as Gumbel points out, they are taken by most American
children as simply natural. This nationalist tendency is greatly encouraged by a
wider decline in historical studies and indeed in general culture (a decline of course
not confined to the United States). As a result, Americans' knowledge of the world,
and their own history, has not declined over the past sixty years—but it also has not
improved from the miserable level of that time. In 2001, 57 percent of American
high school students were graded "below basic" in history, with only 11 percent
rated proficient or advanced.[69] In many individual cases, the result is pure ignorance; but this cannot be true of a society as a whole, which needs some kind of

basic cultural operating principles in order to function. For America as a whole, the absence of historical knowledge does not mean ignorance, but the presence of myth.

Michael Lind has argued cogently that a combination of political correctness with a system of (very limited and selective) positive discrimination for minorities actually serves the interests of what he calls the "overclass." This overclass is still overwhelmingly White, and even WASP, but creams off and co-opts small numbers of the Black and other elites while diverting the energies of radicals into essentially pointless struggles over symbols—and away from concrete transracial issues such as immigration control and raising the minimum wage, which would genuinely help ordinary members of the racial minorities, who on average remain markedly poorer than the White population.[70]

Political correctness of this type is not simply the result of a swing to the Left in academia on one hand meeting a newly radicalized Right on the other. It also reflects profound changes in American society from the 1960s on: the freeing of Blacks as a serious political force and the resumption of mass immigration without racial restrictions. The resulting new society is one to which Americans of many different political allegiances have had to respond.

Thus not just official American patriotic propaganda, but the visual propaganda of the nationalist and religious Right is in general deliberately multiracial (Lynne Cheney's patriotic primer is full of drawings of Black and Asian American toddlers waving flags and playing at being soldiers).[71] Indeed, to be fair, one could almost say that America over the past generation or so has become so complicated that its educational system is more or less *forced* back to simplistic myths, for trying to teach or discuss the full reality would be physically impossible.

This connection between diversity and conformism is not only involuntary but also quite deliberate. American public culture is so conformist *because* the nation is so diverse and also because concerning other races, its history before the 1950s was so foul. In this sense, political correctness can be seen as an aspect of what the classical French analyst of nationalism Ernest Renan (1823–1892) said about the creation of modern nations: "Forgetting, I would almost say historical error, is a crucial factor in the creation of a nation, which is why progress in historical studies often constitutes a danger for [the principle of] nationality....The essence of a nation is that all individuals have many things in common, and also that they have forgotten many things."[72]

Precisely because a good many of the people and groups making up contemporary America actually have very little in common, in order to become a nation it may be necessary for Americans to be even more forgetful than other peoples.

The example Renan used was that of the French religious wars of the past. Had he still been around in France after World War II, he could have used the treatment of the memory of the German occupation and Vichy; and this need to forget in order to build the nation is true with even greater force of past racial oppression in the United States. In this sense, Americans can be said to be "held together only by ideas" in the same way that Soviet citizens were. The ideas of American civic nationalism are, happily, much more positive and valuable ones than those of Soviet communism—but that does not change the fact that they cannot be seriously questioned without endangering the stability of the entire structure. Their absolutist character influences in turn the underlying ideology of American foreign policy, making it more difficult for even highly educated and informed Americans to form a detached and objective view of that policy; for to do so would also risk undermining the bonds uniting diverse Americans at home.[73]

Messianism, Exemplary and Dynamic

So pervasive is the American Creed or Ideology in American culture that even Henry Kissinger, no great idealist, has been moved to write that "the rejection of history extols the image of a universal man living by universal maxims, regardless of the past, of geography, or of other immutable circumstance....The American refusal to be bound by history and the insistence on the perpetual possibility of renewal confer a great dignity, even beauty, on the American way of life. The national fear that those who are obsessed with history produce self-fulfilling prophecies does embody a great folk wisdom."[74]

The American Ideology, then, like classical Marxism, believes that it is possible to make a sudden "leap from the realm of necessity to the realm of freedom." Or as Reagan used to say (quoting the polemicist of the American Revolution Thomas Paine), "We have it in our power to begin the world over again." As another illustration of the underlying pervasiveness of the American Ideology, this was also a favorite phrase of 1960s radicals.[75]

But Kissinger also writes of the need for America in the twenty-first century to express its power and influence as far as possible by multilateral means if it does not wish its dominance to falter.[76] And here the American Creed and its attendant myths, and the kind of nationalism they support, can constitute serious problems. The intense identification of the American Ideology with the American nation also feeds American national messianism, a belief in the nation's duty to save the world. This belief makes it much more difficult for most Americans to imagine the United States as a country among others or an "international community" that includes America as a member rather than a hegemon.[77]

This messianism contributes to the shortage of true internationalists in the United States. For reasons which will be set out later, it can even contribute to a kind of racism. Richard Hughes has written that "there is perhaps no more compelling task for Americans to accomplish in the 21st Century than to learn to see the world through someone else's eyes." The messianism inherent in a combination of the American Creed and American national myths makes the development of such a capacity even more difficult.[78] It feeds "our inveterate tendency to judge others by the extent to which they contrive to be like ourselves."[79]

63

However, it would be quite wrong to think that American messianism necessarily implies a desire to save the world by action. Equally strong, and indeed historically more common, has been the belief that America's mission to humanity consists above all of the force of its example.[80] In the debates between Al Gore and George Bush in the presidential election campaign of 2000, both candidates stressed America's mission to the world, but both also stressed that it should be exercised above all by example, with Bush famously declaring that "I think they [the people of the world] ought to look at us as a country that understands freedom, where it doesn't matter who you are or how you're raised or where you're from, that you can succeed....So I don't think they ought to look at us in any other way than what we are. We're a freedom-loving nation. And if we're an arrogant nation, they'll view us that way. But if we're a humble nation they'll respect us as an honorable nation."[81]

One of the earliest and most famous expositions of this view was by President John Quincy Adams in 1821:

> America does not go abroad in search of monsters to destroy. She is the well-wisher to the freedom and independence of all. She is the champion only of her own. She will recommend the general cause by the countenance of her voice, and the benignant sympathy of her example. She well knows that by once enlisting under other banners than her own, were they even the banners of foreign independence, she would involve herself beyond the powers of extrication, in all the wars of interest and intrigue, of individual avarice, envy, and ambition, which assumed the colors and usurped the standards of freedom....She might become the dictatress of the world. She would be no longer the ruler of her own spirit.[82]

As these words imply, one underlying concern of many Americans who have opposed overseas interventions—including ones in the name of the American Creed—has been that they would tarnish the force of the nation's example and thereby in the long run make it more difficult to spread the lessons of the Creed around the world.[83] I would endorse this argument from my own observation of how the prestige of American democracy and material culture destroyed the faith even of the younger Soviet elites in the Soviet system and thereby helped destroy that system. This bore out the prediction of George Kennan: "The most important influence the United States can bring to bear upon internal developments in Russia will continue to be the influence of example: the influence of what it is, and not only what it is to others but what it is to itself."[84]

Nevertheless, the rich vein of messianic belief in American political culture also provides a continuous latent resource which particular historical events can bring to the surface and particular political forces can exploit. So it proved after 9/11, when the Bush administration was able to base much of its public rhetoric on a belief in American exceptionalism and in America's right and ability to bring freedom, democracy, human rights and progress to other nations.

American academia and quasi-academia have played an important but complex role in the maintenance of the illusions and myths underpinning "dynamic messianism." The world of academia in general is a great exception to the patterns of myth and conformism sketched earlier. It has produced not only distinguished centrist critics of these tendencies, but even an intellectual Left which continues to be highly influential within academia itself and in parts of the world of non-governmental organizations (NGOs). The progressive and left-wing liberal world also supports a number of respectable intellectual journals.

This is why hatred of the nationalist Right is particularly directed at the universities. And indeed, as everywhere else, some of the attacks of the intellectual Left on the U.S. ideology and ruling system deserve severe criticism, being extremist, foolish and occasionally downright wicked. Powerful, however, they are not. Left-wing intellectuals are almost completely excluded from the American mainstream media and from those branches of academia with close government dealings. Their only role in these fields is to act as convenient whipping boys for the Right.

With time this picture may change, as products of the pluralist university worlds find their way into politics and government; but as yet there are few signs of this happening. It might indeed seem natural that the radical Left should be excluded from the "mainstream," except for one thing: the radical Right is not so excluded. Even in the comment pages of newspapers widely viewed as liberal, such as the *New York Times* and the *Washington Post*, hard-line, right-wing nationalists such as George Will, William Kristol, Robert Novak, William Safire and Charles Krauthammer are to be found day after day.[85]

In the areas of foreign relations and security, a capacity for truly open debate on underlying principles has been discouraged by the close links among government, particular university departments, think tanks and journalists working in the field. Paradoxically, the American system of political appointments, whereby a president chooses some four thousand officials from outside the civil service, has worked if anything to limit the advice coming to government. Rather than opening the bureaucracy, the system has tended to bureaucratize those sections of academia with a role in the foreign policy debate. Because they are divided into two political tribes, these parabureaucrats retain a capacity to criticize specific policies of particular administrations. With very few exceptions, however, like most bureaucrats they lack completely an ability to distance themselves from the supporting myths of the state system which supports them.

As a result of this complex of factors, in the view of the American historian and former soldier Andrew Bacevich, the basic American consensus on foreign policy "is so deep-seated that its terms have become all but self-evident, its premises asserted rather than demonstrated," and much of the public and media debate on international issues within the country is no more than "political theatre."[86] Outside the United States, however, these generally accepted premises are thought to be highly debatable assertions, given certain aspects of America's actual historical record.

The effects of the American Ideology and the mating of bureaucracy and sections of academia have run together with wider currents in sections of contemporary academia. These sections have tended to downgrade history and regional studies in favor of "disciplines" based not on empirical research but pseudoscientific general theories, which are generally mere facades for Western ideological and cultural assumptions. The most extreme of these, but also one of the most influential within the theoretical sections of international relations studies, is Rational Choice theory.[87] Said Professor Michael Lehmann, protesting in 1994 at the growing domination of this trend within the University of California: "I have never understood how a timeless, non-historical analysis that removes itself from technological, institutional and other social developments can be employed to discern the course of human events. Nor can I fathom the ideological orthodoxy that insists on such a path to the exclusion of others."[88]

This tendency is much more easily understood if it is seen in part as a particularly florid growth from the soil of the American Ideology and American civic nationalism, fertilized after 1989 by America's triumph over communism. In the 1950s, American commentators such as Louis Hartz and Reinhold Niebuhr were already lamenting how the nation's vastly increased international involvement after World War II had gone hand in hand with increasing isolation, determinism and dogmatism in the "social sciences." This ideological dogmatism has always been increased still further by the overwhelming tendency, at universities as well as in schools, to study American history in isolation and to treat it as if no other country's experience could be of any relevance to America—something which, as Herbert Bolton warned, risks raising a "nation of chauvinists."[89] Three generations after Herbert Butterfield began the intellectual demolition of the Whig Theory of History among serious historians, a naive nineteenth-century belief in the inevitable march of human progress along a fixed path continues to dominate much of history teaching in the United States.[90]

Rational Choice theory really is founded on an almost theological faith in the universal validity of a dogmatic (and in part imaginary) American-style economic individualism. In the traditional Christian faith, all human beings, if taught properly and protected from the lures of the devil, will become Christians. That is their default mode. In Rational Choice theory—and in the instinctive belief of many ordinary Americans—the default mode of humanity is to become Americans. This quasi-religious, utopian belief was strengthened still further by the fall of communism.[91]

The extremely abstruse, "scientistic" style of this and other related approaches makes it very easy to hide such basic assumptions within the model.[92] As Edward Shils commented two generations ago, "It is not difficult to understand how the adoption of the scientist tradition can prepare the way to the acceptance of a secularized millenarianism and thus lead on to ideological politics." He was speaking of the link between scientism and communism, but it is no less true with regard to the American Ideology.[93] Thus all too many of the official and semiofficial discussions on the subject of democratization which I have attended in Washington have been conducted as if no serious work of history, sociology, or political anthropology had ever been written.

As in the case of communism, the severe intellectual limitations of this approach when it comes to understanding actual developments and other societies can lead rather quickly to what the American radical historian Charles Beard called "the Devil Theory of Politics," attributing most problems to "manipulation" by essentially external and contingent causes: agitators, communists, terrorists, cynical and exploitative elites, foreign regimes. This tendency is encouraged still further by a naive liberal belief in the natural goodness and perfectibility of "the people," of whatever country.[94]

Moreover, if "history is bunk," if the study of religion and political culture is to be dismissed as foolish or even wicked "essentialism" (often a barely veiled cover for charges of racism), then the only remaining explanation for a country's successes and failures must lie in "leadership" and the capacity of leaders to understand and adopt the right (U.S.-inspired) policies.[95] This analysis essentially means reliance on a form of the "Great Man theory" of history, a superficial and stupid paradigm abandoned or heavily qualified by serious historians half a century ago. As Michael Lind notes, "The devil theory is rather optimistic. Replace devils with angels, and everything will be fine."[96]

I have lost count of the number of times I have heard commentators on Afghanistan speak of "the warlords" there as if they are some kind of Martian implant, rather than the leaders of powerful groups and the products—vile, but authentic—of local Afghan society, the Afghan heroin trade and the wars which afflicted Afghanistan since the 1970s. From this approach comes the belief that if such devils could somehow be spirited away by a sufficient effort of outside will, then that will could also implant new angelic local leaders. Of course, just as these intellectual trends described are by no means limited to the United States, neither are such illusions. They are widely shared in Europe too. The difference is that because America is so much more powerful militarily than Europe, and has not suffered so much from past wars, Americans may believe that they actually have the power to bring such fantasies to life through military intervention. The consequences for the dynamic or interventionist form of American national messianism are all too clear.

The inability or refusal seriously to study other societies also makes Americans horribly vulnerable to being told what they want to hear by foreign representatives with their own political axes to grind. Others work for U.S.-funded institutions in their own countries and therefore are understandably anxious to please their benefactors. Of course, all great empires have faced this problem; but the absolutism of the American Ideology, and the international hegemony of liberal democratic ideology among intellectuals around the world, makes the risk especially great in the case of the United States. At best, the combination of this factor with U.S. dogmatism and ideological hegemony can lead to a kind of mirror game, a copulation of illusions in which Americans and their foreign informants passionately misconceive together. At worst, the United States is seduced by contemporary versions of

Queen Cartimandua, who sought Roman legions to put her back in power over her unwilling British subjects.

In recent years, a range of American dissident intellectuals, including George Kennan, Samuel Huntington, Andrew Bacevich, William Pfaff, Michael Lind, Fareed Zakaria and others, have landed very heavy blows on such illusions; and more important, so have the experiences of trying to bring progress to Somalia, Afghanistan and now Iraq. But so deeply rooted are these premises in American civic nationalism that after every blow they arise again. As we have seen, even Vietnam seemed only to flatten them for a while. This may also prove true in the future after the blow of Iraq.

The collapse of Soviet communism greatly helped in the restoration of the American ideological and mythical self-image after Vietnam. It also reduced still further any perceived need to take the opinions of the rest of the world into account. The collapse of communism combined with the messianic elements in the American tradition to produce an attitude summed up in Fukuyama's "End of History" thesis.

This proposition was so extreme that it was widely challenged, and indeed eventually Fukuyama himself moved to much more moderate and sophisticated positions. However, as I wrote in 1996, the spirit which it reflected became so omnipresent in the U.S. media and political discourse that it was rarely noticed, let alone analyzed or criticized. Above all, the spirit consisted of a belief in a monolithic version of progress defined by the American experience and involving in turn a monolinear "path to democracy and the free market." The religious overtones of the word "path" are especially indicative. In the 1990s at least, this whole approach had distinctly theological aspects, being largely impervious to argument and evidence, and promising limitless future benefits which would transcend the miserable present.[97]

Characteristic of the radical market theories of the past generation and the Rational Choice theory which helped feed them has been a failure in "the basic philosophical test of functioning intelligence and ethics—the ability to imagine the Other."[98] I can certainly confirm from my own experience that in the case of Russia, only a very small number of American (and, to be fair, Western European) officials and semiofficial experts spent any time imagining themselves in the shoes of ordinary Russians, let alone trying to meet those Russians. The indifference to their physical well-being, indeed survival, was both striking and deeply shocking; but just as serious was the phenomenon noted by the American sociologist and historian Robert Bellah concerning past American views of the Native Americans: "For a long time, indeed for centuries, the new settlers failed to appreciate the fact that the people who lived here lived in a different dream. Whether the Indian was seen as noble or noble savage, he was treated as if he were a character in the European's dream, as if he had no dream of his own."[99]

There is therefore a very strong tendency in America, now institutionalized in the mandates and approaches of the various state and NGO bodies devoted to world democratization, to live in what Frances FitzGerald and others have called the "eternal present."[100] According to this way of looking at the world—which has become so deeply internalized as to be usually beyond self-awareness and therefore beyond discussion—not only is humanity in general on one linear path of progress, but all of its different sections are potentially at exactly the same point at exactly the same time; just as in the missionary view, all peoples are naturally capable of hearing and apprehending the Gospel. This attitude to history and society is quite as distant from any observable historical reality as were the assumptions of doctrinaire communism.

This attitude may well be rooted in a genuine desire to liberate other peoples from their history. Its proponents claim that it is also antiracist, because it suggests that all people can make rapid progress toward democracy regardless of their race, culture, or economic level. But what if the peoples concerned are unwilling or incapable of accepting such liberation? In a pattern familiar to all students of the missionary tradition and mentality, this attitude can all too easily slip into an aggressive, chauvinist and ultimately even racist contempt for such peoples. This tendency is fed enormously by the strong currents of ethnoreligious nationalism which exist in American life alongside American civic nationalism.

After all, if the Message is self-evidently true, universal and universally apprehendable, then any failure cannot be due to the Message. It must be due to some failure on the part of the audience, whether because of innate wickedness or because its collective heart has been hardened by some wicked agents: manipulating nationalist elites, former communists, emissaries of Satan....

To assert the unique morality of the political culture of one's country is already to adopt a position which the rest of the world will find very difficult to accept and will be strongly tempted to challenge by reference to the darker episodes of one's past—thereby setting off ugly national exchanges. To assert this and then derive from it, as have William Kristol and Robert Kagan, the belief that America's "moral goals and its fundamental national interests are almost always in harmony" is to come rather close to saying "my country is always right."[101]

Yet this basic attitude characterized most U.S. foreign policy "ecology" long before 9/11. In dealing with Russia in the 1990s, the great majority of writers assumed that Russian democrats would self-evidently identify not just with the promotion of U.S. national interests in international affairs but with U.S. geopolitical ambitions in the former Soviet Union—because, consciously or unconsciously, their assumption was that these were indeed identical with justice, progress and the real interests of Russia itself. Attempts to challenge this absolutely lunatic assumption often were met with either outrage or total incomprehension. And this, be it noted, was under the Clinton administration, not the Republicans, which emphasizes the extent to which these illusions extend across the U.S. political spectrum.

And while "my country, right or wrong" may be morally disagreeable, it is a rational statement of loyalty.[102] Consequently its proponents can appreciate and negotiate with other peoples who have the same feelings toward their own countries. By contrast, "my country is always right" admits no negotiation. It is self-evidently destructive of the bases of international law and belief in any form of international community.

This identification of the principles and spread of democracy with the American nation is a key link between the ideological bases of American Creedal nationalism and American imperialism. Insofar as they can use this rhetoric in support of their plans, the imperialists have a tremendous means of seduction, as far as many Americans are concerned. This is America's version of the missions of the great civilizational empires of the past: of the duties of Rome and imperial China—as seen by their rulers, elites and intellectuals—to spread their civilizations to the barbarians beyond their borders; of the Spanish to christianize the New World; of the "civilizing missions" of the nineteenth-century European empires; of the Soviet Union to bring the light of communism to the rest of humanity. And as already pointed out, America is in fact a not unworthy heir of Rome and China in this regard, and the lessons that America has to teach are of real value to humanity—although they are, of course, ones in which other Western democracies also have a share.

And that is a key point. The Roman and Chinese state models, although universalist, were authoritarian and bureaucratic, and there was no contradiction in Rome and China spreading their own rule by force or in other authoritarian monarchies adopting their form of rule. The American model is supposed to be democratic and to be adopted voluntarily by peoples. How far then can these lessons be presented as exclusively American and used to feed American pride and power? How far can they be spread by force of arms, how far they can be associated with American national prejudices, interests and geopolitical ambitions without losing their value and attractive power? How can an approach supposedly rooted in democratization succeed if it displays a brazen contempt both for international public opinion in general and for the democratic votes of particular nations?

Inside America, this strategy works very well in terms of political appeal and consolidation of the political elites behind American strategy. Outside, it gives the impression that the American conscience can be flicked on and off according to tactical advantage like a strobe light in a particularly seedy disco. This international perception of hypocrisy is increased enormously by very strong and all-too-visible American national hatreds of other countries and peoples.

This tendency is exemplified by Freedom House, a politically independent but officially sanctioned body whose annual survey of freedom and democracy in the world is treated as a kind of biblical authority by many American journalists and commentators. Yet this is an institution which over the past thirty years has advanced China precisely one grade in its freedom rating, from seven to six. That is to say, according to Freedom House, after a generation of economic liberalization and the transition from fanatical totalitarianism to authoritarianism, in 2004 Chinese were only very slightly more free than they were in the depths of the Cultural Revolution in 1972. In 2002 India rated a two, despite severe repression in Kashmir and the massacre in Gujarat of more than two thousand members of the Muslim minority, with the active complicity of the local government and police. And so on.[103] In this, Freedom House was simply following the pattern of many U.S. institutions during the Cold War, when a range of abysmal dictatorships in Africa, Latin America and elsewhere were classified as part of the "Free World" because their allies were geopolitical allies of the United States.[104] A similar approach was adopted by former U.S. ambassador Mark Palmer, in his book setting out a "strategy" for ending the world's dictatorships by 2025—a work characterized by an extreme degree of superficiality in its analysis of the countries concerned and an incredible air of ideological ambition.[105]

And of course, at the level of policy discussions, human rights abuses, whether real or exaggerated, can be cited in almost any circumstances as a reason to display hostility against a given country. Thus in a small but typical example, a writer in the *New York Times*, arguing for a hostile American attitude to the Chinese space program, declared "amid calls for joint scientific or commercial ventures in space to improve Chinese-American relations, officials in Washington should consider what kind of cooperation is appropriate with a regime that does not share the United States' tradition of freedom and respect for human rights."[106]

This kind of thing filters down through society. In February 2004 *Parade* magazine asked its readers, "Who Would *You* Say Is the World's Worst Dictator?" lumping together indiscriminately—just as Freedom House does—Hu Jintao of China with Kim Jong-il of North Korea, Robert Mugabe of Zimbabwe, Than Shwe of Burma, Teodoro Obiang Nguema of Equatorial Guinea and Crown Prince Abdullah of Saudi Arabia. In other words, the selection was made with no reference whatsoever to the nature of the given regime, the role of the leader within that regime, or most of all the success of the regime in advancing the material well-being and economic freedom of its subjects—areas which, when applied to themselves, Americans have defined as part of the essence of liberty.[107] Hu Jintao came third, counted as worse than the leaders of the catastrophic regimes in Zimbabwe and Guinea and the Wahabi Islamist totalitarianism of Saudi Arabia. Coupled with the incessant rhetoric of politicians, the media and human rights groups concerning freedom in other countries, the effect is both to feed American chauvinist hostility to other countries and to pour a continual nourishing rain of self-praise on Americans' belief in their own country's superiority.

Many people from the former colonial world in particular are bound to see this mixture as simply a repeat of former European *missions civilisatrices*, as a hypocritical cover for imperial aggrandizement; and they are often right to do so. Moreover, America's universal mission contains certain elements of "universal values" which are in fact not universal at all but very visibly part of a purely American culture and "way of life."[108] Many people in the countries which Americans propose to liberate in the name of these supposedly universal values perceive this fact clearly.

Bush and the American Thesis

Bush administration rhetoric after 9/11 portraying America as a vital force of freedom and democratization both embodied and exacerbated many of these problems. This rhetoric was messianic and rooted in the American Creed, and—like the Creed itself—it was also universalist. It stressed that American values represent the salvation of all humanity. The opening words of the new National Security Strategy of 2002 read:

> The great struggles of the twentieth century between liberty and totalitarianism ended with a decisive victory for the forces of freedom—and a single sustainable model for national success: freedom, democracy and free enterprise. In the twenty-first century, only nations that share a commitment to protecting basic human rights and economic freedom will be able to unleash the potential of their people and assure their future prosperity. People everywhere want to be able to speak freely; choose who will govern them; worship as they please; educate their children—male and female; own property; and enjoy the benefits of their labor. These values of freedom are right and true for every person, in every society—and the duty of protecting these values against their enemies is the common-calling of freedom-loving people across the globe and across the ages.[109]

Bush and his leading officials therefore possessed, and expressed, a boiled-down, simplified and extreme version of a vision of America which is in fact held very widely in American society and has deep historical roots: "The US primarily goes to war against evil, not in its self-perception, to defend material interests."[110] The Bush administration and its supporters used the messianic argument that America needed to invade Iraq to liberate its people as a subsidiary justification for going to war. After the overthrow of the Ba'ath regime and the failure to find Iraq's alleged weapons of mass destruction, it became the principal justification.[111]

In Harry Truman's words, America had become great but had renounced self-aggrandizement, and his task was to "mobilize the people who believe in a moral world against Bolshevik materialism." Truman's messianism coexisted strangely with his savagely chauvinist attitudes toward almost all other nations, as it does today in the attitudes of many American democratizers both toward the Arabs they profess to want to democratize and toward other countries which are already democracies but disagree with the United States.[112]

Such words as Truman's are inspiring, but also embody very grave dangers for analysis and policy. The dubbing of the enemy as an enemy of civilization itself and the embodiment of evil—although accurate enough in the case of Stalin—also suggested that it was pointless to seek to understand his motives, even if doing so was in order the better to resist him; the exact opposite, in other words, of the approach advocated by Kennan and other pragmatic Cold Warriors. This approach also involved the homogenization of different national communist movements into one giant united global communist enemy.

As noted by William Fulbright and others, this attitude contributed directly to the debacle of Vietnam, where before the war U.S. analysts and policymakers, seeing the North Vietnamese simply as "communists," had completely failed to understand their real nature, their immense strength and the depth of their underlying historical enmity toward their Chinese communist backers—despite the fact that regional experts such as Bernard Fall had long pointed out this fact.[113] Similarly, they wholly failed to appreciate the depth of the Sino-Soviet split, which within a few years would bring the two communist states to the verge of nuclear war.[114]

In consequence, the United States missed repeated opportunities to use one communist country as a bulwark against another. A few years after Fulbright launched his critique, Nixon and Kissinger implicitly recognized its wisdom by their reconciliation with Communist China. In the Middle East, however, the Bush administration has had to learn this lesson all over again, and many American commentators and politicians—in part for reasons related to Israel—are determined that it should *not* be learned.[115]

The tendency both to demonize and to homogenize different kinds of "enemy" has had a specific and very damaging aspect in the context of 9/11 and the struggle against terrorism. Immediately after 9/11, Bush eliminated any discussion of the concrete issues at stake between the United States and Islamist radicals from his own and the administration's public statements. Indeed, avidly abetted by most of the media and the political class, public discussion of these issues was to a great extent suppressed. Instead a Manichean discourse was promoted which identified American values as the terrorists' target, with those values both absolutely good in themselves and identical with the good of the world. When the language of the "Axis of Evil" (the phrase comes from Bush's State of the Union address of 2002) extended this approach to a range of different states, the effect was to shut down discussion of negotiation and accommodation in the more nationalist sections of the American public mind.

Or as the populist tabloid *New York Post* put it, reflecting a very widespread view in the U.S. media and society: "Why do they hate us? That's what the so-called deep thinkers are asking about America's Islamic enemies....Who cares? Osama [bin Laden] ordered the deaths of some 6,000 innocent people, mostly Americans, on American soil. What difference does it make why? There's no justification for such evil. There's no excuse. And the only question that matters is how can they be eradicated most quickly."[116]

By encouraging this kind of attitude, the Bush administration forgot the oldest and wisest rule of strategy: "Know thine enemy." In doing so the administration actually has made "eradicating" that enemy much more difficult. This did not matter so much as far as al Qaeda itself is concerned, because its implacable aims and ideology rule out any attempt at compromise. But by refusing to discuss sources

of Muslim grievances, such as U.S. support for Israel and U.S. military domination of the Middle East, Americans alienated ordinary Muslims and created more
recruits for Islamist terrorism.

The approach of both the Bush administration and leading Democrats tended
therefore to undermine and even cripple the political struggle against Islamist
extremism and push the nation toward a reliance on purely military options. The
darkening of the American mind was worsened by Bush's identification of the
enemy as "terrorism"—a bizarre formulation, as has so often been pointed out,
equivalent to declaring "aerial bombing" or "tanks" the enemy.

Thus in an address to the Congress on September 20, 2001, Bush identified
America with Freedom, and said that that was why America had been attacked:
"Americans are asking, why do they hate us? They hate what they see in this
chamber—a democratically elected government....Great harm has been done to
us. We have suffered great loss. And in our grief and anger we have found our
mission and our moment. Freedom and Fear are at war. The advance of human
freedom—the great achievement of our time, and the great hope of every time—
now depends on us."[117]

Like the opening of the National Security Strategy document, such words represent a general consensus of the American people, with only a limited number of dis-
senters. Like the Soviets and like so many Americans—liberal as well as
conservative—Bush also cast America as the agent of a historical teleology.[118]
Statements that "our nation is on the right side of history" echo the Soviet communist cliché, "the wind of history is in our sails."[119]

And as with Soviet rhetoric, this ideological element in Bush's language was
also universalist in nature, appealing to America and the world in the name of the
American Creed. This belief found an even more strident and messianic expression in Bush's speech to graduates at the U.S. Military Academy at West Point on
June 1, 2002, which also ushered in the "doctrine" of preventive war: "Wherever
we carry it, the American flag will stand not only for our power, but for freedom
(applause). Our nation's cause has always been larger than our nation's defense. We
fight, as we always fight, for a just peace—a peace that favors human liberty....The
twentieth century ended with a single surviving model of human progress, based on
non-negotiable demands of human dignity, the rule of law, limits on the power of
the state, respect for women and private property and free speech and equal justice
and religious tolerance."[120]

This language on the part of Bush and other administration officials might
have come—word for word—from the Clinton administration, as expressed by
Madeleine Albright and others; and indeed from President Woodrow Wilson, who
declared in January 1917 that "these are American principles, American policies.
We could stand for no others. And they are also the principles and policies of
forward-looking men and women everywhere, of every modern nation, of every
enlightened community. They are the principles of mankind and must prevail."

Wolfish Wilsonians

This mood of national messianism was however the work not only of the Bush administration and its media and intellectual supporters, but also of leading intellectuals from the Democratic camp. It had its roots both in very old American traditions and in a convergence of Republican and Democratic attitudes to democratization as a weapon against communism during the Cold War.[121] After 9/11 these attempts were directed above all toward U.S. policy in the "greater Middle East." However, they also had wider implications.

The merger of the selective use of "democratization" with strategies based on ruthless "Realism" has been central to the approach of neoconservatives since this political tendency began during the first decades of the Cold War. In the neoconservative program, the Soviet Union was to be driven to destruction by a mixture of military and economic pressure, the ruthless repression of communist-backed rebellions against U.S. client regimes—including U.S. military intervention where necessary—and the rigorous preaching of democracy and liberty to Soviet subjects.

The selective or instrumental use of moral outrage and calls for liberation— what Jeanne Kirkpatrick, the leading neoconservative and Reagan administration ambassador, candidly enough called "the utilitarian value of democracy" to U.S. foreign policy—is a very old pattern in human affairs and especially perhaps in the Protestant and Anglo-Saxon worlds.[122] Rarely, however, has it been used so systematically, or with such contempt for even the appearance of consistency or intellectual honor, as by American nationalists, especially from the neoconservative camp. Thus in 1980, when attacking President Jimmy Carter's attempts at consistency in the treatment of U.S. allies and rivals concerning their human rights abuses and lack of democracy, Irving Kristol sounded like George Kennan, Samuel Huntington or other Realist conservative critics of American messianism:

> It is the fundamental fallacy of American foreign policy to believe, in face of all the evidence, that all peoples, everywhere, are immediately "entitled" to a liberal constitutional government—and a thoroughly democratic one at that….As a matter of fact, it is only since World War I—a war fought under the slogans of "self-determination for all nations" and "make the world safe for democracy"—that American foreign policy began to disregard the obvious for the sake of the quixotic pursuit of impossible ideals. Before World War I, intelligent men took it for granted that not all peoples, everywhere, at all times, could be expected to replicate a Western constitutional democracy.[123]

Two years earlier, as part of the same hard-line campaign against Carter, Kristol had expressed himself categorically in favor of America's mission as example, not intervention: "The proper extent of political rights in any nation is not something that our State Department can have any meaningful opinion about. It can only be determined by the people of that nation, who will draw on their own political and cultural backgrounds in arriving at a suitable disposition of this matter. We can try to set them a good example by making our democratic republic as admirable as possible—as our Founding Fathers urged. But that is about all we can do—as our Founding Fathers recognized."[124]

But Kristol and his school have reserved such moderation for U.S. allies, however savage. Neoconservatives have attacked precisely such Realist statements as Kristol's when these have been applied to countries which they wish to weaken or undermine, and these attacks have been not only ferocious, but also phrased in terms of the most strident version of America's messianic mission as intervention, not merely example.[125]

The most shameless example of this is the way in which neoconservatives and other former anticommunists in the United States have played around with the distinction between "totalitarian" and "authoritarian" regimes. During the 1980s, a number of anticommunist intellectuals advanced this notion as a key difference between the dictatorial but still culturally, intellectually and economically open pro-American regimes of Latin America and the communist states. And this distinction is indeed a valid one.[126]

The amusing thing is that when Russia and China both in their different ways abandoned communism, it turned out that many of the Americans who had argued most fiercely for the distinction between totalitarian and authoritarian regimes did not really take it seriously themselves. Instead, in these and other cases, like Iran, they did their utmost to blur the line between totalitarianism and authoritarianism. For them, this distinction had been nothing more than a cheap debating trick, intended to demonstrate that Washington's Latin American scum were better than Moscow's eastern European scum.

In the wake of 9/11, a number of intellectuals still belonging to the Democrat Party and calling themselves liberals set off on the same well-worn path as the neoconservatives had done two generations earlier, when most future neoconservatives were Democrats and followers of the bitterly anticommunist, pro–Vietnam War and pro-Israel Democratic Senator Henry "Scoop" Jackson.[127] Thus in 2003 Michael Tomasky declared that the Democrats needed to adopt a new conception of foreign policy as a strong, clear alternative to that of the Republicans:

> The hard part is backing up the critique [of the Republicans] with an alternative vision. That too should be simple, and for consistency's sake it should follow from the critique: The world's leading democracy should support… democracy. The Cold War is over; the twentieth century, the century in which all the "isms" became "wasms," is over. It's the 21st century; the United States should declare it to be—American liberals should declare it to be—the century of democracy….
>
> Picture a Democratic president, or even a presidential candidate, making such a case forcefully on the world stage; for the purpose of showing that he (or she) *really* means business, he (or she) might choose one test case that

highlights some outrage to which the United States has heretofore turned a blind eye—the plight of the Kurds in Turkey, or, better still for the purposes of domestic political consumption, oppression of women in Saudi Arabia. There will be initial resistance, but ultimately, who can afford to buck the United States? The world will start, in its lumbering, petulant way, to change.[128]

In 2003, very similar passages could be found in the writings of numerous other supporters of the Democratic Party. They were summed up in *Progressive Internationalism: A Democratic National Security Strategy* drawn up by a group of former officials, think tank members and academics with a view to influencing the Democratic election campaign and the policies of a future Democrat administration. This strategy was drawn up under the aegis of the Progressive Policy Institute (PPI) in Washington, a grouping which in U.S. domestic policy advocates a form of Blairite "Third Way" for America. Some of its domestic proposals are quite sound.[129] Like other works by members of this school, this document also differs from works by the right-wing nationalists in that it stresses, no doubt sincerely, the theoretical need for multilateralism. The problem is, however, that its other statements on the use of force to improve the world are so alien to predominant European and other thinking that, if implemented, they would make such multilateralism very difficult.

In a related essay Dana Allin, Michael O'Hanlon and Philip Gordon call for a future Democrat administration to show "respect" for leading allies, unlike the Bush administration.[130] It is difficult to show respect, however, while categorically rejecting someone's advice. In this regard, much of the content and even the language of the *Progressive Internationalist* declaration is indistinguishable from neoconservative tracts.[131] Several of the signatories to this document had joined with neoconservative and other right-wing Republican commentators in supporting the Iraq War.[132]

One of the signatories of the "Progressive Internationalism" statement, Professor Michael McFaul of Stanford, has written that "during the twentieth century, the central purpose of American power was to defend against and when possible to destroy tyranny"—a description almost Soviet in its omission of inconvenient but crucial facts. Advocating adoption of a "liberty doctrine" as the guiding principle of U.S. foreign and security policy, McFaul writes in terms identical to those of the neoconservatives: "to promote liberty requires first the containment and then the elimination of those forces opposed to liberty, be they individuals, movements or regimes....To effectively promote liberty abroad over the long haul, the United States must maintain its overwhelming military dominance over the rest of the world."

In McFaul's view:

> The United States cannot be content with preserving the current order in the international system. Rather, the United States must become once again a revisionist power—a country that seeks to change the international system

77

as a means of enhancing its own national security. Moreover, this mission must be offensive in nature. The United States cannot afford to wait and react to the next attack. Rather, we must seek to isolate and destroy our enemies by eliminating their regimes and safe havens. The ultimate purpose of American power is the creation of an international community of democratic states that encompasses every region of the planet.[133]

Elsewhere McFaul and colleagues called for the toughest possible U.S. policy toward Iran based on opposition to engagement and a demand for regime change and democratization—thereby aligning themselves with neoconservative hardliners and the Israeli lobby and against both Colin Powell's State Department and the views of leading European allies, including Britain. Yet all this was supposed to be somehow compatible with "multilateralism."[134]

Strangest of all is the idea expressed by Tomasky and other self-described liberals that such an approach would constitute an "alternative" to that of the Bush administration. As is evident from the passage from the National Security Strategy quoted earlier in this chapter, their words in fact differ hardly at all from those of the Republican administration. All Tomasky and his colleagues can claim is that they would implement these principles more consistently and effectively—but then that is precisely what the neoconservatives also claim. Moreover, this kind of rhetoric has been a staple of American international propaganda for many years and is to a considerable degree implicit in the American Creed and its attendant myths.[135]

The hawkish Democrats' line was not even distinguishable from that of Bush when it came to the Iraq War. By the time Tomasky's words were written, numerous intellectual supporters of the administration had already declared that support for democratization was now at the core of its foreign policy. George Will, Max Boot and others had trumpeted George Bush's supposed conversion to "Wilsonianism" and nation building.[136] Democratization, human rights and the liberation of women had already been used as part of the justification of war in Afghanistan; and the first two aims were becoming part of the administration's *casus belli* for war with Iraq.

The language of liberal Democrats like Tomasky about the supposed failings of the Republican "Realists" in this regard was even echoed almost word for word in Newt Gingrich's virulent attacks on the internationalism of Colin Powell and the State Department. Gingrich's statements use the need for the United States "to promote freedom and combat tyranny" as a mantra: "The United States should actively stand for and promote its values around the globe. Every person deserves safety, health, prosperity and freedom. The United States supports the core values of constitutional liberty, the right to free speech (including a free press), independent judiciaries, free markets, free elections, transparency in government, the equality of women, racial equality and the free exercise of religious beliefs. Without these values, it is very hard to imagine a world in which U.S. safety can be secured. We should not confuse respect for others with acceptance of their values if they violate these principles."[137]

78

This passage formed part of a determined attempt by the Republican Right to reduce still further respect in the U.S. government for the opinions even of democratic Western allies, to undermine the chief government department entrusted with international relations, to open the door wider to unilateral American military actions and to reduce genuine support in the administration for President Bush's "Road Map" for peace between Israel and Palestine.

After the conquest of Iraq and the failure to find the promised weapons of mass destruction, motives of democratization and human rights were turned post facto into *the* central justification for the war.[138] Nor was the ostensible support for democratization limited to those countries under American military occupation. It was also argued that the democratization of Afghanistan and Iraq would initiate the democratization of the entire Middle East, beginning with Iran.

And, of course, the emphasis on democratization among powerful sections of the modern American Right does not date from 2002. The most important historical moment in this regard was Ronald Reagan's adoption of the language of democratic revolution and human rights as a key part of his struggle against the "Evil Empire" of the Soviet Union, involving a deliberate and open repudiation of the "Realist" considerations which had supposedly governed the policies of the previous Republican administrations of Ford, Nixon and Eisenhower.

Largely in consequence of this, leading intellectual Scoop Jackson Democrats completed their drift away from the Democratic Party and into the ideological camp of the neoconservatives and the political camp of the Republicans. In other words, Tomasky and his colleagues in 2003 were simply following a path already marked out by Richard Perle, Irving Kristol and others a generation before.[139]

The vision of the Democrat "progressive internationalists" does genuinely differ from that of the nationalist Right on a range of other vital international issues including the environment, foreign aid, various international treaties and in general the need to display a "generous vision of global society and America's role in it."[140] And if actually implemented—highly dubious, given the past record of the Democratic Party in Congress regarding these issues—such policies would not only be very good in themselves, but would improve the entire atmosphere between the United States and Western Europe in particular.

However, when it comes to the specific issues of the conduct of the war against terrorism and the use of force to improve the world, the progressive internationalists present no real "alternative" to Bush administration policies. Rather, like the neoconservatives, they represent a form of liberal imperialism of a kind which characterized much of the liberal scene in the United States and Europe a century ago. Although this picture obviously has specifically, even uniquely, American features, it also has melancholy antecedents in the history of relations between nationalist and liberal movements in previous ages and other parts of the world.

The psychological ascendancy of nationalism over liberalism in this relationship is vividly demonstrated by the macho nationalist language used in the passages from Tomasky and McFaul, the spirit of which differs very little from that of the neoconservatives. America "eliminates" the enemies of liberty. It declares unilaterally what it wants, and the rest of the world has to follow, for "who can afford to buck the United States?" The "world" is seen as inevitably responding "petulantly," thereby delegitimizing any criticism and demonstrating yet again the need for firm American command over the rest of humanity.

The "test cases" are chosen carefully to appeal not to world but to U.S. public opinion and to suit America's diplomatic and security needs of the hour: to punish the Turks for failing to help the Americans in Iraq and the Saudis for hostility to Israel and insufficient toughness against al Qaeda and its allies. Like the other examples already quoted, such passages are also nationalist in their profound national solipsism, amounting almost to autism, when it comes to the likely response of non-Americans to this kind of language, let alone to the political realities of other countries. When combined with the inability of the Democrats to criticize Israel, these attitudes have a disastrous effect on that party's ability to formulate coherent alternative strategies for the struggle against terrorism.

Jacobin Internationalism

In his book *Barbarian Sentiments*, William Pfaff records a historically rather piquant exchange in 2000 between Senator Jesse Helms and a senior member of the French National Assembly, Paul Quiles. Helms had told members of the UN Security Council that "states, above all the United States, that are democratic, and act in the cause of liberty, possess unlimited authority, subject to no external control, to carry out military interventions."

After 9/11 the following year, this stance became part of the so-called Bush Doctrine, enshrined in the National Security Strategy of 2002. Quiles warned in *Le Monde* that if the United States did take such a course, the result could be "greater and greater defiance by countries such as Russia and China, and still others, American refusal of collective security; recourse to solutions of force by an increasing number of states; intensification and generalization of conflict...."[141]

The piquancy of this exchange comes from the fact that Senator Helms, although an ultra-conservative representative of the dominant world hegemon, was expressing a revolutionary philosophy of international upheaval coined by Quiles's French revolutionary ancestors more than two centuries earlier. According to the great historian of nationalism Elie Kedourie:

> The [traditional] society of European states admitted all varieties of republics, of hereditary and elective monarchies, of constitutional and despotic regimes. But on the principle advocated by the [French] revolutionaries, the title of all governments then existing was put into question; since they did not derive their sovereignty from the nation, they were usurpers with whom no agreement need be binding, and to whom subjects owed no allegiance. It

is clear that such a doctrine would envenom international quarrels, and render them quite recalcitrant to the methods of traditional statecraft; it would indeed subvert all international relations as hitherto known.[142]

The revolutionary or Jacobin aspect of this approach in the United States is indeed openly acknowledged by some of its proponents.[143] If such statements were truly honest, they would be bizarre indeed coming from representatives of the world's dominant capitalist hegemon. In fact, as we have seen, the intention is that their application should be highly selective, weakening certain states while ignoring American allies: hence moral outrage concerning Iran, silence on the much worse crimes of Uzbekistan. But even if this philosophy is of limited and cynical application, it is still extremely dangerous to international order, peace and cooperation.

Indeed, the history of revolutionary and Napoléonic France itself should be enough to remind us of this. If on one hand the French armies did bring genuine progress to many parts of Europe, they also stirred up ferocious resistance leading to wars which ravaged Europe for a generation. These conflicts not only led in the end to the crushing defeat of France, they weakened her so badly that she never recovered her preeminence in Europe and the world. And this resistance was not only from the forces of the old European resistance, but also from peasant partisans in several countries and from a German popular uprising in 1813 which helped lay the foundations for German radical nationalism. As Robespierre himself admitted, "No one likes armed missionaries." When the French Revolution generated Napoléon, even liberal allies turned against the French, sickened by supposedly democratic invaders who in fact only produced a new crop of hereditary monarchs from among the ranks of Napoléon's brothers and marshals.

In our own day, such a messianic revolutionary attitude on the part of Americans has three ill effects, even if in practice it is rarely expressed in action. The first is the way in which it fuels self-righteous nationalist extremism in America itself, the *chauvinisme cocardier* (flaunting chauvinism) with which the Jacobin tradition in France was reproached. Such attitudes openly despise the interests and views of other nations, and—glorying in American righteousness—believe at heart that "it is not necessary to keep faith with heretics," in the precept of the Catholic Counter-Reformation.[144]

In particular, the authoritarian nature of most states in the Arab and Muslim worlds is used as an excuse to dismiss out of hand not only the views of their rulers, but those of their peoples—with potentially catastrophic results for the struggle against Islamist terrorism. More widely, this messianic attitude leads to a curious but historically very familiar mixture of rampant idealism and complete absence of charity, in the wider biblical sense.[145] C. Vann Woodward warned of this during the Vietnam War, in words which directly recall those of Kedourie:

> The true American mission, according to those who support this view, is a moral crusade on a worldwide scale. Such people are likely to concede no

81

validity whatever and grant no hearing to the opposing point of view, and to appeal to a higher law to justify bloody and revolting means in the name of a noble end. For what end could be nobler, they ask, than the liberation of man....The irony of the moralistic approach, when exploited by nationalism, is that the high motive to end injustice and immorality actually results in making war more amoral and horrible than ever and in shattering the foundations of the political and moral order upon which peace has to be built.[146]

The second evil consequence of this ideological stance is explored in Chapter 6 with reference to U.S. policy in the Middle East. It distracts the United States from taking measures which are urgently needed to strengthen the struggle against terrorism: namely, a real push for peace between Israel and the Palestinians, and serious economic steps to help the region. And indeed, in the first case, the stance is to some extent intended as just such a diversion.

The third evil consequence of an American messianic ideology has profound implications not only for the Middle East but for American relations with much of the rest of the world. This is the way in which, as Kedourie and Woodward indicated and as its proponents themselves admit, this ideology encourages contempt for and hostility to states; not only particular states, but to some extent, states as such—at least, that great majority which do not conform to American standards of democracy and economic success; and even those that do, such as those of Western Europe, can be damned for being too cowardly, cynical and decadent to support America's courageous and idealistic mission to the world.

This hostility represents a serious threat to U.S. strategy in the war on terrorism. Thus the revelations of former counterterrorism coordinator Richard Clarke in March 2004 concerning the relative indifference of the Bush administration to terrorism before 9/11 led to much of the U.S. media and political class being drawn into a courtroom-style questioning of the details of "who knew what and when" in the summer of 2001. In doing so, they are at risk of missing the deeper and much more important question of why the Bush administration and so many other Americans from both main parties have been so obsessed with the alleged threat from states which have a tiny fraction of the power of the United States and can also be deterred by the threat of massive retaliation.

This hostility to foreign states also embodies a number of different elements. These include an obsession with rival states among proponents of the Realist philosophy of international relations, which continues to dominate much of the American foreign policy world, and the hostility of specific American ethnic groups to particular states in the world—most notably, that of the Israeli lobby to Muslim states which are hostile to Israel (which means the vast majority of Muslim states).

This hostility to states, and ignorance of other political cultures, is also fueled by Western NGOs and human rights organizations. The downside of their often sincere and passionate commitment to human rights and democratization is of-

82

ten an inability to listen to voices from non-Western cultures, a dismissal of bitter memories of Western colonialism and above all a profound ignorance of history.[147]

Such Western groups by their nature are concerned with oppression by states rather than anarchy among peoples. They are philosophically incapable of even addressing the question of whether in some societies—and historically speaking, almost everywhere—a strong, even brutal state may not be necessary to hold down and transform the even more savage forces of heavily armed, anarchic, predatory and mutually hostile warlords; barons (both of the traditional variety and in the modern form of capitalist "robber barons" like the Russian oligarchs); clans; and ethnic groups; and to protect ordinary people from their depredations. This was true of America in the past and could be true again. As Francis Lieber, "father of American political science," wrote in 1838, "a weak government is a negation of liberty."[148]

In this context, I recall a Pakistani woman working for a Western NGO who informed me that the Pakistani army and police were so horrible that it would be better for Pakistan if they were to disappear completely—the implication being that the country then would be a place where democracy and human rights would be better respected. In fact, of course, in these circumstances Pakistan would become Afghanistan. This would not be a step forward in any respect, and would result quickly in the woman's own death or exile.

Thinking along such lines has been encouraged by the idea in the NGO world that a "global civil society" is emerging as an alternative to state sovereignty.[149] This proposition is exceptionally dubious, given the complete inability of NGOs not merely to administer or police any society, but even to protect themselves without the help of state forces, either from within the country in question or in the form of international intervention. NGOs only briefly and partially replace states when states have already collapsed. As they are, wholly unsuited to perform state functions, they inevitably make an unholy mess of things.[150]

The notion of a global civil society is also a profoundly elitist one. Although this is rarely recognized, it is based on the idea that enlightened elites can and should modernize and civilize uncivilized peoples whether they like it or not. Historically speaking, this is indeed just how progress has often occurred. The failure of the NGO world is to recognize that it can usually only do so if the elites and elite groups in question are backed by a strong state. The women and Western-educated technocrats who became members of the Afghan grand national assembly (Loya Jirga) did so not because they were elected, but because they were appointed by the Afghan government at the insistence of its Western protectors. In Turkey under Ataturk, Iran under Reza Shah, Iraq under Saddam Hussein, and to a lesser degree even Pakistan under President Pervez Musharraf, the position of women has been advanced by the decree of authoritarian states—sometimes very savage ones.

The absolutist nature of the American Thesis also contributes to discussions of "democracy" and "freedom" among liberal interventionists which are not so much

idealized as etherized: stripped of history, economics, political culture, class interests, ethnic interests, political interests and above all nationalism, that most critical historical element in both successful economic development and the creation
of mass democratic politics.[151]

Indeed, this blindness to nationalism is reflected in the very term "nation building." *States* sometimes can be built, or reconstructed with the help of outside military intervention—although even then, there need to be some strong existing
foundations on which to build. America achieved such reconstruction in Germany
and Japan after World War II. There were also a few notable British imperial achievements in state building, although the process took decades or even centuries.

The successful genesis of true nations, however, takes vastly longer and is vastly
more complicated, and has not been achieved across most of Africa and large
parts of the Muslim world. In the case of Germany and Japan—which are the *only*
truly successful examples to date of rapid democratization through American military occupation—the German and Japanese nations had existed in some form for
many centuries and had been developed as self-conscious modern nations by their
elites in the nineteenth century.[152]

The idea that the United States "built nations" in these cases is historically grotesque. The fact that the Bush administration and considerable parts of the American political class and media used the history of Germany and Japan as serious
parallels with Iraq is a terrifying comment on the quality of knowledge and understanding brought by these elements to the analysis of other societies and the
formulation of U.S. policies toward them.[153]

Instead, empty phrases like "governance" (defined by the leading Africa expert
Alex de Waal as "government minus politics"—in other words, an intellectual absurdity) and "civil society" are advanced to take the place both of serious analysis
of other political cultures and serious programs of development. In this, the effects of the American Ideology are akin to those of communism, whose proponents also found themselves idealizing communist systems whose real contents
bore little resemblance to their public shells. These effects are a common failing in
Western thought. Once again, however, this failing is more important regarding
the United States because it is only in the United States that these beliefs actually
contribute to interventionist war and debacles like Iraq.

This hostility to states brings liberal interventionists from the nongovernmen-
tal world together with liberal imperialists in an alliance which much of the world
sees as highly reminiscent of the alliance between Christian missionaries and Western imperial soldiers in the nineteenth century.[154] Despite all their often genuine
idealism and good intentions, in the end the missionaries depended on soldiers
and had to abide the colonial orders which the soldiers created—however utterly
these conflicted with Christian ethics.

As Martin Jacques has argued (in a review of *Empire Lite* by Michael Ignatieff),
what too many liberal interventionists have done is to take the admittedly miser-

able example of most of postcolonial Africa (plus Yugoslavia and Afghanistan) and extrapolate it to the former colonial world as a whole. As a result, they often grossly denigrate the achievements of many postcolonial states in Asia. Because the great majority of states are imperfect from a democratic point of view, this conflation of failed states with undemocratic ones risks giving a moral carte blanche to U.S. military intervention—irrespective of a state's achievements in other fields. In taking this "liberal imperialist" line, as Jacques also points out, these writers forget that "some of the greatest difficulties these countries have faced have been a direct result of the imperial legacy."[155]

The Western colonial empires overwhelmingly failed to develop most of their colonies, as witnessed by the catastrophic decline in Indian industries and share of world trade under British colonial rule. Indeed, that was part of the point, as the colonies were intended to be captive markets, not competitors—an approach replicated in the Bush administration's policy of distributing contracts to rebuild Iraq to American corporations rather than to Iraqi ministries.

The only empires which successfully developed their imperial possessions were those of Russia and Japan, which treated them economically as part of the imperial metropolis itself. Japanese rule over Taiwan and (South) Korea, for all its cruelty, laid the foundations for these countries' later economic and social progress.[156] America's former colony in East Asia, the Philippines, by contrast, is the economic basket case of the region.

Reasonably strong states, drawing legitimacy from state and national traditions and infused with a sense of national purpose and direction, are in fact essential to human progress and, most immediately, to success in the struggle against terrorism. As the disastrous example of much of the former Soviet Union in the 1990s demonstrates, such states are essential not only for the protection of ordinary people and the maintenance of basic order, but for the stable functioning and growth of market economics. Even if the state should not be more than Adam Smith's "night watchman," it certainly cannot afford to be less. As the SARS (sudden acute respiratory syndrome) and bird flu epidemics in East and Southeast Asia in 2003–4 reminded us, the wider interests of humanity also require states strong enough to adopt tough public health policies. Of course, successful states are not just a matter of brute force; public legitimacy is also of critical importance. But it is difficult to deny, historically speaking, that a capacity for force, even savage force, is also often essential.

We should remember that the creation and development of states has rarely been a pretty sight. Morally speaking, Bismarck's statement that states are constructed from "blood and iron" is disagreeable. As a historical description, it is simple truth. It is true even in the Anglo-Saxon world if we go back a few centuries—witness the history of England under the Tudors. It is even truer of non-Western countries, many of which have been compelled to try to imitate Western success by adopting forms of state organization that may have no roots whatsoever in local tradition. In the words of Henry Kissinger in April 2004:

To say that democracy has cultural prerequisites does not deny it ultimate applicability to other societies, but only takes note of the fact that compressing the evolution of centuries into an inappropriate time frame risks huge unintended consequences. Where societies are divided by faith and ethnicity, our practices run the risk of ratifying a permanent distribution of power based precisely on those ethnic divisions. Where the minority has no prospect of becoming a majority, elections may often result in civil war or chaos—the very breeding ground for militant terrorist organizations....

The advocates of the important role of a commitment to democracy in American foreign policy have won their intellectual battle. But institution-building requires not only a doctrine but a vision recognizing cultural and historical circumstance. Such humility is not an abdication of American values; it is the only way to implement those values effectively.[157]

A good many countries are in effect trying to jump, in a few decades, to twenty-first-century Britain from something like the Britain of the fifteenth or even the fifth century. It is hardly surprising that so many countries make a mess of it and that so often the process is bloody. Historically speaking, there is little reason to believe that many of these societies are capable of supporting true democracies now or that the kind of democracies they might create would be able to bring about rapid and stable economic growth. This is not to say that authoritarian rule is any kind of universal recipe for economic success either. What it indicates rather is that we actually know very little about universally applicable rules for human progress, assuming such rules exist at all.

In these circumstances, the U.S. and Western approach to democratization in other societies should be governed by rigor of the intellect and generosity of the spirit: rigor in studying the history, political culture, and social, economic and ethnic orders of other societies to determine what kind of political system they can support at present and in the near to medium term; generosity of the spirit, from both success and modesty. The West's immense wealth and security compared to most societies on this planet makes lecturing them rather than giving them serious economic aid singularly indecent; and if we look back only a few decades, we will find our own societies guilty of monstrous crimes of racism, aggression and oppression. If we look back not much more than a century, we will often find them guilty of what would now be called genocide.

If we have any sense at all of history, we should know that our system does not represent the "end of history," is not divinely ordained, and will not last forever. It is already clear, for example, that if the environmental challenges facing us reach really severe dimensions, then Western free market democracy in general, and the American version in particular, will fail to meet these challenges just as completely as the Chinese Confucian order failed to meet the challenge of Western modernization in the nineteenth century and many Muslim societies are failing in this regard today.

Julien Benda called for Western intellectuals to liberate themselves from the service of their respective nationalisms. American Creedal nationalism has identified the nation absolutely with the achievement of successful modernity and even with the "end of history" through the achievement of a perfect and permanent model for the world. This means that for many American intellectuals to liberate themselves from the service of nationalism, they also need to liberate themselves from their present slavery to Time.

They need to develop an intellectual capacity to step outside the current age and contemplate the broader sweeps of human history; to situate themselves somewhere between Conrad's fictional British Captain Marlowe, remembering that the Thames, like the Congo, was once "one of the dark places of the earth," and Macaulay's imaginary future visitor from New Zealand to the archaeological ruins of London.[158] This is, of course, a terribly difficult task. It is not however an inappropriate one for the intellectual elites of a country which has defined its own role in the sweep of human history as equivalent to that of Rome, the "Eternal City."

Instead of the rigor of the intellect and generosity of the spirit which might result from such detachment, the contemporary U.S. approach to democratizing the rest of the world all too often strangely combines sloppiness of intellect and meanness of spirit: rose-colored sloppiness of the intellect when it comes to progress and democratization in general combined with a bitter meanness of spirit toward specific countries which fail to measure up to American standards or demands. To this is added an acute lack of generosity when it comes to giving real economic help to peoples less fortunately endowed than the United States—the exact opposite of the "generous vision of global society and America's role in it" rightly called for by Allin, Gordon and O'Hanlon.

The sloppiness of intellect stems from the absolutist character of the American Thesis, explored in this chapter, and the intellectually and the morally tawdry consequences of mixing that thesis up with the short-term objectives of U.S. administrations and U.S. ethnic lobbies. The meanness of spirit is more surprising, for in Senator Fulbright's words, "a nation whose modern history has been an almost uninterrupted chronicle of success…should be so sure of its own power as to be capable of magnanimity."[159]

But as we shall see, while America as a whole may have a history of repeated triumphs, this is certainly not true of very large groups of people within the country. As in so many other nations throughout modern history, their sense of inherited defeat and humiliation fuels hatreds which not only envenom domestic politics, but have grave consequences for the character of their country's nationalism.

Three

Antithesis Part I:
The Embittered Heartland

Defeat of the aspen groves of Colorado valleys,
The blue bells of the Rockies,
And blue bonnets of old Texas,
By the Pittsburg alleys.
Defeat of the alfalfa and the Mariposa lily.
Defeat of the Pacific and the long Mississippi.
Defeat of the young by the old and silly.
Defeat of tornadoes by the poison vats supreme.
Defeat of my boyhood, defeat of my dream.

—Vachel Lindsay, "Bryan, Bryan, Bryan, Bryan"
(on the defeat of William Jennings Bryan's
populist campaign for president, 1896)[1]

R adical nationalism has many fathers, but its mother is defeat, and her milk is called humiliation. From this poisoned nourishment comes in part the tendency to chauvinist hatred which has streamed through so many of the world's nationalisms. This is self-evidently true of the nationalisms of the former European colonies, nationalisms which grew out of their conquest and occupation by European and other empires and the destruction or forced transformation of their previous economic structures and traditions of moral and political authority.

It is no less true, however, of those countries which avoided direct conquest, but were forced to defend themselves, to imitate Western forms of government, economics, society and culture as best they could and reshape themselves radically in the process. Religiously ordered social and state traditions were particularly threatened. Where such traditions survived, it was often by associating themselves with modern nationalism, sometimes—as in Japan—of a quasi-totalitarian kind.

Russia, Japan and Turkey are the best-known examples in this category. In the case of Russia, despite great military victories, the repeated failure of the country as a whole to catch up with its Western European and North American rivals pro-

88

duced an inferiority complex which has haunted Russian society and culture for almost three centuries.

In a wider sense, this pattern has been true not only of most of the globe, but even of most European countries: in recent centuries all have been forced to adapt as best they could to a model of modernity and progress which they did not create and over the shape of which they have had little say, whether that model was set by Holland, France, Britain or most recently the United States.

The tensions, insecurities and hatreds produced by this pattern sometimes endure long after the country concerned has liberated itself from its oppressors and even in those rare cases where it has caught up with its Western rivals. Thus German nationalism was born in the later eighteenth and early nineteenth centuries in large part out of a profound sense of inferiority and vulnerability to France. Culturally speaking, this sense was produced by the overwhelming dominance of French language and culture in eighteenth-century Europe, leading in Germany to that humiliating aping of French words and forms which was so bitterly denounced by Herder, Fichte and others.

For ordinary Germans, there was the repeated and unpleasant experience of invasion by French armies, culminating in those of Revolutionary and Napoléonic France. And for the German elites, there was the ruthless reshaping of Germany's political and social structures by French diktat—all of which was made possible by Germany's radically disunited condition, compared to the *Grande Nation*. The resulting resentments were watered by a steady drizzle of French contempt for German boorishness, drunkenness and general absurdity, which was well publicized by German nationalists.[2]

As a consequence, Germans developed a national inferiority complex which persisted even after Germany's unification in 1871 and emergence as Europe's most militarily powerful and economically successful nation: the psychological pattern by which, as Bismarck put it sardonically, "A German generally needs to drink two glasses of champagne before he feels himself to be his full height." This legacy was not least among the causes of the edgy arrogance, restlessness and paranoia of Wilhelmine German foreign policy, which, when combined with overwhelming German power, did so much to alarm other European states and unite them against Germany.

In the case of the United States, such tendencies are extraordinary not in the context of the history of nationalisms in the world, which obviously has thrown up infinitely worse examples. What makes it remarkable is once again the fact that the U.S. population seems at first sight to have had so little underlying reason—when compared to the historical sufferings and humiliations of other peoples—for a spirit of embittered, mean-spirited resentment of the outside world, and in particular of foreign countries which have in any way crossed their national will.

Regarding particular animosities, one needs to examine the role of specific U.S. ethnic lobbies and that of the American military-industrial-academic complex.

These two factors for example combined in sections of the U.S. establishment to prolong a widespread spirit of inveterate malignity against Russia for a decade after the Soviet Union collapsed and Moscow ceased to form any real threat to the United States. Clearly the Israeli lobby has also played its part over the decades in generating hostility to Arabs and Muslims.

However, it would be a mistake to accord either of these factors a central place in the overall pattern, which was shaped long before World War II and the Cold War transformed the American state and before the ethnic lobbies attained their full power. These groups would not have achieved their objectives had they not been able to tap the support of much larger bodies of Americans who have a natural tendency in the face of any disagreement to adopt harshly adversarial stances and who, when confronted with opposition from any other country, feel impelled automatically to take up positions of fear, hostility, militancy, intransigency and self-righteousness: in other words, classically nationalist positions.

This nationalist culture, and not only public ignorance, helps to explain how the Bush administration could transfer the anger Americans felt after 9/11 to targets which had nothing to do with that attack and why the opposition by much of the world to the Iraq War caused such an outburst of chauvinist fury in sections of the American media and public opinion.

This capacity for chauvinist nationalism in the United States can be explained largely by the fact that the role of defeat in the genesis of nationalism resides not only in the defeat of nations as a whole, but of classes, groups and indeed individuals within them. The hatred and fear directed abroad by nationalism often emanates from hatreds and tensions at home, and this is strikingly true in the case of the United States.

The appearance of nationalism in many countries has been correctly attributed in large part to the ascendancy and needs of new bourgeois classes; but it is equally true that many of nationalism's darker features have been produced by classes in relative or absolute decline, or with good reason to fear such decline, ones that have seen not only their status and security but their cultural worlds undermined by economic and social change.[3] These sentiments are especially liable to become radicalized if a period of economic growth ends and is replaced by depression or stagnation; thus many of Europe's modern radical conservative and radical nationalist movements had their origins in the first "Great Depression," which lasted from the mid-1870s to the 1890s.[4]

If one defining feature of many nationalisms has been a belief in a glorious future for the nation, another equally common feature has been the desire for a return to an idealized past, of a culturally and ethnically purer nation, a stable, traditional society and a "moral economy" in which decent, hardworking people are guaranteed a decent job: a shimmering, golden, ungraspable mirage, ever present, ever receding. In Germany, for example, this was the old world of the independent small towns, with their homogenous religious cultures and their guilds guaranteeing employment to respectable insiders and the exclusion of outsiders.

In the United States, this sense of defeat and embattlement resides in four distinct but overlapping elements of the American national tradition: the original, "core" White Anglo-Saxon and Scots Irish populations of the British colonies in North America; the specific historical culture and experience of the White South; the cultural world of fundamentalist Protestantism; and the particular memories, fears and hatreds of some American ethnic groups and lobbies.

Daniel Bell's words of 1963 remain true today: "What the right wing is fighting, in the shadow of Communism, is essentially 'modernity'—that complex of beliefs that might be defined most simply as the belief in rational assessment, rather than established custom, for the evaluation of social change—and what it seeks to defend is its fading dominance, exercised once through the institutions of small-town America, over the control of social change. But it is precisely those established ways that a modernist America has been forced to call into question."[5]

Nativism and White Middle-Class Anxieties

In America, the vision of an ideal past has developed and changed with almost every generation, as formerly "outsider" groups join the White middle classes and form a new synthesis with the older Protestant culture. Like the Hindu nationalist tradition in India, today this tendency is no longer narrowly ethnic. The stream of feelings of dispossession, however, has flowed continually from one cup to another, from the old "Protestant nativism" through McCarthyism to the Christian and nationalist Right of our own day.

In each generation, a new fear of being "swamped" or invaded arises. Nor is this fear by any means restricted to poorer or more ignorant Whites. In 2004 Samuel Huntington issued a stern warning that the United States is in danger of losing its political culture and even its language as a result of Mexican immigration, and declared roundly that both the American Creed and the American Dream are purely products of "a distinct Anglo-Protestant culture." He warned of the risk of a fierce White "Anglo" backlash if this trend continues. The same theme was present less explicitly in his *Clash of Civilizations*, in which Huntington effectively classified not only American Latinos and Asians but even Blacks as members of non-American civilizations.[6]

The radical edge that this fear lends to American conservatism also allows us to speak of the associated American right-wing nationalism as a "nationalism" and not merely a "patriotism."[7] Hence the phenomenon—so strange at first sight, but perfectly sincere, and entirely characteristic of the history of radical nationalism worldwide—of deeply conservative defenders of the American capitalist system such as Newt Gingrich describing themselves as "revolutionary Republicans," and adopting a style and rhetoric of radical alienation from the supposed ruling elites and dominant culture. Hence the popularity on the American Right of speeches, books and manifestos on the theme "Taking Back America"—a most revealing formulation.[8]

As the right-wing conservative politician Patrick Buchanan put it at the 1992 Republican Convention, "We must take back our cities and take back our culture and take back our country," the way (he said) that the U.S. military had recently "taken back" Los Angeles from the Black and Latino mobs during the Rodney King riots.[9] Ralph Reed of the Christian Coalition has spoken of the need for Christians to "take back this country, one precinct at a time." This kind of radical Rightist sentiment was perfectly expressed by Charles Maurras, who declared in the 1930s that "in order to love France today, it is necessary to hate what she has become."

As such words reflect, this attitude stems from a feeling of dispossession and even alien occupation. It is common in this segment of American politics to hear talk of the nation being ruled by a "liberal (or gay, or feminist) dictatorship." Such sentiments feed dark fantasies about the United States being secretly ruled by the United Nations or other international conspiracies, and contribute to the general apocalyptic tendency found in parts of American culture. The right-wing nationalist and populist Barry Goldwater, who exploited this tendency in America in the 1960s, was once called "the favorite son of a state of mind."[10]

This tendency can be summed up by the wonderful name of a Texas-based right-wing organization of the 1960s: the National Indignation Committee. It is a tendency with numerous dangerous parallels in the history of radical conservatism and nationalism in Europe. Like such movements in the late nineteenth and early twentieth centuries, it also stems from the moral and cultural confusion of deeply traditional people (largely but by no means exclusively petty bourgeois and peasants) desperately trying to make sense of a world which has become alien, and doing so with the help of the only culture available to them.

One could say, therefore, that the ethnic anxieties of sections of the original American stock created an enduring cultural mood in American society, a rich layer of sediment which was later added to by other assimilated ethnic groups and in which, over the generations, many different kinds of paranoia, fanaticism and national ambition have been planted and have flourished.[11]

In the mid-nineteenth century, the nativist "Know-Nothings" dreamed of a return to an earlier Protestant America without Irish Catholics and without the growth of the new capitalism.[12] In the early twentieth century, a complex of Protestant nativist tendencies dreamed of an America without a whole set of new immigrant groups and also without the automobile (or at least its backseat) and its corrosive effects on sexual morality. Today much of the White middle classes in general (including, of course, Irish and many other ethnicities and mixtures) dream of an idealized version of the Eisenhower years of the 1950s, before the sexual revolution and the rise of Blacks, gays, feminists and other hated groups. This particular nostalgia suffused the language of the "Republican Revolution" of the mid-1990s and memoirs by Pat Buchanan and other Rightists.[13]

The real or perceived defeats fueling such nostalgia have affected and harmed important groups within America just as badly as they have similar groups elsewhere. The American middle classes may not have suffered so badly economically—although that situation may be changing as the economy ceases to generate adequate numbers of "middle-class" jobs—but the nation's openness to immigration means that the middle classes have suffered even more from demographic pressure and the cultural tension and change that immigration has encouraged.

This clash has generated much of the electricity which drives the turbines of nationalism and other radical political tendencies across the world. A classic example is the role of the endangered and declining nobility, peasantry and traditional middle class (*Mittelstand*) of Germany in generating German "radical conservatism," and the new nationalism which was its intimate partner, in the later nineteenth century.[14] These social strata generated movements which often combined radical economic protest against the new capitalism with intense nationalism and cultural conservatism.[15] And as the example of the Prussian nobility shows, absolute decline does not necessarily have to occur to drive an old elite in a radical direction—the threat can be enough.

Anti-Semitism has been described as the "socialism of the petty-bourgeois," but in fact it formed part of a much wider complex of radical attitudes and resentments. Ultra-nationalism and reproaches to "cosmopolitan elites" for not being nationalist enough have long formed one path for the expression of socioeconomic grievances on the part of groups that for whatever reason could not turn to socialism: "Having gained a foothold in the world of bourgeois respectability, they stood in danger of being plunged back into what they viewed as an abyss of powerlessness and dependence. It was that fear that made the middle class, even more than those who were truly rootless and indigent, a politically volatile group."[16]

The United States is not only the home of rapid, unceasing capitalist modernization and unceasing change; it also contains large middle-class groups which at certain times in history—including today—have suffered badly as a result of the workings of this same capitalism: especially since, compared to other developed societies, American capitalism is also less restrained and softened by state controls and state-funded social support mechanisms.

Over the centuries, the socioeconomic anxieties of the White middle classes and rural populations often have fused with ethnic and racial fears. These fears stemmed originally from what used to be called the "native" Americans—not the American Indians, but the White Anglo-Saxon and Scots Irish populations of the eighteenth-century British colonies.[17]

At the time of independence from Britain, the thirteen colonies, far from representing great diversity of ethnicity and culture, were if anything rather less diverse than the kingdoms of Britain or France. This statement is not true if one includes Blacks and Indians—but then, non-Whites were *not* included in the American states as they then understood and defined themselves, nor would they be for almost another two hundred years.

Leaving aside the Blacks and Indians, White America at independence was overwhelmingly made up of two ethnicities, Anglo-Saxon and Scots Irish (Protestant Scots and northern English who had settled in Ireland as part of the wars against the native Gaelic Catholic Irish). Significant numbers of Dutch lived in New York and Germans in Pennsylvania and a few other places. Despite being overwhelmingly Protestant, these Germans attracted considerable hostility and fear from the English colonists, including the supposedly pragmatic and tolerant Benjamin Franklin, who was not even sure that the Germans and other Europeans were really White: "The number of purely White people in the world is proportionally very small.... In Europe, the Spaniards, Italians, French, Russians and Swedes are generally of what we call a swarthy complexion, as are the Germans also, the Saxons only excepted, who with the English make the principal body of White people on the face of the earth. I could wish their numbers were increased."[18]

The vast majority of the White American population spoke English and, equally importantly, were Protestants. These were divided into different churches and sects, and displayed very considerable cultural differences (especially between the English of New England and the Scots Irish of the Frontier and the South). They also however shared a great many attitudes, not least their deep distrust of Catholicism. Especially in the South and on the Frontier, Americans perpetuated not just the Protestant religious culture of sixteenth- and seventeenth-century England and Scotland, but also aspects of their language and folk culture. And the English had developed strong elements of a common national identity even before the first settler set foot in North America.[19]

Compared to Britain and France, America lacked the huge Gaelic-speaking Catholic population of most of Ireland, the still–Welsh-speaking population of Wales, the numerous mutually incomprehensible languages and dialects spoken by ordinary French, and even the suppressed but still considerable and deeply disaffected Protestant minority of central and southern France.

By historical standards, then, the population of the new United States was relatively homogenous ethnically and culturally. By European standards, it was also relatively homogenous socially. Except for the great plantation owners of the Southern states, there was no aristocracy—and even the Southern planters were vastly closer to the mass of the White population than the Duke of Norfolk and the Prince de Rohan were to their tenants.

In reality if not legally, the United States was a Protestant nation in which Catholics and others were protected and tolerated, and for many years even toleration "was regarded more as an arrangement among the Protestant sects than a universal principle." (For that matter, John Locke, philosophical father of the American political Enlightenment and national Creed, had explicitly denied toleration to Catholics in Britain.)[20] "Most of the proponents of the various religious positions did not really believe in either freedom or toleration. Freedom came to the Western world by the providence of God and the inadvertence of history."[21]

This belief was, if anything, only encouraged as more and more German Protestants immigrated and later joined the elites. The view of the United States as "an essentially Protestant nation with free exercise rights constitutionally guaranteed to minorities" remained widespread well into the twentieth century, and in many ways up to the election of the nation's first (and as of mid-2004, only) Catholic president, John F. Kennedy, in 1960.[22]

Of course, this nativist stream has changed greatly over time. Most notably, it has continually attracted to itself sections of those immigrant populations which formerly were precisely those which stoked the fears of the "true stock." In the process however, it has infected these immigrant groups with some of its own "paranoid style."[23]

Although sections of the old core groups felt embattled and even defeated, such was the strength and conviction of their culture that over two centuries they were able to turn even a largely immigrant America into a "Protestantoid" nation. Today across large parts of the country, the White middle classes (including the upper proletariat) share a culture which is rather homogenous and above all, as already noted, very conformist.

As Walter Russell Mead has written, the American sense of "folk community" (in the German sense of *Volk*), gradually has become synonymous in the minds of its proponents with "the American middle class." It has still, however, retained the meaning of a community of shared and narrowly defined cultural values, closed to many categories of outsider.[24] This conformism gives tremendous opportunities to any political force which can seize on key symbols of public consensus for its own ends.

Furthermore, from the first, both the size of America and the nature of the American system made compromises between these groups a necessity. Thus despite pathological fears of Catholicism among nineteenth-century American evangelical Protestants, since the 1820s a political alliance has existed on and off between the Jacksonian tradition in the South and West and sections of the Catholic Irish in the Northeast. One essential ingredient in the glue holding this alliance together has always been common hatred of the "East Coast elites."[25] In our own time too, a determined and partially successful attempt has been made to create an alliance between this tradition and American Jewish groups on the basis of support for Israel and a strong U.S. military policy in the Middle East, and of hostility to Muslims and Arabs, and to Americans and Europeans who criticize Israel.

One aspect of this history has been the attempt of older immigrant groups to ingratiate themselves and deflect hostility by attacking either more recent immigrants or racial minorities, or both. The Jacksonian alliance of Southern Whites with the Irish and other Northern "ethnics" has always owed much to shared fear of and hostility to Blacks. After World War I, "even liberals such as Fiorello LaGuardia [mayor of New York City] and Representative Samuel Dickstein began to bait Asians and Mexicans in order to protect Jews and Italians."[26]

In the mid-nineteenth century, the most important targets of nativist protestant movements like the Know-Nothings were Irish Catholics. A century later, the descendants of this tradition had taken up a German Irish Catholic as one of their great heroes. Progress? Not entirely. His name was Senator Joseph R. McCarthy. Similarly, it is at first sight wonderful that the Christian Right tradition has shed much of its ancestral anti-Semitism and come to identify closely with Israel. The problem is that the Israel in question is that of Ariel Sharon, Likud and even more extreme forces in Israeli society and among the settlers in the Occupied Territories.

The "Jacksonian" and Frontier Traditions

As Chapter 5 explores, sympathy for Israel on the part of the American nationalist Right owes a great deal to the ferocious history of racial conflict on the North American continent. This history also created the figure who more than any other has been seen to symbolize the populist nationalist tradition in the United States and who has indeed given his name to one of its dominant elements: President Andrew Jackson (1767–1845).

The Jacksonian tradition stems above all from the experience of the American Frontier, an experience which at one time or another affected all the states of the nation and which remains strong to this day in the South and West.[27] But as recorded by David Hackett Fischer and other historians and cultural demographers, it also has older roots in the traditions and experience of the Scots Irish Protestants, who after settling Ulster and largely exterminating its Gaelic Irish Catholic population, later brought both their fundamentalist Protestantism and their ruthless attitude to warfare with them to the Americas. In the words of one of Jackson's early biographers, which would be endorsed by any student of recent Northern Irish history, "It appears to be more difficult for a North-of-Irelander than for other men to allow an honest difference of opinion in an opponent, so that he is apt to regard the terms opponent and enemy as synonymous."[28]

Born in North Carolina into a prominent Scots Irish lineage, and later settled in Tennessee, Jackson's entire career was shaped by conflict with the American Indians of the South and their British, French and Spanish backers. Although General Jackson's greatest victory was against the British at New Orleans in 1815, most of his campaigns were against the Cherokee, Creek and others. It was as an Indian fighter and leader of local militias that Jackson emerged to prominence in Tennessee. And although "Jacksonian nationalism" contains other important elements, including nativism, antielitism, anti-intellectualism and dislike of the Northeast, a strong sense of White identity, and violent hostility to other races, was long at its core.[29]

A classic collision between this strand of Jacksonian nationalism and the core principles of the American Creed as publicly formulated occurred in 1831, during Jackson's presidency. The Cherokee nation, resident in what had become northern Georgia and parts of Tennessee and Alabama since long before Whites landed in the Americas, appealed to the U.S. Supreme Court against new laws passed by the state of Georgia making them subject to its law and laying the basis for the Indians' expulsion beyond the Mississippi to make way for White settlers. Lawyers for the Cherokees argued—quite correctly—that this was in violation of several treaties with governments of the United States. In accordance with the unarguable legal facts, a majority of the Court, led by Chief Justice John Marshall, ruled in favor of the Cherokees.

To this Jackson reportedly replied, "John Marshall has made his decision; now let him enforce it." Although the president may not actually have said this, these words certainly reflected the spirit in which he acted. The U.S. government refused to defend the Cherokee against Georgia, Jackson warned them that they had no choice but to leave, and within a few years (although after Jackson himself had left office) they were driven out of their ancestral homeland onto the "Trail of Tears" to Oklahoma, on which a great many died of disease and malnutrition.[30]

Jackson's reported words reflected not only his own implacable hostility to the Indians. More important, his statement was descriptive of the actual situation in the South and West and of the attitudes of the vast majority of Jackson's constituency, the White inhabitants of these sections. They were determined to drive out the Indians irrespective of what the U.S. government or U.S. law said. Folk law called for the expansion of White land and civilization at the expense of the "Savages" and the protection of the White community from any possibility of a revival of the Indian raids of the past or Indian alliances with foreign enemies of the nation.

This folk law took precedence over the written code of the United States (even when the Indians concerned had been allies of the nation in war and had in fact made long strides toward the adoption of "civilization," including the creation of a written language). Together with these attitudes came a deep hostility to humanitarian East Coast, or "Yankee" lawyers and intellectuals, who having gotten rid of their own Indians more than half a century before, now felt free to criticize and restrict the behavior of the West and South in this regard—a regional hostility which has replicated itself over numerous different issues up to our own day.

The other elements which over time have shaped the populist-nationalist tradition in America include the Southern experience of slavery, the specific cultural and historical traditions of the Protestant Scots Irish who dominated on the Southern Frontier; and a communal culture heavily influenced by evangelical Protestantism.[31] This tradition has reflected the culture, interests and anxieties of the original Anglo-Saxon and Scots Irish settler stock, although its proponents have also been willing to forge political alliances with specific immigrant groups and over time, to accept as full members of the community aliens who are held to conform to communal and "civilized" values. In the past, this always meant White aliens, but in the last three decades it has expanded to include some non-Whites as well.

Another element is a "producerist" ethos with very strong resemblances to the ideologies thrown up by lower-middle-class and agrarian-based radical conservative and nationalist movements in Europe of the past. This ethos involved bitter hostility to "parasitical" elements of society—concentrated in the Northeast—which supposedly drained away the wealth from those who actually produced it: "finance capitalists," snobbish "silk stockings," hereditary *rentier* elites, overpaid intellectuals, "experts," bureaucrats and lawyers—all of them with suspect foreign contacts, influences or antecedents (in the past, this tradition often involved anti-Semitism). There has been equal hostility to the "parasitical," shiftless, lazy, drunken (or addicted) urban lower proletariat, above all when of alien or immigrant origin. Hostility to the elites stemmed from the society of the Frontier and the newly settled areas, but it also had roots in seventeenth-century English and Scottish Puritan hostility to the Anglican (and sometimes crypto-Catholic) English elites of that time, not only in the nobility and the clergy, but also in the universities and the legal profession.[32]

In America, these attitudes are also closely related to regional interests and prejudices; the hostility of the "honester South and West," as Thomas Jefferson phrased it, to the decadent, exploitative and above all commercial East.[33] In our own time, some of these sentiments have found expression through the term "the Heartland." Geographically, this means the states of the Midwest and the high plains, from Ohio to the Rockies. However, as its name indeed suggests, in political rhetoric it often carries with it the suggestion that this territory is also the home of true, core American people and values, of which nationalism is one of the most important.[34]

Jacksonian language pitting these regions against the East Coast elites continued in the Democratic Party for more than a century: in the 1948 elections (drawing also on bitter Confederate memories), Harry Truman declared in North Carolina that the Republican Party and business elite "treats the South and West as colonies to be exploited commercially and held down politically."[35] Over the past forty years, this attitude has been taken over by the Republican Party. For obvious reasons having to do with the economic interests of their own leadership, the Republicans have taken a somewhat different group of Jacksonian hate objects—Washington bureaucrats and liberal intellectuals rather than bankers—but the appeal to regionalist hatred of the metropolitan elites remains the same.

These hate objects were always somewhat flexible and protean. Thus Thomas Jefferson has been seen as in many ways a precursor of Jacksonianism, in his thoroughly racist version of an egalitarian white society and Herrenvolk democracy based on the "healthy" producerist farmers and artisans. However, Jefferson—Virginia aristocrat, former ambassador to France and admirer of the French Revolution—was also attacked by his enemies both as a frenchified Jacobin revolutionary atheist and as a frenchified, decadent, parasitical intellectual aristocrat.[36]

Indeed, the association of France not only with atheism and decadence but also with East Coast elitism dates back to American reactions against the French Revolution. Notable among these was the first "Great Fear" of independent America, the hysteria surrounding the passage of the Alien and Sedition Act of 1798, directed against supposed French revolutionary plotters in the United States.[37] Hostility to European decadence, when contrasted with American purity and honesty, found its way into the American education system at an early date through one of its fathers, Noah Webster.[38] The attacks on France in the context of the war with Iraq therefore have had a long pedigree. Some of the language about French decadence, atheism and elitism has remained much the same. In the words of one right-wing nationalist attack on France after 9/11: "Most Americans find it difficult to take the French critique seriously, coming as it does from men who carry handbags."[39]

In his classic work on the populist tradition in America, Michael Kazin characterized Jacksonian ideology as one of American populism's most important and enduring elements. Jacksonian beliefs and rhetoric were rooted in a particular moral framework the elements of which were drawn from a mixture of Scots Irish Calvinism and the Frontier experience. This morality championed the honest producers against "the consumers, the rich, the proud, the privileged" and American "aristocrats" corrupted by European atheism and decadence. It advocated equal *access* to wealth—above all, Indian lands—for all White Americans, but certainly not economic egalitarianism; and it celebrated "toughness, maleness, and whiteness" in defense of family, race and nation.[40] In the later 1960s and 1970s, the Republican Party revived the Jacksonian alliance of Southern Whites and Northern "ethnics" (in Jackson's own time and after, Irish Catholics) in hostility to Blacks.[41]

It was on the strength of this appeal that Andrew Jackson won election to the presidency in 1828. His election has been taken as symbolizing, in myth and to some extent in reality, America's transition from the oligarchical rule of the founding elites to mass democracy. The transition was closely related to the emergence of new forms of evangelical Protestant popular religion, which radically downgraded the position of the old elite-dominated churches and which had strong anti-intellectual and antimodern biases. This democracy categorically excluded Indians, Blacks and women.[42]

As Jackson's own mixture of Southern and Frontier origins indicates, the American Frontier and the American South might be treated almost as one cultural complex in terms of their cultural impact on American nationalism. Gunnar Myrdal in 1944 described the South as a "stubbornly lagging American frontier society."[43] What we have been taught by Hollywood to think of as the classic Frontier, in the West, was settled largely by Southerners with Southern cultural traits.

The mingling of the Southern and Western traditions is at its most obvious in Texas, the home state of George W. Bush and the source of much of his political culture and attitudes. Texas has been described as "a southern state masquerading as a western state."[44] It was one of the Confederate states, and its eastern section, close to the border with Louisiana, has a strongly Southern flavor, with a large Black population and a plantation tradition of agriculture. Central and western Texas, however, were still Indian territory at the time of the Civil War.

Western Frontier culture had been molded by the previous experience of the Southern Frontier in the Appalachian Mountains and the Southern forests. Yet the Frontier tradition as a whole also had aspects which had nothing to do with the South. The northeastern states had an Indian Frontier from their foundation in the early seventeenth century to the expulsion of the French and then the British 150 years later. The Western Frontier also generally lacked the other defining factor in the South, namely a Black population and (before 1865) an institution of Black slavery to be defended. The need to defend slavery and Black subordination produced a Southern tradition of conformism—enforced democratically and spontaneously, but with ruthless determination—which has not been as characteristic of the West.[45] Closely connected with this difference is the fact that the West is also far more religiously diverse than the South.

One of the most important legacies of the Frontier for American nationalism was a history of exceptionally ferocious warfare, often amounting to genocide, in which both sides committed appalling atrocities. This legacy has bred in sections of the American tradition both a capacity for ruthlessness and a taste for absolute and unqualified victory of the kind which was in the end won over all the indigenous adversaries of White America. A second legacy was constant expansionism, often pushed for by the Frontier White populations against the wishes of administrations in Washington.

In the South especially, this expansionist spirit was directed not just toward the Indian and Mexican lands but also to European colonial possessions in the Caribbean. In the twentieth century, as T. R. Fehrenbach has written, it carried over into support for far wider agendas: "Since 1900, Texas had increasingly fused back with the nation in foreign policy, especially when foreign policy was basically imperial—whatever name was put upon it. Texans instinctively supported anything that seemed to support American power and prestige. Both the domination of the banana republics and the destruction of Imperial Germany were parts of the same policy, blended of self-interest, self-defense, and an arrogant form of goodwill.... Those who had in some sense carried the American flag West did not metamorphose overnight when they had no more worlds to conquer on their shores."[46]

Moreover, as far as the American mainland was concerned, this expansion was completely successful—in part because it very cannily stopped short of annexing regions with large Catholic, Spanish-speaking populations which could not be exterminated, swamped or assimilated.

By contrast, the record of successful settlement on the part of other White nations has been a mixed one. In regions of the world where the indigenous peoples were similar to those of the Americas (and had been decimated by Eurasian diseases before the settlers even arrived), White settlement was successful and seems quite likely to prove long-lasting. Everywhere else, eventually the White settlers have been kicked out, as from Algeria, Zimbabwe and Soviet Central Asia, or subordinated to the indigenous population, as in South Africa and Kazakhstan. In America, the record of settlement has been one of unqualified victory through ruthless violence—with all the effects that this is bound to have on a nation's psyche.

The bestial atrocities to which Indian tribes such as the Comanche and Kiowa subjected their prisoners also did much to shape long-term attitudes to aliens in Texas and elsewhere: "Survivors of Indian raids were unable to rationalize a brotherhood of man that included American Indians....The dominant view of the Amerindians among the English became one of inhuman savages who were unpredictable and dangerous predators. Since the whole Frontier population—not a protecting line of soldiers—became involved in endemic Indian wars, the entire population was predictably brutalized. Suffering terrible wrongs themselves, the Frontier people inflicted terrible wrongs on the Amerindians."[47]

The Scots Irish in particular had already experienced one savage Frontier war with genocidal overtones. Their ancestors (together with some English Puritans and French Huguenots) initially had settled in Ireland as part of the Elizabethan and Jacobean clearances of the native Irish population of Ulster and the Cromwellian and Williamite settlements of the rest of the island. There they had mixed with Protestantized elements of the Irish population.[48]

From their original settlements in central Pennsylvania, the Scots Irish eventually settled much of the old Frontier of Virginia and the Carolinas (where Jackson was born), before moving on to Tennessee, the lower South, Texas and the Southwest. Indeed, the Southern historian Grady McWhiney has gone so far as to attribute most of the cultural difference between the South and the rest of the United States to Southerners' Celtic cultural heritage.[49] Discriminated against by the Anglo-Irish Episcopalian elites on the grounds both of class and religion, the Scots Irish brought with them to America a legacy of dislike of educated elites, whether English or Yankee (Northeasterners of overwhelmingly English origin).[50]

This tradition in America remains closely akin to the Ulster Protestant community from which it stemmed, in its conflation of religion and nationalism and (until recently) its bitter hatred of Catholicism. Now that the Boer tradition of South Africa has surrendered to the Black majority, today the Ulster Protestant Loyalists are the only people anywhere else in the developed world whose culture and ideology resembles that of American evangelical Christianity.[51]

The Old Testament gave these settlers in Ireland, America and South Africa both a language and a theological framework to describe and justify their dispossession of the land's native inhabitants. The biblical tones of Jackson's addresses to the Cherokee and Creek demanding their removal across the Mississippi River were prefigured 150 years earlier in Cromwell's addresses to Irish Catholics demanding their removal "to Hell or Connaught."[52]

The Frontier also helped continue into the modern age a cult of personal weaponry, closely associated with a certain kind of egalitarianism and belief in every man's right and duty to defend his personal and familial honor—a classic theme of Hollywood versions of the West, but one with a real existence and with real roots in the Southern and Frontier traditions.

These traditions in turn derive ultimately from the world of late medieval and early modern England and Scotland, which was extremely violent by contemporary standards. Especially in northern England and Scotland, crimes were very often crimes of "honor," or forms of the *lex talionis* (law of retaliation): collective family revenge or self-defense, often on the part of respectable gentry families.

"Stuart England was a country in which violence was endemic even when it was not being torn apart by Civil War."[53] Gentry and poor alike displayed the "ferocity, childishness and lack of self-control of the Homeric age."[54] Stuart Scotland and Ireland were a great deal worse. As in the southern and western parts of the United States—or in many tribal societies across the world—this concern with honor was often indistinguishable from intense quarrelsomeness. The duel proper lasted in the South for several decades after it had died out in most of the Western world in the mid-nineteenth century.[55]

Writing in the 1960s, the Texan journalist and author Warren Leslie described the traditional Texan character:

> Frontier days in Texas are not so far in the past....Challenged, [the Texan] fought with his gun or his fists, and he fought the land, too, as he would an enemy. He was a man of action rather than contemplation; he was an individualist, and he took great pride in victory—over the land and over other men. His life was made up of elemental facts, and fundamentalist preaching confirmed his conviction that things were either Black or White....The man who acts, who fights, who resists trespass, who takes no orders from groups or from other men and who will not compromise—he is the frontier man, and he is still around in Dallas, and in Texas.[56]

This picture is a tremendously important part of the self-image of George W. Bush, of Dick Cheney (from Wyoming, another tough Frontier state) and indeed of their administration as a whole, and it has shaped that administration's aggressive stance in international affairs—although, of course, unlike their ancestors, its leading members show no desire to fight themselves.

As John Shelton Reed remarked of Appalachian society in the mid-twentieth century, "It has been found impossible to convict men of murder...provided the jury is convinced that the assailant's honor was aggrieved and that he gave his adversary notice of his intention to assail him." In other words, the code of the duel: once again, an essentially premodern cultural tradition continuing to exist in parts of the standard-bearer nation of world "modernity."

Reed has described this as "lawful violence," in the sense of violence which is socially sanctioned, is a predictable response to certain actions and observes codes and limits. It is, in other words, another aspect of community or "folk" law, as opposed to that of the state. It is closely related to the right of the community as a whole to administer its communal version of "justice" whenever the state for whatever reason is unwilling or unable to follow the popular will. The resulting tradition of lynching has been associated above all with the terrorization of Blacks in the South in the century after the Civil War, but the tradition on the Frontier was much older, and usually was deployed against deviant Whites (and Indians, of course).[57]

This culture of violence has declined greatly in the South and the West over the past century, but remains very noticeable compared to the rest of the United States (except for the inner cities, which were largely peopled by Blacks from the South), let alone the rest of the developed world; and has carried over into attitudes to the outside world.

As W. J. Cash wrote in his great study of 1941, *The Mind of the South*, Southern violence was not only personal: "The Southerner's fundamental approach carried over into the realm of public offences as well. What the direct willfulness of his individualism demanded, when confronted by a crime that roused his anger, was immediate satisfaction for itself—catharsis for personal passion in the spectacle of a body dancing on the end of a rope or writhing in the fire—now, within the hour—and not some ponderous abstract justice in an abstract tomorrow. And so, in this world of ineffective social control, the tradition of vigilante action, which normally lives and dies with the frontier, not only survived but grew."[58]

In one respect, the Frontier, like the South, embodies a tradition quite at variance with the popular image of a triumphant march westward, a tradition that links the roots of American populist nationalism to radical nationalisms elsewhere in the world. This is a tradition of repeated and sometimes shattering defeats, although on the Frontier these defeats were at the hands of nature, provoked by human mismanagement and greed: the defeat of whole populations on the agricultural frontier by soil exhaustion, erosion and drought.

The most internationally famous episode of this was the "dustbowl" created on the lower Great Plains by the 1920s, which led to the westward migration of "Okies" (people from Oklahoma) and others described by John Steinbeck in *The Grapes of Wrath*; but this was only part of a much wider and longer pattern. Indeed, many of the Okies moved to the plains from the lower South in the first place not only because they were drawn by the lure of land taken from the Indians, but also because they were *driven*: driven first from the fertile lands of the South to the thin soils of the hills by the spread of slave-worked commercial plantations; then driven from the hills by the erosion of that soil due to deforestation and overcropping. When they arrived on the plains, the same pattern would repeat itself.

When the Okies arrived in California, they found themselves treated by the existing White Californian population (itself originally very largely from the Midwest) as an inferior and despised underclass, almost like the Mexicans, and this treatment lasted into the 1960s—with inevitable results for Okie alienation, antielitism and of course racial hatred of the Mexicans. This Southern and Midwestern background of "Anglo" southern California explains in part the flavor of religious and political conservatism in that region and its differences from northern California, with its far more mixed White population.[59]

A brilliantly evocative picture of this process of defeat in one section of the agricultural frontier, the Texas Hill Country (Edwards Plateau), is to be found in Robert Caro's monumental biography of President Lyndon B. Johnson, who came from that country. Caro describes the deceptively fertile soil of the Hill Country as "a trap baited with grass and water," which having attracted the settlers, doomed their descendants to generations of poverty and a continual, grinding struggle against drought and erosion.[60]

In the late 1880s, a decade or so after the trap began to close on the inhabitants of the Hill Country, a defeat by drought more sudden and on a much larger scale struck the new settlers of the high plains of the Dakotas, Nebraska, Colorado and western Kansas. Hundreds of thousands of people had to abandon their dream of an honorable life of farming for wage slavery in city factories. Those who remained on the land fell deeper and deeper into debt to the hated banks.[61] This pattern was repeated in a less dramatic way across large parts of the rural Midwest in the last decades of the twentieth century.[62]

This defeat (repeated in a fresh drought after 1910) produced one of the great Heartland revolts against the East Coast elites in American history, the Populist movement led by William Jennings Bryan. His defeat as Democratic candidate by the Republicans (backed by a combination of East Coast financial-industrial interests and the big-city populations) in the presidential elections of 1896 was mourned by Vachel Lindsay in the poem quoted at the beginning of this chapter.[63] Just as the Democrat Al Smith was defeated in 1828 in large part because of his Catholicism, which led to the defection of many Protestant Heartland and Southern supporters, so Bryan lost in part because his intense evangelical Protestant culture and barely veiled dislike of the cities and the Catholic immigrants alienated the Democrats' big-city voters, especially among the Irish.

In fact, Bryan picked up and reunited a good deal of the Protestant nativist tradition of the American Party or Know-Nothings, which had collapsed when their Northern and Southern wings split in the run-up to the Civil War. In the interval, however, the number of immigrant voters—and especially Catholics—in America had increased manifold, greatly increasing the difficulties of this approach for anyone wishing to run for national office.

The 1880s and 1890s were years in which, overall, not just the American economy but American agricultural production grew enormously. My point therefore is not to suggest that the American tradition of national and individual success is somehow imaginary. I mean only to point out that this tradition also contains within it innumerable personal and collective defeats, defeats that also have had their place in shaping the American national psyche.

For every family that moved West and made good, there was another "decent, feckless family that had left a century of failed farms, male suicides, and infant graves across the land from Ohio to the Coast, pushing always unprofitably westward."[64] Furthermore—although this is something which cannot be established statistically—the sting of defeat probably has been more bitter in a country where success really does depend to a much greater extent than elsewhere on character and determination—not just on the Frontier, but in the cities as well. Thus in America, failure has been attended by both shame and Protestant-flavored guilt; for "to fail is to acknowledge some deep flaw in the self, for responsibility cannot lie with a society whose promise of happiness and possibility is its reason for being."[65]

In the still hierarchically influenced societies of Europe, no small German farmer needed to feel bad about not being a Prince von Hohenlohe or a Count Preysing. A new Texan settler who had remained a small farmer—or was forced off the land altogether to become an urban proletarian—while Charlie Goodnight created in less than a generation a ranch larger than some European countries would naturally have a different feeling about himself. He would seek all the harder, perhaps, to soothe this feeling by a conviction that despite everything, he was part of God's chosen elite, culturally, religiously and nationally.

The White South

Both foreign analysts and Americans themselves have often treated the South as a culturally quite separate part of the United States, without influence on the nation's wider national identity. And the South does indeed have a very special historical and cultural character—one which, however, cannot be somehow cut out from America's wider political culture and American nationalism: "No small part of the reactionary nationalism of the twentieth century United States can be directly attributed to the South's pronounced conservatism and its comparative isolation from contact with foreigners and foreign ideas."[66]

The White South occupies a very considerable section of the United States and a very much bigger one of what I have called the American Nationalist Party or Republicans.[67] According to the 2002 census, the eleven former Confederate states made up 30.21 percent of the U.S. population, with the Greater South (including Oklahoma, Missouri, Kentucky and West Virginia) making up 35.44 percent. Only 19.79 percent of the former Confederate Old South and 18.13 percent of the Greater South was Black; 17.91 percent and 15.71 percent respectively were Latino, Asian and Native American.

This means that White Southerners make up over one-fifth of the total U.S. population—not a dominant section, but certainly a potentially very powerful one. In terms of political power, the position of the South (and the often-allied West) is strengthened by the American federal system, which gives disproportionate weight to states with small, mainly traditional White populations.[68] Since the 1970s, only a handful of Southern states have ever voted Democrat in presidential elections.

As Michael Lind, Kevin Phillips, Peter Applebome and others have pointed out, over the past two decades the "southernization" of the Republican Party has given these traditions a very considerable new importance in the politics of America as a whole and consequently in U.S. international behavior.[69] Among the effects of this "southernization" has been a harsher form of nationalism. The growing Southern-style religiosity of the Republicans also has had its effect, both in alienating the United States from "atheist" Europe and in increasing commitment to Israel. This transformation of the Republicans has contributed greatly to the increasing polarization of Americans along party lines. As indicated in the introduction, party lines also reflect strongly contrasting attitudes to religion, morality, culture, economics and nationalism.

This division was symbolized in 2003 by the public condemnation of the Democrats for moral decadence and lack of patriotism by their last senior conservative Southern representative, Senator Zell Miller of Georgia. Or as Thomas Schaller put it in 2003, "Trying to recapture the South is a futile, counterproductive exercise because the South is no longer the swing region. It has swung: Richard Nixon's "'Southern strategy' of 1968 has reached full fruition."[70]

The White South has not of course regained the political dominance enjoyed by Virginia's aristocracy from the 1780s to the 1820s, but it has recovered and indeed exceeded the power exercised by the region's representatives from the end of post–Civil War Reconstruction in the late 1870s to the era of Civil Rights and the collapse of the South's allegiance to the Democratic Party in the mid-1960s.

A key reason for Southern power is the way in which the South has been able to exercise disproportionate political influence through its grip on one of the two major parties. From 1877 to the 1960s (albeit with diminishing strength from the 1940s on), the White South was solidly Democratic, thanks to Southerners' bitter hostility toward the Republican Party of Abraham Lincoln. However, during that entire period, lingering Northern and Midwestern prejudices related to the Civil War and unease about the South's racial record meant that no Southerner from the eleven Confederate states could aspire to the presidency (unless, like Woodrow Wilson, he had moved north in his youth).[71]

Because a majority of the White South switched its allegiance to the Republican Party in the 1960s and 1970s in reaction against Democratic advancement of Civil Rights and multiculturalism, its role has become a good deal more activist. The critical importance of the White South to Republican hopes has been demonstrated in a series of presidential elections—most notably in 2000, when Al Gore's failure to win a single Southern state (despite coming from Tennessee himself) doomed his presidential hopes.[72]

The region's importance to hard-line conservative influence in the Republican Party is indicated by the fact that in a survey compiled by the *National Journal* of senators and congressmen in 2004, of the sixteen senators dubbed "most conservative" (one-third of the Republican total), ten came from the Greater South; of twenty-one senators dubbed "centrist," only five were from the South.[73]

If only because Southern Blacks now have the vote and use it to vote solidly Democratic, the South today is not as overwhelmingly Republican as it was once Democratic. The recent end of discrimination and the economic rise of the South (compared to the "Rust Belt" cities of the Midwest and Northeast) has led Blacks to return to the South. If this process continues and intensifies, eventually it will seriously undermine the grip of White conservatives on the South.

As of 2004, however, Southern Whites form the most solidly and reliably major Republican voting bloc in the country, which naturally gives them immense influence. The political power and longevity of the Southern conservatives in Congress has been unintentionally increased by the redivision of congressional districts to create solidly Black areas and therefore strengthen Black representation; the result of which has also necessarily been to create more solidly White districts. From the late 1970s, and particularly since the Republican Revolution led by the Georgian Newt Gingrich in 1994 and the formation of the Texan-led Bush administration in 2001, this influence has been used to advance programs with their roots in White Southern culture.

As noted by Applebome, Mead and others, this process has been greatly facilitated by the fact that important parts of White Southern culture have in recent decades spread far beyond their original homelands; consider the Southern evangelical Protestant religion; the cult of personal weaponry; country and western music; and stock car racing (which apparently originated among Appalachian Mountain bootleggers of moonshine whiskey). The South has also long been the home of a particularly intense form of American nationalism, strongly flavored by respect for the military and military values, and part of a wider culture which believes in traditional values of religion, family, manhood and honor.[74]

The South in this cultural sense was never coterminous with the eleven states which in 1861 seceded from the Union and for four years formed the Confederate States of America. The Greater South extends beyond the borders of the former Confederacy and even the Mason-Dixon Line (the parallel that separated slave from free states before 1861) to cover large parts of the Midwest and the West. According to some cultural geographers, the northern cultural border of the Greater South lies roughly along Route 40, which runs from east to west across the middle of Ohio, Indiana and Illinois. In the West, the Greater South includes Oklahoma and other states largely settled from the Old South.[75] In his run for the president, the radical conservative populist (and formerly racist) George C. Wallace appealed to Southerners "from Baltimore to Oklahoma City to St. Louis."

This region forms the heartland of evangelical Protestant religious belief, or the so-called Bible Belt, and the picture of America as a deeply religious country is to a considerable extent derived from the Greater South.[76] Until fairly recently this region lacked many large cities and consequently did not undergo the massive immigration pouring into the cities of the North and East from the mid-nineteenth century on. In many areas, and especially in the countryside and small towns, the White population of the Greater South remained homogenous.

W. J. Cash declared that the White South "is not quite a nation within a nation, but it is the next thing to it."[77] He wrote those words in 1941, but decades later, the leading Southern sociologist John Shelton Reed could still speak of Southern Whites constituting a form of ethnicity and possessing a form of ethnic consciousness.[78] And it is worth remembering in this context that if a couple of battles in the Civil War had gone the other way—by no means a historical impossibility—the South would in fact have become an independent nation, with its own (White) national consciousness.

Because the White South's bid for nationhood was crushed in war, and the region's particular nationalism was later reincorporated into that of the United States as a whole, students of nationalism have never properly addressed the development of Southern identity before 1865. This is a pity, for in many ways it provides a fascinating case study and adds interesting nuances to the debate between the "primordial" and "constructivist" approaches to the explanation of nationalism's origins.

On one hand, the Southern "national identity" was clearly a "constructed" one. It was constructed moreover in response to a particular threat: to the South's "peculiar institution," slavery. Moreover, although Southern Whites genuinely hated and feared Blacks, slavery was an issue which affected above all the Southern slave-owning elites. The antebellum South can well be seen therefore as a good example of the model of elite construction of modern nationalism argued for by Eric Hobsbawm and other left-wing scholars of the "constructivist" tradition in nationalism.

Of course, issues other than slavery were also involved in the North–South split before 1861. Nonetheless, take slavery, and Northern antislavery, out of the equation, and there is no real reason to think that the Southern elites would have devoted such intense effort to the construction of a separate identity, or that the Southern states would have gone so far as to fight for independence through four years of catastrophic warfare.

But the South is also an example of the fact that while national identities can be "constructed," they cannot—*pace* Hobsbawm—be "invented." They have to be put together, or "imagined," out of certain previously existing elements; and if these elements are not old and strong, then the resulting nationalism will be a weak one for which few are willing to sacrifice and die. This is one key reason why the invented nationalisms of postcolonial Africa, based on completely artificial colonial territories, usually have proven so weak, while many old tribal and religious loyalties have proven so strong.[79]

The antebellum White Southern "proto-national" identity was based on three main foundations. The first, obviously, was a Herrenvolk determination to keep Blacks in a subordinate and helpless position—what Cash called the "Doric" tradition of the South, after ancient Sparta and its ferocious suppression of the Helot population. The second, closely linked to the first, was a desire to preserve the South's agrarian economy and with it the domination of the plantation-owning class. This desire in turn generated intellectual and cultural defenders who self-consciously looked to European traditions of aristocratic conservatism, very different indeed from the kind of liberal pseudoconservatism prevalent elsewhere in the United States.

As in Europe, rather than explicitly defending aristocratic rule, this tradition instead attacked the soullessness, atomization and exploitation of Northern capitalism and contrasted it with real or invented Southern values of continuity of tradition and rootedness in the soil.[80] (Or in the words of T. R. Fehrenbach about twentieth-century Texans, "the great majority knew where their grandparents lay buried."[81]) This kind of critique of Western capitalism has been very characteristic not only of declining agrarian and aristocratic social orders, but of nationalist movements from wholly or partially "defeated" societies throughout modern history, from German ideas of Teutonic community (*Gemeinschaft*) against soulless, exploitative French and British "society" (*Gesellschaft*) to the nineteenth-century Slavophils in Russia and a host of "Third World" writers in our own time.[82] Thus already by 1825 there had been created among the South Carolinian gentry "just that atmosphere of pride, poverty and resentment which in the twentieth century has favored the growth of Arab and African nationalism."[83]

This tendency in the Southern identity overlapped with one which has been obscured both by the South's Civil War defeat in 1865 and by the fact that in that war, Americans of Anglo-Saxon and Scots Irish descent fought on both sides, as did evangelical Protestants: Namely, the specifically ethnic elements, in the White Southern tradition. I believe that if the White South had prevailed in the Civil War and established itself as an independent nation, the assertion of an ethnic identity based on a composite of the Anglo-Saxon and Scots Irish strains and fundamentalist Protestantism would have emerged as *the* central public face of White Southern nationalism.

As the North, or remaining United States left after Southern secession, became more and more ethnically mixed due to immigration, so the "purity" of the Southern ethnic tradition would have been asserted against Northern "mongrelization." Indeed, this purity/mongrelization opposition was already widely used in Southern rhetoric during the Civil War. It was shared to a degree by the Southerner Woodrow Wilson, and was continued in rabid form by Southern anti-Semitic nativists of the late nineteenth and early twentieth centuries like Governor Tom Watson of Georgia.[84] In these circumstances, the South would have lost its remaining liberals to the North, but would have attracted conservative northern Whites appalled by the nation's transformation by immigration; whites such as the novelist Owen Wister or the painter Frederic Remington, with his ferocious talk of "Jews, Injuns, Chinamen, Italians, Huns—the rubbish of the Earth I hate."[85]

But as recent scholars of American historical demography have stressed, the Scots Irish ethnic tradition at least was at bottom neither constructed nor invented, but very ancient, perpetuating until well into the twentieth-century folkways which long predated the modern age and in some cases even Christianity. Moreover, the violent circumstances in which the Scots Irish found themselves on the American Frontier in the eighteenth and nineteenth centuries replicated in many ways circumstances they had left behind, both in the savage wars against the Gaelic Irish and in the much older tradition of feuding along the English-Scottish border and among Scottish and North English clans.[86] This was a tradition of which the Scots Irish themselves in the nineteenth century were well aware. Andrew Jackson reportedly "required his wards to read the history of the Scottish chieftains whom he deeply admired and made the models for his own acts."[87]

The figure of Sir Walter Scott is a fascinating one in this regard. The craze for his historical novels and poems in the antebellum South generally has been seen—and mocked—as part of the attempt of the Southern plantation-owning class to invent a British aristocratic and "Cavalier" tradition for themselves. For the Scots Irish frontiersmen, however, Scott's role was rather different: to "reimagine" in suitably sanitized form their own historical tradition and thereby also to romanticize their actual lives on the Southern Frontier, which as noted reproduced in many ways those of their wild ancestors.

If the White South had gained its independence, Scott might be studied today from some of the same angles as those nineteenth-century nationalist poets and novelists who helped "imagine their nations" by weaving genuine but fragmented stories and legends into nationalist myths—novelists such as Elias Lonnnrot in Finland or Andrejs Pumpurs in Latvia. As a nineteenth-century Estonian nationalist declared, "Let us give the people the epic and the history, and everything is done!" That Sir Walter had no idea that he was performing this role in the American South only indicates the extremely tortuous cultural paths by which nations come into being.[88]

A Vignette of the Deep South

In 1979 I spent several months at a college in the small town of Troy, in southern Alabama, on an English-Speaking Union scholarship named for the soon-to-retire governor, George C. Wallace. At that time, not only was society rigidly divided between Blacks and Whites, but the absolutely overwhelming majority of locally born Whites I met were of mixed Anglo-Saxon and Scots Irish descent, and Southern Baptist by religion. A 1982 survey shows religious adherents in Pike County, where Troy is situated, as 67.5 percent Southern Baptist and 15.7 percent United Methodist. No other church reached 5 percent of the total. Eighteen years later, the figures for the Southern Baptists and Methodists were almost identical. Fundamentalist believers in the Assembly of God and Church of Christ had grown to 3.8 percent and 4.9 percent respectively.[89]

The public spirit of the place was strongly marked by this religious tradition. Thus the county was "Dry" (not completely, but alcohol could not be advertised or drunk in public, and bars were highly restricted). Neither this nor the fact that we students were mostly under twenty-one, the legal drinking age, seemed to have the slightest effect on the drinking habits of my peers. The great majority of White students were self-described "rednecks," and proud of it. They were very far indeed from the centers of American wealth, power, culture and influence. They knew this, and their response differed from prickly pride to bitter resentment.

They possessed a very strong sense of ethnoreligious community and local tradition. Although very few were of wealthy or aristocratic descent, very many were able to trace their ancestry back beyond the creation of Alabama, to settlers who

110

had originally moved from Tennessee, Georgia, or the Carolinas. Surprisingly, some were even proud of the possession of Cherokee or Creek ancestry, since this constituted proof of ancient establishment—whereas Black ancestry, although perhaps sometimes present, was emphatically not talked about. Despite state relief programs, a large part of the rural population, White as well as Black, was also still appallingly poor by the standards of the "developed" world, with extremely high levels of illiteracy.

Except for time spent in military service, a quite astonishing number had never been outside Alabama, except for visits to nearby Pensacola and the beaches of the Florida Panhandle, and still more had never traveled outside the South. Given the greater distances in the United States compared to Europe, Troy's isolation was in some ways comparable to that of small European towns before the coming of the railroads.

People were extremely kind and hospitable to the individual visitor (at least from Britain, a land which seemed to enjoy an almost mystical prestige both as an ally in war and as their own ancestral land of origin), but many were deeply suspicious of outsiders in general and deeply ignorant of America beyond the lower South. The world beyond America's shores was a kind of magic shadow play, full of heroes and demons, but without real substance. "Demons" in some cases is a literal rendering of how they saw America's enemies, for millenarian views of history were also present, although of course less at the college than among the surrounding population.

This was therefore a society as different from the common image both of American prosperity and of the American "melting pot" as could be imagined; and this picture was and to a considerable extent still is mirrored in small towns across the Deep South and certain parts of Texas and the West, reflecting what Oran Smith has called the continuing "incredible homogeneity among White Southerners."[90] Blacks had been accepted into the university and were not subject to overt discrimination, but they were still in a thoroughly subordinate position, with little local influence.[91]

Over the past sixty years, the tremendous economic changes initiated by World War II have changed the South greatly. The shift of industries from the Rust Belt of the Northeast and Midwest have transformed parts of the South into some of the most industrialized areas in America, and this transformation has been widely publicized by boosters from the region and beyond.[92] Economic development has sucked in new immigrants, including not only Latinos but also South Asians, so that for the first time since the expulsion of the Indians, Southern society is not simply split along Black-White lines.

However, a glance at the political, religious and ideological map of the White South reveals a society which has not changed nearly as much as figures for economic change would suggest. Although both the Latino and South Asian minorities have grown enormously, in 2000 the Southern Focus Poll still found that 65 percent of Southerners declared themselves Protestant, and more than half the population of Mississippi, Alabama and Georgia belonged to one denomination, Southern Baptist. Six out of ten Southerners still say that they prefer the biblical account of Creation to evolutionary theory (this figure of course includes Southern Blacks).[93]

The region has continued to elect a range of politicians of strikingly conservative, religious and nationalist cast. Older representatives of this culture such as Strom Thurmond and Jesse Helms have retired, only to be followed by younger figures such as Tom DeLay, Newt Gingrich, Trent Lott, James Inhofe and Dick Armey, who perpetuate their tradition. These are indeed "lively dinosaurs," as one observer put it. They are no fading remnants of a dead tradition and a lost cause.

One reason for this continuity may be that in one respect, the South has become if anything more homogenous over the past century. Before the Civil War, Blacks were a majority in two Southern states (South Carolina and Louisiana) and very close to a majority in two more (Alabama and Mississippi). By the 1960s Black emigration to the North, pulled by Northern jobs and pushed by Southern White oppression and harassment, had radically reduced these figures—a change which helps explain why the achievement of civil rights for Blacks under federal pressure, savagely resisted though it was by many Whites, did not lead to the Balkan-style eruption of White mass violence of which Southern racists and conservatives had so often warned. According to the census of 1880, Blacks made up 41 percent of the population of the Old South. By the 1960s this figure had fallen by more than half.[94]

For a century and a half, however, the desire to preserve first slavery and then absolute Black separation and subordination had contributed enormously to the closing of the Southern mind, with consequences for America as a whole which have lasted down to our own day. Both before the Civil War and in the mid-twentieth century, the social system of the South was "on the defensive against most of the Western world" and White Southerners saw "outside aggression" against the South everywhere.[95] The effects of this long experience of embittered defensiveness continue to this day.

Racial solidarity gave poor Whites pride in belonging to the superior, ruling race and helped deflect resentment against the wealthy plantation owners. Cultural, racial, political and economic defensiveness reached the point in the 1850s where the South became the pioneer in the modern world of the mass public burning of "dangerous books"; in this case, attacks on slavery from the abolitionist North. "In place of its old eagerness for new ideas and its outgoing communicativeness the South developed a suspicious inhospitality toward the new and the foreign, a tendency to withdraw from what it felt to be a critical world."[96]

Southern Defeat and Reconciliation

The defense of slavery and its effects on culture, combined with the other specific features of Southern culture already noted, led the South into its attempt at independent statehood in 1861 and to crushing defeat. The losses suffered by the South during the Civil War were fully comparable to those of European nations during the great wars of the twentieth century. Some 260,000 Confederate soldiers—more than one-fifth of the entire White adult male population—were killed in action or died of disease. (Some 350,000 Union soldiers died, but from a much larger population.)

Hundreds of thousands of civilians, White and Black, also died of disease brought on by malnutrition. Several of the South's largest cities were destroyed, along with numerous smaller towns, and extensive tracts of the countryside were deliberately stripped bare by the strategy of Sherman, Sheridan and other Northern generals. The real value of all property dropped by 33 percent; the number of horses by 29 percent; the number of pigs by 35 percent. The South's cotton production did not recover its prewar levels until 1879, fourteen years after the war ended.[97] Moreover—as in so many neocolonial monoculture economies around the world—the Southern economy as a whole was depressed by a fall in the price of cotton which lasted for several decades, just as the economy of the Great Plains was depressed by a fall in wheat prices.

It was more than a century before parts of the Confederate South caught up with the rest of America, both in terms of income and development and in access to supreme political power. Extensive areas have not done so yet, for much of the countryside and small-town world of the South has still to share in the glittering modernity of Atlanta or Huntsville. For a century, the South was reduced, in reality and still more in the perception of its inhabitants, to a position of almost colonial dependence on the North and the East Coast, symbolized above all by railway freight rates which discriminated against the South and in favor of the Northeast—a gross injustice not rectified until World War II.[98]

Moreover, the period of Radical Reconstruction under military rule in the South, with its establishment of Black voting rights and advancement of Blacks to political office, was a terrible shock to the White South. The "tragic legend of Reconstruction," focused on Black crimes, corruption and "tyranny," was immensely exaggerated and embroidered in subsequent Southern propaganda (most famously in Thomas Dixon's novel *The Clansman* and the film *Birth of a Nation,* which was based on it). Nonetheless, it had a solid basis: if not in real Black behavior, then certainly in real Southern White fears.[99]

Absolute White dominance was reestablished in the 1870s with the help of a campaign of terrorism by the Ku Klux Klan, directed against supporters of the Republican administrations in the South, both Black and White. Thereafter, a determination to eliminate any possibility of even limited Black political power led to the establishment at a formal level of the "Jim Crow" apartheid laws which were to rule in the region until the 1960s. Informally, these were reinforced by the application to the Blacks of the tradition of public lynching which in the antebellum South had been used more often to control White criminals (slaves being valuable private property and punishable by their owners).[100]

113

Typically for colonized territories, with a feeling of economic exploitation came bitter resentment of cultural patronization and insults, focused chiefly but not exclusively on criticism of the South's racial record and habits. This resentment lingers on, although now rather than regarding race, the resentment is at a general sneering at the South by East Coast and Californian liberals, intellectuals and film-makers. And such sneering has occurred continuously—albeit at varying levels of intensity—since the 1830s, with a new crescendo being reached in the 1960s.

A century earlier, in the run-up to the Civil War, a Northern supporter of Abraham Lincoln had called the South "the poorest, meanest, least productive, and most miserable part of creation, and therefore ought to be continually teased and taunted and reproached and reviled."[101] The great satirist H. L. Mencken derived much pleasure from slashing at Southern barbarity, ignorance and fatuity, with fundamentalist religion coming in for the sharpest strokes. Even when justified, such approaches are unlikely to create good feeling.

During his campaign for the presidency in 1968, George Wallace declared: "Both national parties have been calling us peckerwoods and rednecks for a long time now...and we gonna show them we resent being used as a doormat." He said that these parties represented "the Eastern moneyed interests that have done everything they could to keep the people of our region of the country ground into the dirt for the past hundred years."[102] The public attack on the contemporary Democrats by Senator Zell Miller of Georgia was motivated in part by what he saw as their elitist Yankee sneering at Southern culture:

> Democrat leaders are as nervous as a long-tailed cat around a rocking chair when they travel south or get out in rural America. They have no idea what to say or how to act. I once saw one try to eat a boiled shrimp without peeling it. Another one gagged loudly on the salty taste of country ham....We're like the alcoholic uncle that families try to hide in a room up in the attic: after the primaries are over and the general election nears, national Democrats trot out the South and show us off—at arm's length—as if to say, "Look how tolerant we are; see how caring? Why, we even allow people like this in our party of the big tent. We still love that strange old reprobate uncle." As soon as the election is over, the old boy is banished to the attic and ignored for another two years.[103]

In Troy, acquaintances would complain bitterly that every Southern character in a Hollywood movie was likely to be a variant on half a dozen stock and hostile types: the sadistic police chief, the bestial swamp-dwelling "cracker," the fanatical and/or hypocritical preacher, the corrupt political boss, or—at best—the corny, simple-minded hillbilly and the eccentric aristocratic lady on her decaying Gothic plantation (of course, certain Southern actors have themselves made careers by playing "white trash" parts, and often celebrating their culture and attitudes—notably Robert Mitchum and Burt Reynolds).[104]

More recently, the Coen brothers' film *O Brother Where Art Thou?*—although praised for its Southern music—was criticized by Southerners for exploiting some of that same old set of shallow stereotypes. The unforgiving reader is admittedly at liberty to find a certain poetic justice in White Southerners sharing some of the cultural experience of American Blacks and Indians at the hands of Hollywood.[105]

As has often been pointed out, this collective regional experience of comprehensive defeat and humiliation is unusual in a White American history characterized by continuous national success. In Richard Weaver's phrase, "The South is the [American] region which history has happened to." Equally unique is the sense of guilt for past collective crimes of slavery and racism felt by more liberal Southerners, including those like William Faulkner, whose pride in their regional tradition was fundamental to their identity and culture. The psychological and cultural anxiety which this produced is comparable to the position of westernized, humane and patriotic Russian serf-owning noblemen in the nineteenth century.[106] As in that case, these profound contradictions and ironies contributed enormously to the richness of the Southern literary tradition after the Civil War.[107]

Once the Southern threat to the United States had been eliminated, and for that majority of Americans who were prepared to overlook the White South's record on race, the attitudes of the rest of America to the Old South were by no means as hostile as Southern defensiveness would suggest—the enormous popularity in the North of the prettied-up Plantation romanticism of the *Gone With the Wind* tradition being one example. As part of the reconsolidation of America as a White Herrenvolk democracy, Northerners joined with Southerners in denouncing the period of Radical Reconstruction as a disastrous mistake and the Blacks as unfit for government.[108]

The Confederacy's glorious military struggle against overwhelming odds was quite soon reincorporated into the military legend of the United States as a whole: a process symbolized by joint meetings of Union and Confederate veterans; by mass Southern enlistment to fight in the War of 1898; and, somewhat later, in a tradition of literary, Hollywood and television portrayals of the Civil War which continues to the present.[109]

This was something in which the White South was glad to join. Having itself abandoned the dream of independence, the South responded to Yankee patronization by seeking to outdo the Yankees in American nationalism and especially to outdo the effete and gutless Yankees in a willingness to fight for America. Linked to this bellicose nationalism was a return to pre–Civil War patterns in which Southerners were the most ardent proponents of American imperial expansion.

At the same time, however, other Americans were beginning to celebrate the South almost precisely for the fact that it had been defeated: as a kind of badge of honor and tradition for those who in a range of different ways felt alienated from or defeated by the dominant values of bourgeois America. This tendency might be dubbed Henry Adams on a Harley-Davidson, and has been heavily colored by the romance of the lost cause.

At one end of the spectrum, it has included Yankees and others who reacted against the greed, corruption, vulgarity, materialism and self-satisfaction of the post–Civil War "Gilded Age" and have continued to react against these features of American life to this day. In the process, some have rediscovered the conservative and aristocratic critique of capitalism that was developed as part of the South's intellectual and cultural defenses by writers like George Fitzhugh before the Civil War and perpetuated by Southern intellectuals like Allen Tate in the mid-twentieth century and to some extent by Eugene Genovese and others in our own day.[110]

At the other end of the social and intellectual spectrum, as John Sheldon Reed has noted, for many Southerners and others Confederate symbols came to represent a version of the "Don't Tread on Me" attitude: "Sometime around the middle of the last century [i.e., the twentieth century], the Confederate battle flag took on yet another meaning: Especially in the South, but not only there, it began to send a message of generalized defiance directed at authority, and to some extent at respectability. People who use it in this way may not care for Black folks or Yankees, but those groups are somewhere behind high-school principals on their list of targets....As one girl said, "When I see the Confederate flag I think of a pickup truck with a gun rack and a bumper sticker that says "I Don't Brake For Small Animals.""[111]

The adoption of Confederate symbolism by alienated members of the Northern White working class (including many Irish, Poles and others from outside the old White core ethnicities) reflects three elements in the Confederate tradition. The first is of course White racial supremacy. The others are more attractive. One is the "Good Ole Boy" or Southern redneck tradition described earlier and celebrated, for example, by the popular TV series *The Dukes of Hazzard* (1979–1985). This is a tradition of great innate attraction to hell-raisers everywhere, and dignified by the Confederate "Rebel" label—as in the choice of name for "Rebel Yell" Bourbon whiskey.

"Redneck" culture, often originally rooted in that of the less respectable Scots Irish, is much more attached to country music, fishing and beer than to evangelical religion, or at least church attendance. This is of course not necessarily the same thing, as the records of many country singers who have mixed deeply religious sensibility with utter wildness tend to demonstrate.[112]

Another aspect of Southern culture which has spread to sections of the wider American working classes, and fed strongly into American nationalism, is the picture of stoicism, tenacity and gallantry against overwhelming odds presented by the Confederate soldiers of the Civil War.[113] This is an image of great emotional force for many White Americans who feel defeated by economic and other circumstances beyond their control and excluded from wealth, power, influence and fashion. And, of course, those who feel defeated are also, by instinct, culture and tradition, American nationalists. When they felt let down by their rulers and generals during and after Vietnam, they listened to ballads of betrayed working-class patriotism by Bruce Springsteen or Johnny Cash, not to the protest anthems of

Don McLean or Bob Dylan. Such people therefore require a symbol which is rebellious and yet part of the American national and especially military tradition.

My acquaintances in Troy, although overwhelmingly of Confederate descent and very proud of it, had by the 1970s moved a long way toward this wider identity and sentiment. They still harbored certain old Southern prejudices against Yankees in general, but these had become something of a self-confessed joke, although one which retained a bitter flavor.[114] Their most intense and vivid loathings had become of a more generic "Heartland" kind: of the "East Coast elites" and unpatriotic liberal intellectuals in general; of the "fruit and nut states" of California and (southern) Florida, and the homosexual and hippie lifestyles they were held to represent; and of New York City, for which the hope was frequently expressed that it would be towed out to sea and sunk. Cultural, religious, ethnic, economic, historical and geographical distance meant that only to a very limited extent did they regard the people of New York as fellow countrymen.

Due to the Iranian hostage crisis, the people of Troy were in a more than usually nationalist mood, and "Iranians" had joined the existing gallery of international hate figures. However, in a sign of what were to prove extremely dangerous confusions after 9/11, a commonly used word for "Iranian" was "Arab."

The General Will

The United States possesses strong elements of an antithesis to its publicly accepted national "creed." Indeed, this antithesis appears to fit all three of what Eugen Weber called the "three Rs" of extreme nationalism: "Reaction against the tendencies of the present; Resistance to Change; and Radicalism, which has radical change in mind."[115]

Compared to conservative and nationalist radicalism in most of the rest of the world, however, one very important and widespread element has been absent in the United States: namely, the impulse to authoritarian dictatorship characteristic of the vast majority of radical nationalist and radical conservative movements. The autocracies pursued by different movements at different times have differed greatly, taking the form of traditional royal autocracies, military *caudillismo*, the Fascist Duce principle, or the charismatic leadership of groups of young nationalist radicals, à la Garibaldi (which later in turn fed into Italian fascism). In most countries the impulse to authoritarianism and the leadership principle has seemed inherent to this kind of nationalist tendency. Nor has this been wholly lacking in the United States, if one remembers the number of successful (and unsuccessful) American generals elected to high office or encouraged to aspire to it.[116]

But in the United States, such threats have in the end always been contained by the institutions of American democratic constitutionalism, thanks not only to the institutions themselves, but to the strength and uniformity of the democratic national political culture and ideology sustaining them. Although at their farther fringes the forces of the American antithesis shade over into fascistic manias like that of the terrorist Timothy McVeigh and the various militia movements, the great majority are not opposed to the formal democratic aspects of the American Creed; on the contrary, they take enormous pride in them and regard them as the core of American grandeur.

This national unanimity behind democracy has formed the essential component of what might be called America's self-correcting mechanism, the country's ability to undergo periods of popular hysteria, moral panic and nationalist extremism without allowing them to become a permanent feature of the national scene or to be institutionalized in dictatorship. At least until now. As later chapters discuss, a combination of the national security state created by the Cold War and a war against terrorism with no foreseeable end may create some worrying possibilities in the long term.

For most of American history, however, tendencies toward authoritarianism have taken what might be called a communal form, and have been phrased and even thought of in terms of a defense of the American liberal democratic system—what Seymour Lipset has called episodes of "Creedal passion"—not a revolt against it. In Louis Hartz's words, America's commitment to an absolute form of liberal nationalism "does not mean that America's General Will always lives an easy life. It has its own violent moments—rare, to be sure, but violent enough. These are the familiar American moments of national fright and national hysteria when it suddenly rises to the surface with a vengeance, when civil liberties begin to collapse, and when Fenimore Cooper is actually in danger of going to jail as a result of the Rousseauan tide."[117]

As this passage suggests, certain collective aspects of democratic America have a close affinity with Jean-Jacques Rousseau's prescription for the ideal state and for the role of the General Will in the life of that state: that each individual citizen should, when making up his or her mind on a public issue, ask what decision would be in accordance with the General Will. In Rousseau's conception, this mechanism is based on the shared moral and ideological consensus of society—which in turn is shaped by a universally held civic religion. This consensus "saves the ideal of liberty, while preserving discipline" and also preserves a national capacity to make decisions.[118] As noted by J. L. Talmon, Rousseau's vision possesses implications which do point to a form of collective authoritarianism—or even totalitarianism, although this suggestion is widely viewed as overdrawn.[119]

Rousseau's portrait of the General Will is not only prescriptive, but also to a degree descriptive—of the ethnically, culturally and religiously homogenous world of his native Swiss city-state of Geneva (an insight that would not have pleased Rousseau himself, at least after Geneva burned his books for immorality). The idea of the General Will as formulated by Rousseau can therefore be seen as an attempt to extend the powerful and admirable but also stifling and repressive atmosphere of a culturally homogenous small town to the life of an entire nation. But as it actually existed in Geneva—and in other closed, homogenous communities where homogeneity is maintained not by repression from above but by the community itself—a form of General Will had emerged naturally from the community's history.

For many populist-nationalist Americans, the General Will and "liberal nationalism" have never been just about an absolutist adherence to liberal democratic institutions. They have also involved a conviction that being American means adherence to a national cultural community, one defined by its values and, in the past at least, also by race, ethnicity and religion. And this has been true from the start. Whatever one thinks of his current agendas, when Christian Coalition leader Ralph Reed writes that "the centrality of faith to the maintenance of democratic institutions was once considered axiomatic," he is being completely accurate historically.[120]

This combination explains how many Americans can combine in themselves elements of both the American Thesis and its antithesis: can, as Louis Hartz has argued, be genuinely devoted followers of the American Creed, on a basis laid down by John Locke and developed by the Enlightenment, and yet can combine this devotion with a sense of cultural, religious and national community which is decidedly pre-Enlightenment. After all, if the Enlightenment contributed critically to the American Revolution and the national institutions which it generated, it is equally true that many Americans felt—as their Parliamentarian ancestors in England had done during the Civil War 130 years previously—that they were fighting for ancient English liberties against the innovations of an autocratic monarch. At least some aspects of the American Revolution itself were founded in a "dread of modernity."[121]

And the numerous descendants of this tradition have had a strong sense, fostered originally by many years of racial warfare in North America, that this community is threatened by alien and savage "others." They also have a sense that they constitute in some way the genuine American people, or folk: the backbone of the American nation, possessing a form of what German nationalists called the *gesundes Volksinn* (healthy consciousness of the People), embracing correct national forms of religion, social behavior and patriotism. Over time they have come to accept people first of different ethnicities, then even of different races as members of the American community—but only if they conform to American norms and become "part of the team."[122]

Although this culture is devoted to freedom, it is not devoted to "negative freedom," as Isaiah Berlin classically defined it, but to a kind of positive freedom. In the first place, freedom is restricted to members of the moral, cultural and (formerly) racial and ethnic communities: "Free, *White*, and Twenty-one" was the old saying. The racial qualification has disappeared, but the sense that freedom can be exercised only in certain ways and by certain kinds of people is still very much alive.[123] In the words of Merle Haggard's song "Okie from Muskogee," the adherents of this culture believe not only in "bein' free" but also in "livin' right." One might almost say that they believe in being free *in order* to live right.[124]

Second, and as a consequence, freedom is tightly circumscribed by communal culture. It is a form of "positive freedom," a freedom to—in Immanuel Kant's phrase—"obey the laws you yourself have made." The freedom of aliens, who do not share this culture, or deviants therefore can legitimately be circumscribed by authoritarian and even savage means, as long as the aim is to defend the community and reflects the will of the sound members of the community.[125] A survey of Southern Baptist ministers with premillenarian beliefs in 1987 revealed rather low levels of willingness to allow socialists, civil liberties activists and "secular humanists" even to speak in public, run for public office, or teach in schools.[126]

The description by Walter Russell Mead has deep implications for American nationalism abroad as well as at home:

> Death to the enemies of the community! It is a legacy from colonial times, confirmed by the experience of two centuries of American life, and one of the most deeply ingrained instincts in the Jacksonian world…Jacksonian realism is based on the very sharp distinction in popular feeling between the inside of the folk community and the dark world without. Jacksonian patriotism is an emotion, like love of one's family, not a doctrine. The nation is an extension of the family. Members of the American folk are bound together by history, culture and a common morality. At a very basic level a feeling of kinship exists among Americans. We have one set of rules for dealing with one another; very different rules apply in the outside world.[127]

This is the tradition which produced figures such as John Ashcroft, former governor of Missouri and attorney general in the Bush administration. Ashcroft has been responsible for formulating laws and measures that have greatly increased federal powers of surveillance, interrogation and detention without trial, powers that would seem hostile to the legalism which is a core element of the American Creed and self-image, ideals in which Ashcroft himself professes to believe passionately.

Nor is this belief in the rule of law on the part of figures like Ashcroft hypocritical. It is merely qualified by two very large conditions: that in a crisis, written laws can be suspended for the sake of the defense of the community; and that the law applies only to a limited extent to aliens, especially in cases of those suspected of being enemies and of having behaved in a "barbaric" manner.

The most dramatic and chilling result of this historically derived attitude has been seen since 9/11 in the approach of the Bush administration to the torture of prisoners captured in the course of the war on terrorism and the response of a section of the American public to what happened. In the spring of 2004, hard on the heels of the evidence of gross maltreatment of Iraqi detainees by U.S. interrogators and guards at the prison of Abu Ghraib, came the exposure of secret memos by administration lawyers advocating the torture of prisoners. This episode also encapsulated some of the contrast between the forces of the American Thesis and those of the American Antithesis.[128]

On one hand, probably a majority of Americans, and certainly a majority of the media, seemed not only outraged by what had happened but also genuinely and deeply surprised that U.S. troops could do such things. Mainstream papers and television channels gave extensive coverage to agonized discussions of the brutalizing effects of war on ordinary, decent people. The outrage was of course both understandable and correct. The surprise, however, was somewhat surprising, given the record of the U.S. military in Vietnam. Certainly Abu Ghraib would not have come as a surprise to the Vietnam veterans with whom I spoke in Alabama.[129]

But another very considerable section of Americans were not surprised at all by what had happened and indeed approved it. In an opinion poll commissioned in May 2004 by the *Washington Post* and ABC News, 34 percent of respondents said that torture is acceptable in the case of "people suspected of involvement in recent attacks on U.S. forces in Iraq or Afghanistan," with 64 percent rejecting this. When asked if physical abuse short of torture is acceptable, 45 percent said yes and 53 percent no.[130]

What happened can also clearly have come as no surprise to White House Counsel Alberto Gonzales, who in a memo to the president of January 25, 2002, described articles of the Geneva Convention regarding the treatment of prisoners as "quaint" and advised that they be abandoned (Colin Powell strongly dissented). Later, lawyers in the Justice Department (August 2002) and in the Pentagon (March 2003) advised the administration that a U.S. President in his capacity as commander in chief has the right to override both U.S. and international law and sanction physical abuse of prisoners as part of the war on terrorism.[131]

These memos were intended to be kept secret. There was nothing secret, however, about the reaction of numerous right-wing politicians and media commentators to the Abu Ghraib revelations. Senator James Inhofe (Republican, Oklahoma) declared to his colleagues on the Senate Armed Services Committee: "I'm probably not the only one at this table that is more outraged by the outrage than we are by the treatment....You know, they [the prisoners at Abu Ghraib] are not there for traffic violations...they're murderers, they're terrorists, they're insurgents."[132]

Senator Inhofe attacked the International Committee of the Red Cross (ICRC) as "humanitarian do-gooders right now crawling all over these prisons looking for human rights violations while our troops, our heroes, are fighting and dying." His fellow Republican senator, Trent Lott (Mississippi), declared: "Frankly, to save some Americans' troops lives or a unit that could be in danger, I think that you should get really rough with them." Reminded that at least one prisoner had been beaten to death by U.S. troops at Abu Ghraib, Lott replied: "This is not Sunday school. This is interrogation. This is rough stuff."[133] Similar statements came from right-wing media figures such as Rush Limbaugh, Bill O'Reilly and Michael Savage. Limbaugh declared:"Maybe the people who ordered this [the abuses at Abu Ghraib] are pretty smart. Maybe the people who executed this pulled off a brilliant maneuver...boy, there was a lot of humiliation of people who are trying to kill us—in ways they hold dear. Sounds pretty effective to me if you look at us in the right context."[134]

Right-wing radio star Michael Savage described Arabs as "non-humans" and declared that "conversion to Christianity is the only thing that can probably turn them [Arabs] into human beings." He said: "Smallpox in a blanket, which the U.S. Army gave to the Cherokee Indians on their long march to the West, was nothing to what I'd like to see done to these people."[135] Savage's talk show is broadcast on 350 radio stations and has an audience of some 7.5 million people. Limbaugh's goes out on 680 stations and has an audience of around 20 million.[136]

Senator Inhofe's attack on the ICRC was echoed two days later by the *Wall Street Journal* in an editorial entitled "Red Double Cross," which decried the organization's "increasing politicization" and warned that it was at risk of becoming "just another left-wing advocacy group along the lines of Human Rights Watch or Amnesty International" (the *Journal* has always been glad to cite these bodies as respectable authorities when it comes to attacking countries which its editors hate and wish to target).[137] Of course, these statements did not represent the views of all Republicans. They drew a sharp rebuke from former prisoner of war Senator John McCain, who praised the ICRC's record and stressed America's duty to abjure torture and respect international conventions.[138]

This tradition is clearly antithetical to the formal aspects of the American Creed when it comes to both the administration of justice and the equality of rights—it certainly does not believe either that fundamental rules of justice are to be found in law books or that "all men are created equal." However, in the past it has usually coexisted comfortably enough with the Creed at home, because the eruptions of popular fury and folk justice have been short-lived responses to particular real or perceived threats.

The exceptions were the Frontier, where the threat from the Indians and the tradition of vigilanteeism and collective punishment which it produced, lasted as long as the Frontier itself, and the South, where the constructed threat from the Blacks required collective repression which lasted from the origins of these colonies to the 1960s. The implication of these traditions for the "war on terrorism" will be among the subjects explored in the following chapters.

Four

Antithesis Part II:
Fundamentalists and Great Fears

Did ever men pretend an higher degree of holiness, religion and zeal to God and their country than these? These preach, these fast, these pray, these have nothing more frequent than the sentences of sacred scripture, the name of God and of Christ in their mouths: You shall scarce speak to Cromwell about any thing, but he will lay his hands upon his breast, elevate his eyes, and call God to record, he will weep, howl and repent even while he doth smite you under the first rib.

—*The Hunting of the Foxes* (England, 1649)[1]

A vital though informal part of the American Creed has long been the belief that the United States epitomizes the triumph of modernity in economics, technology and culture as well as in its democratic arrangements. This successful modernity, with the economic opportunities, the material culture and the consumerism it generates, is also at the heart of what has been called the American Dream. And although recently the European Union has presented itself as an alternative model of capitalist modernity, America's defining image is still by and large accepted by most of the world, including among groups such as al Qaeda, which are in violent revolt against just this U.S.-led modernity.[2] This is true above all of consumer culture and mass entertainment. In East Asia, for example, Europe is hardly present as a trend-setter in these fields.

America is also seen as the country which has tended to undergo the fastest economic and cultural change of any country in the developed world, and the one which is the most open to change. Closely connected to this is the fact that the United States is exceptionally open to immigration and consequently has experienced the most radical demographic change of any country in the Western world. It is still generally believed that "there has from the start been a marriage of true minds between the American and the type-man of the modern era, the New World Man."[3]

And all these things are true to a great extent. Yet amid all this change, America is also home to by far the largest and most powerful forces of conservative religion in the developed world. The attitude of these forces to key aspects of modernity as

123

this is usually understood was summed up in the 1960s by the leading Pentecostalist preacher A. A. Allen: "The most treacherous foe in America isn't Communism (as perilous as it may be), Nazism, Fascism or any alien ideology, but MODERNISM" (capitals in the original). Allen's call to arms appeared in a booklet entitled "My Vision of the Destruction of America." The title in itself brings out the contrast between the optimism of the American Creed and the profound pessimism of Protestant fundamentalism as far as progress in this world is concerned.[4]

As Samuel Huntington has observed, "Those countries that are more religious tend to be more nationalist." Looking at the contrast between the United States and the rest of the developed world, Huntington and others have explained early twenty-first-century America's greater nationalism partly in terms of its greater religiosity. This link to nationalism is especially true of American fundamentalist Protestantism, which, as described in Chapter 3, has particular roots in the nationalist culture of the White South.[5]

American conservative religion evangelicalism and fundamentalism have not remained unchanged over the years; indeed, much of their modern history and growth has been produced precisely by *reaction*. Evangelicalism is "a religious persuasion that has repeatedly adapted to the changing tones and rhythms of modernity," especially when it comes to the employment of modern mass media and modern techniques of mass mobilization.[6] Furthermore, across large parts of America, the eighteenth- and nineteenth-century churches played a central part in civilizing—and therefore to a great extent modernizing—what might otherwise have remained quasi-medieval Frontier societies.

By no means all evangelicals are either fundamentalist in religion (although evangelicalism and fundamentalism share most core beliefs) or right-wing nationalist in politics. For example, belief in the literal truth of the whole of the Bible (known as inerrancy) is critical to fundamentalist belief, but many members of the broader evangelical tradition take a more nuanced position. They are also less conservative in politics. Moreover, Blacks make up a very considerable proportion of the evangelical population in the United States and in the American South; for obvious historical reasons they are not often led by their religious beliefs into right-wing political positions.[7]

At the same time, the fundamentalist wing of the evangelical tradition is a very powerful ideological force in large parts of the United States and retains elements of thought which have come down with relatively few changes from much earlier eras. Its origins are pre-Enlightenment, and its mentality to a very great extent anti-Enlightenment. It has also retained a strong element of geographical continuity. While conservative religious belief is strong in Kansas and other parts of the Midwest, and many new adherents to fundamentalist groups are from the heterogeneous ethnic and cultural worlds of newly growing cities in the Southwest and California, the heart of their support remains what it has long been: the White South and its outlying regions.[8]

A religious map of the United States in 2000 still shows an unbroken belt of Southern Baptist majority counties stretching from central Virginia to eastern Texas, and taking in northern Florida and much of Kentucky and Missouri. Many others adhere to other evangelical and/or fundamentalist churches, such as the Pentecostalists.[9] As already explained, this area is not just religious, but also home to some very tough, strongly held and ancient social and cultural traditions, the roots of which predate not just the nation's independence but the first settlements in North America. A particular form of nationalism is one of the most important of these traditions.

The greater religiosity of the United States compared to Europe at the start of the twenty-first century, and the strength of Southern-based fundamentalist churches in particular, is rooted in key differences between North American and European history over the past two hundred years or so. These differences involved not only the explosion of American Protestantism into a multiplicity of churches and sects (which at the same time were very homogenous in their basic beliefs and cultural attitudes), but also the role played by those sects in the development of society on the Frontier and in the backcountry of the Greater South.

The formation of these churches followed the old American tradition of settlers in the wilderness spontaneously creating their own churches. Although church membership was voluntary, it involved taking on serious duties to the church and the community as a whole. And because the church often in effect embraced the entire community, membership was often not truly voluntary. Leaving the church was easy only in the sense that it was relatively easy to leave the local community itself, by moving west.[10] Although the religious culture of these churches was derived from that of the Protestant sects of seventeenth- and eighteenth-century England and Scotland, each also presented itself as sprung directly from the Bible and the word of God, without historical precedent or intermediary.

The growing pluralism of sects in the early and mid-nineteenth-century South was accompanied by a sharp decrease in cultural pluralism and a growing culture of orthodoxy, conservatism and conformism in religion and in social and cultural life more generally. "By 1860, religious liberalism was virtually dead in the South."[11] The greatest beneficiaries of this religious wave were the Baptist churches, which have continued to predominate in the region to this day, followed by the Methodists. Of course, individualism of a kind has been a key part of Southern culture since its beginnings, but it is an individualism of action, not of thought.

In seeking to understand the deep cultural differences between much of the United States and Western Europe, a combination of the American Frontier and the role of the American Protestant churches is of central importance. In both America and Europe, much of the rural population remained largely medieval in its thinking and behavior until the eighteenth and even the nineteenth centuries (the last burning of a witch in France, with the apparent collusion of local officials, took place in 1835). In Europe, first the local upper classes, then the state, often through the upper classes, played a leading role in civilizing the rural populations. The churches played only a subsidiary role and by the later nineteenth century were in full retreat across much of Western Europe.

In the newly settled parts of the United States, neither a truly functioning state nor traditional upper classes existed. In these areas, it was above all the churches which prevented the settlers from lapsing into not only complete barbarism but isolation—very often the church was literally the only social institution in the entire district and the only place where the local population met regularly; and it also was responsible for the local school. Without the Protestant churches, the societies of the American Frontier would have remained much more backward, violent and medieval than has been the case. Thus the churches have played an ambiguous role with regard to the modernization of large parts of the United States: on one hand, they chastened frontier medievalism and laid the basis for a modern social and economic order; on the other, they created a religious culture which has been in many ways at odds with modern culture as understood in the rest of the Western world.

And in the South and West, these were churches which local people had literally made themselves. As a result, these populations retained all the traditional European peasant fear and hatred of the state, without being exposed to the dense web of state influences, institutions and benefits which in Europe later diminished this fear; or at least, not until the twentieth century, by which time some basic features of these American societies had long since been set.[12]

The power of religion in America also played a critical part in preventing the establishment of any strong mass socialist tradition. Thus William Jennings Bryan and the Populists of the 1890s were bitter critics of American capitalism; but Bryan's deeply held fundamentalist Protestantism made even the slightest tinge of ideological Marxism utterly alien to him.[13]

Hector St. Jean de Crevecoeur wrote more than two centuries ago that "the American is a new man who acts on new principles." Richard Hofstadter wrote of America as "the country of those who fled from the past." In the 1960s, the Canadian observer George Grant wrote that "the United States is the only society on earth that has no traditions from before the age of progress," and this was repeated approvingly by Seymour Martin Lipset in 1996.[14] They are all quite wrong as far as this section of Americans is concerned.

Hard-line evangelical Protestants in the United States coined the name "fundamentalists" for themselves in the 1920s because of their desire for a return to what they viewed as the "fundamentals" of Christianity, including a literal, word-for-word belief in the Bible. Their origins were "reactionary" in the strict sense; they were reacting against key aspects of twentieth-century modernity.[15] These religious elements form part of the wider world of American radical conservatism and radical nationalism, of which Hofstadter wrote that "their political reactions express a profound if largely unconscious hatred of our society and its ways....The

126

extreme right suffers not from the policies of this or that administration, but from what America has become in the twentieth century."[16]

There were indeed certain elements of this tendency even in the American revolt against Britain, which has been seen as motivated partly by the hostility of "a provincial people, [who] regarded their style of living as not only good but of God" to cosmopolitan, latitudinarian and modernizing British rule.[17] And from the very first days of the American colonies, the settlers' belief that they were a people chosen by God was accompanied by an Old Testament belief that God was a "God of Warre." The image of the ancient Israelites and their battles with their neighbors was used to justify wars against latter-day "Amelekites," whether Indian or French, and God was held to fight for the Americans in those wars.[18]

This body of belief is therefore one of the "huge political icebergs" of American life, which "move through time with massive stability, changing slowly and surviving in their essential form for many generations."[19] For several decades now, the evangelical and fundamentalist churches have been growing while the "mainline" Protestant churches have declined, a process symbolized in 1967 when membership in the churches of the Southern Baptist Convention overtook the Methodist Church, hitherto the biggest Protestant church in the country.

Many American liberals have been disappointed and also deeply puzzled by the way in which so many American workers, farmers and shopkeepers have been led by conservative cultural affiliation to vote for right-wing Republicans and against the (largely imaginary) "liberal elites" which are hostile to all the values they hold dear. It is said, quite rightly, that the radical capitalism espoused by the Republicans is directly contrary to the real economic interests of those same workers.[20]

To explain this political behavior, one must understand that these voters belong to coherent and immensely strong religious and cultural worlds, which are genuinely under attack as a result of social, cultural and economic changes. The political importance of the religious factor is of course not peculiar to the United States. As long as religious belief and adherence remained of great importance in certain Western European societies, it also had a critical effect on political allegiances in those countries—sometimes, unfortunately, in extremist directions. The tragicomic aspect of the situation of politically conservative American religious believers is that the laissez-faire capitalism which they support is not only undermining their economic world, but through the mass media and entertainment industries is also playing a central role in biting away at their moral universe.

Godly Republicans

Conservative religiosity thus plays a very important part in U.S. politics, and especially in the Republican Party. Its growth has formed part of the "southernization" of that party in recent decades. According to the Christian Coalition, the leading grassroots political organization of the American Christian Right, 29 senators out of 100 and 125 House members out of 435 voted 100 percent of the time in accordance with the Christian Coalition's own principles in 2001 (the last year for which figures are available); in other words, more than a quarter of the members of both houses of the U.S. Congress. Of these, 15 senators and 64 congressmen were from the Greater South, or just over half of the Christian conservative bloc in both cases (more than double the South's percentage of the U.S. population as a whole).[21]

The influence of this segment of the U.S. population on the Bush administration, and its link to American nationalism, was well expressed in a *Newsweek* article of early 2003:

> Every president invokes God and asks his blessing....But it has taken a war, and the prospect of more, to highlight a central fact: this president—this presidency—is the most resolutely "faith-based" in modern times, an enterprise founded, supported and guided by trust in the temporal and spiritual power of God. Money matters, as does military might. But the Bush administration is dedicated to the idea that there is an answer to societal problems here and to terrorism abroad: give everyone, everywhere, the freedom to find God, too....
>
> Bible-believing Christians are Bush's strongest backers, and turning them out next year in even greater numbers is the top priority of the president's political adviser Karl Rove....The base is returning the favor. They are, by far, the strongest supporters of a war—unilateral if need be—to remove Saddam.[22]

With a view to this constituency, but also apparently reflecting his own beliefs, President Bush repeatedly cast the struggle against terrorism and America's place in the world in explicitly religious terms. Not just the terrorists, but a range of other rivals of America were cast as "evil." A religiously inspired messianic spirit colored even those passages where Bush was ostensibly speaking of secular and universal values. Bush himself has been reported as seeing himself as an instrument of divine Providence.[23]

The statement that "if you are not with us you are against us," so endlessly repeated by the president and other officials, was originally Christ's, and has been repeated by American preachers and politicians down through the centuries.[24] This religious element in Bush's thought fed into wider patterns of American moral absolutism and produced statements like Bush's promise to "rid the world of evil" and the insane title of a book on terrorism cowritten by his former speechwriter David Frum, *An End to Evil*.[25]

Addressing Congress, Bush declared that "the course of this war is not known, yet its outcome is certain. Freedom and fear, justice and cruelty, have always been at war, and we know that God is not neutral between them." A form of religious nationalism permeated the whole address. Bush took words from a hymn, "There's Power in the Blood," to refer to the "power, wonder-working power," of "the goodness and idealism and faith of the American people"—words which in the hymn are used of the lamb, Jesus Christ.[26] The identification of the nation with Christ himself (whether suffering or victorious) has a long pedigree in the nationalism of Poland, Serbia and certain other countries, but it is a striking image to find in the mouth of a president of the United States, the supposed embodiment of all that is modern, at the start of the twenty-first century.

The specifically Anglo-American lineage of this mode of thought and its implications for views of the rest of the world were well set out by a Puritan minister during the English Civil War of the mid-seventeenth century: "All people are cursed or blessed according as they do or do not join their strength and give their best assistance to the Lord's people against their enemies."[27]

As the neoconservative intellectual Norman Podhoretz wrote before the Iraq War: "One hears that Bush, who entered the White House without a clear sense of what he wanted to do there, now feels that there was a purpose behind his election all along; as a born-again Christian, it is said, he believes that he was chosen by God to eradicate the evil of terrorism from the world. I think it is a plausible rumor, and I would even guess that in his heart of hearts, Bush identifies more in this respect with Ronald Reagan—the President who rid the world of the 'evil empire'—than with his own father, who never finished the job he started in taking on Saddam Hussein."[28]

An American patriotic artist best known for his popular "paintings of heroic firemen and policemen superimposed over images of Americana and faith" was encouraged by the White House to produce a painting of George Bush at prayer while leaning on a podium. At his side are Lincoln and Washington, each also praying, and each with a hand on Bush's shoulders.[29] Bush himself has written of his "belief in a human plan that supersedes all human plans."[30]

According to Bob Woodward, "The President was casting his vision and that of the country in the grand vision of God's master plan."[31] As a sympathetic Christian writer, Stephen Manfield, notes, Bush is one of the very few American presidents "to have undergone a profound religious transformation as an adult":

> He was already engineering a religious renovation of the executive branch when the country suffered a traumatic terrorist attack that placed religion unashamedly at the center of American political and social life. The secular state seemed to recede for a time. Congressional leaders sang hymns on the Capitol steps and even introduced legislation to adopt "God Bless America" as the official national hymn.
>
> What followed was a freer rein for religion in American society. Bush seemed to embody it. He prayed publicly and spoke of faith, divine destiny, and the nation's religious heritage more than he ever had. Aides found him face down on the floor in prayer in the Oval Office. It became known that he refused to eat sweets while American troops were in Iraq, a partial fast seldom reported of an American president. And he framed America's challenges in nearly biblical language. Saddam is an evildoer. He has to go. There must be a new day in the Middle East. Isaac and Ishmael must shake hands in peace.[32]

At home, this tendency has caused considerable alarm to secularist Americans and contributed to the growing cultural-political rift in American society. Fundamentalist religiosity has become an integral part of the radicalization of the Right in the United States and of the tendency to demonize political opponents as traitors and enemies of God and America.[33]

In the rest of the developed world, it has contributed a new element to fear and distrust of the United States. In the past, these feelings were concentrated mainly on the Left, and were concerned with American capitalism, imperialism and militarism. But although these tendencies were often portrayed as wicked, they were not seen as inherently irrational, as far as the motives and interests of the American elites were concerned.

Moreover, outside the Left, a majority of Europeans looked on these tendencies with relative indifference, since they were entirely characteristic of modern Europe's own previous relations with the rest of the world. Furthermore, many Europeans also saw most of the targets of American policy—communists in the past, Muslim extremists more recently— as enemies. And, of course, the populations of the developed world were becoming more and more dominated by a basically American popular culture.

But this culture was and is *secular* American popular culture. American fundamentalist Protestant missionaries have made considerable inroads among the poor of Latin America, but have gotten nowhere at all in the centers of the developed world and among America's key allies. America as civilizational empire and America's thesis about itself and the world is represented by secular American culture: America as the embodiment of successful modernity. The radical religious element in American nationalism is something new and deeply disquieting to non-Americans.

To the old anti-American prejudices elsewhere in the West, it adds the suspicion that powerful sections of the United States are driven by motives which are both wholly culturally alien to the rest of the developed world and fundamentally irrational. It risks creating a degree of fundamental alienation from America among other Western elites which was never true in the past.

Moral Panics

Although the Southern and Northern churches divided bitterly over slavery (with abolition becoming a great crusade for parts of Northeastern Protestantism), after the Civil War the Southern churches were also closely associated with some of the Northern and so-called mainline Protestant churches of the United States in certain moral crusades. These movements frequently reflected a desire to preserve the cultural dominance of the old "core" Protestant populations in the small towns and countryside over the new Catholic and Jewish populations of the great cities, and hostility to "aliens" in general.

The consequent anxieties often took the form of concern over sexual promiscuity, especially when linked to drugs, drunkenness and venereal disease; and in the South, the anxieties fed into perennial fears concerning Blacks.[34] Since the 1970s, this tradition has been revived in the Christian Right's crusade against abortion. As in the past, abortion is a real moral issue in itself, an issue which has helped perpetuate the alliance between Southern and Heartland Protestant conservatives and Catholic conservatives. It also, however, acts both as a metaphor for wider anxieties and as a rallying cry for a wider political mobilization against a wider set of political and cultural enemies.

As with such past panics, it is also closely associated with fears of national decadence leading to national weakness. This situation is reflected in most directly and traditionally religious terms by the fear that if such wickedness continues, God will either abandon or smite America—a suggestion made directly by Christian Right leader Jerry Falwell after 9/11, an event he attributed to God's punishment of America for its sins, including the sins of abortion and homosexuality. (He was later forced to apologize for this.)

These recurrent cultural "panics" with ethnic and racial overtones have been chronicled by James A. Morone in a recent book, *Hellfire Nation*.[35] Thus starting in 1909, a panic swept Protestant America concerning a supposed huge growth in the number of brothels, with alien "White slavers" roaming the countryside to seduce and even abduct innocent White rural maidens.

Much of the language of this particular panic was anti-Semitic, with anti-Chinese, anti-Catholic ("Secrets of the Convent") and anti-French feeling playing a secondary role: in the words of *McClure's* magazine, "Out of the racial scum of Europe has come for unnumbered years the Jewish *kaftan*, leading the miserable Jewish girl to her doom." Now, with the help of urban "Tammany Hall" Irish and other politicians, they had set their sights on American womanhood. In an effort to target two ethnoreligious enemies with one slur, it was alleged that sometimes these Jewish White slavers dressed as Catholic priests! It was claimed as established fact that 60,000 American girls were lured or kidnapped into brothels every year and that a similar number of prostitutes perished annually—a fantastic exaggeration.

These fears were closely linked to paranoia about the White race committing "race suicide" through decadence, birth control and so on, and being overwhelmed by the yellow and brown tide. The result of this movement was the closure of most of America's red-light districts and the Mann Act of 1910 banning the transport of women across state lines for "immoral purposes," a means of harassment and oppression of Blacks for decades thereafter.[36]

The most powerful of these movements was that for the prohibition of alcohol. The passage of the Volstead Act of 1919 and the Eighteenth Amendment in 1920 (greatly helped by wartime hysteria) was the greatest victory for the old "core" Protestant groups over the Catholic immigrants (Irish saloon keepers and German brewers), the decadent, cocktail-sipping East Coast elites, and the forces of

131

social, cultural and demographic change. Later Prohibition became in practice—or rather lack of practice—their greatest defeat. It has been called "a Kulturkampf [struggle of cultures] between two opposing religious-cultural lifestyles."[37]

Of course, it must be recognized that as in the case of other such movements, such as the current one against drugs, Prohibition targeted a real problem of "inner city" alcoholism, leading in turn to unemployment, child abuse and so on—and it may have had some real success in reducing these abuses.[38] It was also linked not only to anti-immigrant feeling, but to concerns about social modernization, linked to America's emergence (according to the census of 1920) as an urban-majority country.

But such genuine concerns—then as now—have also been mixed up with much darker emotions. Morone quotes the temperance crusader Alphonse Ava Hopkins, in words the anti-European tone of which has echoed down to our own day:

> Our boast has been that we are a Christian people, with Morality at the center of our civilization....Besodden Europe, worse bescourged than by war, famine and pestilence, sends here her drink-makers, her drunkard-makers, and her drunkards, or her more temperate and habitual drinkers, with all their un-American ideas of morality and government; they are absorbed into our national life but they are not assimilated; with no liberty whence they came, they demand unrestricted liberty among us, even to license what we loathe....they dominate our Sabbath, they have set up for us their own moral standards, which are grossly immoral; they govern our great cities...until foreign control or conquest could achieve little more through armies and fleets.[39]

Similar emotions and fears powered the appearance of the second Ku Klux Klan in the 1920s. Unlike its predecessor of the 1870s in the South, this short-lived but widespread movement was based chiefly in the Midwest and was devoted above all to anti-immigrant, anti-Semitic, anti-Catholic and antimodernist sentiment, with Negrophobia present but of lesser importance. It was deeply steeped in evangelical Protestantism and reflected, among other things, the agricultural depression of the decade and the pressure it was putting on the old farming communities from the old "core" populations (plus German Protestant).[40]

The end of open immigration in 1924 reduced the appeal of such movements.[41] This measure in turn owed a great deal to two passages of public hysteria which were strongly fed by nativist and anti-immigrant sentiment: the wave of anti-German feeling which swept the country in 1917–18 after America entered World War I and the "Red Scare" of 1919–20. During the first, the religious preacher Billy Sunday declared: "If you turn hell upside down, you will find 'made in Germany' stamped on the bottom."[42]

These two movements both saw the widespread use of the term "Americanism," or "One hundred percent Americanism," and demands that immigrants either must be rapidly assimilated or deported. Hysteria and even violence against

German Americans was especially strong in Texas. Stanley Coben has written that the Red Scare drew on certain enduring tendencies among many Americans: "Hostility towards certain minority groups, especially radicals and recent immigrants, fanatical patriotism, and a belief that internal enemies seriously threaten national security."[43]

Prohibition itself, of course, was later perceived to fail utterly even in its own terms; not merely to be rejected by so much of the population as to be unenforceable, but to have corrupted the police and judiciary and given a critically important boost to the growth of organized crime. However, as Morone argues, even when such laws as the Volstead or Mann acts failed, they left behind a new layer of federal bureaucracy and above all police—as in more recent times have done the "war against drugs" and now the "war on terrorism." Far from being the work of ultimately irrelevant fringe groups, these movements mobilized millions of people, greatly influenced wider political behavior, and helped transform the American state.

Irish American Nationalism

However, so deep had been the defeat of Prohibition and the humiliation of the controversy over Evolution that for some fifty years after Congress (under pressure from President Roosevelt) repealed Prohibition in 1933, it was assumed that no extensive movement of this kind could ever again take place in America.[44] Thus Daniel Bell wrote in 1979 (just as the new Christian Right was about to make its appearance in response to the cultural, sexual and Black revolutions of the 1960s and the defeat in Vietnam) that while this kind of "backlash" continued, it had been compelled to take a new form, that of nationalism, in the specific form of McCarthyite "Americanism" and anticommunism.[45]

McCarthyism was indeed the classic example of a movement which brought together previously mutually hostile groups of White "middle-class" Americans behind an essentially nationalist program strongly marked by traditions of Protestant cultural paranoia, but in ostensible defense of the American Creed of freedom, democracy and law.[46] It succeeded in uniting ultra-nationalism, "Lockean absolutism" (in Louis Hartz's phrase), psychological hysteria, religious-cultural reaction, bitter class resentment and (to a lesser and more ambiguous and veiled extent) anti-Semitism in one mass of hatred. McCarthyism was in some ways a precursor of the alliance between the White South and culturally conservative Northern and Midwestern White ethnic groups which at the start of the twenty-first century forms a key foundation of the Republican Party, and of which nationalism is a vital element.

McCarthyism thus also symbolizes the way in which certain previously excluded ethnicities have been able to merge with the old "core" groups through militant nationalism. McCarthy was prefigured by the fascistic "radio priest," Father Charles

Coughlin, in the mid-1930s, who similarly mixed anticommunism and antielitism, although in his case—due to the Depression and the legacy of Catholic social thought—he also included explicit attacks on capitalism and was much more overtly anti-Semitic.[47]

McCarthy himself was a Catholic Irish petty bourgeois from a farming background in Wisconsin (with a German American mother). His alliance with Protestant WASP (White Anglo-Saxon Protestant) reaction was created by a mixture of anticommunism and bitter class resentment. Viewed in its own terms, McCarthyism seems like a modern version of the irrational "Great Fears" of peasant Europe (as the "witch hunt" analogy is of course meant to suggest). Viewed as a rather typical petty bourgeois nationalist maneuver to displace existing WASP elites by accusing them of a lack of patriotism, it becomes much more comprehensible, and even rational.[48]

As noted in the last chapter, one aspect of populist nationalism in the United States has always been a very strong element of class antagonism against the East Coast elites. This is a hatred in which old "core" Protestant populations and newer immigrants can join, and has helped the populist-nationalist tradition to become multiethnic. The origins of the strong strain of anti-intellectualism in this American tradition owe much to a fusion of class hostility to the educated elites and religious-cultural fear of their supposed culture of atheism.[49]

McCarthy can also be seen as in some ways the high—or low—point of a certain set of patterns in Irish America which had been developing for well over a century. Of course, his stance also reflected the strong anticommunism of the Catholic Church at the time, in part because of the savage oppression to which it was being subjected by Stalinist rule in Eastern Europe.

Also of great importance, however, was bitter Irish American ethnic and class resentment of the old Northeastern Protestant elites, stirred up by the quasi-racist contempt with which they were treated for so many years by those elites: the term "White nigger," the vicious racist cartoons portraying the Irish as subhuman monkeys, the notices reading "no Irish need apply," the continual, ostentatious social contempt—as well, of course, as wider anti-Catholic sentiments which in 1928 contributed to the humiliating defeat of Al Smith, the first Irish American candidate for president.

One way in which the Irish sought integration in the nineteenth century was by stressing their whiteness, to escape the hated "White nigger" epithet and join the ruling race. This established a pattern of cooperation in racial matters between the Irish and the White South which during the Civil War—and especially in the New York conscription riots of 1863—posed a real threat to Union victory. Always present under the surface, it became of great political importance once again from the 1960s on, when many Irish and other White ethnic working-class groups joined the White South in quitting the Democratic Party partly in protest at supposed Democrat pandering to the Blacks.[50]

Class, however, was always almost as important as race. "From start to finish, McCarthy got his largest response from the New York Irish when he attacked the institutions of the White Anglo-Saxon Protestant Establishment."[51] This rhetorical appeal to the masses against the treacherous elites and intellectuals has been a characteristic of radical nationalist movements since their beginnings.[52] Rarely, however, has it been so explicit as in the United States. As a recent defender of McCarthy, Ann Coulter, has written: "[McCarthy's] appeal was directed to a sturdier set—the mass of ordinary Americans....From McCarthy to Richard Nixon to Ronald Reagan, it is conservatives who appeal to workers. When Republicans ignite the explosive power of the hardhats, liberals had better run for cover.... McCarthy was beloved by workers. He had a gift for appealing to the great common sense of the American people."[53]

This hatred of the intellectual elites was strengthened by the failure of the Irish Catholics as a group to advance beyond a certain socioeconomic level—lower middle class and upper working class—even as a much more recent immigrant group, the Jews, went rocketing past them as the twentieth century progressed. It became strongly associated with a measure of anti-intellectualism, in part because for a long time the Irish of America—in striking contrast to their compatriots at home in Ireland— failed to produce an intellectual class in proportion to their numbers.[54]

McCarthyism also appeared at a point where the Irish Americans as a group had reached the maximum political power they were to achieve in America and had begun to decline politically. John F. Kennedy's presidency and Thomas P. "Tip" O'Neill's Speakership of the House (1977–1987) were both a number of years in the future, but at the local level in New York and the other great Northern cities, the power of the old Irish Democratic machine was already in decline, whittled away by other immigrant groups.[55]

One other factor should be kept in mind, because it fits into wider American patterns of defeat and the embittered nationalism which they help produce: the Irish sense of historical defeat, oppression and dispossession by England. For if the Confederate South's historical experience of defeat is unique among America's geographical sections, this is certainly not true of its ethnic sections: Irish, Poles and other American immigrants all brought with them ethnic memories of defeat much worse than those of the South. Even the southern Italians had been conquered, despised and exploited by northern Italians, while Jews and Armenians had suffered infinitely more horrendously. Indeed, in many cases it was precisely the attacks and oppression they had suffered which brought the immigrants to America's shores.

All these groups have had a certain tendency to compensate for past humiliation and suffering by glorying in American national power—and, of course, in many cases (the Irish included), by seeking to harness that power to the achievement of their own national aims. Many have sought to overcome their exclusion from the centers of national power, wealth and prestige by becoming "200 percent" American nationalists.[56]

The Irish American novelist and essayist Thomas Flanagan has attributed the contradictions in the character and work of director John Ford (John Aloysius Feeney) to "his double sense of himself as both American and Irish....Like Eugene O'Neill, he believed that being Irish carried with it a burden of moods, stances, loyalties, quarrels with the world. Working with the most popular of American cultural forms, he was conscious of a majority culture, from which the Irish, despite their bellicose loyalty to it, stood somewhat apart."[57]

Ford's *Fort Apache* is a fascinating summary of some of these contradictions. The U.S. Army is portrayed as a kind of Irish clan, with a smattering of former Confederate soldiers and WASP officers. Toward the WASP upper classes, symbolized by Colonel Owen Thursday (Henry Fonda) and his daughter, there is a mixture of resentment, contempt, admiration and desire for intermarriage.[58]

As shown in Ford's work, and in accordance with their self-image, cultural tradition and economic status, Irish Americans sought to overcome their exclusion not only through militant nationalism but specifically through being "First in War."[59] They have sought with great success to turn the image of the fighting Irishman from a drunkard in a saloon to that of Colonel "Wild Bill" Donovan leading his regiment into the Argonne in 1918 and the Sullivan brothers dying to a man on the USS *Juneau* off Guadalcanal in 1942. This success was rooted in the fact that it reflected something real about the Irish Americans—as demonstrated by Ford himself, who though well past the age of military service, showed conspicuous courage and determination as a documentary filmmaker for the U.S. Navy in World War II. In Hollywood, the Irish American actor James Cagney played both Irish criminals and Irish soldiers.[60]

In seeking prestige and national integration through bellicose nationalism, the Irish strongly resembled the White South after the Civil War—and according to Grady McWhiney, came from the same ultimate roots anyway.[61] John Ford's admiration for the military record of the Confederacy emerges both from some of his westerns and from his biopic of "history's most decorated Marine," Lieutenant General "Chesty" Puller, whose grandfather was killed fighting for the Confederacy.[62]

For part of the twentieth century, the Irish Americans, like other ethnic groups, had a particular need to assert their military nationalism because it had been made suspect by their stance in the early years of both world wars. In the run-up to both wars, hostility to Britain had led many Irish Americans to take up positions of fierce isolationism, which led to accusations of treachery when America did go to war.

However, during the anticommunist hysteria of the early 1950s, "The Irish derived a strong temporary advantage from the McCarthy period....In the era of security clearances, to be an Irish Catholic became *prima facie* evidence of loyalty. Harvard men were to be checked; Fordham [a Catholic college in New York with a mainly lower-middle-class Irish American intake] men would do the checking."[63]

This image still is exploited by blowhard nationalist Irish American media figures such as Sean Hannity and Bill O'Reilly, with their talk of America being "the greatest best country God ever gave man" (*sic*).[64] Although both are of middle-class origin, in an effort to appeal to their specific audience, both have adopted a proletarian style, and O'Reilly has even allegedly constructed a fake Irish American working-class background for himself.[65]

For a long time the Irish-dominated American Catholic Church itself was thoroughly nationalist, a spirit which only increased in the first years of the Cold War: "Irish, Catholic and American became almost identical in the Irish-American mind."[66] Since the 1960s, however, this nationalistic orientation of the American Catholic Church as a whole has changed.

First Vatican II licensed the development of liberal and reformist tendencies which have survived through subsequent decades of reaction. Then these tendencies were mobilized by opposition to the Vietnam War. But equally important, the Catholic Church is of course a universal church. Its inevitable and instinctive tendency to a certain internationalism and respect for international institutions is seriously at odds with American nationalism. This fact has become apparent since the end of the Cold War, when positions taken by a great hero of anticommunism, Pope John Paul II, on international affairs, such as his strong criticism of Israel and his opposition to the Iraq War of 2003, have seriously angered American nationalists, including Catholics. No such international inhibition has affected the American fundamentalist churches, which are indeed now the most purely national Christian churches outside the Orthodox world.

The Christian Right

From the end of Prohibition to the 1970s, however, these fundamentalist churches were largely absent from direct politics. They were almost in a form of "internal emigration," so completely did the dominant culture appear to have shifted against them. One book of essays on the new religious Right of the 1980s and 1990s is revealingly entitled *No Longer Exiles*, and a 1979 essay on the Jewish tradition in America described demands to define the United States as a Christian nation "local eccentricities." Max Lerner's monumental work of 1957, *American Civilization*, devotes only 14 pages (703–717) out of 950 to a systematic examination of Christianity in America.[67]

This process was encouraged by the waves of mockery which fell on fundamentalists after the so-called Monkey Trial in 1925, when a teacher, John Thomas Scopes, was prosecuted by the state of Tennessee for teaching Darwin's theory of evolution. Although the state won the case, the defense and the media (with H. L. Mencken inspired to some of his most ferocious sallies) made the arguments of the populist and evangelical leader, former Secretary of State William Jennings Bryan, who appeared for the prosecution, appear utterly foolish. Bryan declared that "all the ills from which America suffers can be traced back to the teaching of Evolution. It would be better to destroy every other book ever written, and just save the first three verses of Genesis."[68]

It seemed for decades that such figures would never again be taken seriously in national politics; in other words, that the United States would in fact take much the same path as the rest of the industrialized world.[69] These decades strengthened still further the feeling among Protestant fundamentalists of being a persecuted minority, "strangers here, as in a foreign land," as the hymn has it. This feeling has old roots in the Christian tradition, but also fed into wider sentiments of defeat, alienation and paranoia on the Right in America.[70]

Thus Lyndon Johnson, whose entire political career was passed in the decades between the repeal of Prohibition and the emergence of the new Christian Right, never had to deal with this particular kind of politics at a national level. In their standard textbook on U.S. history, published in 1969, Samuel Eliot Morison and his colleagues entitled the section on Prohibition, the Scopes Trial and the revived Ku Klux Klan "Nineteenth Century America's Last Stand."[71]

This of course has proved a grave mistake. Although "it would be almost a half century before large numbers of evangelicals again discovered an elite diabolic enough to make the building of their own mass movement seem both imperative and possible," the fundamentalist churches were not really undermined in their geographical and cultural heartlands. There, the insults and contempt of the metropolitan elites blended with other resentments to make fundamentalist views if anything even more popular.[72] By the 1990s the fundamentalist counterattack against the teaching of evolution in schools was back with a vengeance.

Although the churches were largely absent from politics and government from the 1930s to the 1970s, they did not withdraw from society. On the contrary, these decades saw the evangelical churches spread both to new media—television—and to new areas of the United States.[73] Even though televangelist Billy Graham himself was in most ways a political moderate, the world he represented also played a great part in McCarthyism.

The American churches, and especially the evangelical and fundamentalist ones, were able not just to retain but in some respects to expand their followings at a time when in the rest of the developed world, religious belief and practice was in steep decline. One reason for this is that the churches have played a significant role in softening some of the harsher aspects of change for many Americans— especially migration from country to cities and consequent social atomization.

Given the speed of socioeconomic change in America, the resulting disruption of existing society, and the lack of welfare and health safety nets comparable to those of other developed countries, this role has been all the more necessary and has helped churches to retain their hold on important sections of society. Across much of America, churches have in a sense therefore continued the formative role they played on the American Frontier, and in doing so, they have helped maintain the cultural worlds which generate American populist nationalism.

Many large American Protestant churches, with their associated web of schools; study groups; parents' groups; children's, adolescents', men's, women's and seniors' clubs; marriage counseling services; excursions; sports activities; and even collective tourism (often to the Holy Land), form dense communities with a strong aspect of social welfare. In fact, they have played a central role in bringing a sense of community to what would otherwise be the flat, arid social plains of many American suburbs—or in the words of humorist Garrison Keillor, "If you want to meet single women in Minnesota, maybe you should join a church."[74]

In this sense, the churches resemble the Catholic Church of the nineteenth century (which played a related role among the new inhabitants of the great cities in Europe and America) much more than the anemic European churches of today.[75] And as with the Catholic Church in the past, this has also given conservative Protestant tendencies a formidable capacity for political mobilization and organization, both in the past and today in the Christian Coalition and associated movements.

The shift of the Southern Baptist Convention to de facto support for the Republican Party from the 1970s has stemmed from a general White Southern move in that direction, but has also reinforced that trend. It has left Democratic Southern Baptists like Bill Clinton and Al Gore in a decidedly minority position within their own church. In most of the South, their faith was of limited help to them among Whites in either 1992 or 1996, and Gore's failure to carry the region in 2000 helped doom his bid for the presidency.[76]

Also of great importance has been the replacement of urbanization with suburbanization. Urbanization around the world has generally marked a radical shift in environment and values from culturally homogenous small towns and rural areas to heterogenous, ethnically, culturally and even racially mixed cities. A transformation in values, including most often a decline in religious faith, has been the general long-term result; stemming of course from the disintegration of small, relatively isolated communities.

Suburbanization is a rather different matter. It allows—and, in its American form, is explicitly or implicitly *intended* to allow—the preservation of a small-town world as far as family life and culture are concerned: racially homogenous and also potentially at least culturally homogenous, traditional, church-going and patriotic. The spread of (softened and modernized) forms of Southern culture, including country music, to much of the rest of the United States can be traced in part to the move of "middle-class" Whites away from urbanism and toward suburbanism.[77] If therefore American nationalism in 2004 sometimes resembles European nationalisms before 1914, the reason is because in some American regions, aspects of society and culture are closer to those of Europe of 1914 than to those of the Europe of 2004.[78]

In the preservation of this re-created small-town atmosphere, the evangelical Protestant churches have played a very important role, which has helped not only to preserve them in their traditional heartlands, but to expand them to much of the rest of the United States.[79] Indeed, the strong recovery of religious belief and practice in the United States after World War II was contemporaneous with the astonishing growth of suburbia, and probably closely associated with it.[80]

The figures both for religious belief in the United States and for the strength within this sector of the "fundamentalist" element are somewhat disputed. A 1993 Gallup Poll showed 42 percent of Americans describing themselves as "born again." This figure, however, includes both many members of the so-called mainline churches for whom this is more a formal statement of theological belief than a deeply felt personal statement, and Black evangelicals, who with rare exceptions are not led by this belief to vote Republican. A 1996 study by George Barna found 66 percent of Americans saying that they had made a "personal commitment to Jesus Christ," up from 60 percent in the 1980s. About one-third of the public attends church (or other places of worship) once a week and another third at least once a month. The remaining third never attends.[81]

According to an authoritative survey conducted in 2000 by the University of Michigan, White evangelical Protestants (including churches defining themselves as fundamentalist) made up 23.1 percent of the U.S. population in that year. This made evangelical Protestants the second largest Christian group, after Catholics with 27.3 percent. Although they have spread all over the United States, by far the greatest concentration of evangelicals remains in the Bible Belt of the Greater South and its outlying regions.

Mainline Protestants (Episcopalians, Methodists, Lutherans, etc.) came third, with 21.2 percent of the U.S. population. Between 1971 and 1990 evangelical churches gained more than 6 million new members; the mainline ones lost some 2.6 million.[82] Black Protestants accounted for 7.6 percent of the population; "other religions," 4.5 percent; Jews, 2 percent. In a striking divergence from Europe, only 14.4 percent of respondents described themselves as "secular."[83] As the term "Bible Belt" suggests, these figures include very noticeable regional variations. In 1986, according to Gallup, 48 percent of Southerners (more than twice the national average) described themselves as "born again" Christians, compared to 31 percent of Midwesterners and only 19 percent of Northeasterners (the wicked, atheist "East Coast" again).

Determining how many of these people possess truly "fundamentalist" beliefs or support the agenda of the Christian Right in politics (closely associated in turn with populist nationalist attitudes) is a difficult question.[84] A Pew poll of March 2004 indicated that 40 percent of Americans believed in the literal, word-for-word truth of the Bible, with another 42 percent declaring that it is the word of God, but not necessarily true.[85] Of course, most of these people do not attempt to match behavior to beliefs, but nonetheless this world of belief does give the more determined minority a wide ocean of public acceptance in which to swim, something that does not exist elsewhere in the developed world. According to Gallup, 18 percent of Americans polled in 1993 believed that floods that year were a punishment by God for the sins of the people living on the Mississippi River.[86]

In Britain, Prime Minister Tony Blair's far more moderate and "mainline" Protestant views have been toned down by his advisers for fear of public mockery and

140

alienation. Advisers would never recommend this in the United States. By 1976 the overtly born-again religious identity of presidential candidate Jimmy Carter of Georgia was already sufficiently appealing to the electorate that President Gerald Ford felt impelled also to declare himself "born again"—even though he was an Episcopalian![87]

With the exception of George H. W. Bush (Bush Sr.), all subsequent U.S. presidents have also declared themselves born again—and in the case of Reagan and George W. Bush (Bush Jr.), it would seem, quite sincerely. In a poll conducted in 1998, 56 percent of Americans declared that they would not vote for an atheist as president (admittedly a big change from 1958, when 82 percent said this).[88] Playing on this sentiment, Bush Sr., like all Republican candidates over the past generation, declared in 1992 that "I believe with all my heart that one cannot be President without a belief in God." In 1996 more than one-fifth of registered members of the Republican Party described themselves as belonging to the Christian Right.[89] In the 2004 Democratic primary campaign, several candidates declared, most improbably, that they had discovered religion while campaigning.[90]

It has been suggested that between one-third and one-half of the White evangelicals (including the fundamentalists), or between about 7 percent and 12 percent of the whole population of America, support the Christian Right or at least share its ideology. However, the strength of the fundamentalists, like the strength of some ethnic minorities, lies not so much in numbers but in relatively greater social and political commitment: high rates of voter turnout, willingness to agitate over particular issues, readiness to make personal sacrifices of time and money, and concentration in politically strategic regions.

As Christian Coalition leader Ralph Reed has noted, over time concern over education and other local issues made Christian conservative activists into a formidable force in local politics (on school boards and the like), laying the basis for their later success in national politics: "The advantage we have is that liberals and feminists don't generally go to church. They don't gather in one place three days before the election."[91] Conservative Christian colleges have also proved a useful source of Republican campaign workers.[92]

The power of the fundamentalists, like that of other highly motivated minority groups, has been greatly increased by the generally very low voter turnout in U.S. elections. Thus in the congressional elections of November 2002, the Republicans made extensive gains in the Senate and House of Representatives with the votes of only some 15 percent of all registered voters. Of a figure this small, the fundamentalists obviously can form a very large and powerful proportion.

The Christian Right of the 1970s arose above all as a reaction to the legalization of abortion. Abortion was a matter of deep concern to Christians, and one which united evangelical Protestants and Catholic conservatives, such as William Bennett. However, as in earlier periods, the fury over abortion also formed part of a much wider sentiment of fear and resentment which motivated both the Christian Right and the wider new Right of which it was part.[93]

The 1960s and 1970s saw defeats for the culture of the White South and the Heartland which, put together, were greater than anything experienced since the Civil War. The term "Negro socio-economic revolution," used by some authors to describe aspects of the 1960s, is overdrawn, but certainly reflects the way many Whites felt then and even to a degree feel today.[94] Civil rights for Blacks, coupled with inner-city rioting and pressure for concessions in education and housing, terrified and infuriated large sections of the White middle classes. Out of this terror arose a new alliance between the White South and the Midwest along lines similar to the original Jacksonian alliance which for more than a century formed the foundation of the Democratic Party. The active celebration of supposed "Black" values and the denigration of "White" ones by the more fashionably radical sections of the intelligentsia hit the very rawest nerves of unfashionable, poor, small-town Whites.[95]

The sexual revolution, of which legalized abortion was part, struck at the very foundations of the conservative idea of the family. The sexualization of adolescence (which sits so oddly alongside savage laws against teenage sex in a number of states) became central to the marketing strategies of vast sectors of American capitalism. Some fundamentalists viewed the appearance of open homosexuality as a sign of the impending end of the world. The reaction of conservative society against public homosexual identification became more, not less, intense in the 1990s as homosexual and lesbian characters began to appear in positive roles on mainstream TV and even have whole shows, such as *Will and Grace*, devoted to them and their society. This potentially brought gay influence into every American family with a television.[96] In 2003–04, a push to legalize gay marriage provided a new stimulus to Christian Rightist mobilization in support of the Republicans.

To conservative Christian America, the "counterculture" in general appeared as an unspeakably hateful, diabolical attack on its idea of society. Limited but vocal sections of American youths revolted against military service and patriotic values; and for the first time in its history, America was defeated in a major war.[97] The Catholics had been hated in the past, but at least their ideas of family, sexual morality and manly behavior were not really different from those of the hard-line evangelicals. To a traditional mind, the American culture which developed after the 1960s by contrast seemed like something out of Hieronymus Bosch, literally a pandemonium of scarcely credible monsters and abominations; and much of television constitutes nothing less than a daily assault on their world of faith and culture. Finally, beginning with the oil shock of 1973, the 1970s saw the end of the long postwar boom and the beginning of three decades of unprecedented long-term stagnation in real incomes for the American middle classes. The old White working class of the Midwest had gotten used to a world in which respectability and steady work guaranteed a steadily rising income and social status. The end of this world has been a dreadful blow to their "moral economy."[98] These defeats provide much of the explanation for the embittered, mean-spirited, defensive and aggressive edge to the contemporary American right wing and to the American nationalism it espouses. Even when apparently in power, these people still feel defeated. They have essentially spent many years trying to wipe out the defeats of the 1960s and early 1970s.

A hope exists—strongly reflected in the Republicans' 1994 election manifesto, the "Contract with America"—that given sufficient will, America can somehow be turned back to the perceived golden age of Eisenhower in the 1950s.[99] Since it cannot be admitted that American capitalist development itself is largely responsible for hated social and cultural change, the failure of this restorationist social and cultural program must necessarily be explained by the "Devil Theory of politics." In this theory, wicked forces at home and abroad—notably the "liberal elites," especially in the media, their supposed allies in Europe and the national enemies they supposedly pamper elsewhere in the world—are the "devils" responsible. And bizarre though it may seem in view of the power of conservative groups, if the standard for a healthy conservative society is the America of the 1950s, then of course the conservatives have been defeated and always will be.

The context of the Vietnam War made the cultural changes of the 1960s and 1970s all the worse as far as many conservative Americans were concerned. The perceived association with military defeat was fatal to the chances of a successful progressive liberalism in appealing to wider sections of the American mainstream. The Christian Right, like the Right in general, was deeply committed to anticommunism, opposing START II agreements with the Soviet Union on limiting nuclear forces, demanding higher military spending and a tough antiradical strategy in Central America, supporting Ronald Reagan's "Evil Empire" rhetoric and also supporting Taiwan against "Red China."[100] And this "anticommunism" formed part of a wider complex of hard-line nationalist attitudes; politicians associated with the Christian Right, like my friends in Troy, also bitterly opposed the abandonment of American rule over the Panama Canal Zone and demanded the toughest possible policies against Iran after the revolution there.[101]

One of Jerry Falwell's most publicized campaigns was entitled "I Love America." The meetings, propaganda and rhetoric of the Christian Right have always been suffused with nationalism and national symbolism. This tendency helps strengthen nationalist hatred of Europe in particular. One evangelical pastor with an apocalyptic bent and considerable influence on the Right, retired colonel Robert Thieme of Houston, became famous for wearing his old military uniform in the pulpit.[102] According to conservative commentator Robert D. Novak, "These Bush backers see the President under worldwide attack as a Christian, particularly in a Europe where atheism is on the rise and religion in decline."[103]

The radical nationalism of the religious Right naturally emerged particularly strongly after 9/11 and fused with religious hostility to Islam as a religion. Bush himself was bitterly criticized by sections of the religious Right for his speech of September 17, 2001, at the Islamic Center in Washington praising Islam as a "religion of peace."[104] Franklin Graham, son of Billy Graham, called Islam "very evil and wicked, violent and not of the same God." Jerry Falwell described Mohammed as a terrorist—remarks from which Bush officially distanced himself and the administration.[105] The influential millenarian Hal Lindsey (author of the best-selling book in American history after the Bible) produced a strikingly hate-filled work which combined Christian and radical Israeli sources to vilify Islam in general.[106] The effect of such rhetoric on the outside world has been severe.[107]

In their identification of religion with the nation, the fundamentalist wings of the American evangelical churches are unique in Western Christendom (except for Northern Ireland, from which much of their tradition is ultimately derived). As mentioned, the Catholic Church as noted is universal by nature. The national Protestant churches of Western Europe have since 1945 been strongly committed to internationalism. Even in England, it is several decades since the Anglican Church was last described as "the Conservative Party at prayer"; in Texas, however, according to Texan novelist and essayist Larry McMurtry, "a flavorless Protestantism seems to have yielded super-patriotism as a by-product."[108]

The American mainline Protestant churches, like their European equivalents, with which they are linked in the World Council of Churches and other international organizations, have come to adopt generally liberal and internationalist positions. To find a Western parallel for the instinctive nationalism of some of the evangelicals, one would once again have to go back to Europe before 1939, or even before 1914. In eastern Christendom, the Orthodox churches are often very closely identified with their respective nationalisms and often with chauvinist positions; but quite unlike in America, these churches have historically been state churches.

Millenarians and Nationalists

Of the American evangelicals, significant numbers also hold millenarian beliefs, beliefs with frightening implications for their holders' attitudes to the world outside the United States. In 1977 the number of American premillennialists alone was conservatively estimated at 8 million. A Pew poll of May 2004 had 36 precent of respondents declaring that the book of Revelations is no metaphor but "true prophesy." Premillennialists believe in Christ's bodily return *before* his thousand-year earthly reign; postmillennialists (a majority of the mainline Protestant churches), on the other hand, believe in his return only after the Millennium has already been established by the power of God working through his people. This is a distinction with crucial implications for attitudes to politics, history and the possibility and desirability of Christians seeking to bring about positive social change in this life.[109] The great majority of the leaders of the Christian Right have been premillennialists, and often from a more extreme variant of this belief known as dispensationalism. In 1987, 63 percent of Southern Baptist pastors declared themselves to be premillennarian.[110]

144

A very much larger number of Americans have some belief in "prophecy": that the Bible—and especially the Book of Daniel and the Revelations of St. John—provides accurate predictions of future events.[111] The widespread nature of this belief is indicated by the popularity of millenarian religious fiction, such as Hal Lindsey's *Late Great Planet Earth* (35 million copies sold by 2004) or, more recently, the Rapture series by Tim LaHaye and Jerry B. Jenkins. To date, this series has sold more than 62 million copies, putting the Harry Potter series to shame and making it by a long stretch the most successful series in the history of American print fiction. LaHaye was a cofounder (with Jerry Falwell) of the Moral Majority, the pioneering Christian Rightist group which laid the foundations for the later and much more successful Christian Coalition.[112]

These readership figures demonstrate once again a profound distance between a considerable part of the American population and modernity as the rest of the world understands it, as well as the rationalist and universalist principles of the American Creed. Not only is this tradition deeply and explicitly hostile to the Enlightenment and to any rational basis for human discourse or American national unity, it cultivates a form of insane paranoia toward much of the outside world in general. Thus *The End of the Age*, a novel by the Christian Rightist preacher and politician Pat Robertson, features a conspiracy between a Hillary Clintonesque first lady and a Muslim billionaire to make Antichrist president of the United States. Antichrist, who has a French surname, was possessed by Satan, in the form of the Hindu god Shiva, while serving with the Peace Corps in India.[113]

These books are also utterly, shockingly ruthless in their treatment of the unsaved—in other words, the vast mass of humanity. In accordance with one strand in prophetic belief, the Rapture series begins with God's elect being taken up to heaven in an instant, and dwells lovingly on the immense casualty rates that results as pilotless planes and driverless cars crash all over the world—with most of the victims presumably going to hell.[114]

The moral tone of such attitudes has real consequences for how these believers think about the world today. Thus I remember the words of my born-again landlady during a stay in Washington in 1996–97. When challenged that the Bible cannot be literally God's word, for in this case sections of the Books of Exodus and Joshua in particular would make God guilty of ordering genocide, she replied, in honey-sweet tones, "But don't you see, if those people had been wiped out 3,000 years ago as God ordered, we wouldn't have all these problems in the Middle East today." Some millenarian language achieves a kind of pornography of hatred in its description of the fate of the damned, especially those from nations hostile to the United States.[115]

As these words suggest, one of the most important effects of millenarian thinking in the religious conservative camp in recent years has been to help cement the alliance of this camp with hard-liners in Israel—a subject explored in Chapter 6. This alliance has become one of the most important practical connections between the religious conservatives in America and aspects of contemporary American nationalism. In the context of American nationalism, of particular interest is

"Dominion" or "Reconstruction" theology—a relatively minor current in itself, but one which has been of great influence in the thinking of leading figures in the Christian Right like Pat Robertson.

This theology is based on Genesis 1:26–29, in which God gives to Adam and Eve dominion over earth and all its plants and creatures. These words have been taken by Christians of the "Dominion" persuasion as giving Christians dominion over Earth and has been used as an antienvironmentalist argument, since God has also given Christians the right of unlimited exploitation of Earth's resources. Because America is in the general evangelical view the world's leading Christian nation, the implications for American power are also clear: "Our goal is world domination under Christ's lordship, a 'world takeover' if you will....We are the shapers of world history."[116]

These beliefs play their part in fueling the tendency of the American Right to implacable nationalist moral absolutism, with a succession of foreign leaders, from Hitler to Saddam Hussein, identified as Antichrist or Antichrist's servant. (Earlier, of course, the Vatican often had played this role.) Because Satan is supposed to be deceitful and alluring, these leaders do not even have to be actively hostile. In these circles, Soviet leader Mikhail Gorbachev was widely identified with Antichrist precisely because of his popularity in the West. Both millenarian belief itself and the tendency of its American exponents to link it to hard-line U.S. foreign and security policies were given a tremendous boost by the Cold War and the much wider image of the Soviet Union as an "empire of evil."

Because Antichrist is supposed to extend his dominion over the whole earth, these millenarian beliefs fuse with nationalist ones in absolute, untrammeled American national sovereignty to produce the widespread and pathological hatred of the United Nations on the American Right, and the dark fantasies associated with these views—which are extraordinarily widespread in American society, and by no means just in the Bible Belt.[117] The European Union too can be made to play this apocalyptic role, for example in the pages of the millenarian journal *The Philadelphia Trumpet*, which sees the EU as a new "Holy Roman Empire" under German rule.[118] The Trilateral Commission and the Council on Foreign Relations have also frequently been portrayed as agencies of Antichrist for world unification and domination. Antichrist himself of course is rarely an American, although his deluded minions may be; and President Kennedy was cast in the role of Antichrist by some millenarians in the South.

Millenarian beliefs also indirectly influence a wider American "ecology of fear," to use the phrase coined by Mike Davis for Los Angeles, and therefore a wider culture of national paranoia and aggression.[119] As Paul Boyer points out in his magisterial book on this subject, the strength of millenarian feelings among a minority of Americans means that they have also had an effect on wider culture, feeding into Hollywood films such as the Omen series, science fiction novels and pop music.[120]

Often these fantasies have a racial edge. Thus in 1999 Jerry Falwell warned his followers to prepare for possible chaos as a result of computer meltdown (consequent on the so-called Y2K or Millennium Bug problem) by stocking up on essential supplies. These he said should include arms and ammunition, to protect the well provided (the Careful Virgins, if you will) against the hungry and improvident others—and we can be pretty sure what colors he imagined those others were going to be. Drawing once again on "Heartland" anti-immigrant and antiurban sentiments, much of apocalyptic literature is set amid urban collapse and upheaval. Hal Lindsey was possessed by pathological fear of the "Yellow Peril"—a fear which he has now transferred to Islam.[121]

Finally, in the context of American traditions of defeat and their link to paranoia and aggression, we must note the strong element of class resentment in the whole millenarian tradition. This resentment was superbly analyzed by Norman Cohn in his famous book *The Pursuit of the Millennium*, in which he saw the millenarian cults of medieval and early modern Europe, with their dreams of an egalitarian kingdom of God and the obliteration of the unrighteous rulers and masters, as acting in some ways as precursors of communism (and in some cases of modern anti-Semitism).[122]

While they were analyzing 500-year-old cults, Cohn and others failed to notice that millenarian groups embodying the same tradition were still alive in the America of their own day. In the United States, there is a very strong correlation between such beliefs and poverty, residence in the countryside and small towns and above all lack of education.[123] This mixture of course fed into wider Southern and Heartland resentments of the East Coast elites and lower-class resentments of the elites in general, especially those widely identified as of "alien" origin, such as bankers. Indeed, some historians have seen U.S. fundamentalism as a whole as a form of "opium of the people," a process which diverts socioeconomic resentments into a form which is hostile to the culture of the elites but does not threaten their actual power.[124]

Again and again in millenarian fiction, wealthy, educated and prestigious figures perish and go to hell because of their wicked lifestyles, while simple, ordinary, God-fearing believers are saved. Millenarian writers equally regularly excoriate American hedonism and consumer culture. As throughout history, American millenarianism is to a great extent a religion of the disinherited, a form of spiritual socialism for people who are not able for whatever reason to be socialist.[125] According to Billy Graham, "Let me tell you something: when God gets ready to shake America, he may not take the PhD and the DD. God may choose a country boy. God may choose a shoe salesman like He did D. L. Moody [a popular fundamentalist preacher earlier in the century].... God may choose the man that nobody knows, a little nobody to shake America for Jesus Christ in this day...."[126]

Evangelical and especially millenarian preachers speak of the future kingdom of Christ on earth in terms strongly reminiscent of those of Karl Marx. The kingdom will be essentially a greatly improved America, stripped of poverty, sinfulness and alien values: "much like the present life…but missing all the imperfections that have destroyed the full and true meaning of life." Christ's reign will bring "labor, adventure, excitement, employment and engagement." There is a very strong stress on the equality—including economic equality—of all believers in this future kingdom, in which all men will be kings.[127]

It would be quite wrong though to portray this segment of belief in America as purely the province of the poor and marginalized. On the contrary, as Boyer, Grace Halsell and other students of the subject have emphasized, it has considerable influence both among the regional elites of the South and West and among the Republican national elites. The Pentecostalist faith, closely linked to millenarian belief, includes in its number John Ashcroft and a row of senior military officers. Pat Robertson, cofounder of the Christian Coalition, who has spoken of liberal America doing to evangelical Christians "what Nazi Germany did to the Jews," is the son of a U.S. senator, from a patrician Virginia family.[128]

The link between millenarianism and radical nationalism was exemplified by Lieutenant General William G. "Jerry" Boykin, a Pentecostalist believer appointed in 2003 as deputy under-secretary of defense for intelligence. A minor scandal developed in that year when the content of some talks Boykin had given to U.S. evangelical church groups made their way into the national media. (President Bush eventually condemned General Boykin's statements, but did not dismiss him from his post—one which, it may be noted, later involved a measure of responsibility for the intelligence-gathering strategy which contributed to the abuses of Abu Ghraib and elsewhere.)

Among other things, General Boykin declared that America is a "Christian nation" and that George Bush had been elevated to the presidency by a miracle—an idea with which many Democrats would agree, but not quite as Boykin meant it. Of judgments by the U.S. Supreme Court of which he disapproved, Boykin said, "Don't you worry about what these courts say. Our God reigns supreme." He informed his listeners that in examining photographs of Mogadishu, where he served as a special forces officer, he found an unexplained black mark, which he explained as a manifestation of evil; and that on 9/11 terrorists actually took over two more planes, but they were "thwarted by the hand of God." [129]

America's enemy in the war against terrorism, he said, is Satan, and Satan will be defeated only "if we come against him in the name of Jesus." Most famously, Boykin said, of a Somali warlord, "I knew that my God was bigger than his. I knew that my God was a real God and his was an idol." This last was widely described as "crude machismo," which it may have been, but it was also a straight biblical reference, to the victorious contests of Hebrew Prophets with the priests of Baal.[130] Similar statements concerning Islam have emanated from several leaders of the Christian Right like Franklin Graham (son of Billy), Jerry Falwell and the Reverend Ted Haggard, president of the National Association of Evangelicals. [131]

Concerning the United States itself, leading officials of the Bush administration made no secret of their belief that the American state rests on essentially religious foundations, that "the source of freedom and human dignity is the Creator," in Ashcroft's words.[132] Even Vice President Dick Cheney sent a Christmas card in 2003 with a message asking, in the words of Benjamin Franklin, "And if a sparrow cannot fall to the ground without His notice, is it probable that an empire can rise without His aid?"[133]

Boykin's remarks indicate two salient features of this sector of American society, as discussed above. The first is their intense nationalism. As for the English and Scottish Puritans of the seventeenth century, from whom they derive their religious culture—as indeed for the Israelites of the Old Testament—their God is essentially a tribal God, a Cromwellian "God of Warre" who fights for them against Amelekites, Irish papists, Red Indians, Mexicans, Spaniards, Germans, Japanese, Communists, Russians, Chinese, Vietnamese, Muslims and any other enemy who comes along.

The second is that their religion-based culture is to a very great extent premodern and definitely pre-Enlightenment. A comparison of Boykin with his equivalents in other contemporary Western armed forces is instructive. A great many French, British and Russian officers would feel more comfortable in the nineteenth century and some surviving aristocratic elements in the eighteenth. British officers in particular sometimes have an affection for horses which trembles on the brink of impropriety. However, the golden ages which they yearn for are still post-Enlightenment. Unlike General Boykin, they would not feel at home in Cromwell's New Model Army. The extent of this ideologically premodern sector in the United States is greater than almost anywhere else in the developed world—except for Northern Ireland. This kind of religious nationalism is fueled both by religious moralism and by a paranoia fed in turn by a feeling of cultural embattlement. In the words of Richard Hofstadter: "Since what is at stake is always a conflict between good and evil, the quality needed is not a willingness to compromise but the will to fight things out to the finish. Nothing but total victory will do. Since the enemy is thought of as being totally evil and utterly unappeasable, he must be totally eliminated....This demand for unqualified victories leads to the formulation of hopelessly demanding and unrealistic goals, and since these goals are not even remotely attainable, failure constantly heightens the paranoid's frustration."[134]

The implications of this belief system for the war on terrorism are among the subjects explored in the next two chapters.

Five

The Legacy of the Cold War

*Where the hell is Cambodia? People see a headline, and suddenly we're in trouble
in Cambodia. It's got to be somebody's fault, so we start attacking somebody. The
news is too fast and too confusing. We see a headline, and we go over to the atlas to
find out where Cambodia is. Then we attack somebody about it. We do more damn
talking about things we don't know anything about than anybody in history.*

—Sam Bloom, Texas businessman, 1960s[1]

The Cold War perpetuated and strengthened the long-standing messianic, paranoid and Manichean strands in American nationalism. It also added a new
element, largely unknown in the United States before World War II, but very important in the history of nationalism elsewhere: a massive military-industrial and
security complex with great influence and a stake in promoting armed rivalry
with other states.

Since the Vietnam War, the impact of this new force in American affairs has
been seen above all in what I have described as the American Nationalist Party, or
Republicans. However, it has had a strong presence among the Democrats as well.
Before the Vietnam War, the Democrats were adept at using "scares" concerning
alleged Soviet military superiority against the two Eisenhower administrations.

In the 1990s, although Clinton reduced the military budget somewhat, he also
presided over both a still greater extension of U.S. military presence in the world
and a geopolitical campaign to "roll back" the influence of Russia within the former
Soviet Union. Concerning the war on terrorism, as of mid-2004 it is not clear that
the Democrats have any serious alternative strategy. If this lack of strategy proves
to be the case, one reason is that they draw their advisers and philosophy from the
same foreign policy and security "ecology" which was nurtured by the Cold War.

This legacy of the Cold War has had a very damaging effect on U.S. strategy
after 9/11 by helping to direct U.S. attention away from the terrorist groups themselves. In the words of the collective biographer of the Bush II foreign and security
policy team James Mann: "The Vulcans [the name Bush's senior foreign and defense policy team gave themselves] were fully prepared to deal with security threats
of the sorts they had confronted in the past—major powers, rogue states, dicta-

tors and land armies, all entities that operated inside fixed territories and identifiable borders—but they were not as ready to combat a stateless, amorphous terrorist organization like Al Qaeda."[2]

Moreover, even in confronting threats from states, their approach was based on a simplistic right-wing Cold War paradigm of building up ever stronger American military forces. "The Vulcans were far less active in developing new institutions, diplomacy or other approaches that could deal with these issues."[3]

The Cold War essentially created all the leading members of the Bush II administration's foreign and security staff. Many had already been senior officials in Republican administrations of the 1970s.[4] As the official White House photographer of the Ford administration remarked concerning the Bush administration which took office in 2001, "I feel like Rip Van Winkle. It's like I woke up twenty-five years later, and not only are my friends still in power, they're more powerful than ever."[5]

The Cold War also produced the neoconservative academic and bureaucratic grouping, whose members between 2001 and 2003 critically influenced the administration of George W. Bush and acted as some of its leading officials and propagandists.[6] The neoconservatives originated in the "Vital Center" group set up by Reinhold Niebuhr and others in the late 1940s to rally American liberals against the threat of Stalinist communism. The Vital Center split over the Vietnam War, with the future neoconservatives generally supporting the war and tough anti-Soviet policies. Via support for the hawkish Democrat senator Henry "Scoop" Jackson, most ultimately moved to the Republican Party (although some remain formally Democrats to this day).[7]

Also of central importance to the development of the neoconservatives was their reaction against the left-wing counterculture of the 1960s, and especially its romantic, pacifist, anti-intellectual and hooligan elements, and against the increasing tendency of the Left to condemn Israel. However, just as many of the original neoconservatives, such as Irving Kristol, had been Trotskyite Marxists, so some of the second generation were former 1960s radicals, such as Stephen Schwartz (of the Foundation for the Protection of Democracy) who later moved to the radical Right. In both generations, these people brought with them from the Left a radical style, a taste for vicarious violence and a certain sense of politics as theater. In this, they closely resembled an old pattern in Europe of members of the radical Left crossing over to the radical Right. (Mussolini is the most famous example of this movement.)[8]

As Irving Kristol admitted in a candid moment, a desire for drama played a part in his shift to the radical Right. In the 1950s he had become "bored with my own sensibly moderate liberal ideas."[9] Like many of the Cold War elites in general, such neoconservatives have proven incapable of dropping this style once the ostensible reason for it—the communist threat—disappeared.

The original neoconservative grouping is now highly fractured.[10] Some of those still occasionally described as neoconservatives, such as Samuel Huntington, in fact differ radically from the remaining core group on key issues, such as the right and ability of the United States to spread its values in the world, especially by force of arms.[11] Others, such as the late Senator Daniel Patrick Moynihan, broke with their former comrades a generation ago.

The remaining neoconservatives are best described as a kind of parabureaucratic grouping which (as Jacob Weisberg has pointed out), given the level of intermarriage and hereditary descent among its members, also somewhat resembles an extended lineage or clan.[12] This kind of grouping is made possible by the American system's blurring of the lines among government, academia, the media and business, which I described in Chapter 2. The group's self-image was encouraged by the Cold War tendency in U.S. security elites as a whole to see themselves as a version of Plato's Guardians, a closed, all-knowing, elect group guiding, protecting (like guard dogs) and when necessary deceiving an ignorant and flaccid populace for its own good, to save it from ruthless enemies.[13]

In the case of the neoconservatives, this tendency was also strongly encouraged by certain secretive and conspiratorial tendencies in the thought of one of their founding intellects, Leo Strauss.[14] He fostered a thoroughly Platonic belief that it is both necessary and legitimate for the philosophical elite to feed the populace religious and patriotic myths in which the elite itself does not believe. This belief may have contributed to the remarkable facility with which neoconservatives over the years have abandoned prior positions (e.g., on humanitarian and democratic interventionism) and formed alliances with groups, such as the Christian Right, which should be quite alien to them.

This inconsistency and opportunism is one reason why despite its harshly ideological tone and radical nationalism and imperialism, neoconservativism today cannot be described as a true ideological tradition. Another reason is that for all their noise, most neoconservatives have not in fact contributed anything truly new to American political culture. Except for the writings of Leo Strauss and Allan Bloom, their works are characteristic of many radical nationalist movements: they often combine fanaticism with dullness and banality. Most indeed are little more than collages of newspaper op-eds.

Rather, what neoconservatives have done is to take some of the existing traditions described in this book and given them a radical and extremist twist. Thus they have turned sympathy for Israel into support for Likud; and they have taken beliefs in America's role as a democratic model and the need for U.S. national security and turned them into arguments for interventionist war. This was only possible for the neoconservatives, however, in the context of a wider feeling of national emergency existing at times during the Cold War and in a more dramatic form after 9/11.

By 2004, as we shall see, the Iraqi disaster meant that the neoconservative influence on the Bush administration was in retreat, compared to both the equally tough but more pragmatic Realism of Dick Cheney and Donald Rumsfeld and the more

Clinton-like and multilateral approach of Colin Powell. However, the deeper tendencies in American political culture which the neoconservatives exploited will remain; indeed, as Chapter 2 explored, their democratizing messianism is widely shared within the Democratic Party. It is essential, therefore, that Americans examine these deeply rooted elements in their political culture and not assume that the dangers they represent will disappear if the neoconservatives lose their grip on power.

Confirmation of Myths

The emergence of America as the leader and bulwark of Western democracies against Nazism and then communism gave a tremendous new strength to messianic feelings stemming from the American Creed. These feelings stressed America's role as the exemplar, leader, protector and savior of the "Free World" in the battle against the evil communist "enemies of Freedom." Indeed, for a number of years these sentiments were justified, at least as far as Western Europe and (to a lesser extent) Northeast Asia were concerned.

The successful democratization of Germany and Japan under U.S. occupation created a fatally alluring image of liberation by force which was to be trotted out later, from Vietnam to Iraq. The historical, economic, geographical, cultural and social positions and experiences of these countries bore no relation whatsoever to those of Germany and Japan; but no matter. The image of the U.S. soldier as conqueror, liberator and modernizer rolled into one had already been firmly established during the Spanish-American War and World War I, and drew on still older roots.[15]

As a result of a combination of old American myths and developments in the mid-twentieth century, this image achieved a power in the American mind which survived what should have been the shattering counter-lesson of Vietnam and which has offset to some extent fears of imperial involvements and military quagmires. The role of America as "guardian of freedom" was played on incessantly by official propaganda, political rhetoric, the media and indeed much of American society. It achieved its most eloquent expression in the speeches of John F. Kennedy and Ronald Reagan—the first a Democrat, the second a Republican, but in this regard not easily distinguishable.

This image was used continuously by Bush and other officials after 9/11, and was of tremendous importance in the mobilization of support for the Iraq War. Even in the case of Afghanistan, the simple and justifiable arguments for war in self-defense against al Qaeda were accompanied by surreal statements about turning that country into a "beachhead of democracy and progress in the Muslim world" (in the words of a U.S. senator at a conference I attended in 2002). As the aftermath of the Taliban's defeat has amply demonstrated, this fantasy bore no resemblance whatsoever to Afghan reality and displayed a complete ignorance of modern Afghan history, society and culture.[16]

But if the Cold War strengthened the messianic aspects of the American Creed, it also poured new sustenance into the maw of America's demons and the "paranoid style" of American politics: an obsession with domestic subversion, belief in an outside world dominated by enemies and potential traitors, reliance on military force and contempt for many of America's leading allies. The Cold War also strengthened messianic nationalism, expressed not only in the quasi-religious terms of adherence to the Creed, but in the explicitly religious ones of belief in America as a nation chosen by God to lead the struggle against the enemies of God. These enemies included, of course, "Godless communism" and any forces associated with it; but by extension the phrase meant any enemies of America.

Coming right after the war against the Nazis, the Cold War strengthened and indeed institutionalized the Manichean elements in the American view of the outside world, a belief in absolute powers of light led by America fighting against absolute forces of darkness. The struggle against a revolutionary and conspiratorial enemy also attracted a certain personality type on the U.S. side, people who saw themselves as an anticommunist revolutionary elite dedicated to fighting the communists: self-described "Bolsheviks of the Right," such as David Stockman, or the curious figure of Grover Norquist, a radical Rightist who reportedly admires Lenin's "iron dedication" and keeps his portrait in his living room—not behavior characteristic of a traditional conservative.[17]

This Manichean tendency in the American right wing and nationalist intellectual world at the start of the twenty-first century was perfectly summed up in a passage about the American Enterprise Institute in 2003 by a horrified British observer, Mark Almond:

> Acting as the ideological enforcers of the Bush administration, the American Enterprise Institute is a kind of Cominform of the new world order. Its so-called scholars are the inquisitors of a global regime. Minutes of their foreign seminars are more like sitting in on a hate session from China's cultural revolution than a political science class at Yale. Participants rise to denounce the hate figure of the day or to endorse a visiting dignitary favoured by the regime. There is an overwhelming stench of ideological conformity. Washington think-tanks promote not pluralism, but a Stalinist-style dogmatism with eulogised conformists and excommunicated heretics. This show-trial mentality is hardly surprising, as the American Enterprise Institute brings the ideological successors of McCarthy and renegade leftists together with emigres educated in the Soviet bloc.[18]

Thus the Cold War both contributed to and legitimated the drives to hysterical hatred in radical conservative circles. In part precisely because these roots are so deep, this tendency outlived the disappearance of communism in the early 1990s and was then directed both against new enemies abroad and "liberals" at home. These radical conservatives and nationalists were people for whom the Cold War atmosphere had become an addiction, irrespective of any intellectually serious analysis of real threats. Or as Irving Kristol wrote in 1993: "There is no 'after the Cold War' for me. So far from having ended, my Cold War has increased in intensity, as sector after sector has been corrupted by the liberal ethos. Now that the other 'Cold War' is over, the real Cold War has begun. We are far less prepared for this Cold War, far more vulnerable to our enemy, than was the case with our victorious war against a global communist threat."[19]

Domestic threats preoccupied the American radical Right for much of the Cold War, often strangely eclipsing the Soviet Union as a menace in their minds.[20] This redirection of an ostensibly national struggle toward attacks on domestic enemies is also a much older and wider pattern in nationalism. As Alfred Cobban remarks of the French nationalists before 1914, "Though the nationalists of the early years of the twentieth century often used bellicose language and were xenophobic, their aggression was directed more against their compatriots than against foreigners."[21]

As Kristol's statement suggests, wars are always morally corrupting, and the Cold War went on for a very long time compared to most "hot" wars. They are corrupting no less in their idealization of their own side than in their demonization of the enemy and in their deliberate and systematic cultivation of hatred, including toward rival compatriots guilty of alleged weakness or treason in the face of the enemy. This has been a staple of American right-wing attacks on liberals throughout the Cold War and its aftermath, and has been taken to lunatic heights in works such as Ann Coulter's *Treason*.[22]

Wars are also corrupting in their encouragement of the belief that "the truth has to be protected by a bodyguard of lies," in Winston Churchill's phrase: that public lying is morally and patriotically justified for the higher good of victory, and that enemy propaganda is to be met not with the truth but with counter-propaganda. Conscious or unconscious falsification of facts and evidence has become a staple of much of the discussion of international affairs in the United States—as demonstrated, for example, in the 2003 media campaign against France. Such publicly funded institutions as Radio Free Europe and Radio Free Asia were founded and have continued in this spirit, even after the end of the Cold War.

The Cold War allowed institutions like the upper-class Public Affairs Luncheon Club of Dallas in the 1960s to weave different paranoias into one seamless web, with speeches on such themes as "The UN Is the Springboard from Which the Great Communist Movements Are Coming"; "International Socialists Still Control the State Department"; and "The Internationalists Have All But Destroyed U.S. National Independence."[23] The fear of communism taking over a defeatist United States seems strongly to have affected even so apparently sober a bureaucratic figure as Dick Cheney.[24] Far from the end of the Cold War liberating the United States from this malign discourse, the victory over communism of 1989 to 1991 sealed it in place. All of these tendencies continued (albeit at a diminished level) during the 1990s and have gained a new and frightening strength after 9/11.

Permanent Mobilization

The Cold War therefore perpetuated and intensified already existing tendencies in American political culture. Coming on top of World War II, however, it also introduced something quite new: a state system of permanent semimobilization for war, institutionalized in the military-industrial-academic complex and the academic bodies linked to it. As the radical U.S. critic and historian C. Wright Mills wrote in 1959: "For the first time in American history, men in authority are talking about an 'emergency' without a foreseeable end . . . the American elite does not have any real image of peace—other than as an uneasy interlude existing precariously by virtue of the balance of mutual fright. The only seriously accepted plan for 'peace' is the fully loaded pistol. In short, war or a high state of war preparedness is felt to be the normal and seemingly permanent condition of the United States."[25]

In typical fashion for security elites of this kind, they became deeply conditioned over the decades to see themselves not just as tougher, braver, wiser and more knowledgeable than their ignorant, innocent compatriots, but as the only force standing between their country and destruction. They are therefore entitled if necessary to deceive their compatriots for their own good; because, after all—so the wisdom goes—if the American people had been left to their own instincts, America would have been left almost defenseless in the face of German and Japanese aggression in the 1940s and Soviet aggression at the start of the Cold War. And in fact there are historical grounds for a limited and prudent form of this attitude. General George Marshall—not a man given to hysterical exaggeration—described the reduction of the armed forces after 1945 as "not demobilization, but a rout."[26]

This "emergency without end" has now been repeated in an intensified form in the war on terrorism; but the nature of the security establishment and military-industrial-academic complex created by the Cold War also helped make the United States poorly fitted to fight against terrorists. Instead, this complex of institutions and attitudes requires states as enemies—and if such enemies are not readily apparent, it will instinctively seek to conjure them up, at least in the American public mind.[27]

So important did military spending and the military-industrial sector become during World War II and the Cold War that—with space exploration as a minor adjunct—they have become fundamental to the U.S. economy, U.S. economic growth and above all U.S. technological development. Despite its often almost incredible wastefulness and corruption, this military spending has also been in some ways a kind of unacknowledged but rather successful state industrial development strategy, in a country whose free market ideology meant that it could not formally adopt or admit to such a strategy.

The growing importance of the military and associated institutions and interests was quite unlike anything that had ever existed before in U.S. history. Hostility to standing armies—involving both high taxes and the threat of royal tyranny—was a central part of the motivation for the American revolt against Britain. This sentiment helped fuel the belief in popular militias as a free and democratic alternative—which, as written into the second amendment to the Constitution, constitutes today the main constitutional defense of the right to bear arms and the U.S. gun lobby.[28] Three times before the Cold War, the United States resorted to conscription to fight wars: in the Civil War and World Wars I and II; but each time, victory was followed by very rapid demobilization. Only with the Cold War did the notion of permanent readiness for war become an integral part of the American system. This was doubtless unavoidable, given the permanent (if often exaggerated) nature of the threat from a permanently mobilized and nuclear-armed Soviet Union; but just because it was unavoidable does not make its consequences any less dangerous.

While new to the United States, this kind of system and atmosphere have been all too widespread in world history. In the decades before 1914, all the major European powers with the partial exception of Britain lived in a state of permanent semimobilization. This condition reflected the objective security circumstances of the European continent at the time; but as in the United States during the Cold War, it also first created and was then itself fed by great military, bureaucratic and industrial blocs with a strong vested interest in the maintenance of a mood of national paranoia, of fear and hatred of other countries, and of international tension.

A classic example is the German Navy League, backed by the great steel and armaments interests, allied to the old military aristocracy and dedicated to the creation of an arms race with Britain.[29] Such groups contributed a good deal to the competing aggressive nationalisms which eventually clashed between 1914 and 1918.

Every country had its version of the U.S. "Committee on the Present Danger" which mobilized fear of the Soviet Union in the early 1980s. Every European country before 1914 had its own repeated and carefully stoked panics concerning the enemy's military capabilities, such as the "Missile Gap" scare that the Democrats created as a weapon against Eisenhower with the help of intellectual allies including the nuclear scientist and arch–Cold Warrior Edward Teller.[30]

In the United States, one of the first employers of this tactic was Senator Lyndon Johnson when chairman of the Senate's Preparedness Subcommittee during the Korean War. Since then it has become a fixed and recurring feature of American political theater.[31] Such moves can be used either by the opposition to discredit the government in power or by the government to whip up patriotic support and discredit the opposition. Lord Salisbury, several times British premier at the height of the British empire, once remarked sourly that if British generals and their political allies had their way, he would have to pay to "fortify the Moon against an attack from Mars."[32]

Indeed, in 1897 a British magazine published a story with a title which could have been written by Charles Krauthammer—"How Britain Fought the World in 1899"—in which France and Russia invade Britain. In the words of its publisher, this story was "no wild dream of the imaginative novelist, this threat of an invasion of our beloved shore. It is solidly discussed in French and Russian, aye and in

German newspapers....The Frenchman and the educated Russian talk of such a thing as coolly as we talk of sending out a punitive expedition to the Soudan or up to the hills of North-West India." [33]

This bizarre fantasy was praised as realistic by senior British officers and was part of a very extensive genre of such stories in Europe at the time. In the United States, such fictional "scares" concerning invasion of the United States by the Soviet Union, China, Cuba and even Nicaragua became a staple of Cold War thrillers, recalling nineteenth-century Protestant fears of a Catholic army invading America by balloon. [34] These old cultural and historical roots of paranoia helped anticommunist hysteria become part of American political culture—a matter of assumptions and fears which exist and operate below the level of political discussion and which are not indeed really open to rational argument. [35]

Such wild fantasies did not appear just in fictional works, but in those of highly influential and respected officials and commentators. In his 1980 book, *The Present Danger*, neoconservative Norman Podhoretz warned of the imminent "Finlandization" of America, involving "the political and economic subordination of the United States to superior Soviet power." He asked if a point had come at which "surrender or war are the only choices." [36]

After what became obvious later about the real condition of the Soviet economy and military at that time, one would have thought either that Podhoretz and his colleagues would have become at least somewhat chastened and modest in their judgments, or that their public would have lost confidence in those judgments. But no. As of 2004, Podhoretz was still there, editor in chief of *Commentary*, a regular pundit on television, and advising the United States on "How to Win World War IV." [37]

Bismarck on occasion used such scares as a tactic in his struggle to control the German parliament, co-opt or emasculate the liberal parties and maintain royal control over the executive. Under his successors, it became a repeated practice. [38] In the United States, such scares concerning Soviet power continued even as the Soviet Union was manifestly collapsing; then they were immediately revived in the form of paranoia about Russian "revanche," even as the Russian armed forces were similarly rotting before our eyes. [39]

The need for major states as enemies stems partly from the fact that only the perceived presence of enemy states can justify military spending at the level which the industries concerned have come to demand. Terrorist groups require a very different set of responses, much more complicated but also very much cheaper. [40] But, the intellectual and institutional framework of the men and women concerned also requires enemies who in some sense are their own evil twins, with similar mind-sets and ambitions: military-bureaucratic-economic state elites, not terrorists driven by a complex and alien mixture of religious, cultural and socio-economic values and motivations. A really thorough reform of the American defense establishment to meet the threat of Islamist terrorism would require the fundamental recalibration of the American security elites—an idea which, not surprisingly, does not enchant them.

This tendency to focus on states has been increased by the dominance of the "Realist" intellectual approach to international affairs among the greater part of the American security elites. This view of the world both tends to direct attention away from the study of societies and can act as a cover for extreme nationalism. "Realism" encourages a view of states as basically pieces on the "Grand Chessboard" of international affairs (to borrow the title of a book by former National Security Adviser Zbigniew Brzezinski) with certain preset and unchangeable attributes and possible moves.[41]

As such, it is rather a comfortable doctrine for a security elite and its intellectual employees and allies, suggesting that great cultural and linguistic knowledge is not really necessary, and so neither is uncomfortable and possibly dangerous travel and research. Together with a similarly limited approach to the study of history among many (but not all) Realists, this belief helps demolish any capacity to put the behavior of one's own country in a wider moral perspective and encourages some of those same solipsistic weaknesses in contemporary American study of the outside world which were analyzed in Chapter 2.

The Obsession with Russia and China

In theory, Realism—as its name suggests—should encourage a cool and distant view of human affairs. In practice, its exponents often have been suffused with nationalist hatreds and prejudices concerning the unchanging malignity of selected other nations. As Owen Harries, editor of the conservative journal *The National Interest,* wrote of widespread U.S. establishment attitudes to Russia in the 1990s:

> The realist case is based largely on the conviction that Russia is inherently and incorrigibly expansionist, regardless of how and by whom it is governed....In arguing this way, these commentators are being very true to their realist position. But they are also drawing attention to what is one of the most serious intellectual weaknesses of that position—namely, that in its stress on the structure of the international system and on how states are placed within that system, Realism attaches little or no importance to what is going on *within* particular states: what kind of regimes are in power, what kind of ideologies prevail, what kind of leadership is provided.[42]

One senior Clinton administration defense official quoted by Chalmers Johnson actively celebrated the fact that in government departments dealing with China, experts on China were being pushed aside by a "new strategic class" of generalists from strategic studies and international relations, who might not know much about

China but would be watchful "for signs of China's capacity for menace"—a most revealing statement.[43]

This combination of tendencies to ignore societies and concentrate on states also helps explain why the Bush administration, and the elites which support it, have been in some ways so strangely indifferent to the terrorists who actually carried out the attacks of 9/11 and continue to threaten America. As Richard Clarke, Paul O'Neill and Bob Woodward have recorded, from the very first days after the attacks, Bush, Cheney, Rumsfeld and especially Paul Wolfowitz were already thinking of using the terrorist attacks to justify war with Iraq.[44] As soon as the Taliban was overthrown, detailed planning for war with Iraq began, although it should have been manifestly obvious that Afghanistan was going to remain an immense problem from which the United States could not afford to avert its eyes.

It is also partly because of this Cold War legacy that, according to Woodward (seemingly drawing on an interview with Donald Rumsfeld), on 9/11 the United States was so unprepared for a campaign in Afghanistan, although that country had already acted as the base for very serious terrorist attacks: "the military, which seemed to have contingency plans for the most inconceivable scenarios, had no plans for Afghanistan, the sanctuary of bin Laden and his network. There was nothing on the shelf that could be pulled down to provide at least an outline."

The drive for national missile defense, which dominated the security agenda of the Bush administration in its first eight months in office, was motivated above all by a desire to nullify the nuclear deterrents of China and other rival states and thereby to create what Walter Russell Mead calls "the holy Grail of Jacksonian foreign policy: a weapons system that defends this nation while intimidating all others, and that would allow the United States to control events around the world without risking the lives of its citizen soldiers."[45] A speech by Bush's National Security Adviser Condoleezza Rice on threats to the United States scheduled for September 11, 2001, "was designed to promote missile defense as the cornerstone of a new national security strategy, and contained no mention of Al Qaeda, Osama bin Laden or Islamic extremist groups."[46]

I can testify to "inconceivable scenarios" of Russian aggression and international war from my own experience of scenario-building sessions and discussions with U.S. officials in the years before 9/11. And if no such scenarios existed for war in Afghanistan—despite the fact that al Qaeda had already launched several bloody terrorist attacks against U.S. targets—surely one reason was that too many of the people who should have been thinking about this were worrying about war with Russia or China.

The memo on security challenges which Rumsfeld drew up for the Bush administration as it took office dwelt on the threat to the United States from Iraq, China, Russia, Iran and North Korea, and from weapons of mass destruction—but not from al Qaeda.[47] Former antiterrorism coordinator Richard Clarke has complained bitterly of the indifference of the Bush administration to the terrorist threat both before and after 9/11, compared to their obsessions with missile defense and with war against Iraq. And in Iraq, the entire obsession was with the defeat of Saddam Hussein, to such an extent that the planners seemingly neglected even to secure that state's civilian nuclear facilities and prevent terrorists from getting radioactive material for a "dirty bomb."

Hence also the concentration on strategy against Russia, to some extent under Clinton, but still more strongly in the first eight months of the Bush administration. In the mid-1990s, the American foreign and security establishment turned the rolling back of Russian influence in the former Soviet Union into an American strategic priority. This aim was despite the fact that the areas concerned had never previously been of the slightest strategic interest to America.

This new strategy also clashed with that of the administration of Bush Sr. from 1988 to 2002 toward the Soviet Union in its years of collapse. That former strategy was based above all on fear of chaos, civil war and loss of control by the state over nuclear weapons and materiel. All of these threats remain in parts of the former Soviet Union to this day, and all should have been given a new importance after 9/11. Some genuine justification for the new anti-Russian strategy in terms of national interest was given by the need to secure access to the energy reserves of the Caspian basin—but to make this idea truly credible, vastly exaggerated reports of the actual proven extent of these reserves had to be promulgated.

Meanwhile, throughout the 1990s, influential commentators also continued to exaggerate both the military power and the aggressive will of Russia and the Russian people.[48] In many circles, this exaggeration was accompanied by historicist and even racist attempts to portray the Russian people as congenitally imperialist, with such statements as "Expansionism is in the Russians' DNA"[49] or "The only potential great power security problem in Central Europe is the lengthening shadow of Russian strength, and NATO has the job of counter-balancing it. Russia is a force of nature; all this is inevitable."[50]

To anyone with a sense of history, there is a certain tedium about such views, which tend to repeat interchangeable phrases used of other nations since the very beginning of nationalism. Thus the following passage is typical of many articles and speeches on the subject of a supposedly congenitally aggressive and malignant Russia which I encountered in America during and after the Cold War—but it was actually written by an American about Britain in the 1890s, and forms of it have been used repeatedly by international critics of the United States: "Restless activity, and wanton aggression—especially when dealing with weaker powers—have been the controlling factors in British diplomacy for centuries. History presents an unbroken record of arrogant and unjust attacks on the integrity of every nation in the world where a pretext could be found for asserting English domination."[51]

I came to Washington on a visiting fellowship in 1996, fresh from covering the immense retreat of Russia from empire—by far the greatest peaceful abandonment of empire in all history, with the partial exception of the British withdrawal from its empire. I had also covered both the Russian military defeat in the first Chechen war (a war not for empire but against the secession of part of the Russian

Federation itself) and the mixture of corruption, cynicism, materialism and political apathy which gripped Russian society after the fall of communism.[52]

On arrival, I was first astonished and then horrified to find large sections of the American elites—serving officials as well as unofficial commentators—dedicated to creating an image of Russia in the minds of the American people which bore only a tangential relation to reality; and this line was swallowed by large sections of the American media and public.[53] With this experience behind me, I was not too surprised by the success of the Bush administration and its media allies in conflating al Qaeda and Saddam Hussein and of the Israel lobby in conflating al Qaeda and the Palestinians.[54]

During the first months of the Bush administration, these views found expression in a set of strongly anti-Russian policies, combined with contemptuous and aggressive language.[55] But within two years, of course, there had been a radical change, above all with regard to Chechnya. U.S. troops had arrived in Georgia in late 2001 with the mission of training the Georgian army to deal with Chechen and Arab terrorists on its soil, and U.S. and European intelligence services were calling on Russian help to deal with Arab terrorist groups allied to the Chechens and trained in Georgia.[56]

Indeed, at the time the U.S. media, Republican politicians and neoconservative hawks were hurling the same charges of harboring and abetting terrorists against Saudi Arabia and other U.S. allies which Russia had hurled at the same target before 9/11—and in consequence, had been accused by these same commentators of mendacity and aggression.[57] The example of Russia demonstrates the flaw in claims by the Bush administration, and much of the U.S. foreign policy and security establishment in general, that their hostility is not to other peoples or states, but only to regimes.

As far as many members of the U.S. establishment are concerned, the fall of communism and the end of the Soviet Union hardly changed at all their hostility to Russia as a state; the situation would change only if Russia adopted a position of complete subservience to American wishes not only in the world as a whole, but in its own region. This is something which no Russian state will ever accept. A future postcommunist Chinese state and a future posttheocratic Iranian state would also be extremely unlikely to accept this kind of American domination—and will therefore go on attracting implacable hostility from important forces in Washington.

The case of U.S. attitudes to China since the end of the Cold War has been more complicated than that of U.S.-Russian relations. The Korean War left many Americans with a legacy of hatred for China analogous to that directed against Russia during the Cold War. The Taiwanese lobby in Washington also played a role which resembled to some extent that of the anti-Russian ethnic lobbies in the United States, although as it lacks an American ethnic lobby on the same scale, it has proven a great deal less effective.

However, the almost two decades of U.S.-Chinese alignment against the Soviet Union, starting with Nixon and Kissinger, left a different background to U.S. relations with China in the 1990s. Even more important has been the tremendous growth of the Chinese economy since the end of the 1970s, and the opportunities that this created for Western investment and trade. This led to pro-Chinese business lobbies in Washington which dwarfed anything that could be generated by the faltering Russian economy during the same period.

Nonetheless, the 1990s saw a determined effort in certain right-wing and security circles to cast China in the role of the new Cold War enemy—and not only in the Republican and neoconservative opposition, but to some extent among Democrats as well. This effort included the usual campaigns to emphasize Chinese human rights abuses and vastly exaggerate China's military capabilities.[58]

The hope was to create a U.S. security strategy of "containing" China, modeled on the "containment" of the Soviet Union during the Cold War; to attempt to bankrupt the Chinese state by forcing it into an unsustainable arms race; and to undermine the Chinese state from within by encouraging movements for democratic revolution and ethnic secession. Meanwhile, the Chinese nuclear deterrent was to be neutralized by an American system of missile defense.

These views were pushed especially hard by the so-called Blue Team, an informal grouping of anti-Chinese junior officials, think tank members and congressional staffers, and had considerable impact in Congress, though much less within the official community. The Blue Team was a conscious attempt to imitate the success of the so-called B Team, a similar (but more senior) group of officials and propagandists of the 1980s who set out to dramatize the supposed extent of Soviet power. The curious thing is, of course, that virtually every proposition advanced by the B Team concerning the Soviet Union has since been proven false.

In 1999 Republicans in Congress mounted a classic scare of the "Missile Gap" type, with the Cox Committee accusing China of having spied so successfully on the United States as to be able in a short time to match American nuclear technology and threaten the U.S. mainland. The report also declared that "essentially all Chinese visitors to the United States are potential spies."[59] The report set off an orchestrated Republican media campaign attacking the Clinton administration for "weakness" and pushing for tougher policies against China. It was replete with phrases like "the greatest nuclear theft since the Rosenbergs" (the Soviet spies who provided Moscow with U.S. nuclear secrets in the 1940s) and "every nuclear weapon in the U.S. arsenal has been compromised." Former UN ambassador Jeanne Kirkpatrick declared—incredibly—that "it renders us immediately a great deal more vulnerable than we have ever been in our history." Former House Speaker Newt Gingrich called it "the largest espionage success against the United States since the Soviet Union in the 1940s."[60]

Echoing "yellow peril" racist stereotypes which long predated the Cold War, the *Washington Times* reported that "both Mrs. Kirkpatrick and Mr. Gingrich believe the Chinese are capable of launching a missile at American troops, allied targets and even American cities. Mrs. Kirkpatrick said the Chinese do not value human life and might be willing to suffer retaliatory consequences for the psycho-logical benefit of striking American soil with a missile."[61]

Among many right-wing politicians, such attitudes to China continued un-abated even after 9/11, with House Majority Leader Tom DeLay in June 2003 pub-licly calling China "a backward, corrupt anachronism, run by decrepit tyrants, old apparachiks clinging to a dying regime."[62]

In the first months of the Bush administration, it seemed that this anti-Chinese approach, like the then–anti-Russia approach, might be adopted as official U.S. policy. Given the ferocious views of the Chinese system which he had expressed in the media, the appointment of John Bolton to the State Department could have been taken in itself as an anti-Chinese act.[63] Like Condoleezza Rice, Bush repeat-edly called China a "strategic competitor" and called for a range of tougher U.S. policies.[64] Rice called on the United States to build up India as a strategic counter to China and to take a more firmly pro-Taiwan stance in its relations with Beijing.[65] *Time* magazine reported that the Bush administration in its first weeks in office was "hosing down China with acid."[66]

If 9/11 had not occurred, many of the officials and commentators who have since used the terrorist attacks as an argument for radical unilateralism in U.S. policy would have directed their energies to stirring up the maximum possible American public hostility to Russia and China and to manufacturing crises in relations with these states. They would have remained just as indifferent to the terrorist threat as they were before 9/11, despite the fact that repeated attacks on American targets outside the United States had already occurred.

Present Dangers, a book of essays by leading neoconservatives and other right-wing hard-liners, edited by Robert Kagan and William Kristol and published in 2000, provides evidence of how Bush administration policy might have developed had 9/11 not intervened. Its title intentionally recalled the already mentioned Cold War era Committee on the Present Danger.

In keeping with the Realist tradition before September 11, the authors are in-different to terrorism and issues of violence and stability within societies; of fif-teen essays, not one is devoted to terrorism as such (with the partial exception of one on Israel). Instead they are obsessed with the threat to the United States from a range of supposedly powerful rival states, all of which must be approached with the maximum degree of toughness. "Appeasement" is a constant theme. The last essay of *Present Dangers*, for example, is a paranoid attempt to suggest that the U.S. position vis-à-vis China resembles that of Britain vis-à-vis Germany in the early 1930s—a "Realist" analysis almost surreal in its indifference to economic, technological, political and ideological realities.[67]

The former British diplomat Jonathan Clarke described the tendency which the authors represent:

> The book advocates a U.S. foreign policy of maximum muscularity. No con-cession is offered to the traditional arts of diplomacy. Indeed, those of us

who have labored in overseas chanceries in the interests of "good relations" find our endeavors ridiculed. The word "stability" is used in quotation marks as if it was somehow a suspect notion of doubtful legitimacy. The conventional ingredients of national interest are attacked as imposing rigid, undesirable limitations on American options. The concept of engagement is dismissed as the equivalent of appeasement.

Far from looking for ways to take the toxicity out of international problems, the authors purposefully seek out trouble spots (the Taiwan Strait, North Korea, Iraq) and then reach for the gas can. "Quiet diplomacy" or "keeping one's powder dry" are anathema. "Steely resolve" is the watchword, with the emphasis on steel. Indeed, it is hardly an exaggeration to say that if the book's combined recommendations were implemented all at once, the US would risk unilaterally fighting at least a five-front war, while simultaneously urging Israel to abandon the peace process in favor of a new no-hold-barred confrontation with the Palestinians....

There is a curious flavor of Nietzchean "will" running through this book. There is a constant appeal to the need to mobilize the people to war. The "present dangers" of the title turn out to be not external threats but the possibility that the American people will not be sufficiently ready to lift up arms. There is a fascination with history's strong men, as if the "Triumph des Willen" was an admirable trait, albeit expressed as evil in certain of them. Whether this is really compatible with American ideals of limited, constitutional government by laws rather than men is a subject for another essay.[68]

This widespread and sinister obsession with national "will" among the neoconservatives is brought out in a striking passage by Charles Krauthammer: "America is no mere international citizen. It is the dominant power in the world, more dominant than any since Rome. Accordingly, America is in a position to reshape norms, alter expectations and create new realities. How? By unapologetic and implacable demonstrations of will."[69]

And once again, these words were not written after 9/11, calling for a tough response to savage terrorism. They appeared in March 2001 and were pegged to what the author at that stage celebrated as a tough new Bush approach to dealing with Russia, a state which since 1991 had posed no direct threat whatsoever to the United States.

In such circles, neither 9/11 nor the bloody occupation of Iraq had much effect on this underlying psychological stance. If anything, it only widened the circle of enemies and intensified demands for America to display its will and toughness by deliberately standing alone. Thus the book *An End to Evil*, by Richard Perle and former Bush speechwriter David Frum and published in 2003, expressed a greater or lesser degree of embittered hostility not just to the Muslim world, but to Russia, China, the United Nations and every country or institution which had in any way questioned or resisted the United States over war with Iraq.

An End to Evil advises the United States to oppose European unity. Most of Western Europe is said to be affected by "the same jealousy and resentment that animate the terrorists"—an astonishingly extreme and provocative statement to come from a man still serving as a senior government adviser. No exception whatsoever was to be made for different terrorist movements, or between their political and military wings—except in the case of Russia, which is accused of having invented its terrorist threat and fabricated its terrorist attacks. The only country treated positively is Britain—whose views and interests are then treated with dismissive contempt.[70]

Bellicose But Not Militarist

However, it would be quite wrong to think of neoconservative figures like Perle and Frum as characteristic of the American security establishment as a whole, let alone the American people. On the contrary, they have been able to mobilize mass support for their imperialist programs only by presenting them in nationalist and defensive guise. Moreover, by 2004 the extremist program which they represent seemed in retreat even within the Bush administration.

The American historian C. Vann Woodward, writing in the 1960s, described the American people as having traditionally been "bellicose but not militaristic." They are willing—even overwilling—to fight if America is attacked or even insulted, but are not committed to the permanent celebration and projection of military power and values.[71] Even after the militarizing effects of the Cold War, this remains true to a considerable extent today. It is closely linked to the fact that many Americans also can be said to be "bellicose but not imperialistic" and are indeed very unwilling to recognize that they possess even an indirect empire.[72] Open exaltation in empire and celebrations of parallels with the British and other empires is restricted to a few neoconservatives and others.[73]

Bellicose nationalism is a different matter, however, and certainly is very widely present. This gut bellicosity, the "Don't Tread on Me" or "Spread-Eagle" position and the opportunities it gives for political manipulation and exploitation were summed up with amazing frankness by Irving Kristol in 1989: "If the president goes to the American people and wraps himself in the American flag and lets Congress wrap itself in the white flag of surrender, the president will win....The American people had never heard of Grenada. There was no reason they should have. The reason we gave for the intervention—the risk to American medical students there—was phony but the reaction of the American people was absolutely and overwhelmingly favorable. They had no idea what was going on but they backed the president. They always will."[74]

The "Don't Tread on Me" response in the U.S. Congress is especially identified with Southern senators and representatives such as Jesse Helms (formerly senator for North Carolina), Trent Lott (Mississippi), James Inhofe (Oklahoma), Tom DeLay (Texas) and Dick Armey (Texas)—and still including a few hawkish Democrats, such as Zell Miller of Georgia—but is also geographically spread across the United States.

While often an embarrassment to U.S. foreign policy, this tendency is extremely useful to any U.S. leader planning a war. Many of these figures can be counted on to support almost any war, as long as they can somehow be convinced that the United States has been attacked or insulted. The stance of some conservative Republicans over the Kosovo War is a revealing example.

Most opposed that war, out of hostility toward the Clinton administration and out of opposition to "humanitarian" wars in which U.S. national interests did not seem to be at stake. (They overlooked the importance of preserving NATO as a vehicle for U.S. influence in Europe, and therefore for giving it something to do.) It might have been expected therefore that when the Chinese embassy in Belgrade was bombed, and the Chinese reacted with bitter criticism of the United States, these men would have used this debacle as a lesson of the dangerous wider "unintended consequences" of supposedly minor, limited military operations. Not at all. Their reaction was one of furious belligerence, strongly flavored with traditional attitudes toward the character and proper treatment of Orientals and lesser breeds, as in this statement by Representative Tom DeLay: "While the bombing of the embassy is an unfortunate example of collateral damage during Mr. Clinton's war, the prestige of the United States has been harmed more by the constant apologies and groveling of the President in its aftermath. It seems that every time the television is on, the President is apologizing to Communist China....No wonder the PRC government thinks it can walk all over the United States. Communist Chinese leaders do not understand weakness in leadership. They respect unquestioned power, firmness of purpose and unquestioned shows of strength."[75]

This instinctive belligerence has been much in evidence since 9/11, and in ways very damaging to the conduct of the struggle against Islamist terrorism. President Bush himself has been careful to avoid this attitude, and to speak of Islam as a religion and Muslim peoples in general with respect. But on the American nationalist Right, there was an explosion of aggressive chauvinism, not just against al Qaeda and the Taliban, or even Saddam Hussein, but against Islam and the Muslim world in general.[76]

Typical of such statements was that of Republican congressman Peter King, that "85 per cent of the mosques in the United States have extremist leadership." In newspapers like the *Washington Times* and on right-wing radio shows, the language descended into appalling depths of hatred. Thus radio personality Don Imus in February 2004 rejoiced in the deaths of Iranians in a civilian plane crash and added, "Too bad it wasn't full of Saudi Arabians."[77]

Certain advisers joined in, with Kenneth Adelman of the Defense Advisory Board declaring that "the more you examine the religion [Islam] the more militaristic it seems."[78] Former *New York Times* executive editor A. M. Rosenthal called for the governments of Afghanistan, Iraq, Iran, Libya, Syria, Sudan "and any other devoted to the elimination of the United States or the constant incitement of hatred against it" to be given a three-day ultimatum to hand over both terrorists and their own leaders to the United States. If they refused, their capitals and major cities should be "bombed to the ground beginning the fourth."[79] Charles Krauthammer made the same demand later concerning Afghan cities: "To restrain our military now in order to placate our diplomats is a tragic reprise of Vietnam."[80] Fox News commentator Bill O'Reilly declared during the first stage of the Iraq War that "there is a school of thought that says we should have given the citizens of Baghdad forty-eight hours to 'get out of Dodge' by dropping leaflets and going with the AM radios and all that. Forty-eight hours, you've got to get out of there, and flatten the place. Then the war would be over....It's just frustrating for everybody to know that we have been fighting this war with one hand behind our back."[81]

As disagreement between the United States and parts of Western Europe (and most of the rest of the world) over war with Iraq intensified in 2002–03, the bitter hostility of American nationalists was extended to any country which refused to follow the United States into war.[82] This spirit led to the U.S. House of Representatives voting to change the designation of "French fries" in its restaurant to "Freedom fries"; but it also affected even some normally moderate and intelligent American analysts.[83]

Even usually moderate figures succumbed to the hysteria, with Thomas Friedman declaring in the *New York Times* that "France is not just our annoying ally. It is not just our jealous rival. France is becoming our enemy." French opinions were moreover worthless in any case because "France has never been interested in promoting democracy in the modern Arab world."

Friedman adopted a mild version of the same position taken up by Krauthammer and others: because other countries hate us, and for ignoble, wicked and illegitimate reasons, their opinions do not count, and we are free to do whatever we like. Friedman wrote those words in September 2003, by which time France's warnings about the consequences of war had been shown to be amply justified. They are an example both of the degree to which even centrist Americans can become the captive of nationalist emotions and of a nationalist insistence that the only acceptable criticism of America is by Americans.[84]

At the time of the Iraq War, not just extremist publications like the *Washington Times,* but the *Washington Post* and *New York Times* became vehicles for "a well-orchestrated campaign of innuendoes, distortions and lies aimed not only at discrediting French arguments but France itself."[85] Articles accused France of harboring fugitive Ba'ath officials, possessing banned stocks of biological weapons and supplying Iraq with weapons—all charges which were later admitted to be completely groundless.[86]

Militarist But Not Bellicose

If the U.S. population and its representatives harbor strong traditions of instinctive bellicosity but are not imperialist, since the Vietnam War at least much of the American military-industrial complex and the institutes and academics associated with it might be described as imperialist and militarist but not bellicose. As Stanley Hoffmann wrote (in a review of Garry Wills's biography of Reagan): "[Reagan's] domestic program precluded activism abroad, as [Alexander] Haig discovered with dismay. Foreign policy was to be just a matter of armed deterrence ('Weinberger was buying arms from all directions and discouraging their use in any sector'), occasional swift and easy coups (Grenada) and verbal thrusts at the evil empire."[87]

This pattern has been reflected in Bush administration policy toward Russia and China, even before 9/11. The terrorist attacks obviously led to a radical shift in U.S. policy toward both Russia and China; and this shift was increased still further by the war of occupation in Iraq and the revelation of the actual military weakness of the United States when it came to the mobilization of large numbers of troops for prolonged campaigns. The terrific drain on U.S. reserve forces risked creating a crisis of morale and recruitment. Evident to all military professionals, and to most (but by no means all) civilian officials and commentators, was the fact that the United States simply could not afford to risk simultaneously another major war elsewhere.[88] Ambitious, imperialist, ruthless these people may often be; insane they are not.

In some respects the administration's mood of hubristic and hostile arrogance toward Russia—and to a lesser and more ambiguous degree toward China—had become more moderate several months before 9/11 and two years before the Iraq War. When an American EP-3E reconnaissance aircraft was forced to land on the Chinese island of Hainan on April 1, 2001, after a collision with a shadowing Chinese fighter, the resulting crisis seemed to act like a cold shock to the administration.

This crisis brought with it the realization that a deliberate escalation of tension with China could lead to actual conflict, or at least a collapse of the U.S.-Chinese trade relationship, with catastrophic consequences for the Asian, American and world economies. *Time* magazine reported that "though some anti-China folks in the White House were eagerly chatting up plans for a revenge move last week, it is likely that Bush will conclude that retaliation is not worth the damage it might do to what may be the most important bilateral relationship in the world."[89]

Accompanying this new sobriety vis-à-vis China was the realization that if increased military tension with China was a real possibility, then it was insanity to infuriate Russia gratuitously at the same time. In consequence, while certain policies (notably the abrogation of the ABM [Antiballistic Missile] Treaty) continued unchanged, there was a much greater willingness at least to help save Russian face, and hostile rhetoric diminished markedly.[90] This shift can be seen by a comparison of administration remarks and administration-inspired op-eds on Russia in March, before the reconnaissance aircraft crisis, and in early May, after it ended.[91]

By late 2003, however, the Bush administration had gone much further. In the case of China, Bush personally recommitted America very strongly to oppose Taiwanese independence.[92] Despite continuing bursts of unilateralist rhetoric from hawks like John Bolton on the issue of preventing North Korea's development of nuclear weapons, the U.S. administration tacitly recognized the bankruptcy of its previous unilateralist strategy and the practical impossibility of following the "Bush Doctrine" of preventive war in East Asia.

In consequence, although still refusing to negotiate with Pyongyang directly, the administration was forced willy-nilly toward a strategy of relying heavily on China to help in restraining and influencing Pyongyang. This new approach recognized not only the impossibility of waging war against North Korea, but also the power of the other regional states, South Korea, Japan and above all China—all of them vastly more formidable countries in their different ways than the feeble dictatorships of the Middle East.

In these circumstances, nationalist unilateralism simply could not even appear to work. In Iraq, too, the growing troubles of the U.S. occupation led to a near about-face toward the United Nations, with the Bush administration seeking the legitimacy given by cooperation with the UN to defuse some of the growing anger of the Shia minority and find alternatives to the original U.S. plans for the country. By 2004, the leading historian of international relations John Ikenberry could write with solid evidence of "The End of the Neoconservative Moment" in U.S. foreign and security policy. Richard Perle's resignation from the Defense Policy Board in March 2004 provided a symbolic marker for this neoconservative decline.[93]

This more multilateralist approach adopted toward a number of issues in the last months of 2003 was seen as a limited victory for the vision and strategy of Secretary of State Colin Powell and the State Department. However, it also reflected the "Realism" of Dick Cheney and Donald Rumsfeld and the institutions and traditions they represent. If this brand of Realism suffers from the faults described above, it nonetheless operates on the basis of rational calculations about power, interest and risk, and derives from ways of looking at the world characteristic of diplomats and strategists since the seventeenth century.

The policy toward Russia and China adopted by the Bush administration after 9/11 fits admirably into this tradition. At bottom, the administration remained strongly distrustful of both countries' motives and plans. Equally, it recognized that it was not in the interests of the United States to seek confrontation with them and that risking war with China would be catastrophic. Washington therefore sought good, cooperative relations, without giving too much away.[94]

Such Realists can make terrible mistakes, as in the case of the occupation of Iraq. They are also hopelessly at sea when faced with challenges falling outside traditional Realist frames of reference: Metternich when faced with rising ideological nationalism, Cheney and Rumsfeld when confronted with the threat of global warming. Nonetheless, they can be distinguished rather clearly from ideologues of the neoconservative type, let alone the Christian Right; and because their views also reflect the views and interests of the complex of institutions and corporations which they represent, they have a tremendous weight which the neoconservatives lack. The triumph of the Realist approach in later 2003 caused deep anguish in hard-line neoconservative circles, and the hysteria of some of their language reflected the depth of their sense of defeat.[95]

This relative caution on the part of Realists in the U.S. establishment reflects in part the nature and interests of the U.S. military-industrial and security elites. These elites are obviously interested in the maintenance and expansion of U.S. global military power, if only because their own jobs and profits depend on it. Jobs and patronage also ensure the support of much of Congress, which often lards defense spending bills with weapons systems the Pentagon does not want and has not even asked for, to help out senators and congressmen whose states produce these systems.[96] And as already noted, to maintain a measure of wider support in the U.S. media and public, it is also necessary to maintain the perception of certain foreign nations as threats to the United States and a certain minimum and permanent level of international tension.

But a desire for permanent international tension is different from a desire for war, especially a major international war which might ruin the international economy. The American generals of the Clinton era have been described as "aggressive only about their budgets."[97] The American ruling system therefore is not a Napoléonic or Moghul one. It does not actively desire major wars, because it does not depend on major victorious wars for its own survival, and it would indeed be threatened by such wars even if the country were victorious. Small wars are admittedly a different matter.

Even in the last decades of the Cold War, under the roiling waves of public anxiety, continually whipped into spray by the winds of political propaganda, the feelings of the security establishment were often actually relatively complacent. As the latest National Security Strategy admits, "In the Cold War, and especially following the Cuban Missile Crisis, we faced a generally status-quo, risk-averse adversary. Deterrence was an effective defense."[98]

As Chalmers Johnson remarks bitterly, it is a pity we were not told this by U.S. official analysts while the Cold War was still on.[99] Indeed, George Kennan's famous telegram and essay of 1947–48, which formulated the intellectual basis for America's Cold War stance against Soviet expansionism, also stated clearly that a direct military challenge to the West was unlikely.[100] Throughout the Cold War, however, powerful voices in the United States alleged not only that the Soviet Union posed a serious threat to the West (which it did), but also that ideological fanaticism and contempt for the lives of their own subjects meant that the Soviet leaders were not fully rational, that they might well launch a reckless war even at the probable cost of their own destruction.

This line was revived in 2002 as a description of the Ba'ath regime in Iraq and a justification of war to topple it, with President Bush repeatedly referring to Saddam Hussein as a "madman."[101] It was also used to justify radical action against Iran and North Korea. As Professors John Mearscheimer and Stephen Walt argued before the war, this portrayal of Saddam Hussein was almost certainly just as false as it is now admitted was the portrayal of Soviet leadership under Leonid Brezhnev.[102]

At least in recent years, however, such exaggerations have not been generally characteristic of one obviously central part of the military-industrial-academic complex. The U.S. uniformed military remains more profoundly influenced by the debacle of Vietnam than perhaps any other section of American society.[103] It was not the uniformed military which pressed for war with Iraq in 2002, but a small group of politically appointed and harshly ideological civilian officials in the Pentagon. Indeed, the army chief of staff, General Eric Shinseki, warned publicly, as did numerous other officers privately, of exactly the type of bloody and troop-consuming war of occupation that would follow—with the result that Shinseki was publicly humiliated by Paul Wolfowitz and other Rumsfeld allies.[104]

When it comes to the real possibility of conflict with the major powers, it is also worth remembering that Rumsfeld's own plans when he took office called for a smaller, lighter U.S. military with a more expeditionary focus and capability. These plans were seemingly predicated on the belief that there would be no land war with another serious military power for a generation at least.[105] Beneath all the talk of Russian and Chinese threats, very few Americans have wished for actual conflict with these states. The desire and need are for tension, not conflict; for large-scale military spending, not full-scale war. Of course, the issue of Taiwanese independence may all too easily bring America and China into conflict; but this will almost certainly be the result of a combination of actions by a third party—Taiwan—with miscalculations in Beijing and Washington, rather than of a conscious decision for war by an American administration.[106]

The Middle East is the great exception to this rule of the ultimate Realist domination of U.S. policy. Here U.S. behavior is colored by nationalist and religious passion to a degree not remotely the case in East Asia, for example. Here the terrible memory of the Holocaust has combined with the long struggle with the Palestinians and Arab states to produce an inflamed nationalism not only among Jewish Americans but in much wider segments of the U.S. population. The resulting influences on American thinking and policy sometimes stand quite outside any Realist—or indeed rational—framework of thought.

Six

American Nationalism, Israel and the Middle East

> *When we look at you from a distance, maybe a little sketchily, we see in you a dangerous threat to what is dear and sacred to us…you threaten to boot Israel out of the union between Jewish tradition and western humanism. As far as I am concerned, you threaten to push Judaism back through history, back to the Book of Joshua, to the days of the Judges, to the extreme of tribal fanaticism, brutal and closed.*
>
> —Amos Oz[1]

In the fall of 2003, two votes were taken in the United Nations General Assembly concerning Israel's policy toward the Palestinians. That of September 19, 2003, demanded that Israel not deport or harm Yasser Arafat. The resolution of October 27, 2003, while condemning Palestinian suicide bombings and calling on both parties to implement the U.S.-designed "Road Map," demanded that Israel cease construction of its "security fence" in the West Bank. The first vote was 133 to 4; the second was 141 to 4. The minority view, rejecting the resolutions, was represented by Israel itself, the United States and two tiny Pacific island states and quasi-dependencies of the United States, Micronesia and the Marshall Islands.[2]

The countries which voted for the resolutions criticizing Israel included some of America's oldest and closest allies, such as Britain; countries which have recently begun to seek close relations with both the United States and Israel, such as India; and of course the whole of the Arab and Muslim worlds. In their absolutely overwhelming nature, these votes find their mirror in resolutions of the U.S. Congress pledging unconditional support for Israel—with the difference that whereas these UN votes condemning Israeli behavior also denounce Palestinian terrorism, votes in the U.S. Congress are almost always completely one-sided.

Consider the U.S. Senate Resolution of May 6, 2002, at the height of Israeli-Palestinian violence. It attacked Palestinian terrorism and declared that "the Senate stands in solidarity with Israel, a frontline state in the war against terrorism, as it takes necessary steps to provide security to its people by dismantling the terrorist infrastructure in the Palestinian areas." Not one clause of the resolution contained even the slightest hint of criticism of any Israeli action. The resolution passed the Senate by 92 votes to 2.[3]

As former National Security Adviser Zbigniew Brzezinski pointed out a few months later, the UN votes illustrated the fact that "American power worldwide is at its historic zenith. American political standing is at its nadir."[4] In the Muslim world especially, American prestige was driven down still further by gestures like those of the Senate.

In April 2004 the Bush administration drove another deep wedge between the United States and Europe over strategy toward the Middle East when Bush unilaterally endorsed Israeli Prime Minister Ariel Sharon's plan to withdraw from the Gaza Strip (although continuing to control its external borders and to dominate it militarily) while retaining control of settlements on the West Bank and ruling out the right of return of Palestinian refugees to Israel. By endorsing Israeli views of key aspects of a final settlement without agreement from Palestinians, Arab regimes or Europe, Bush effectively tore up his own Road Map for peace and made nonsense of U.S. claims to be working with the "Quartet" (of the United States, the European Union, the UN and Russia) in seeking a solution to the conflict. His move was bitterly condemned by most European governments—at a time when Washington was wooing those same governments and the UN to help combat the deteriorating situation in Iraq.[5] It was also denounced in public letters by over one hundred former U.S. and British diplomats who had served in the Middle East.

Even more depressing was the fact that Bush's move was promptly and unconditionally endorsed by his Democratic rival for the presidency, John Kerry, who also approved Israel's assassination of Hamas leaders.[6] Kerry's approach to this issue was completely incompatible with his campaign's central foreign policy emphasis on the need for the United States to adopt "multilateral" approaches and improve relations with its European allies and with the UN.

In fact, as of June 2004, beyond such platitudes, the Kerry campaign had no serious alternative strategy for the war on terrorism or the war in Iraq, and above all had no strategy for appealing to the Muslim world for support. The Democratic inability to criticize Israel lay at the heart of this potentially disastrous failure, not only because of the direct role of U.S. support for Israel on Muslim opinion, but also because the United States' relationship with Israel makes seeking rapprochement with Iran and Syria, two states critical to any stabilization of the situation in Iraq, vastly more difficult. Unusually, the Bush-Sharon agreement was criticized quite widely in the mainstream U.S. press—but in an election year, such criticism obviously had no effect on the calculations of the rival electoral teams.[7]

Since 9/11, U.S. relations with the Muslim world have become central to American strategy and American security. At the time of this writing, the United States actually is ruling one large Muslim country (Iraq) and playing a critical part in the government of a second (Afghanistan). Most important, through Sunni Islamist terrorism, Muslim societies are generating the only truly serious threat of a catastrophic attack on the American mainland. Success or failure in the struggle against this terrorism may be of existential importance for the survival of Western liberal and pluralist democracy: For given certain tendencies observable in the wake of 9/11, it is not difficult to imagine how even worse attacks in future, with or without weapons of mass destruction, could push Western political cultures in a much harsher, more chauvinist and authoritarian direction; in America, away from the Creed and toward its various antitheses.

As repeated polls and surveys have indicated, the Israeli-Palestinian conflict is also central to how Muslims perceive the United States and how Europeans and others view U.S. strategy in the Middle East. Large majorities in every Arab country view the Palestinian issue as "the most" or a "very important" issue facing the Arab world today.[8] According to the Bush administration's most important international ally, British Prime Minister Tony Blair, "There is no other issue with the same power to reunite the world community than progress on the issues of Israel and Palestine," and "This terrorism will not be defeated without peace in the Middle East between Israel and Palestine. Here it is that the poison is incubated. Here it is that the extremist is able to confuse, in the mind of a frighteningly large number of people, the case for a Palestinian state and the destruction of Israel; and to translate this moreover into a battle between East and West; Muslim, Jew and Christian."[9]

The European Union's Security Strategy of December 2003 declares that "resolution of the Arab/Israeli conflict is a strategic priority for Europe. Without this, there will be little chance of dealing successfully with other problems in the Middle East."[10]

Unfortunately, as the UN votes cited above indicate, of all important world issues, this is probably the one on which the United States is most completely isolated from the rest of the international community. Thus this issue has contributed significantly to weakening the U.S. capacity for leadership by persuasion and consent. America's position, and isolation, on this issue has fed the spirit of unilateralist nationalism in the United States and helped draw large sections of the U.S. liberal intelligentsia (not just Jewish Americans, but sympathizers with Israel in general) away from previously held internationalist positions. For if on this critical issue it is believed that America need not and should not listen even when the whole of the international community tells it something, how long can any genuine sense of internationalism, or "decent respect to the opinion of mankind" (in the words of the Declaration of Independence), survive with regard to other issues?

The effort to explain how the United States can be justified in the face of such a unanimous weight of world opinion against it has encouraged a view of the international community in general as irredeemably malignant, anti-Semitic and by extension anti-American. This has fed into much older hatreds and paranoias on the Right in the United States concerning the outside world in general and international institutions in particular. It has contributed to the kind of vicious attitudes to "the world" displayed by people like Charles Krauthammer and Phyllis Schlafly in the passages quoted in the introduction and elsewhere.

In the view of the British scholar and journalist Timothy Garton Ash, the new split between the United States and Western Europe after the unity created by 9/11 began with the escalation of the Israeli-Palestinian conflict in early 2002:

> The Middle East is both a source and a catalyst of what threatens to become a downward spiral of burgeoning European anti-Americanism and nascent American anti-Europeanism, each reinforcing the other. Anti-Semitism in Europe, and its alleged connection to European criticism of the Sharon government, has been the subject of the most acid anti-European commentaries from conservative American columnists and politicians. Some of these critics are themselves not just strongly pro-Israel but also "natural Likudites."...Pro-Palestinian Europeans, infuriated by the way criticism of Sharon is labeled anti-Semitism, talk about the power of a "Jewish lobby" in the United States, which then confirms American Likudites' worst suspicions of European anti-Semitism, and so it goes on, and on.[11]

The Israeli-Palestinian conflict in turn contributes to wider tendencies to U.S. national autism, an inability either to listen to others or to understand their reactions to U.S. behavior. As noted, this is a strange feeling to encounter in a country as powerful, wealthy and open as America. It is, however, very characteristic of small and embattled nations, especially when their populations have in the past been subjected to ferocious massacre and persecution—as in the case of Israel. The aggrieved and embattled sentiments of Israel have spread back to the United States and strengthened already existing tendencies to paranoia, resentment and chauvinism examined earlier.

For this and other reasons, contemporary U.S. policies toward Israel and toward the Middle East in general fit all too well into the thesis-antithesis duality set out in this book, and are perceived to do so by Muslims and Europeans. On one hand, President Bush committed the United States to what he called "a forward strategy of freedom in the Middle East," a strategy solidly rooted in the universalist values of the American Creed: the encouragement of liberty, democracy, free speech, the rule of law and "healthy civic institutions." Although these hopes will doubtless be qualified by the bitter lessons of Iraq, this basic approach seems likely to be followed by succeeding U.S. administrations of whatever party. As Bush said, the commitment to democracy in the Middle East must be "a focus of American policy for decades to come."[12]

On the other hand, the U.S. Congress, and to a very considerable extent successive U.S. administrations, have pursued policies of largely unconditional support for Israel, irrespective of Israeli behavior in the Occupied Territories—behavior often completely incompatible with the ideals which the United States professes and the standards it demands elsewhere. The reasons for this almost unanimous stance by U.S. politicians in support of Israel are rooted partly in genuine identification with that country, as well as in some cases sympathy with Israeli ideologies. Thus the dominant elements of the Bush administration proved especially close to the Likud-led government of Ariel Sharon.[13] There is also, however, a strong element of political calculation, opportunism and indeed fear related to the real or perceived strength of the Israel lobby.

In the words of M. J. Rosenberg of the Israel Policy Forum:

> The fact is that both Democrats and Republicans are very adept at this game and sometimes the sheer effrontery of it is astonishing. Democrats attack a Republican for "selling out" Israel even though the policy advocated by the Republican is the same one they supported when a Democrat advanced it. And Republicans do the exact same thing. Is it any wonder that candidates seem to go to great lengths to avoid saying anything remotely substantive on the Middle East?…Knowing that any substantive statement could be used against them, candidates just play it safe. And segments of the pro-Israel community encourage them by criticizing constructive suggestions as anti-Israel, and by giving ovations to candidates who tell them what the candidates think they want to hear.[14]

The right-wing commentator Robert D. Novak summed up the domestic political factor in American policy very cogently in May 2003, describing

> serious GOP [Republican] efforts to end absolute Democratic domination over the small but important Jewish constituency. The question is whether that constrains President Bush's pursuit of Israeli-Palestinian peace. The private assessment by important Republicans is that it should and that it does…
>
> [Republican leaders]…argue that social and economic liberalism now runs a poor second to support for Israel and that they have for the first time outdone Democrats in cheering the Jewish state. There is no more unyielding supporter of Israeli Prime Minister Ariel Sharon's policies than House Majority Leader Tom DeLay, the exemplar of muscular Republicanism.
>
> But what about Bush's advocacy of the Road Map? He surely had to embrace it to retain Britain in the Iraq War coalition and to keep moderate Arab states friendly. The question is whether he will risk Jewish votes by pressing for Middle East peace.
>
> Republican activists leave no doubt about their views. DeLay has called the Road Map "a confluence of deluded thinking" between European elites, the State Department bureaucracy and American intellectuals. Former House Speaker Newt Gingrich, an intimate adviser of Defense Secretary Donald H. Rumsfeld, called the Road Map "a conspiracy by the State Department and foreign powers to work against U.S. policies."…
>
> This confronts Bush with a classic presidential decision that may forge his place in history. Should he follow Powell's advice that American leadership on creating a Palestinian state is essential for peace in the Middle East? Or should he follow the path urged by his party's leaders to guarantee his reelection?[15]

This Republican strategy can be seen as a continuation of Reagan's strategy of the 1980s in trying to draw away the votes of "Reagan Democrats," comprising mainly "Southern [White] evangelicals, Northern 'blue collar' workers and pro-Zionist Jews."[16] This alignment was based on thoroughly Jacksonian principles of conservative populism at home and aggressive nationalism abroad (although under Reagan, as noted, this nationalism was to some degree more rhetorical than real).

That is not to say that this Republican strategy has necessarily been successful after Reagan left the scene. In general, voting patterns and surveys suggest that when it comes to elections, most Jewish Americans remain true to their liberal traditions, with 51 percent recorded in 2003 as Democrats to only 16 percent Republicans (with 31 percent independents). In the 2000 elections, 79 percent of Jewish Americans voted for Gore to only 19 percent for Bush.[17] The alliance of Jewish American supporters of Israel with Christian fundamentalists often makes Jewish American liberals very uneasy; as the liberal Jewish American writer Roberta Feuerlicht has noted, "In Jewish history, when fundamentalists came, Cossacks were not far behind."[18] No one can say for sure though how Jewish American voters would react to a Democratic administration which took a really tough line with Israel. They certainly punished Carter severely in 1980 for his moves toward dialogue with the Palestine Liberation Organization (PLO).

If Bush had wanted his administration to be taken seriously as a force for peace in the Middle East, he would have had to fire those of his own senior officials who during the 1990s had opposed the Oslo peace process and advised the Israeli government to abandon it.[19] In their policy paper of 1996, "A Clean Break," Richard Perle (later chairman of the Defense Advisory Board in the Bush administration), Douglas Feith (later deputy under-secretary of defense in the Bush administration) and other members of the Project for the New American Century (PNAC) advised the Israeli government of Benjamin Netanyahu to abandon both the Oslo process and the whole idea of land for peace in favor of insistence on permanent control of the Occupied Territories: "Our claim to the land—to which we have clung for hope for 2000 years—is legitimate and noble....Only the unconditional acceptance by Arabs of our rights, *especially* in their territorial dimension, *'peace for peace,'* is a solid basis for the future" (italics in the original).[20]

The paper makes clear that it rules out the "peace for land" idea on which the whole "two-state" solution is based, describing this as "cultural, economic, political, military and diplomatic retreat"; and what it means by "peace for peace" is to go on attacking Arab regimes until they accept Israeli rule over the whole of Palestine. The authors were thereby opposing, in the name of "our" claim to the whole of Palestine, not only the then current policy of the Clinton administration, but that of all previous U.S. administrations and that formally adopted later by the George W. Bush administration of which some of them were to be officials. Elliott Abrams, appointed by Bush in 2003 as chief official for the Middle East at the National Security Council, had also argued—before the collapse of talks in 2000 and the second Intifada—that Oslo should essentially be abandoned in favor of a new crackdown on the Palestinians.[21]

It is true that U.S. policy and the U.S. public discourse concerning the Palestinians have improved greatly since the 1970s, when Washington essentially echoed Israel in declaring that no such separate people existed.[22] A critical moment in this regard was the peace initiative of President Anwar Sadat of Egypt in 1977, when for the first time an American poll showed more Americans approving of an Arab leader's policy than that of the Israeli government, by 57 to 34 percent.[23]

Since the Iraq War, public figures such as Zbigniew Brzezinski and General Anthony Zinni have argued strongly that the new U.S. role in the Middle East demands a serious change of emphasis in dealing with the Israeli-Palestinian conflict. On the other hand, the attacks of 9/11 and the link made between anti-American and anti-Israeli terrorism mean that much of the American political classes and public opinion have once again become strongly anti-Palestinian and are willing to see Israeli actions simply as part of the war on terrorism. As a result of this and the Israeli lobby's iron grip on the U.S. Congress, American support for Israel, including support for its occupation of the Palestinian territories, has continued unchanged—with all that this means for the image of the United States in the Muslim world and for U.S. chances of success in the struggle against Islamist terrorism.

Israel and the American Antithesis

One of the principal arguments made in defense of unconditional U.S. support for Israel over the past generation is rooted in the American Creed: namely, that Israel is a fellow democracy and the "only democracy in the Middle East," and therefore it deserves American support.[24] But as this line becomes more and more difficult to square with Israeli actions—most especially, the occupation of the West Bank and Gaza Strip and the planting of Jewish settlements there—other arguments, which have always been present, may gain greater prominence. These arguments are closely related to the values and beliefs which I have described as forming part of the American antithesis.

Indeed, even the argument that Israel is a "bastion of democracy" is often paired with the spoken or unspoken view, more reminiscent of the nineteenth century, that it is also "an island of Western civilization in a sea of savagery." Indeed, the use of "democracy" in this context sometimes seems more a contemporary version of the nineteenth-century use of the word "civilization" than a reference to actual behavior.[25]

Arguments rooted in the American antithesis were admirably summarized in a speech to the U.S. Senate in March 2002 by Senator James Inhofe (Republican, Oklahoma) setting out seven reasons why "Israel alone is entitled to possess the Holy Land," including the Palestinian territories. These views are widely shared among other members of the Christian Right in Congress. As described earlier, members of the Christian Right make up a significant proportion of senators and congressmen and a very powerful proportion of the Republican Party. Their numbers include both of the last Republican leaders in the House, Dick Armey and Tom DeLay, both of them very strong supporters of Israel. Thus in May 2002 Armey, then House Majority Leader, called during a television interview for the deportation of the Palestinians from the Occupied Territories.[26] Tom DeLay has also expressed unconditional support for Israel, without reference to Palestinian rights.[27]

Democracy was not among the arguments set out by Senator Inhofe; indeed, the only argument compatible with U.S. official public values as currently understood, let alone with the official policies toward the issue of every U.S. administration, was that of "humanitarian concern" for the Jewish survivors of the Holocaust. Instead, the senator set out archaeological and historical arguments proving that the Jewish claim "predates any claims that other peoples in the region may have"— the same arguments so often used by nationalist intellectuals in the Balkans and Caucasus. By contrast, in 1913 "Palestinians were not there." Two of Inhofe's reasons were Realist ones: Israel is a "strategic ally of the United States" and "a roadblock to terrorism."

Other of his arguments concerned civilizational superiority, the idea that Israel took desert land which "nobody really wanted" from its supposedly nomadic native inhabitants and made it bloom. Despite all the years since the conquest of the West, this idea still has great resonance for Americans from the Jacksonian tradition or influenced by it. After all, both this belief and the explicit parallel between the American settlement of the New World and the Israelites' occupation of Canaan go back to the first days of White settlement in North America.[28] In the words of T. R. Fehrenbach concerning the Texan consciousness of Texan history (and remembering that Oklahoma borders Texas and was largely settled from there): "The Texan did not shed his history in the twentieth century; he clung to it. Texas history was taught in Texas schools before the study of the United States began....This Anglo history was shot through with the national myths all such histories have; it had its share of hypocrisy and arrogance. Parts of its mythology made both ethnic Mexicans and Negroes writhe. But in essence, it rang true. *We chose this land; we took it; we made it bear fruit,* the Texan child is taught" (italics in original).[29]

Or in the words of John Wayne: "I don't feel that we did wrong in taking this great country away from them [the Indians]....Our so-called stealing of this country from them was just a matter of survival. There were great numbers of people who needed new land, and the Indians were selfishly trying to keep it for themselves."[30] Leo Strauss, one of the intellectual fathers of the neoconservatives, asserted that "theft of land" has been the basis for *all* states, while arguing that this unpleasant truth should be veiled from the masses.[31]

In this vein, like so many American supporters of Israel over the decades, Inhofe quoted a passage from Mark Twain about his travels through a desolate Palestine: Such long-held views of Palestine's backwardness before the start of Jewish settlement, and therefore the Palestinians' inferiority, hark back directly to nineteenth-century attitudes.[32]

Inhofe's final argument also stems directly from another key strand in the American antithesis. In his words: "This is the most important reason; because God said so. As I said a minute ago, look it up in the book of Genesis. It is right up there on the desk....The Bible says that Abram removed his tent and came and dwelt in the plain of Mamre, which is in Hebron, and built an altar there before the Lord. Hebron is in the West Bank. It is at this place where God appeared to Abram and said 'I am giving you this land'—the West Bank. This is not a political battle at all. It is a contest over whether the word of God is true."[33]

Such an argument not only removes this critical issue from the sphere of nego-tiation; it removes it from any possibility of rational discussion based on univer-sally accepted criteria. This argument in fact rejects the Enlightenment as a basis for political culture and, in doing so, also rejects modern Western civilization. The rejection of the Enlightenment tradition is especially true of the millenarian Chris-tians in the United States, who believe that the restoration of Israeli rule over the entire biblical Kingdom of David is an essential precondition of the Apocalypse. (This belief is a very old one among Protestant fundamentalists, and was shared by Oliver Cromwell.)[34]

As recorded by Donald Wagner, Grace Halsell, Gabriel Almond and other lead-ing students of this tradition, especially sinister are the links between these forces in the United States and the powerful mixture of fundamentalist and ultra-nationalist forces on the Israeli radical Right. The latter share the moral absolutism of their American Christian counterparts without necessarily sharing their commitment to democracy. Such Israelis are of course represented especially strongly among the settlers on the West Bank.

Israeli radical fundamentalists and nationalists are implacably opposed to a state for the Palestinians and in many cases are committed to the most radical of all solutions to the Israeli-Palestinian conflict: the ethnic cleansing ("Transfer") of the Palestinians from the Occupied Territories. According to opinion polls, in 2003 some 46 percent of the Jewish population of Israel in general also believed in this solution, with 33 percent calling for the deportation even of Arab citizens of Israel.[35] In 2003 the possibility of future deportation was raised by a leading Israeli liberal historian, Benny Morris.[36] Such a move would mark a definitive break with "the Democratic West," as this has been defined in recent decades. If America were to support such a move, it would mark a triumph for the forces of the American antithesis over the American Creed.

Ian Lustick has written of this fundamentalist element in Israel—with funda-mentalism defined as "political action to radically transform society according to cosmically ordained imperatives"—as forming "a key element on the Israeli side of the Middle Eastern equation."[37] In 1991 the Israeli scholar Ehud Sprinzak de-scribed how "one of the great successes of the [Israeli] radical right has been its ability to penetrate the Likud and the National Religious Party. Thus, approximately a quarter of the leaders and members of the Likud look at the world today through the ideological and symbolic prism of the radical right. The most outstanding example is cabinet member Ariel Sharon, a person with great charisma and a large following, who thinks and talks like the ideologues of the extreme right."[38]

Or in the simple words of the Reverend Jerry Falwell: "To stand against Israel is to stand against God."[39] Over the past decade, unconditional support for Israel has become increasingly strong on the Republican Right, in tandem with the rise of the Christian Right "from an irrelevant fringe into a centerpiece of the conservative movement." This is a very marked change from the days of Eisenhower and indeed of George Bush Sr.[40] As Inhofe's and Falwell's words indicate, the origins of this belief lie by no means only in the political opportunism analyzed by Novak, but also in profound religious, ideological and cultural identification.

Millenarian author Hal Lindsey produced after 9/11 a book on Arabs and Muslims which repeats the same biblical and pseudohistorical arguments as those of Inhofe. (Lindsey quotes extensively from a work by the pseudoacademic Arabophobe Joan Peters purporting to "prove" that Arabs actually immigrated to Palestine in the nineteenth century.) Lindsey adds a strong element of hatred and contempt for Islam and for "the nature and genetic characteristics of Ishmael and his descendants, the Arabs." These he identifies with "the donkeys of the wilderness" mentioned by God in the Book of Job—in other words, rootless nomads with no attachment to place. He speaks of hate as a Muslim "religious doctrine."[41] A symposium of the Christian Coalition on Islam in Washington on February 15, 2003, which I attended (the historian and leading Israeli partisan Daniel Pipes was among the speakers) was a phantasmagoria of hatred. One speaker declared that the reason why there would always be conflict between Christians and Muslims was that Muslims denied the truth of the Resurrection. The Christian Rightist journalist and polemicist Don Feder said that "Islam is not a religion of peace. It is a religion which, throughout its 1,400-year history, has lent itself well to fanaticism, terrorism, mass murder, oppression and conversion by the sword."[42]

Of course, such views represent a distinctly minority opinion in the United States as a whole concerning the Israeli-Palestinian issue. But the rise of the Christian Right within the Republican Party means that on this wing of U.S. politics, these views are becoming more and more significant. The Israeli fundamentalist Right is developing a closer relationship even with more moderate sections of the Christian Right in the United States.[43] Indeed, it would seem that from the mid-1990s, Likud governments have come to rely more on the Christian Right than on "unreliable" liberal Jewish Americans in their attempts to mobilize support in the United States for its policies.[44] Thus the *Washington Times* reported a series of visits to the United States by the Israeli tourism minister in 2003:

> Israeli tourism minister Benyamin Elon has embarked on a "Bible Belt tour" to exploit evangelical Christian enthusiasm for Israel, to lure Christian tour-

ists back to Israel and to derail President Bush's "road map" to Middle East peace.…"We either have to oppose the road map or oppose the Bible," says Mike Evans, founder of the Jerusalem Prayer Team, a coalition of 1,700 churches. "Evangelicals have no debate on this issue."… Thus Mr. Elon is averaging one trip per month to make Israeli views known in states where the Jewish state sees a receptive audience. "The Bible Belt is a very important target for Israel," he says, adding that Israel is raising its annual tourism budget for North America from $1.1 million to $3 million.

"We wish to thank those who have not abandoned us," he says. "In the past three years, those who have come were Jews—out of solidarity—and evangelical Christians. They are saying to Arafat: 'You cannot force us to change our way of life to uproot Israel from the Holy Land.'" [sic]

He opposes a Palestinian state on the West Bank and suggests Palestinians either relocate to Jordan or live under Israeli sovereignty.[45]

The importance of the "Christian Zionists" to the Bush administration was underlined by an episode at the White House on March 25, 2004. Leading members of the Apostolic Congress, a pro-Israel group affiliated with the United Pentecostal Church, received an off-the-record briefing (later leaked to the press) from Elliott Abrams, the Near East and North Africa director at the National Security Council, and other administration officials.

The Apostolic Congress had bitterly opposed the Bush administration's own "Road Map" for peace between Israel and the Palestinians, because of the Road Map's support for the idea of Palestinian statehood and at least partial Israeli withdrawal from the West Bank ("Judea and Samaria"). Abrams sought to assuage their concerns about the U.S.-backed Israeli plan for withdrawal from the Gaza Strip by telling them that unlike the West Bank, "the Gaza Strip had no significant Biblical influence such as Joseph's tomb or Rachel's tomb and therefore is a piece of land that can be sacrificed for the cause of peace." In other words, to please this lobby—and doubtless from his own convictions—a senior U.S. official was essentially briefing against his own administration's declared policy of supporting Israeli withdrawal from large parts of the West Bank.[46]

In almost any other truly vital area of U.S. international policy, such views would have few consequences for policy.[47] But in the case of Israel, a variety of factors have made such marginalization impossible. These factors include the depth of American historical and cultural sympathy for Israel, the power of the Israeli lobby and the particular limitations on the discussion of Israel in the political arena and mass media.

Together these factions have made it impossible for liberal or Realist forces in the United States—including sections of Jewish America—to isolate and overcome such ideas politically, however much they may argue against them in parts of the educated media.[48] It is not that the extremist ideas held by Inhofe, DeLay and others are shared by anything resembling a majority of Americans; rather, in the case of Israel, both the Democratic Party and the liberal intelligentsia have been disabled from presenting strong and coherent opposition to these ideas; whether by sincere identification with Israel or by fear of being attacked by the Israeli lobby. As a result, there is in effect no real political alternative or opposition in the United States concerning the Israeli-Palestinian conflict and U.S. policies toward it.

Over the past four decades U.S. policy has in consequence become bogged down in a glaring contradiction between American public ideals and partially U.S.-financed Israeli behavior. On one hand, America preaches to Arabs contemporary civic ideals of democracy, modernity and the peaceful resolution of disputes. On the other, it subsidizes not only a brutal military occupation but the seizure of land from an established population on the basis of ethnoreligious claims which in any other circumstances would be regarded by U.S. governments and a majority of public opinion as utterly illegitimate.[49]

The most truly tragic aspect of all this, as more and more Israelis and Jewish Americans have begun to argue, is that this kind of unconditional U.S. support, coupled with continued Israeli occupation of Palestinian territory, is also proving disastrous for Israel itself and for the noble ideals which motivated the best elements in the Zionist enterprise. These critics include not just liberals, but senior retired military and security officials, such as the four former directors of the Shin Bet domestic security service who in November 2003 warned the Sharon government that if Israel does not withdraw from the West Bank and Gaza Strip, Israel's very existence will ultimately be endangered. They also said that this withdrawal is necessary even if it leads to a clash with Jewish settlers. According to one of the four, Avraham Shalom, "We must once and for all admit that there is another side, that it has feelings and is suffering, and that we are behaving disgracefully....We have turned into a people of petty fighters using the wrong tools."[50]

In the words of former Knesset Speaker Avraham Burg:

> The Zionist revolution has always rested on two pillars: a just path and an ethical leadership. Neither of these is operative any longer. The Israeli nation today rests on a scaffolding of corruption, and on foundations of oppression and injustice. As such, the end of the Zionist enterprise is already on our doorstep. There is a real chance that ours will be the last Zionist generation. There may yet be a Jewish state in the Middle East, but it will be a different sort, strange and ugly....
>
> We cannot keep a Palestinian majority under an Israeli boot and at the same time think ourselves the only democracy in the Middle East. There cannot be democracy without equal rights for all who live here, Arab as well as Jew. We cannot keep the territories and preserve a Jewish majority in the world's only Jewish state—not by means that are humane and moral and Jewish....
>
> Do you want the greater Land of Israel? No problem. Abandon democracy. Let's institute an efficient system of racial separation here, with prison camps and detention villages. Qalqilya Ghetto and Gulag Jenin....

Do you want democracy? No problem. Either abandon the greater Land of Israel, to the last settlement and outpost, or give full citizenship and voting rights to everyone, including Arabs. The result, of course, will be that those who did not want a Palestinian state alongside us will have one in our midst, via the ballot box.

Israel's friends abroad—Jewish and non-Jewish alike, presidents and prime ministers, rabbis and lay people—should choose as well. They must reach out and help Israel to navigate the road map toward our national destiny as a light unto the nations and a society of peace, justice and equality.[51]

The Israeli lobby in the United States is well aware that the settlements—which have been condemned in principle by successive U.S. administrations—are by far the weakest element in its entire argument. Determined attempts have been made to distract attention from this issue, described in one advisory paper as "our Achilles heel" in terms of wooing U.S. public support.[52]

Because of the way in which America and Israel are entwined spiritually, politically and socially, and because so many people in the world treat the Israeli-U.S. relationship as a litmus test of U.S. behavior, the choices that Israel makes will have very grave implications not only for the security of the United States and its Western allies, such as Britain, and for America's role in the world, but also perhaps for the political culture of the United States itself.[53]

From an American point of view, Israel cannot be compared with Russia, China, or other authoritarian states which have waged crueler wars against national secessionist movements. The Israeli lobby makes this comparison repeatedly in an effort to prove that demands for U.S. pressure on Israel are hypocritical and/or anti-Semitic, because the authors of these demands do not ask that the United States apply similar pressure to states like Russia or China.

This argument, however, fails in both ethical and realist terms. Most U.S. and European critics of the U.S. relationship with Israel are not asking that the United States impose trade sanctions against Israel or expel it from international bodies, but only that the United States use its aid and support as a powerful lever to influence Israeli behavior: For most other states do not receive massive subsidies, military support and diplomatic protection from the United States. Israel as of 2004 receives more than a quarter of the entire U.S. aid budget (excluding that for the reconstruction of Iraq).

The figure for U.S. aid to Israel in 2002 was around six times that to the entire desperately impoverished continent of Africa and ten times the proposed U.S. share of aid for the reconstruction of liberated Afghanistan—the latter being both a U.S. moral imperative and supposedly a vital U.S. strategic interest.[54] This radical imbalance clearly makes Israel a special case. It makes the United States morally complicit in Israel's crimes, not only in the eyes of the world but in reality; and it gives Americans both the right and the duty to put pressure on Israel to end the occupation of the Palestinian territories.

The U.S. need to bring about an end to the Israeli-Palestinian conflict is also dictated on purely Realist grounds, especially in the context of the war on terrorism. Israeli strategies and tactics in that conflict, and U.S. support for Israel, are central to how a large majority of Muslims view the United States and U.S. policies in the Muslim world. This fact has been attested to by an almost endless procession of opinion polls and media reports, including surveys by the U.S. State Department, and it is not or should not be open to serious question.[55]

This combination of factors also critically affects how Europeans view U.S. strategy in the region and contributes enormously to European doubts about the wisdom or even sanity of American leadership. The refusal among many Americans to recognize this, and the vilification of European motives for unease at Israel's behavior also help to drive a deeper wedge between the United States and Europe. Thus in the debate in Europe in 2003–04 on Bush's plan for developing the Middle East, the role of Israel and unconditional U.S. support for Israel featured prominently as reasons for skepticism. This factor was barely mentioned in many U.S. reports and analyses of the difficulties regarding the issue between the United States and Europe—leaving the impression that European resistance was motivated chiefly by "petulance" or "anti-Americanism."[56]

The "Love Affair"

The widespread failure in the United States to address these issues has become especially striking and especially dangerous since 9/11 emphasized with dreadful force the threat to the United States and the West from terrorist groups based within Muslim societies. For to most outside observers, including ones in countries and governments closely allied with the United States, it is apparent—as implied by Tony Blair in the remark quoted earlier in this chapter—that Israel has ceased to be the "vital strategic ally" of the United States that it was during the Cold War.[57] It has become instead a very serious strategic liability to the United States and its allies in their effort to fight Islamist and Arab nationalist terrorism.

This is indeed demonstrated by Israel's role, or rather nonrole, in the Iraq wars of 1991 and 2003, in which Israeli forces did not participate. Of course they were begged by Washington not to participate, so as not to infuriate the Arab world and risk disastrously spreading these conflicts. Strategic allies are supposed to come into their own when there is a conflict in their region. It is a funny kind of ally which has to be asked to go away and keep quiet so as not to cause vastly increased trouble. Before 1991 the major U.S. military intervention in the Middle East was that in Lebanon in 1983—a debacle made necessary by Israel's earlier invasion of that country. This intervention led to hundreds of unnecessary American deaths and increased hostility to America in the region, while bringing the United States no strategic or political gain whatsoever. The terms of the U.S.-Israeli alliance are

not a case of the tail wagging the dog; they represent the tail whirling the unfortunate dog around the room and banging its head against the ceiling.

Under the Bush administration, U.S. world policy, as defined by Donald Rumsfeld, became that "the mission defines the alliance:" The United States will decide
its goals and then put together as many allies as possible in support of those goals.[58]
This principle has become very obviously the case in U.S. relations with Europe
and even NATO, for example. The one area where America's alliance continues
absolutely to define America's mission, to the extent that the mission itself has
almost vanished from view, is in the U.S. alliance with Israel.

The nature of this alliance is a matter of concern not only to the United States
but to any U.S. ally in the war on terrorism. If one thing must be apparent to all
but the most prejudiced observers, it is that this war cannot be won—cannot even
be waged—without strong support from Muslims. Even if the United States suc-
ceeds somehow in extricating itself from Iraq, it is extremely doubtful that thereafter it could successfully occupy even one more Muslim country, let alone the
entire Muslim world. The United States can, of course, try to retire behind protec-
tive walls. If, however, these walls become indefinitely higher and higher, sooner
or later they will begin to undermine the U.S. and world economies and America's
cultural and political prestige in the world, and therefore the vital underpinnings
of U.S. hegemony. The impact of Israeli behavior on the sentiments of Muslim
societies is therefore of critical importance not just to the war on terrorism but to
American power and America's success as a civilizational empire.

In the context of either a realist or an ethical international tradition, there is
nothing wrong in a U.S. commitment to Israel based on a sense of cultural and
ethnic kinship, nor in U.S. willingness to make geopolitical sacrifices for the sake
of defending Israel. This, after all, was the position of Britain vis-à-vis its former
White colonies long after they had become politically independent, and even when
some had ceased to be real strategic assets.[59]

In the case of Israel's role in the U.S.-Israel alliance, alas, a darker historical parallel suggests itself. If anything, the alliance is beginning to take on some of the same
mutually calamitous aspects as Russia's commitment to Serbia in 1914, a great power
guarantee which encouraged parts of the Serbian leadership to behave with criminal irresponsibility in their encouragement of irredentist claims against Austria, leading to a war which was ruinous for Russia, Serbia and the world.[60]

One might almost say that as a result of the way in which the terms of the
Israeli-U.S. alliance have become set, Israel and the United States have changed
places. The United States, which should feel protected both by the oceans and by
matchless military superiority, is cast instead in the role of an endangered Middle
Eastern state which is under severe threat from terrorism and which also believes
itself to be in mortal danger from countries with a tiny fraction of its power. Meanwhile, thanks largely to support from the United States, Israel has become a kind
of superpower, able to defy its entire region and Europe as well. This situation is
bad not only for the United States; it is terribly bad for Israel itself, for reasons

which will be set out later. For Israel is *not* a superpower. It is rich and powerful, but it is still a small Middle Eastern country which will have to seek accommodations with its neighbors if it is ever to live in peace. Blind and largely unconditional U.S. support has enabled Israeli governments to avoid facing this fact, with consequences which prove utterly disastrous for Israel itself in the long run.

As in the case of Serbia and powerful Pan-Slavist sections of pre-1914 Russian public and official opinion, so in the case of Israel important sections of U.S. opinion (by no means only Jewish) have over the past half century come to view the United States and Israel as almost one country, so tightly identified with each other as to transcend America's own identity and interests. They genuinely believe in an "identity of interests between the Jewish state and the United States."[61] The relationship has been described as a "love affair." In the words of Jerry Brown (former Democratic governor of California), "I love Israel. If you would show me a map and ask me to identify Israel, I probably wouldn't find it. But Israel is in my heart."[62]

The roots of this love affair long precede the foundation not only of Israel but of the United States itself and lie ultimately in the Old Testament–centered religion of the American Protestant tradition. The acknowledgment (conscious or subconscious) of Israel as a chosen nation was closely related to the long tradition in American thought examined in Chapter 2, and dating back to the first settlers, which also identifies America as God's New Israel. In the words of a sermon by the Reverend Abiel Abbot in 1799: "It has often been remarked that the people of the United States come nearer to a parallel with Ancient Israel, than any other nation upon the globe. Hence *Our American Israel* is a term frequently used; and common consent allows it apt and proper."[63]

This affinity has continued down the generations, and must be set against the former tradition of snobbish WASP anti-Semitism (directed mainly against the East European Jewish immigrants who arrived in the United States from the 1880s on, rather than the longer-established Germans and Sephardim). To it was added a strong liberal identification with the Western democratic culture of Israel's founding generation.[64]

Less openly acknowledged, but immensely important, has been a "Jacksonian" respect for Israel's tough, militarist society and its repeated victories in war, and for the military achievements and the macho personal style of Israeli soldiers turned politicians, such as Ariel Sharon. This factor became especially important after 1967, when Israel's crushing victory over superior odds in a morally justified war of self-defense provided a measure of psychological compensation for America's own defeat in Vietnam.

There is, however, a darker side to this identification, recalled by T. R. Fehrenbach's words on Texan memory. The conquest of land from savage enemy peoples remains central to most of the history of White North America. Gordon Welty among others sees a strong affinity between the "muscular theology" of the Israeli fundamentalist Right and that of the American pioneer tradition: "Since the 'frontier' of America is gone, they seek to recreate it elsewhere."[65] This tradition is reflected in Donald Rumsfeld's notorious remark of 2002 concerning the Jewish settlements on the West Bank: "Focusing on settlements at the present time misses the point....Settlements in various parts of the so-called occupied area...were the result of a war, which they [the Israelis] won."[66]

The circumstances of the Israeli-Palestinian conflict since the 1930s, and the creation of Jewish settlements in the Occupied Territories since 1967, have also created a parallel between the situation of Israel and that of the American Indian frontier. In such cases, soldiers and civilians are mixed up together and fight, and the distinction between them often becomes blurred. Media attention has been focused on terrorism by Palestinians, but this activity takes place against a backdrop of continual low-level civilian violence on both sides: stone throwing and other attacks on settlers by Palestinian youths, vigilante-style behavior by the settlers.[67]

Thus the Israeli writer and commentator Amos Elon described Meir Har-Zion, the famous paratrooper who combined his official military service in the 1950s with private freelance raids and reprisals against the Arabs: "Unsparing of himself and others, he was brutally indiscriminate in inflicting punishment upon his adversaries. He began to personify an Israeli version of the Indian Fighters in the American Wild West. Laconically killing Arab soldiers, peasants and townspeople in a kind of fury without hatred, he remained cold-blooded and thoroughly efficient, simply doing a job and doing it well."[68]

Of course, in this case as in that of the Indian Frontier, to recall the ferocity of the Israeli fighters does not involve in any way an attempt to gloss over the barbarity of their Palestinian and Arab opponents. Yet by its settlement policy, Israel has passed up the chance to end the conditions exacerbating the conflict, as have the Palestinian groups through their continued pursuit of terrorism.

Israel's development since 1967 into what the former Deputy Mayor of Jerusalem and Israeli commentator Meron Benvenisti has called a Herrenvolk democracy, with power and status held by a ruling ethnicity, corresponded to a core part of the Jacksonian ethos in the United States, at least until the 1960s.[69] Such beliefs formed a strong subtext to works such as Leon Uris's fantastically popular novel *Exodus* (20 million copies sold by the 1990s, placing it in the same top category of success as the millenarian novels of Hal Lindsey and Tim LaHaye) and the film based on it.[70]

This identification with Israel would not matter much to U.S. and Western security, except that over the same period the wider Arab (and to a lesser extent Muslim) worlds have come equally to identify with the Palestinians in their struggle with the Israelis. The United States has a separate hegemonic agenda in the region, focused on control of access to oil, the deterrence or removal of hostile states, and the attempt to develop states and societies so as to ward off state failure, anti-Western revolution or both. This task would be difficult enough in itself, but it is made immeasurably more difficult by the embroilment of the United States in an essentially national conflict with the Palestinians and their Arab backers.

As a result of a combination of Israel and oil, the United States finds itself pinned to a conflict-ridden and bitterly anti-American region in a way without precedent in its history. In all other regions of the world, the United States has been able either to help stabilize regional situations in a way which broadly conforms to its interests (Europe, Northeast Asia, Central America), or, if regional hostility is too great and the security situation too intractable, to withdraw (as from Mexico in 1917 and Indochina in the early 1970s).

If the result of U.S. entanglement in the Middle East is also unprecedented embroilment in a series of conflicts, then this is likely to severely damage not only U.S. global leadership, but the character of U.S. nationalism and even perhaps of U.S. democracy. Prolonged war may bitterly divide American society and create severe problems for public order, as it did during the Vietnam War; and it also may help push the U.S. government in the direction of secretive, paranoid, authoritarian and illegal behavior.

America's regional position is not only worsened by the increased hostility which support for Israel arouses among Muslims and in the former colonial world in general. Equally important perhaps is that the violent nationalist passions which this conflict has engendered within U.S. society have made it much more difficult for America to think clearly about its strategy in the Middle East and its relations with a range of countries around the world. As with Pan-Slavism's role in Russian nationalism before 1914, the nature of the identification with Israel has become an integral part of the entire U.S. nationalist mixture and has helped influence U.S. nationalism toward more radical and chauvinist positions.

Once again, this is not to criticize the principle of American identification with and support for Israel, which is in itself entirely legitimate, just as it is in the case of Armenia, Poland, or other countries with which large numbers of Americans retain close ethnic ties.[71] It is a combination of the unconditional terms of this commitment with Israeli policies which are so dangerous.[72] To compare this issue with the role of other ethnic lobbies: partly as a result of the influence of the Polish lobby; the United States strongly supported the accession of Poland and other Central European countries to NATO and the European Union. A condition of these accessions was, however, that the countries concerned should be fully democratic, should give fair and equal treatment to their ethnic minorities, and should have no unresolved territorial disputes with their neighbors.

To put it more concretely: the United States should be committed to support and defend Israel only within its 1967 borders. As a senior retired U.S. diplomat put it to me in 2003, the present situation by contrast is rather as if during the Cold War, the United States had committed itself to defend a West Germany whose political and ethnic borders with Eastern Europe were both open and violent—which would have been a recipe for geopolitical disaster.

A Tragic Imperative

The above propositions would be assented to by the overwhelming majority of the educated populations of Britain and America's other key allies in the world, and indeed by the great majority of people in the world who observe the Israeli-Palestinian conflict. They are very difficult to refute from the standpoint of the American Creed, at least as the Creed has been defined during the decades since World War II.

It may well be the difficulty of defending their position within the scope of basic liberal principles that explains in part the hysteria among Israeli partisans which too often surrounds—and suppresses—attempts at frank discussion of these issues in America, and which is one of the most worrying aspects of the U.S. foreign policy scene. Of course, the principal reason for this atmosphere is the appalling crime and the terrible memory of the Holocaust, and the effects of this memory in deterring criticism of Israel and creating a belief in the legitimacy of Israeli demands for absolute security. The image of the Holocaust has been used deliberately by the Israeli lobby to consolidate support for Israel in the United States and elsewhere; but it also emerges quite naturally and spontaneously from Jewish and Jewish American consciousness, and indeed that of any civilized and honorable citizen of the West.

However, whatever the natural, legitimate and understandable roots of unconditional loyalty to Israel, its effects often resemble wider patterns of nationalism in the world. One of the saddest experiences of visits to countries undergoing national disputes and heightened moods of nationalism is to meet with highly intelligent, civilized and moderate individuals whose capacity for reason and moderation vanishes as soon as the conversation touches on conflicts involving their own nation or ethnicity. Otherwise universally accepted standards of behavior, argument and evidence are suspended; facts are conjured from thin air; critics are demonized; wild accusations are leveled; and rational argument becomes impossible.

I observed this as a journalist in the southern Caucasus in the run-up to the wars there in the early 1990s and more than a decade earlier when visiting the then Yugoslavia as a student. It was therefore with dismay that I found exactly the same pattern repeating itself at dinner parties in Washington as soon as the conversation touched on the Israeli-Palestinian conflict. Also immensely sad and troubling is to see ethical principles and intellectual standards crumble at the touch of national allegiance among scholars and thinkers whose work you deeply admire.

Any condemnation of the pro-Israeli liberal intelligentsia in the United States, both Jewish and non-Jewish, must be tempered not only by the terrible impact of the Holocaust but by an awareness of the extremely difficult ideological and ethical position in which they have found themselves since 1945, a position which is nothing short of a tragic dilemma. This dilemma stems from the fact that for equally valid and legitimate reasons, Western Europe and parts of the liberal intelligentsia of the United States on one hand and the greater part of the world's

191

Jewish population on the other drew opposing conclusions from the catastrophe of Nazism. And this split ran straight through the individual consciousnesses of most of the Jewish diaspora intelligentsia. This is not an enviable situation to be in.

The Western European elites and many U.S. liberal intellectuals essentially decided that the correct response to Nazism and to the hideous national conflicts which preceded, engendered and accompanied it was to seek to limit, transcend and overcome nationalism. Hence the creation of common European institutions leading to the European Union and the great respect paid in Europe, and by many liberal Americans, to the United Nations and to developing institutions of international law and cooperation. Given the strong past connections between chauvinist nationalism and anti-Semitism (even to a degree in the United States) and the role of nationalism in Fascism, most of the Jewish diaspora intelligentsia naturally also identified with these attempts to overcome nationalism around the world.

However, given the failure of the Western world (including the United States) in the 1930s and 1940s to prevent genocide, or even—shamefully—to offer refuge to Jews fleeing the Nazis, it is entirely natural that a great many Jews decided that guarantees from the international community were not remotely sufficient to protect them against further attempts at massacre. They felt that, in addition, a Jewish national state was required, backed by a strong Jewish nationalism. This nationalism embodied strong and genuine elements of national liberation and social progressivism, akin to those of other oppressed peoples in the world, and it was from this that Zionism drew its powerful elements of moral nobility, as represented by such figures as Ahad Ha'am, Martin Buber and Nahum Goldmann.[73]

Israel also developed a central importance for Jewish diaspora communities because of the decline of religious belief and practice, of ethnic traditions and of the Yiddish language concurrent with the steep rise of intermarriage. Due to these trends, these communities fear that they themselves may be in the process of dissolution.[74] Judaism had always been what the German Jewish nineteenth-century poet Heinrich Heine called "the portable Fatherland of the Jews"; its eclipse threatened a form of soft extinction, unless a substitute could be found.[75]

Jacques Torczyner of the Zionist Organization of America declared during the Carter administration that "whatever the administration will want to do…the Jews in America will fight for Israel. It is the only thing we have to sustain our Jewish identity."[76] Or according to religious historian Martin Marty: "As other bases of Jewish identity continued to dwindle…Israel progressively became the spiritual center of the American Jewish experience."[77]

But although the bases for this sacralization of the nation were specifically, and tragically, Jewish, the advancement of nationalism as a substitute for fading religion and the transmogrification of religious passions into nationalist ones also form part of a wider pattern in nationalist history, one which in the past has contributed to national and international catastrophes: "Our most blooming life for Thy most withered tree, Germany!"[78]

Unlike most other national senses of martyrdom, the Jewish sense was truly justified—unlike that of France after 1871 or Germany after 1918. But that fact has not saved many Jews from the pernicious results of such a sense of martyrdom in terms of nationalist extremism and self-justification—any more than it has the Armenians, for example. It has produced an atmosphere which has shaded into and tolerated the religious-nationalist fundamentalism of Israeli extremist groups and of ideological settlers in the Occupied Territories, as well as crude hatred of Arabs and Muslims.[79]

Furthermore, while Zionism of course originated in the late nineteenth century and is a classic example of the modern "construction" of a nation, the Jewish ethnoreligious basis on which it originated represents the oldest and deepest "primordial" national identity in the world. As demonstrated by a series of clashes within Israel over the definition of who is a Jew, who can become a Jew and who has the right to decide these questions, this identity is a basis for nationalism which if not necessarily completely antithetical to notions of civic nationalism based on the American Creed, certainly has a complex and uneasy relationship to them; and this too is perceived by Muslim peoples to whom the United States wishes to spread its version of civic nationalism.

An appeal to religious and quasi-religious nationalist justifications for rule over Palestine was also implicit in the entire Zionist enterprise. Given the large majority of Palestinian Arabs throughout Palestine—even at the moment of the declaration of Israeli statehood in 1948—the claim to create a Jewish state in Palestine could not easily be justified on grounds of national liberation alone. It needed also to be backed by appeals to ancient ethnic claims and religious scripts and by civilizational arguments of superiority to the backward Arabs and "making the desert bloom." These appeals could not be readily assented to by other peoples around the world, and indeed they made even many Western liberals think uneasily of their own nationalist and imperialist pasts. [80]

Following one original strand of Zionism, great Zionist leaders and thinkers such as Nahum Goldmann originally dreamed that Israel, like other civilized states, would also be anchored in international institutions and might even form part of a multiethnic federation with the Arab states of the Middle East, thereby resolving the dilemma in which Jewish diaspora liberalism found itself.[81]

Tragically, the circumstances in which Israel was created made any such resolution of the Jewish intellectual and moral dilemma exceptionally difficult, and would have done so for any group in this position. The intention here is not to condemn or vilify, simply to point out the nature of the dilemma and the sad and dangerous consequences that have stemmed from it.

Amos Oz has written of the Israeli-Palestinian conflict:

> Zionism is a movement of national liberation, which has no need of any "consent" or "agreement" from the Arabs. But it must recognize that the conflict between us and the Palestinians is not a cheap Western in which civilized "goodies" are fighting against native "baddies." It is more like a Greek tragedy. It represents a clash between two conflicting rights. The Palestinian Arabs have a

strong and legitimate claim, and the Israelis must recognize this, without this recognition leading us into self-denial or feelings of guilt. We are bound to accept a painful compromise, and admit that the land of Israel is the homeland of two nations, and we must accept its partition in one form or another.[82]

It cannot be emphasized too strongly that if the Palestinian Arabs in the 1930s and 1940s had agreed that a large part of Palestine—where they were still a large majority and had until recently been an overwhelming one—should be given up to form the state of Israel, they would have been acting in a way which, as far as I am aware, would have had no precedent in all of human history. It is not as if intelligent and objective observers did not point this fact out at the time. As Hannah Arendt wrote in 1945, three years before Israeli independence, the war with the Arabs and the expulsion of the Palestinians:

> American Zionists from left to right adopted unanimously, at their last an-
> nual convention held in Atlantic City in October 1944, the demand for a
> "free and democratic Jewish commonwealth...[which] shall embrace the
> whole of Palestine, undivided and undiminished." The Atlantic City Resolu-
> tion goes even a step further than the Biltmore Program (1942) in which the
> Jewish minority had granted minority rights to the Arab majority. This time
> the Arabs were simply not mentioned in the resolution, which obviously leaves
> them the choice between voluntary emigration or second-class citizenship. It
> seems to admit that only opportunist reasons had previously prevented the
> Zionist movement from stating its final aims. These aims now seem to be
> completely identical with those of the extremists as far as the future political
> constitution of Palestine is concerned....By stating it with such bluntness in
> what seemed to them an appropriate moment, Zionists have forfeited for a
> long time any chance of *pourparlers* with Arabs; for whatever Zionists may
> offer, they will not be trusted.[83]

Throughout history, only rarely were even the great assimilating religious-national movements and empires able to incorporate new peoples without some violence; and—despite the dreams of Herzl and others concerning a multiethnic Jewish state—Zionism is very explicitly *not* a force for the assimilation of non-Jews.

In other words, however one might condemn the Palestinians and Arabs for their long delay in coming to terms with the reality of Israel, to blame them for initially resisting that reality is to engage in moral and historical idiocy. While condemning the Arabs as demons, it suggests that they should have acted as saints. The tragedy of 1948 is not only that of a clash of valid rights, but also that neither side in the conflict could have acted otherwise. Years later former Israeli Foreign Minister Abba Eban (1905–2002) said just as much: "The Palestine Arabs, were it not for the Balfour Declaration and the League of Nations Mandate, could have counted on eventual independence either as a separate state or in an Arab context acceptable to them....It was impossible for us to avoid struggling for Jewish statehood and equally impossible for them to grant us what we asked. If they had submitted to Zionism with docility, they would have been the first people in history to have voluntarily renounced their majority status."[84]

Thus it is surprising that self-styled Western liberals, scholars and intellectuals among Israel's partisans go on using the Palestinian rejection of partition in 1948 as a form of permanently damning original sin. The reasons why most Americans have had such difficulty recognizing this fact, however, go beyond the desire to support Israel and edit out anything which might qualify that support or give any ammunition to its enemies. They are also related to features of American culture well summed up by T. R. Fehrenbach concerning the deep unwillingness of Americans to look seriously at the fate of the Native Americans: "The culmination of the Indian wars was a tragedy, with all the classic inevitability of tragedy, and against true tragedy the North American soul revolts."[85]

Thus to his great credit, Saul Bellow in the 1970s joined Walter Laqueur, Leonard Bernstein and other leading Jewish American cultural and intellectual figures in publicly opposing the establishment of settlements in the Occupied Territories. (Then Senator Abraham Ribicoff took the same line.)[86] In his memoir *To Jerusalem and Back*, Bellow acknowledged that "a sweeping denial of Arab grievances is an obstacle to peace." At the same time, he agrees with Laqueur as saying of the Zionists that in seeking to establish a state, "Their sin was that they behaved like other peoples. Nation states have never come into existence peacefully and without injustices." [87]

Yet these writers did not follow up with the obvious corollary, which is that the Palestinians too "behaved like other peoples" in fighting to hold on to their ancestral land where they were a large majority. Even Norman Mailer, while strongly criticizing current Israeli policies, has suggested that the Palestinians are at fault for not having welcomed Jewish refugees in the 1940s.

Instead, self-described liberals like Alan Dershowitz, professor of law at Harvard University, have explicitly used arguments of collective Arab and Palestinian guilt as a justification. This is not only false historically but is also incompatible with contemporary liberal values, and feeds into American chauvinism toward Muslims and Arabs. According to Dershowitz, "The Arabs bore sufficient guilt for the Holocaust and for supporting the wrong side during World War II to justify their contribution, as part of the losing side, in the rearrangement of territory and demography that inevitably follows a cataclysmic world conflict."[88]

Saul Bellow, in the passage cited earlier, immediately slips into familiar tropes about Arab hostility to Israel being akin to German cruelty toward the Jews, both of them reflecting a kind of "insanity," and ends on a plangent note which simply sweeps away concrete issues of Israeli behavior and Palestinian suffering: "Israel must reckon with the world, and with the madness of the world, and to a most grotesque extent. And all because the Israelis wished to lead Jewish lives in a Jewish state." Such statements, which in one form or another I have heard repeated again and again in conversations in America, laid the foundations for a view of "the world" itself as the mad and evil enemy of Israel and the United States.

By contrast, Israeli Prime Minister David Ben-Gurion himself is reported (by Nahum Goldmann) to have asked in private, "Why should the Arabs make peace? If I were an Arab leader I would never make terms with Israel. That is natural: we have taken their country. Sure, God promised it to us, but what does that matter to them? Our God is not theirs. We came from Israel, it's true, but two thousand years ago, and what is that to them? There has been anti-Semitism, the Nazis, Hitler, Auschwitz, but was that their fault? They only see one thing: we have come here and stolen their country. Why should they accept that?"[89]

Together with the establishment of the Jewish state came the war of 1948 and the expulsion of most of the Arab population of Palestine from the territories of the new Jewish state. So intolerable to the liberal conscience was this action, and so deeply did it seem to call into question the legitimacy of the new state, that for two generations it had to be denied, with absurd arguments being advanced instead—in the face of logic and both Palestinian and Jewish testimony—that the Palestinians had somehow fled voluntarily on the orders of the Arab governments and their own leaders. Indeed, some leading Israeli partisans in the United States are in essence still arguing this.[90]

For my own part, although I deeply regret the human suffering caused by the expulsions of 1948, I have never been especially shocked by them—if only because the facts were largely available, from Israeli sources quoted in various books, long before Israeli revisionist historians "revealed" from the late 1980s on that the expulsion of the Palestinians was in large part a process deliberately planned by the Israeli leadership and accompanied by numerous atrocities.[91] And with regret— and without in any way endorsing the infamous collective guilt argument advanced by Dershowitz and others—I must on the whole accept Benny Morris's recent arguments that this cruel process was necessary if the state of Israel was to be established and its Jewish population to avoid renewed extermination or exile: "Ben-Gurion was a transferist. He understood that there could be no Jewish state with a large and hostile Arab minority in its midst. There would be no such state. It would not be able to exist....Ben-Gurion was right. If he had not done what he did, a state would not have come into being. That has to be clear. It is impossible to evade it. Without the uprooting of the Palestinians, a Jewish state would not have arisen here....There are circumstances in history that justify ethnic cleansing. I know that this term is completely negative in the discourse of the twenty-first century, but when the choice is between ethnic cleansing and genocide—the annihilation of your people—I prefer ethnic cleansing."[92]

This was after all the 1940s. At the end of World War II, some 12 million Germans were expelled from eastern Germany when these lands were annexed to Poland and Russia, and 3 million from Czechoslovakia, amid immense suffering, atrocity and loss of life. Hungarians were deported from Czechoslovakia and Rumania. And allied peoples also suffered. As Poles moved westward into former

German lands, so millions were deported by Stalin into Poland from the Soviet Union, to create more ethnically homogenous populations in Soviet Lithuania, Byelorussia, and Ukraine. In 1947, a year before the creation of Israel and the expulsion of the Palestinians, more than 10 million Hindus, Sikhs and Muslims had fled from their homes, amid horrendous bloodshed, as a result of the partition of the British Indian empire. A generation earlier Greece and Turkey had conducted a great exchange of populations after repeated national conflicts involving great atrocities on both sides.

Horrible though these events were, they did in some ways lay the groundwork for a future absence of war, which is difficult to imagine if these populations had remained mixed up together. Certainly it is difficult to imagine how a Jewish state could possibly have been established and consolidated with such a huge and understandably hostile Palestinian minority.[93] Finally, Israel does have a legitimate case that the subsequent expulsion to Israel of hundreds of thousands of Jews from Arab countries created a kind of rough justice between Israel and the Arab world.

Today it should also be quite clear that if one of the absolute preconditions for peace between Israel and the Palestinians is Israeli abandonment of many settlements in the Occupied Territories, the other is Palestinian abandonment of the "right of return" for those Palestinians who were expelled in 1948.[94] Note by contrast that I strongly support the Jewish "right of return" to Israel within the borders of 1967, as an ultimate fallback line in the event of a real return of anti-Semitism elsewhere in the world.

But while the expulsions may have been necessary for Israel's survival, the lies which they have generated over the succeeding generations, and which continue to this day, have been extremely dangerous for both Israel and the United States. It would have been far better if Israel and its partisans in the United States had—as Ben-Gurion did in private—accepted the truth of what happened in 1948 and then used it as the basis for thinking seriously about compensation and laying the foundations for future peace. Instead, the pro-Israel camp committed itself to an interlocking set of moral and historical falsehoods.[95] Over time, the intellectual consequences of these positions have spread like a forest of aquatic weeds until they have entangled and choked a significant part of the U.S. national debate concerning relations not only with the Muslim world, but with the outside world in general, and thereby have fed certain strains of American nationalism.

To the refusal to consider the Palestinian case before 1948 and to acknowledge the expulsions of that year was added for several decades a widespread refusal even to admit the existence of the Palestinians as a people, with consequent national rights. Such an attitude was summed up in Israeli Prime Minister Golda Meir's notorious statement (echoed by innumerable Israeli partisans in the United States) that "it was not as though there was a Palestinian people and in Palestine considering itself a Palestinian people and we came and threw them out and took their country away from them. They did not exist."[96]

Thus in 1978 Hyman H. Bookbinder of the American Jewish Committee de-nounced the Carter administration for even using the words "homeland" or "le-gitimate rights" with reference to the Palestinians.[97] This meant in turn that the real bases of Arab grievances against Israel could not be considered, and Arab hostility had to be explained away either by inveterate hatred and malignity ("anti-Semitism") or by the sinister and cynical machinations of Arab regimes.[98]

Of course, both these elements have been present among enemies of Israel. But the necessity of making them the *only* real explanations for Arab and Muslim hostility led inexorably to the demonization of Arab and Muslim societies and culture—and later, by extension, of sympathizers with the Palestinians in Europe and elsewhere. Such demonization was by no means always a deliberate strategy of Israeli partisans. In many cases, the sin was rather one of omission. By keeping silent on the subject of what had happened to the Palestinians and on the roots of the Israeli-Palestinian and Israeli-Arab conflicts, intellectual supporters of Israel left irrational, cynical and implacable hostility as the only available explanations of Arab behavior. Or as the Palestinian scholar and polemicist Edward Said has written, "To criticize Zionism...is to criticize not so much an idea or a theory but rather a wall of denials."[99]

The position of the pro-Israeli liberal intelligentsia in the United States toward the Israeli-Palestinian conflict came somewhat to resemble the position of many enlightened mid-nineteenth-century Americans toward the clash between slavery and the American Creed, as described one hundred years ago by Herbert Croly: "The thing to do was to shut your eyes to the inconsistency, denounce anyone who insisted on it as unpatriotic, and then hold on tight to both horns of the dilemma. Men of high intelligence, who really loved their country, persisted in this attitude." [100]

One result of this uneasy moral situation has been a tendency to launch espe-cially vituperative attacks on anyone who draws attention to the radical inconsis-tencies between the stances of many American liberals on the Israel-Palestine conflict and the attitudes of the same people to other such conflicts. Backed by the tremendous institutional power of the Israeli lobby, this has had the effect of se-verely limiting discussion of the conflict in the United States. Reporting of the conflict is generally fair enough, but unlike the U.S. coverage of the Chechen wars, for example, it tends to lack all historical context, thereby allowing Palestinians to be portrayed simply as terrorists with no explanation of why they are fighting. Much more serious however is the general bias of the editorial pages toward par-tisans of Israel. Unconditional, hard-line partisans of Israel such as William Safire are given regular space even in the *New York Times* (which emerged as a moderate critic of Likud policies and Bush administration support for them.) By contrast, hard-line critics of Israel never appear. Such criticism as is permitted is usually by moderates and is highly qualified and restrained.[101]

As Arnaud de Borchgrave (himself a strongly conservative journalist for the *Washington Times* and in part of Jewish descent) has written bitterly: "For many American Jews, anyone who writes disapprovingly of the policies of Israeli Prime

Minister Ariel Sharon and of his Dionysian neo-conservative backers in Washington is evidence of 'classic anti-Semitism.' The mere reference to 'neo-cons' is interpreted to mean an attack against a 'Jewish cabal.'...Israeli newspapers—particularly *Ha'aretz,* the *New York Times* of Israel—make our own critiques tame by comparison."[102]

With time, freedom of debate in the United States might have increased; and indeed it did improve markedly in the 1990s, until the collapse of the Israeli-Palestinian peace process, the resumption of Palestinian terrorism and 9/11 turned the clock back again. For in the decades since its foundation, Israeli military victories and technological advances assured it of security against invasion, and Israel became a more and more firmly established and indeed brilliantly successful state and society. These successes should have diminished fears that by discussing the circumstances of its birth one would somehow be calling its legitimate existence into question.

Even since 9/11 the editorial pages of the *New York Times* and a number of other American journals have taken a much more fair and balanced view of the Israel-Palestinian conflict than they did twenty years ago. Yet few mainstream writers have gone on from criticism of Israel to adopt the logical consequence of their criticisms and call for pressure on Israel by Washington through the threat of a withdrawal of U.S. support—which they would certainly have done with any other state which received massive U.S. aid and defied U.S. wishes. As a result, their criticisms are deficient in both political and moral content.[103] Even the U.S. State Department each year produces a human rights report on Israel and the Occupied Territories which is often very critical of Israeli behavior. The problem is, however, that the United States takes no action as a result.[104]

Starting with President Anwar Sadat of Egypt in 1977, more and more of the Arab world itself has admitted that Israel is here to stay, and ideas of driving it into the sea are an empty fantasy. This process culminated in the peace plan drawn up by Prince Abdullah of Saudi Arabia in 2002 and approved by an overwhelming majority of the Arab League, offering to recognize Israel within the borders of 1967.

In the meantime, however, successive Israeli governments had made the fateful decision to encourage the creation of Jewish settlements in the territories conquered in the Six-Day War.[105] This decision necessitated a continued denial of the national existence of the Palestinians, long after it had become obvious that the Palestinians had in fact developed a coherent national consciousness separate from that of other Arab peoples. Indeed, one of the tragicomic aspects of the Israeli hard-line camp is that it might be described as Pan-Arabist, since it professes to believe that the Arabs are all one people and therefore that Palestinians have no homeland of their own and might as well live anywhere in the Arab world.

The issue of the settlements helped add another thick layer of evasion and chauvinism to the politics and rhetoric of the Israeli lobby in the United States; as a result of their creation and the need to defend their presence, Arab states and individuals could not be admitted to be moderate and reasonable *even if* they offered to sign a peace treaty with Israel within the borders of 1967. Any such offers had therefore either to be as far as possible ignored, or their authors had to be demonized as inherently mendacious, untrustworthy and devoted to Israel's destruction. Discussions with Arab and Palestinian moderates had to be either prevented or drowned in a torrent of denunciation. Offers like that of Prince Abdullah had to be first as far as possible brushed aside, and then their authors discredited by a flood of attacks on Arab countries in general and Saudi Arabia in particular as regressive, barbarous, dictatorial and therefore inherently untrustworthy.[106]

The question of Israeli occupation of the West Bank and Gaza Strip had to be presented as vital to Israel's very survival. This in turn required a constant exaggeration of existential threats to Israel and hence of the power and malignity of Israel's (and America's) Muslim enemies. The result has been a paranoid discourse of permanent emergency with all too many precedents in the history of militarist nationalism.

And too much of this discourse is not focused where it should be, on the real terrorist threat to Israel and the need to reduce this threat by ending settlement construction and withdrawing from most of the West Bank and Gaza Strip. Nor is it focused on the equally real demographic threat to Israel if it continues to rule over huge numbers of Palestinians. On the contrary, it portrays a quite unreal military threat to Israel from Arab states and is used to divert public debate away from the real issues of settlements and occupation. Thus in February 2003 Daniel Pipes wrote that "the existence of Israel appeared imperiled as it had not been for decades." Yaacov Lozowick of the Israeli Holocaust Museum has written a book in which all Israel's conflicts, whether of genuine self-defense and survival or of invasion and occupation, are subsumed under "Israel's Right to Exist."[107]

Remarks like this feed the paranoia of American nationalism as well; and they go to the heart of what has gone wrong with Israeli strategy and U.S. support for that strategy in recent decades. During its first 25 years of existence, Israel was repeatedly attacked, but in consequence won a series of great victories, first military, then political. For most of its early history Israel was indeed threatened by militarily powerful Arab states which rejected Israel's very existence and were backed and armed by the Soviet Union. However, Israel crushingly defeated these states in 1967 and then again to a lesser extent in 1973.

Thereafter, the defection of Egypt from the anti-Israel bloc, and the Egyptian regime's adoption of the United States as supplier and protector, made any further serious conventional military threat to Israel inconceivable for the foreseeable future. In addition, Israel developed a powerful nuclear deterrent as an ultimate and effective guarantee against any threat to its existence from Muslim states (although not of course against catastrophic terrorist attack). After 1989 the collapse of the Soviet Union not only reduced the threat to Israel still further by depriving the remaining Arab rejectionist states of their superpower backer, it released a huge flood of Soviet Jewish emigrants, securing Israel's demographic position within the borders of 1967.

If the Occupied Territories are kept in a "Greater Israel," the demographic picture looks utterly different, and Israel really will be in terrible danger as a Jewish state, or as a democracy, or both. Henry Siegman of the Council on Foreign Relations has written of the Palestinian demographic threat, in words which remind us of the falsity of claims concerning continued existential threats to Israel within the borders of 1967:

> Morris's account points to the sorry fact that there is not much that distinguishes how Jews behaved in 1948 in their struggle to achieve statehood from Palestinian behavior today. At the very least, this sobering truth should lead to a shedding of the moral smugness of too many Israelis and to a reexamination of their demonization of the Palestinian national cause.
>
> The implication of the above for the territorial issue is that it would be irrational for Palestinians *not* to believe that the goal of Sharon's fence is anything other than their confinement in a series of Bantustans, if not a prelude to a second transfer....
>
> Unless Israelis are willing to preserve their majority status by imposing a South African–style apartheid regime, or to complete the transfer begun in 1948, as Morris believes they will—policies which one hopes a majority of Israelis will never accept—it is only a matter of time before the emerging majority of Arabs in Greater Israel will reshape the country's national identity. That would be a tragedy of historic proportions for the Zionist enterprise and for the Jewish people.
>
> What will make the tragedy doubly painful is that it will be happening at a time when changes in the Arab world and beyond...are removing virtually every strategic threat that for so long endangered Israel's existence. That existence is now threatened by the greed of the settlers and the political blindness of Israel's leaders.[108]

Abba Eban's famous line that the Palestinians have "never missed an opportunity to miss an opportunity" to seek peace or gain political advantage has been proven true all too often. Certainly the PLO's record has often been both politically lamentable and morally revolting, and the same is true of leading Arab regimes. Palestinian leadership has been generally abysmal. Palestinian terrorism in recent years has been disastrous and unjustifiable from every possible point of view. But this does not excuse the policies of successive Israeli governments toward the Palestinians. In the words of Amos Elon, "It does not condone terror and murder to say that the Palestinians have a case."[109] If until the 1990s most Arab governments refused to recognize Israel under any circumstances, Israel similarly refused to recognize the existence of the Palestinians as a separate people enjoying rights of self-determination and genuine self-government.

If Israel had respected the Geneva Convention and maintained a military occupation of the West Bank and Gaza Strip pending a peace treaty without planting illegal settlements there, it could have responded positively to later Arab offers to recognize and make peace with Israel within the borders of 1967—like those of King Hussein of Jordan in the 1970s and Prince Abdullah of Saudi Arabia in 2003.[110] Israel would also have been in a position to negotiate both quickly and sincerely on the basis of the Oslo accords, focusing on the establishment of international guarantees for Israeli security and Palestinian abandonment of the right of return.

Instead, Oslo was frittered away in endless haggling while the settlements expanded further—giving the Palestinians the feeling that the whole process was only a delaying tactic to allow more land to be stolen from under them. This eventually contributed greatly to the disastrous Palestinian decision to reject Barak's peace offer of July 2000 and Clinton's proposal of January 2001, and to the catastrophe of the second Intifada.[111]

"Anti-Semitism" and Hatred of the World

Closely linked to systematic exaggeration of the degree of contemporary geopolitical threat to Israel by the Israeli lobby in the United States has been the recent campaign in both countries alleging that criticism of Israel is overwhelmingly anti-Semitic in motivation. It is also stated that this reflects a great wave of new anti-Semitism in Europe and around the world which is closely linked to hatred of America. Or in the simple title of an essay by Manfred Gerstenfeld: "Anti-Semitism: Integral to European Culture."[112]

The savage history of anti-Semitism culminating in the Holocaust makes this subject one of unparalleled moral gravity, and the accusation of anti-Semitism is one which should carry crushing moral weight. Indeed, the very grave consequences which can occur for an academic or public figure in the United States who is accused of anti-Semitism also make this matter an extremely serious one. Unfortunately, all too often in the United States today, the issue of anti-Semitism is not being seriously treated. Thus Andrew Sullivan, former editor of the *New Republic* magazine, attacked the opponents of war with Iraq in this way: "America's antiwar movement, still puny and struggling, is showing signs of being hijacked by one of the oldest and darkest prejudices there is. Perhaps it was inevitable. The conflict against Islamo-fascism obviously circles back to the question of Israel. Fanatical anti-Semitism, as bad or even worse than Hitler's, is now a cultural norm across the Middle East. It's the acrid glue that unites Saddam, Arafat, Al-Qaeda, Hezbollah, Iran and the Saudis."[113]

This attempt at creating monstrous guilt by association was directed not at American neo-Nazis, but at millions of ordinary Americans, good democrats and citizens, who opposed the Iraq War, often for reasons which have turned out to be entirely justified. According to a survey by the American Jewish Committee, 54 percent of Jewish Americans opposed war with Iraq; in fact, the proportion of Jewish Americans who supported the war (43 percent) was much lower than that of the population as a whole (62 percent).[114] As for Sullivan's attempt to link very different and often mutually hostile countries and groups in the Middle East, it ignores the Saudi peace offer to Israel and Iranian official statements that Tehran will accept any settlement with Israel that is accepted by the Palestinians.

This statement of Sullivan's was quoted approvingly by Alan Dershowitz in his book defending Israel, and it forms part of a much wider campaign suggesting that the threat from anti-Semitism in the world is greater than at any time since the 1930s and 1940s—or even as bad as then. Thus Abraham Foxman of the Anti-Defamation League: "I am convinced we currently face as great a threat to the safety and security of the Jewish people as the one we faced in the 1930s—if not a greater one."[115] The American feminist critic Phyllis Chesler has written: "I fear that the Jews may again be sacrificed to a world gone mad and in search of a sacred scapegoat."[116] Representatives of the Christian Right in the United States have joined in these warnings.[117]

This language is itself more than a little mad. America is the world's only superpower and a stable liberal democracy. It is committed to support and defend Israel. Unlike the situation in the 1930s, the American political classes are overwhelmingly opposed to anti-Semitism in any form. The major European states are also stable and successful democracies, in which Jews enjoy the same rights as all other citizens. With very rare exceptions, such as Austria, anti-Semitic parties are tiny, marginal, or even illegal. Among the larger extreme right-wing parties, such as the National Front in France and the Liberal Democrats in Russia, anti-Semitic feeling is now dwarfed by hatred of Muslims. In fact, Muslim minorities seem to have pretty definitively taken on the role of alien and disliked "Other" in European right-wing thinking. It is overwhelmingly thugs from these Muslim minorities who are carrying out physical attacks on Jews in Europe, while these Muslim communities themselves are being targeted by right-wing thugs from the majority European populations. This situation is worrying and disgraceful, but it is not the 1930s.

The leaders and main political parties in these countries have repeatedly denounced anti-Semitism, and their programs or ideologies bear no resemblance whatsoever to those of the Nazis or the other extreme Rightist movements before 1945. Indeed, the entire European project, including the enlargement of the Union to the former Soviet bloc, has been explicitly based on a repudiation of those past crimes and errors. Although there is a historical strain of anti-Semitism in certain sections of the European Left, the absolutely overwhelming majority of mainstream left-wing critics of Israel in Europe—among whom are many Jewish Europeans—would never contemplate the introduction into their own states of even the mildest of the anti-Semitic measures of the past. Such steps as restrictions on entry into universities or exclusion from leading social institutions would be utterly alien to their traditions and ideology, which stress openness and equality for people of all races, ethnicities and religions.

Thus in the course of vilifying the contemporary French Left as anti-Semitic, American critics have forgotten that it was the Left that defended Dreyfus and Frency Jewry against their right-wing anti-Semitic persecutors, that three socialist premiers of France have been Jewish and that though there certainly were anti-Semites on the Left, the defining hostility of the French Left historically was not anti-Semitism but anti-clericalism. Whatever writers like Gabriel Schoenfeld may allege, there is in fact *no* "clear fit between...anti-Jewish hatred and the general ideological predispositions of the contemporary European Left.[118]

Russia of course is not a stable democracy, but even there the government has condemned anti-Semitism and sought good relations with Israel. This had led for example to excellent relations between Vladimir Putin and Natan Sharansky (the former Soviet dissident turned extremist Israeli politician). Jewish Russians hold leading positions in the state and economy. Since the fall of the Soviet Union, three Russians of Jewish origin have been prime minister of Russia: Sergei Kiriyenko, Yevgeny Primakov and Mikhail Fradkov. How on earth can this situation be rationally compared to the world of Hitler, Mussolini, Stalin and Antonescu?

Such charges are in part natural and spontaneous, stemming from the ghastly history of Jewish persecution culminating in the Holocaust. Thus Seymour Martin Lipset notes that in 1985, according to a poll, a majority of Jewish Americans in San Francisco were sincerely convinced that no Jew could be elected to the U.S. Congress from San Francisco—when in fact all three members of Congress were Jewish Americans, plus the two state senators and the mayor![119]

In the words of Irving Howe, which also have relevance for the wider feelings of hereditary defeat and persecution among many Americans, described in this book that:

> Haunted by the demons of modern history, most of the immigrants and many of their children kept a fear, somewhere in their minds, that anti-Semitism might again become a serious problem in America. By mid-century, it was often less an actual fear than a persuasion that they *should* keep this fear, all past experience warranting alertness even if there was no immediate reason for anxiety....It is crucial to note here that even in the mid-twentieth century many American Jews, certainly a good many of those who came out of the east European immigrant world, still *felt* like losers. Being able to buy a home, or move into a suburb, or send kids to college could not quickly dissolve that feeling. Black antagonism...was linked in their minds with a possible resurgence of global anti-Semitism and the visible enmity of Arabs toward Israel. And who could easily separate, in such reactions, justified alarm from "paranoid" excess?[120]

Accusations of anti-Semitism are also, however, being used consciously and deliberately as part of a strategy to try to silence critics of Israel. This was in effect admitted in a backhanded way by Norman Podhoretz, Nathan Perlmutter and Irving Kristol, who urged that anti-Semitic statements on the part of Christian conservatives such as Pat Robertson should be forgiven because they are support- ers of Israel: "After all, why should Jews care about the theology of a fundamental- ist preacher when they do not for a moment believe that he speaks with any authority on the question of God's attentiveness to human prayer? And what do such theological abstractions matter as against the mundane fact that the same preacher is vigorously pro-Israel?"[121]

Or in the words of Perlmutter: "Is it good for the Jews? This question satisfied, I proceed to the secondary issues....Jews can live with all the domestic priorities of the Christian Right on which liberal Jews differ so radically because none of these concerns is as important as Israel." [122]

The Israeli lobby, like the American nationalist Right, pays special attention to U.S. academia, which is the one major section of U.S. society where a genuine debate on this subject does take place.[123] It should be noted that, as in Europe, left- wing and Arab groups on college campuses do all too frequently engage in rheto- ric and actions which are not only excessively anti-Israeli but also on occasions anti-Semitic.[124] On this wing of American academic politics: "Many of the speeches have a mindless quality which repels the listener. The speakers are loud in their denunciations of American and Israeli policy, but they lose moral force and po- litical effectiveness by maintaining a tight-lipped silence about terrorism and dic- tatorship in the Middle East and elsewhere."[125]

American teachers and administrators on campuses where such propaganda is prevalent have a duty to combat it and, where appropriate, to suppress it. How- ever, no matter how revolting the forces guilty of these rhetorical excesses may be, they are utterly powerless beyond the narrow confines of some U.S. university campuses, and they are not dominant even there. In the world of politics, lobby- ing and think tanks in Washington, they are, in my experience, virtually nonexist- ent. They do not even remotely begin to compare in influence on American society, politics and government with the Israeli lobby.[126]

Indeed, it often seems that their most important role is to be used by partisans of Israel in the West as "straw men" whose extremist arguments can be easily de- molished and as a diversionary tactic to avoid engaging with the serious argu- ments of Israeli liberals and patriots like Burg, Oz, Yossi Beilin or General Shlomo Gazit.[127] In the words of Akiva Eldar, in the Israeli newspaper *Ha'aretz*: "It is much easier to claim the whole world is against us than to admit that the State of Israel, which rose as a refuge and source of pride for Jews, has not only turned into a place less Jewish and less safe for its citizens, but has become a genuine source of danger and a source of shameful embarrassment to Jews who choose to live be- yond its borders. Arguing that it takes an anti-Semite to call the Israeli government's policies of 2003 a danger to world peace is a contemptible cheapening of the term anti-Semitism."[128]

The campaign to brand critics of Israel anti-Semites and to portray a monstrous and terrifying wave of anti-Semitism in Europe and the world has effects on the United States which go far beyond the specific issues concerned. It contributes to wider American hostility to the outside world, made worse by the levels of ignorance described in Chapter 2. To judge by the comments of university teachers with whom I have spoken, for all too many American students the entire history of France has been reduced to the Dreyfus case and Vichy, the whole history of Germany before 1945 to the Holocaust and the whole history of tsarist Russia to Cossacks and pogroms.

In the Muslim world and among Muslim immigrant groups in Europe, hatred of Israel certainly has spilled over into hatred of Jews in general; and this hatred is being fed by recycled anti-Semitic myths from the darkest pages of Europe's past. This tendency must be combated as part of general efforts to bring peace to the Middle East, to improve its level of education and public discourse, to lay the foundations for democracy and help it develop in other ways—and in Europe, to help integrate the Muslim immigrants into Western society.[129]

However, to use these vile beliefs as a means of absolving Israel from any responsibility for its actions is just as wrong—and just as bad for Israel—as to suggest that the existence of anti-Americanism in the world means that it does not matter what the United States does. All the evidence suggests, for example, that the flare-up in anti-Semitic violence by Muslims in France stemmed directly from what they saw as Israeli atrocities against the Palestinians. Now, their views of these atrocities were exaggerated; but equally, their criminal behavior was a response to events as well as the product of a warped intellectual background.

It is entirely clear that while Muslim prejudice against Jewish and Christian "infidels" (prejudice which historically speaking has much less than that against Hindu and other "heathens") existed in the past, modern anti-Semitism in the Muslim world stems overwhelmingly from the creation of Israel and its real or perceived crimes against the Palestinians. In answer to charges by Dershowitz and others that it was the other way around, and that Muslim anti-Semitism led to anti-Israeli feeling, Brian Klug, a scholar and founder-member of the Jewish Forum for Justice and Human Rights, has proposed the simple counterfactual question: What if a state had been established in Palestine by Christian European settlers, as in French Algeria? Would the Muslim world not have opposed it just as fiercely? And in these circumstances, would there have been any strong degree of anti-Semitism in the Muslim world?[130]

Equally, if as a matter of just compensation for the Holocaust, Germany east of the Oder-Neisse line had been given to Jews for a state in 1945 rather than being divided between Poland and the Soviet Union, would Muslims or anyone else in the world (other than Germans and some Poles) have denounced this as unjust or a Jewish crime? In this case, could there conceivably have been a wave of anti-Semitism among Muslims?

As Klug argues, hostility to Israel in the developing and former colonial world (leading to repeated votes in the UN condemning Israel and the infamous—and later reversed—equation of Zionism with racism), although it is colored by anti-Semitism, stems fundamentally from anticolonial feeling related to hostility to Western colonists and the circumstances of Israel's gestation under British imperial rule.

Of course, much of this left-wing anticolonial attitude to Israel may well be wrong, cynical and even wicked. For that matter, this is true of a good part of "anticolonial" politics and rhetoric in general, both in the past and today. But the repellent and cynical use of such rhetoric by President Robert Mugabe of Zimbabwe or the rulers of Burma is not generally held to compromise the positive, enlightened, state-building anticolonialism of a Nehru of India or a Mandela of South Africa: The failure in the U.S. mainstream to understand the anticolonial roots of hostility to Israel in much of the world has wider effects in fueling a contempt for world public opinion. It also contributes to an American blindness to the reasons why many former colonies and dependencies around the world which are by no means instinctively anti-American are nonetheless deeply hostile to the idea of American (or Western) military intervention in other states and to any hint of new Western "civilizing missions."

But the damage done by much of the present discourse in the United States concerning anti-Semitism goes beyond its results in terms of increasing hostility to Muslims, Europeans and others and thereby undermining the war on terrorism. It also corrodes American political culture in general, by increasing nationalist paranoia, arrogance, hatred and irrationality. When people can be anti-Semites without even knowing it and without proposing or believing anything which would have been regarded historically as anti-Semitic; when highly decorated Israeli soldiers become traitors and "self-hating Jews;" when anti-Semitism itself loses all historical or cultural context and becomes a kind of free-floating miasma, drifting unchanged down the centuries; when it is argued that "Arab pre-Islamist persecution of the Jews began as early as the third century BCE;" then rational debate is at an end.[131]

In the words of Hannah Arendt in 1945, words which remain true in 2004: "The Zionists likewise fled the field of actual conflicts into a doctrine of eternal anti-Semitism governing the relations of Jews and Gentiles everywhere and always, and mainly responsible for the survival of the Jewish people. Thus both sides [i.e., the Zionists and the Assimilationists] relieved themselves of the arduous tasks of fighting anti-Semitism on its own grounds, which were political, and even of the unpleasant task of analyzing its true causes."[132]

Because by their nature such charges of anti-Semitism, not backed by concrete evidence, can be neither proved nor disproved, they lead discussion away from the clearly lit arena of rational public discussion and toward the dark corridors of paranoia and conspiracy theories, evil spirits and demonic possession—regions of the mind which in the past have been precisely the breeding grounds of anti-Semitic madness.

Nationalism and Democratization

When directed at the Muslim world, these beliefs and accusations are having a truly terrible effect on America's capacity successfully to wage the war against terrorism, let alone to bring democracy to the Middle East.[133] Indeed, much of the discourse on the latter issue on the American Right and among partisans of Israel in the United States is characterized by deep and repellent moral and logical contradictions.

It is in the relationship between the policies of support for Israel and democratization of the Middle East that the clash between the American thesis and antithesis reaches its greatest, its most enduring, and its most dangerous proportions. This is a mixture which unfortunately seems unlikely to change under Democratic administrations.[134] A belief in the necessity of developing and eventually democratizing the Middle East if terrorism and extremism are to be defeated there is both correct and laudable.[135] The widespread inability to readdress the U.S. relationship with Israel as part of this effort not only gravely undermines it in Arab eyes, but also adds to the confusion of American thought concerning the necessary bases of modernization—of which nationalism is one of the most important.

Amid U.S. professions of a desire for democracy in the region, U.S. administrations and much of the U.S. political class and media have treated the opinions of the vast majority of Arabs concerning the Israel-Palestinian conflict and U.S. strategy in the region with open contempt. It is suggested that these feelings are the product of cynical manipulation by cynical Arab elites; but when relatively free, modern and liberal Arab media outlets like *Al Jazeera* reflect the same opinions, they are equally condemned. And in the matter of attitudes to Israel, ordinary Arabs are treated as at best deluded and ignorant sheep, at worst as filled with primeval, irrational malignancy.

Yet these are the people to whom the Bush administration professes to want to bring democracy and also declares are *ready* for democracy. Meanwhile, all too many American op-eds, essays and books which call for the democratization of the Middle East skirt round the question of Israeli treatment of the Palestinians, condemn this treatment briefly and formally while devoting incomparably more space to Arab anti-Semitism, ignore this issue altogether, or simply take Israel's side.[136]

In a book of 214 pages on the ideology and roots of Islamist totalitarianism, in which he bitterly condemns a range of Muslim targets and sections of the European Left, the self-described liberal Paul Berman devotes precisely two lines to a suggestion that America should act against "the manias of the ultra-Right in Israel"—not, it should be noted, against the Israeli government or state as such. Elsewhere, Berman espouses without qualification the view that all blame for the collapse of the Israeli-Palestinian peace process in 2000–01 lies with the Palestinians.[137]

By behaving in this way, such writers discredit themselves in the eyes of Muslims and Europeans; but their effect is also much worse than that. By suggesting to Muslims and others that on this issue liberal intellectuals in the United States, the supposed role model of international democracy, are motivated not by genuine democratic idealism but by ethnic chauvinism, moral cowardice or both, they undermine not only American prestige in the world but the democratic model they are seeking to propagate.

The seemingly bipartisan U.S. rhetoric of democratizing the Middle East also goes to the heart of wider failings of U.S. analysis, rooted in aspects of American political culture examined in this book. The absolutist nature of the American Creed, with its ideological faith in Democracy and Freedom, tends to produce etherized, contentless versions of both these concepts. This tendency is strongly evident in the rhetoric of the Bush administration, with its talk of the "freedom-loving" people of wherever, and so on. In turn, by making democracy look both so universally applicable and so easy, this approach feeds American messianism and militant interventionism.

Within the United States today, and even more if one looks at the history of the nation or of other democratic states, two things are obvious: Our contemporary version of democracy has emerged only after long struggle among different races, ethnicities and social groups; and this struggle was often bloody, and not at all democratic in form. As the American historian Eric Foner has recorded, the concept of freedom has meant radically different and even contradictory things to different groups of Americans, and at different times in American history. Second, even today, democratic institutions and even judicial systems remain forums for competition between different ethnic and other groups—not only for power, but for the fruits of power in terms of the distribution of state patronage.

Yet when it comes to the world outside the United States, "democracy" is all too often treated not as a procedure, but as an end; not as a way of posing a set of questions about the state and society, but as an answer to those questions—and as a quick answer, which, once achieved, will allow the United States to pull out of a country again, leaving behind a stable and reliable U.S. ally. It is in part due to this mind-set that large sections of U.S. public opinion were convinced to support the Iraq War by the argument that this would bring democracy to Iraq as a prelude to democratizing the Middle East as a whole. In this discourse, the inevitable embitterment of the disempowered Sunni minority, ethnic tensions between Arabs and Kurds, the persistence of Shia religious networks as the last civic institutions left by Ba'ath totalitarianism, and the rivalries between these networks—all these perceptions were simply obliterated by the simple mantras of "democracy" and "freedom."[138]

Most important of all in this context is the way in which too many commentators have forgotten the very frequent and important connection between nationalism and the birth both of mass politics and of successful socioeconomic development. This obliviousness stems in part from wider failings of analysis which are by no means restricted to the United States. It is in America, however, and especially with regard to the Middle East, that the failure to appreciate this link has achieved its most dangerous proportions.

This blank spot in much of U.S. thought stems in part from the etherealization of democracy mentioned above, in part from the difficulty that all nationalist countries have in appreciating other people's nationalisms, and in part from the U.S. inability to focus on the role of Israel both in fomenting Arab anger and in focusing wider Arab and Muslim frustrations and resentments on Israel and the United States: "The hidden [U.S.] agenda most commonly identified by Arab writers is the [alleged] United States' decision to allow Israel to control the region and to give Prime Minister Ariel Sharon *carte blanche* in dealing with the Palestinian territories and the Intifada."[139]

It is quite true, as many commentators argue, that the ultimate roots of these Arab sentiments very often have nothing whatsoever to do with Israel or Israeli behavior. The humiliation of the Arab and Muslim worlds by Israel is so infuriating to them in part because it is only the last in a long history of defeats beginning in the seventeenth century at the hands of the Christian or Western world. The central reason for these defeats has been the prolonged and continuing socioeconomic and technological decline of the Muslim world relative to the West—defeats which were already producing radical Muslim responses (whether in Sufi or Wahabi guise) as early as the last decades of the eighteenth century. It is the pathologies produced by these failures, as well as the appearance of Israel and the United States as objects of hatred, which have produced the phenomenon of modern Muslim extremism and terrorism.[140]

But to say this is not to declare that Israel and its occupation of the Palestinian territories are somehow "irrelevant" to Arab attitudes and behavior, that the "real" roots of Arab resentment and hostility to America are different and that change in Israeli actions would have no effect. This is no more true than it would be to say that because French nationalism after 1871 or German nationalism after 1919 were fed by domestic political, social and economic factors, the German annexation of Alsace Lorraine or the territorial terms of the Versailles Treaty were somehow "irrelevant" to what happened later.

For a central feature of nationalism is precisely its ability to feed off a very wide range of other resentments, loyalties, identities, hopes and fears. The sheer breadth of its ability in this respect, together with its quasi-religious ability to offer mortal humans an identity which transcends the short span of their own lives, has helped give nationalisms around the world their decisive edge over socialism.

Nationalism is also critical to an understanding of many examples of successful socioeconomic progress in the twentieth century, and may well be in the twenty-first century as well. Thus there has been a good deal of talk in the United States about a parallel between President Bush's "plan" for democratizing the greater Middle East and the Helsinki process which contributed to the fall of the Soviet empire. The idea is that the United States can play a comparable role in bringing democracy to the "oppressed" peoples of the Middle East. The real comparisons to be made between the Middle East and Eastern Europe over the past twenty years are, however, very different, and the role of nationalism is at their heart.

The lessons of successful development in the Cold War and post–Cold War periods for Western policy are in fact threefold. The regimes concerned obviously need to have both the right economic policies and a state strong enough to regulate and guide economic development; the West needs to have a strong local nationalism on its side; and it has to be prepared to make real economic sacrifices for the sake of the countries it wishes to help develop.

Democracy as such, by contrast, is not of central importance, although law and social freedom certainly are. After an economy has modernized successfully, democracy often follows; but outside parts of Europe, the correlation between democracy and the process of modernization is very weak.

The correlation between modernization and a strong, united and determined nationalism by contrast is very strong.[141] Within the Muslim world, this has been preeminently true of Turkey where Ataturk's Kemalist ideology dictated the modernization and westernization of Turkey by authoritarian means. This took place in the name of a fierce ethnic nationalism which veered over into genocidal violence against minority groups which contested Turkish rule over the Anatolian heartland. Democratic forms were established, but for many decades were constrained and managed by the Turkish military, and interrupted by military interventions and coups. Full democracy has come only in recent years, after critical steps in modernization had been achieved; it is still quite a fragile plant.

Nationalism was of critical importance to the development of two of the crucial theaters of the Cold War, the Far East and Eastern Europe. In the cases of Taiwan and South Korea, the United States backed homogenous authoritarian elites with a strong military element and a very strong sense of national purpose, closely linked to their fear of communism. Later this was also true of Thailand. Take away the military element, and it was true of Japan, Singapore and Malaysia. By contrast, in ethnically divided elites with a weak sense of common national purpose, development was very much less successful.[142]

In the case of Eastern Europe after 1989, the role of nationalism is the great unsung element in the region's generally successful development. Most countries that make up Eastern Europe had strong ethnic nationalisms which long predated communist rule and which were indeed the most important factor in bringing about repeated attempts at anti-Soviet and anticommunist revolution.

Because of their passionate desire to escape for good from Moscow's imperial clutches, after 1989 these countries benefited from a tremendously strong nationalist "push" toward the West. This desire neutralized what might otherwise have been strong nationalist and populist tendencies both to oppose economic reform and to favor authoritarianism. For the Western institutions and alliances which the Central Europeans and Balts so greatly wished to join are defined by democracy and regulated free market economics. This provided the "pull" in terms of modernization.

This means that only really in the case of Eastern Europe and the Baltic states is it legitimate to use the ideological and teleological cliché of a "path" to democracy and the free market. Across the world, there have been and are many paths of development with different outcomes. Thanks to the European Union and NATO, in the case of Eastern Europe however, there has been a fixed path with a fixed goal.

Their inability to acknowledge the role of nationalism in destroying the Soviet communist empire helps undermine efforts by Daniel Pipes, Paul Berman and others to create analogies between the Western struggle against Islamist extremism and the Cold War struggle against communism; and this inability stems above all from a rejection of any suggestion that Israel, and U.S. support for Israel, is a source of strong, real, and legitimate Arab mass anger.[143] The real parallel to be made with the Cold War is that whenever communist parties were able to draw on a strong local nationalism in fighting the United States, as in Vietnam, the communists won; and when local nationalism worked against Soviet rule, the West won, albeit only after several decades.[144]

Even genuinely honorable, well-informed and sincere American works advocating a democratization strategy for the Middle East often suffer badly from the failure to confront the question of nationalism.[145] This was not a problem for nineteenth-century liberal imperialists, who believed in bringing progress through conquest and long-term rule of "lesser breeds" by civilized states; but it is a colossal problem for twenty-first-century liberals who believe in spreading democracy and therefore in gaining the consent of those they wish to improve, and whose capacity for conquest and long-term occupation is much more limited. Furthermore, even if the old liberal imperialist paradigm is accepted, Israeli behavior is still a problem. Douglas Porch, Alastair Horne and other historians of the French colonial empire have recorded how the "liberal imperialist" program of enlightened French colonial administrators in North Africa was continually undermined by the other face of French imperialism in the region, "proletarian colonization": the seizure of land and brutish treatment of the native population by French *pied noir* settlers.

The other critically important point about the parallel between the former communist world and the Middle East is that the economic and democratic development of postcommunist Eastern Europe has not been cheap for the existing EU countries. Subsidies to the region have seemed grossly inadequate to the recipients, but they were colossal compared to the paltry sums Washington has spent or is talking of spending in the Middle East ($29 million for the Middle East Partnership Initiative in 2003, some $200 million in the years to come). And even aid was secondary compared to the most important factor of all: the opening of West European markets—including to a lesser extent labor markets—to the exports and workers of the East European candidates for accession to the Union.

These factors were also central to the successful development of some of the East and Southeast Asian countries. First because of the Korean War in East Asia, then because of the Vietnam War in Southeast Asia, the United States transferred huge sums in aid to states which it viewed as crucial bulwarks against communism. And once again, even more important was the fact that for geopolitical reasons, the United States kept its markets wide open to these countries' products, even when doing so contributed to the collapse of great swathes of U.S. industry.

The contrasts with the greater Middle East are bleak. With the exception of · Iran, none of these states is truly national, and in all their sense of real common national purpose is weak. They are either multinational, like Pakistan, or fragments of a wider ethnolinguistic culture, like the Arab states. As Charles Glass quoted an Arab friend in saying, among the Arab countries, only Egypt is a true nation. All the others are "tribes with flags": heterogeneous populations ruled formally or informally by dictators backed by oligarchic clans—the houses of Saud and Hashem, the various royal dynasties of the Gulf, the Alawite leadership of the Ba'ath Party in Syria, and, until their overthrow, the Tikriti leadership of the Ba'ath in Iraq. Beneath these ruling clans, sections of their populations have often owed their primary allegiance to substate traditions, whether lineage groups or religious communities like those of the Shia in Iraq.[146]

And where state nationalism does exist, the Israeli-Palestinian conflict and U.S. support for Israel means that it is very difficult to mobilize it on the side of the West. What the American formulators of the Helsinki parallel cannot seem to grasp is that all too many Arabs see the United States plus Israel as playing the Soviet role of detested regional hegemon. As long as Arab TV stations can show daily images of Palestinian suffering, it will be difficult even to begin to dispel this impression. According to Marina Ottaway of the Carnegie Endowment in March 2003 (drawing on surveys of the Arab press by the U.S. State Department): "First and foremost, it is clear that the United States cannot hope to be taken seriously when it talks of its commitment to democracy in the Arab world unless it renews its efforts to revive negotiations between Israel and the Palestinians, puts pressure on Israel to allow Palestinian elections to take place, and is prepared to deal with Yassir Arafat if he is elected. The consistent way in which these issues were mentioned leaves no doubt about this."[147]

U.S. rhetoric of democratizing the Middle East therefore risks becoming a cheap way of avoiding looking at the really critical issues facing the region—because to deal with them would be very costly, both for the United States and the European Union as a whole and for individual members of the U.S. political classes.

Helping lay the foundations of future democracy through economic progress would mean massively increased American aid. Openness to trade would mean confronting extremely powerful lobbies. One of the best ways the United States could help Pakistan, for example, would be by reducing severe restrictions on Pakistani textile imports. Doing this, however, would mean having the political and moral courage to confront the American textile industry and trade unions. The whole of the greater Middle East would benefit from a reduction of agricultural barriers and subsidies by the United States and the EU—but this would mean that Western governments would have to confront even more powerful agricultural lobbies.

Above all, resolving the Israeli-Palestinian conflict requires serious American pressure on Israel, including the threat of a severe reduction of U.S. economic, diplomatic and military support. To advocate such a strategy would take real political and moral courage on the part of a U.S. president and administration, but also on the part of individual members of the American political classes and media. Such a stance is, however, their clear duty—especially if they are going to encourage "brave individuals fighting for democracy" in the Muslim world to risk their employment, freedom, or even lives.[148]

For a genuine solution to this conflict is a vital American national interest. It is an essential precondition both for success in the struggle against terrorism and for the long-term democratizion of the Middle East. As long as the Israeli-Palestinian conflict continues as a full-scale national struggle, Arab westernizers will go on being discredited as traitors, Arab nationalism will go on working against reform and all the worst elements of Arabic and Muslim political culture will continue to be fed and nurtured.

Unfortunately, strong elements in the Israeli lobby in the United States appear to be using the language of democratization precisely as a way of evading or even permanently blocking a just and stable Israeli-Palestinian peace. This fact emerges quite clearly from the already mentioned 1996 paper "A Clean Break" by several future Bush administration officials, which originated this approach in the Israeli lobby and the U.S. establishment. This paper combined its strategy of "democratizing" the Middle East with the fantastic proposal that a U.S. invasion of Iraq be used to restore the Hashemite monarchy in Iraq.[149]

In October 2003 Frank Gaffney (of the Center for Security Policy in Washington) declared:

> Authoritarian and for that matter totalitarian regimes have a compelling need for external enemies. This is particularly true because in the absence of external justifications for their generally very repressive domestic behavior, there's no other way to justify the suffering that is entailed on their population, particularly the failure—the manifest failure—of their economic and social policies.
>
> I believe, having said that, that even if there were no West, no United States, no Israel, you would have these same imperatives of external enemies for domestic consumption driving bloodletting in the Middle East and making our world a more dangerous place....This ought to inform the policies we pursue, especially as we are told endlessly that if only we make Israel make territorial concessions to its Palestinian Arab neighbors, that will end the problem. It won't end the problem between Israel and the Palestinians, let alone transform this region into the sort of peaceful arena we hope it would be.[150]

The argument is entirely clear: that Israeli territorial concessions are irrelevant to Israeli-Palestinian peace and Arab attitudes to Israel and the United States, and that in any case no peace is possible until the Arab and Muslim worlds become fully democratic—in other words, at some point so far in the future that it is not worth even discussing. Although Gaffney is a neoconservative radical, the same dynamic seems to be at work with some self-described liberals like Paul Berman, to judge by the complete lack of any balance in the attention they pay to Israeli and Arab policies.

The sincerity of some of these democratic advocates is also highly questionable when it comes to the promotion of democracy and freedom. In 2002 I attended a discussion at the State Department on this subject. Confronted with the evidence of strong opposition to U.S. policies toward Israel and Iraq on the part of ordinary Arabs, a leading U.S. partisan of Israel and critic of Arab tyranny replied that it did not matter, as the United States had more than enough force to crush any Arab opposition, whether from states or peoples: "Let them hate us, as long as they fear us," he declared. *Oderint dum metuant*: the motto of that distinguished humanitarian democratizer, the emperor Caligula.

In the articles for the *New Yorker* magazine that brought the abuses at Abu Ghraib and elsewhere into the open, Seymour Hersh attributes part of the philosophy behind the interrogation techniques to a book by an Israeli and American cultural anthropologist, Professor Raphael Patai, called *The Arab Mind*. This work is characterized by deep contempt for Arab culture and traditions, and was described by Hersh's official sources as "the bible of the neoconservatives on Arab behavior." From it, they said, members of the Bush administration drew beliefs that Arabs only understand force and that their greatest weakness is sexual shame. Mark Danner in the *New York Review of Books* also suggested that the methods used to "soften up" the prisoners at Abu Ghraib and elsewhere reflected not just random sadism but an analysis of Arab culture.[151]

The combination of these attitudes to Arabs on the part of the neoconservatives with their loudly professed belief in democratizing the Arab world is one for which terms such as "hypocrisy" and "cognitive dissonance" are quite inadequate. This is Orwellian doublethink, an offense against fundamental human standards of intellectual decency. That such an incoherent and morally repellent mixture could be taken seriously and exert influence on U.S. policy and the U.S. national debate reveals starkly the hideous muddle into which American thinking about the Muslim world has fallen.

In the Middle East, therefore, American policy at the start of the twenty-first century is an attempt to combine the promotion of values and behavior among Arabs based on the American Creed and American civic nationalism with support for an Israeli state whose policies are based on the American antithesis: strong and exclusive ethnoreligious nationalism, a dominant militarist ethic and rule over another people based on a mixture of claims none of which is related to universalist liberal values.

The result is not a synthesis, but a horrible moral and political mess. It resembles the behavior of nineteenth-century Western powers in preaching Western economics and politics to Japan while somehow assuming that Japan would not pick up their obvious accompaniments at that time, Western racism and imperialism. If this combination of U.S. approaches to the Muslim world continues in the years and decades to come—and the strength of just this mixture among many Democrats as well as Republicans suggests that it well may—then the struggle to stop the spread of Islamist revolution and terrorism could actually be lost, with consequences that hardly bear thinking about.

A book that liberal friends of Israel in the United States could read with profit to themselves, to Israel and to the world is Lewis Namier's *1848: The Revolution of the Intellectuals*. This work examines the record of the German liberal deputies elected to Germany's first democratic parliament in Frankfurt as a result of the revolution of that year. These were genuine liberals, and honorable, civilized men. But they were also German nationalists, and when the Poles, Czechs and other non-German subjects of German monarchs began to state their own national claims, the liberal principles of these German deputies withered before the fiery blast of their own nationalism. Namier's work was published in 1944, amid a world catastrophe originating in large part from that liberal failure.[152]

Conclusion

Gnothi Seauton *(know thyself)*

—Epigraph in the Temple of Delphi

In the past, the demons of American radical nationalism have always been bound again sooner or later by the power of the American Creed. For all their faults, the American Creed and American civic nationalism, and the American democratic system which they sustain, are a great force for civilization in the world. Within the United States, they have up to now provided what might be called America's self-correcting mechanism, which has saved the nation from falling into authoritarian rule or a permanent state of militant chauvinism.

Periods of intense nationalism—such as the panic leading to the passage of the Aliens and Sedition Act in the 1790s, the Know-Nothings of the 1840s, the anti-German hysteria of World War I, the anti-Japanese chauvinism of World War II and McCarthyism in the 1950s—have been followed by a return to a more tolerant and pluralist equilibrium. Chauvinist and bellicose nationalism, although always present, has not become the U.S. norm and has not led to democratic institutions being replaced by authoritarian ones. Moreover, imperialist tendencies in the United States have been restrained by the belief, stemming from the Creed, that America does not have and should not have an empire; as well as by isolationism and an unwillingness to make the sacrifices required to have an empire.

Given the power of the American Creed in American society, there are good grounds to hope that this self-correcting mechanism will continue to operate in future. Indeed, by the middle of 2004 the wilder ambitions of the Bush administration had already been considerably reduced as a result of public disquiet over the aftermath of the war in Iraq and of the fundamental rationality of the greater part of the American establishment.

However, there are also grounds for concern that in the future this self-correcting mechanism may fail, and America be drawn in a more and more chauvinist direction. The reasons for this can be summed up by saying that in the past, the United States went out to shape the world, while being itself protected from the world.

Militarily, it was protected by the oceans. Economically, it was protected by the immense strength and dominance of the American economy. Hence in no small part the unique American combination of power, omnipresence, idealism, innocence and ignorance vis-à-vis the rest of humanity.

This happy situation is no longer the case.

The first change is obviously that like most other countries in the twenty-first century, the American Heartland is now at real risk of terrible attack in a way with no precedents since the French-backed Indian menace disappeared after 1763. The Soviet nuclear menace was obviously a terrifying one, and had a seriously disturbing effect on U.S. politics and political culture; but no attack ever actually occurred. Throughout the Cold War, not one American was ever killed by communism on American soil.

A monstrous terrorist attack on the U.S. mainland has now occurred. It whipped aspects of American nationalism to fury, and this fury was then directed by a U.S. administration against quite different targets. If attacks like 9/11 are repeated, chauvinist nationalism may become a permanently dominant feature of the United States, with everything that this would mean for the country's international behavior, for the prestige of the American system in the world and indeed for the American system at home.

If, as seems all too likely, more such attacks do occur, the mood of the American population could become one of a permanent state of siege and atmosphere of war, with civil liberties restricted and chauvinist politicians fishing assiduously for opportunities in the stew. In this context, it should be remembered that vigilantism and racial justice on the U.S. Frontier ended only with the Frontier itself. The atmosphere of racial fear and a belief in potential conflict in the South also lasted for by far the greater part of American history and ended only when the Southern racist system was overthrown by intervention from the rest of the nation in the mid-twentieth century. September 11 knocked U.S. pluralist democracy off balance. Further terrorist attacks might increase the tilt and make it permanent. In the very worst of outcomes, such attacks could one day capsize the whole American democratic ship of state.

Closely connected with this new threat is the fact that the United States is involved in the greater Middle East in a way with no real precedent in history. In the case of all its other international military involvements, as noted in the last chapter, the United States was able either to pacify an area or to withdraw from it, or both. In the case of Western Europe, Japan and South Korea after World War II, the U.S. military remained present, but in peaceful countries which accepted the U.S. presence. In the case of Indochina, once it became clear that pacification was impossible, the United States was able to make a completely clean break and withdraw. This was, of course, very humiliating, but in the end it proved politically acceptable within the United States and led to no truly harmful results for the nation's security.

In the Middle East, by contrast, the United States appears hopelessly and permanently bound to an unstable, violent and hostile region by two immensely strong

218

ties. The first is the defense of the American Way of Life as presently defined, insofar as this has come to be associated with the gas-consuming automobile. This requires continued American access to cheap and guaranteed supplies of oil, most of which for the foreseeable future will come from the Middle East. The second is the American attachment to Israel, which involves the United States in a national struggle with Arab nationalism and Muslim radicalism—also, so it would seem, for the foreseeable future.

Equally important, if continued, will be the fading of the American Dream as far as large sections of the American middle classes are concerned, due to economic change and the effects of globalization. Over the past thirty years, incomes in this central part of American society have stagnated or even fallen, with the skilled and semiskilled working classes suffering particularly badly.[1] Meanwhile, incomes at the lower end of the scale have been held down by the resumption of mass immigration, both legal and illegal. Median family income rose by 40 percent in the 1950s and 1960s, but in the 1970s, 1980s and 1990s by only some 7 percent, despite the fact that a vastly greater number of women entered full employment over the latter period. Meanwhile income inequality increased considerably. In 1969 the richest 5 percent of families earned 15.6 percent of all income. In 1996, the figure was 20.3 percent.[2]

Ruthless competition, the lack of state regulation and a minimum wage, the increase in temporary and informal employment, the use of unregistered illegal immigrants and the decline of the trade unions have meant that many jobs which once kept people in the middle classes now barely maintain them at subsistence level. This process was symbolized in 2003 by moves on the part of supermarket chains to freeze salaries and slash benefits.[3] The effect of wage cuts and of job insecurity and frequent changes of low-paying jobs is not only to impoverish many working Americans and corrode their family lives; it is also deeply to undermine their personal dignity, their image of themselves as members of the respectable middle classes.[4]

This combination of factors has undermined the "moral economy" which prevailed for most of American history, whereby a man who worked hard, was honest and did not drink or take drugs could be assured of a steadily rising income, enough to support himself and his wife in their old age and to give his children a head start in social advancement through education.[5]

Just as in the past America, unlike other countries, was spared the threat of attack on its homeland and civilian population, so most of the nation (except the South) was also spared for most of its history from the economic disasters inflicted by wars, revolutions and externally driven economic transformations that afflicted so many other countries. In the twentieth century, except for the Depression after 1929, U.S. economic sufferings were mild compared to those of most of the world. It was the United States that went out to overturn and transform other countries' economies.

Within the nation there was, of course, radical economic change, but even in the medium term it was change which generally succeeded in generating new jobs in other areas to replace those that had been destroyed.

This economic history has been of critical importance for U.S. political stability and the character of American nationalism, given the international history of radical nationalism's socioeconomic origins sketched in this book. The specific history of the U.S. economy created the moral economy of the American Dream, which in turn has underpinned so many other positive aspects of America: generally rational and moderate politics at home, relative restraint and benevolence abroad. The success of the American Dream joined with the American Creed to form the American Thesis and to tie up the demons of the American Antithesis, when from time to time these got loose.

If secure working and middle class jobs continue to get rarer and rarer as a result of economic change and globalization, the resulting economic suffering and anxiety concerning social status and security will be gravely worsened by the lack of remotely adequate state-funded safety nets, especially in the area of health. The pathetic fate of elderly former employees of Bethlehem Steel and other great conglomerates, who have seen their health insurance vanish after the companies closed or were sold, is a grim warning of a possible future.[6] In politics, the 2003 California recall election which brought actor Arnold Schwarzenegger to the governorship is also a warning of a mood of desperation in sections of the middle classes and their lack of faith in the existing political class. The danger to the ability of the American economy to serve a majority of the people is increased both by the expense of America's international hegemony and by the curiously insatiable nature of American capitalism, as demonstrated by the Bush administration's tax cuts.

American liberal writers have expressed a certain bewilderment about the way in which, over large areas of the United States, growing economic and social desperation on the part of many White workers leads them to vote not for progressive liberals, but for right-wing Republican candidates. The radical capitalist economic policies pursued by these politicians then contribute still further to precisely those economic trends which are corroding working-class incomes, status and self-respect, leading to yet more radical conservatism, and so on and on: a kind of political *perpetuum mobile.*

Most of these American workers (at least, most of the nonunionized ones from rural, small town and above all religious cultures) are, however, passionately attached to the image of themselves as middle class, not working class. Seen from this point of view, and in the context of wider historical patterns, there is nothing at all surprising about an embattled and declining lower middle class voting for radical conservatism. This has always been the pattern in Europe. The most famous of all novels dealing with lower-middle-class anomie as a result of economic upheaval is Hans Fallada's *Kleiner Mann, Was Nunn?* (Little Man, What Now?), set in Germany during the Depression. We know how the German lower middle classes voted as a result of this experience.[7]

220

Admittedly, most of the European radical conservative parties made at least a token bow in the direction of restraints on capitalism, national social solidarity and so on. In most of the U.S. White lower middle classes, this ideological option has been ruled out so far by the tremendous power of the idea of economic individualism—in effect, part of the American Creed as far as many Americans are concerned—as well as by the sheer grip of U.S. capitalist elites and corporations on American culture and especially the mass media.

This aside, however, the fact that lower middle classes tend to vote according to culture and class self-image rather than class interest is a very well-established one historically. So too is the fact that this self-image has usually included nationalism, and that the more embattled the middle classes become, the more radical their nationalism tends to become.

Should large sections of the self-perceived American "middle class" follow this historical pattern, the consequences could be sinister indeed. In his book *What's Wrong with Kansas? How Conservatives Won the Heart of America* Thomas Frank draws an often hilarious but also tragic picture of the cultural hysteria and paranoia which has gripped sections of White middle-class, churchgoing Middle America.[8] Frank concentrates on religious extremism and illusions about oppression by "liberal elites," but this political culture also includes malignant and hate-filled fantasies about the outside world.

Of course, Kansas is not the whole of the United States, nor is this kind of political culture characteristic even of most Kansans. There is therefore no need for apocalyptic despair in the face of these trends, which a majority of Americans do not share. They are, however, sufficiently widespread in the White "middle classes"—in their own self-perception, still the core and backbone of the American polity—to be a matter of concern and a cause of changes in national policy. Faced with the economic upheaval and misery of the early 1930s, America elected a great democratic reformer and defender of civilization, Franklin Delano Roosevelt, and developed the New Deal. The responses of other countries were much darker and grimmer. Of course, the social effects of changes in the U.S. economy are much more ambiguous and above all very much slower than those of the Slump on various countries after 1929. Nonetheless, history has given us plenty of unpleasant examples of the effect on middle-class political behavior even of slow and partial decline.

If the middle classes continue to crumble, they may therefore take with them one of the essential pillars of American political stability and moderation. As in European countries in the past, such a development would create the perfect breeding ground for radical nationalist groups and for even wilder dreams of "taking back" America at home and restoring the old moral, cultural and possibly racial order. Such developments might lead to unrestrained strikes against America's enemies abroad, or they might lead to isolationism. Or, if past patterns are anything to go by, they might lead to first the one and then the other. This would be a dangerous scenario for America and for the world as can easily be imagined.

Clearly America is no longer immune from the ills of the world. As the twenty-first century progresses, the nation will be more and more vulnerable to a variety of international infections. The dangers posed to America and humanity by America joining the world in this way are greatly increased by certain features of American nationalism which I have described in this book: not only the strength of this nationalism and its alternation between messianic idealism and chauvinism, but also its highly unreflective character. In the past, because America was so victorious, so isolated and so protected, even most American intellectuals never had to reflect on their own nationalism in the way that was forced on Europeans by the disasters of the twentieth century. It is now urgently necessary that they begin to do so, and I hope that this book has provided a small impetus toward such reflection.

To examine their own nationalism in this way, it will however be necessary for Americans to learn from the often terrible example of other nationalisms in modern history and around the world. Doing so will require an ability to step outside American national myths and look at the nation with detachment, not as an exceptional city on a hill, but as a mortal nation among other nations, better than most, no doubt, but also subject to the moral hazards, temptations and crimes to which many peoples have been exposed.[9]

The disastrous outcomes that I have sketched are certainly not inevitable, given the tremendous resilience and dynamism of American society, American values and the American democratic tradition; but preventing them will require not just thought but serious action by the U.S. political classes. At home, action is required to restrain the excesses of capitalism and to reshape the economy so as to serve the American people. Abroad, it requires action to make America once again a leader by consent, concerned for the health, stability and longevity of the current international system and dedicated to working with other responsible states to achieve these goals.

Most important of all, the American elites should have both more confidence in and more concern for the example their country sets to the world, through their institutions, their values and the visible well-being of ordinary Americans. This example forms the basis of America's "soft power" and makes possible a form of U.S. hegemony by consent. These institutions and values constitute America's civilizational empire, heir to that of Rome. Like the values of Rome, they will endure long after the American empire, and even the United States itself, has disappeared. The image of America as an economically successful pluralist democracy, open to all races and basically peaceful and nonaggressive, has been so powerful in the past because it has largely been true. Americans must make sure that it continues to be true.

Notes

Introduction

1. Alexis de Tocqueville, *Democracy in America*, trans. Henry Reeve, intro. Joseph Epstein (New York: Bantam Classics, 2000), p. 662.
2. Cf. G. John Ikenberry, "America's Imperial Ambition," *Foreign Affairs* 81, no. 5 (September/October 2002): 44–60.
3. Cf. Stephen Walt, "Keeping the World Off Balance: Self Restraint and US Foreign Policy," John F. Kennedy School of Government, Harvard Research Working Papers Series (October 2000); Joshua Micah Marshall, "Power Rangers: Did the Bush Administration Create a New American Empire—or Weaken the Old One?" *The New Yorker*, February 2, 2004.
4. Don Siegel (director), *The Shootist*, starring John Wayne and Lauren Bacall, 1976.
5. Cf. PIPA (Program on International Policy Attitudes, University of Maryland), "Americans on Foreign Aid and World Hunger: A Study of US Public Attitudes," February 2, 2001; Robert Bellah, foreword to Richard Hughes, *Myths America Lives By* (Urbana: University of Illinois Press, 2003), pp. ix–xii.
6. Erik Erikson, *Childhood and Society*, quoted in Robert Bellah, *The Broken Covenant: American Civil Religion in a Time of Trial* (New York: Seabury Press, 1975), p. 63.
7. Figures in the public opinion survey "Evenly Divided and Increasingly Polarized: 2004 Political Landscape," The Pew Research Center for the People and the Press, Washington, DC, released November 5, 2003. See www.people-press.org.
8. For profiles of Jacksonian nationalism, see Walter Russell Mead, *Special Providence: American Foreign Policy and How It Changed the World* (New York: Routledge, 2002), pp. 218–263; Michael Kazin, *The Populist Persuasion: An American History* (New York: HarperCollins, 1995), pp. 21–22, 166; Samuel Eliot Morison, Henry Steele Comager, and William E. Leuchtenburg, *The Growth of the American Republic* (New York: Oxford University Press, 1969), pp. 419–443; Robert V. Remini, *The Life of Andrew Jackson* (New York: Harper Collins, 2001), passim.
9. Irving Kristol, *Reflections of a Neo-Conservative* (New York: Basic Books, 1983), p. xiii. See also Kristol, *Neo-Conservatism, Autobiography of an Idea* (New York: Free Press, 1994), p. 365; and Shadia B. Drury, *Leo Strauss and the American Right* (New York: St. Martin's Press, 1997), pp. 149–153.
10. Kenneth Minogue, *Nationalism* (New York: Basic Books, 1997).
11. Richard Hofstadter, *The Age of Reform* (New York: Vintage Books, 1955), p. 15.
12. Figures in "Global Attitudes 2002: 44-Nation Major Survey," The Pew Research Center for the People and the Press, Washington, DC, released November 5, 2003. See www.people-press.org.
13. Gunnar Myrdal, *An American Dilemma: The Negro Problem and Modern Democracy* (New York: Harper and Bros., 1944), p. xlviii.

14. Cf. David H. Bennett, *The Party of Fear: From Nativist Movements to the New Right in American History* (New York: Random House, 1988), pp. 7–8; for a succinct recent statement of the nativist position on the Creed from a leading conservative intellectual, see Samuel Huntington, "The Hispanic Challenge," *Foreign Policy* (March/April 2004), and "Dead Souls: The Denationalization of the American Elite," *National Interest*, no. 75 (Spring 2004).

15. Ralph Reed, "Separation of Church and State: 'Christian Nation' and Other Heresies," in *God's New Israel: Religious Interpretations of American Destiny*, ed. Conrad Cherry (Chapel Hill: University of North Carolina Press, 1998), pp. 373–379.

16. Tocqueville, *Democracy in America*, p. 51; for the decline of religious belief in Germany before 1914, see Hans-Ulrich Wehler, *The German Empire 1871–1918* (Leamington Spa, Germany: Berg Publishers,), p. 115.

17. "Among Wealthy Nations, the US Stands Alone in its Embrace of Religion," Global Attitudes Project report, 2002, released November 5, 2003.

18. Seymour Martin Lipset, *American Exceptionalism: A Double-edged Sword* (New York: W. W. Norton, 1976), p. 62.

19. Cf. Richard Hofstadter, *The Paranoid Style in American Politics and Other Essays* (Cambridge, MA: Harvard University Press, 1996 [rpt]); Michael Lind, *The Next American Nation: The New Nationalism and the Fourth American Revolution* (New York: Simon and Schuster, 1995), p. 99.

20. D. G. Hart, "Mainstream Protestantism, 'Conservative' Religion, and Civil Society," in *Religion Returns to the Public Square: Faith and Policy in America*, ed. Hugh Heclo and Wilfred M. McClay (Washington, DC: Woodrow Wilson Center Press, 2003), p. 197.

21. Speaking of House Speaker Sam Rayburn of Texas. Quoted in Robert A. Caro, *The Years of Lyndon Johnson* (New York: Alfred A. Knopf, 2002), vol. 1, *The Path to Power*, p. 759.

22. Hofstadter, *The Paranoid Style in American Politics*, p. 3.

23. Clinton Rossiter, *Conservatism in America* (New York: Random House, 1962), p. 206.

24. Sheldon Hackney, "The Contradictory South," *Southern Cultures* (Winter 2001); cf. also Jerome L. Himmelstein, "The New Right," in *The New Christian Right: Mobilization and Legitimation*, ed. Robert C. Liebman and Robert Wuthnow (New York: Aldine, 1983), pp. 21–24.

25. Garry Wills, *Reagan's America: Innocents at Home* (New York: Doubleday, 1987), p. 382.

26. Karl Marx and Friedrich Engels, *The Communist Manifesto*, translated Samuel Morse (London: Penguin Books, 1967 [rpt]), pp. 222–223.

27. Sacvan Berkovitch, *The Puritan Origins of the American Self* (New Haven, CT: Yale University Press, 1975), p. 185.

28. For a definition of hegemony, see G. John Ikenberry and Charles A. Kupchan, "Socialization and Hegemonic Power," *International Organization* 44, no. 3 (Summer 1990); for the original definition of this term, see Antonio Gramsci, *Selections from the Prison Notebooks*, ed. and translated by Quintin Hoare and Geoffrey Nowell Smith (London: Lawrence and Wishart, 1971), pp. 52–120, 206–276.

29. Perry Anderson, "Force and Consent," *New Left Review* (September/October 2002). For the views of the Clinton administration on policy toward "rogue states" as a precedent for Bush's "Axis of Evil" approach, see Anthony Lake (national security adviser), "Confronting Backlash States," *Foreign Affairs* (March/April 1994).

30. Cf. William Appleman Williams, *The Tragedy of American Diplomacy* (New York: Dell Publishing,1959); Andrew J. Bacevich, *American Empire: The Realities and Con-*

sequences of US Diplomacy (Cambridge, MA: Harvard University Press, 2002); Chalmers Johnson, *The Sorrows of Empire: Militarism, Secrecy and the End of the Republic* (New York: Metropolitan Books, 2004).

31. Phyllis Schlafly, "Beware of Clinton's 'Web' of Treaties," speech to the Christian Coalition, Washington DC, September 18, 1998, on www.eagleforum.org.

32. Ikenberry, "America's Imperial Ambition."

33. For Bush's abandonment of Roosevelt's international framework, see Peter Gowan, "US:UN," *New Left Review* (November-December 2003).

34. Cf. Melissa August et al., "Unilateralism is U.S.," *Time,* August 6, 2001; Ivo Daalder and James Lindsay, *America Unbound: The Bush Revolution in Foreign Policy* (Washington, DC: Brookings Institution Press, 2003), pp. 71–79, 189–193; Dana Milbank and Dan Morgan, "Some Pet Programs Are Targeted for Cuts," *Washington Post,* February 5, 2004.

35. Richard Clarke, *Against All Enemies: Inside America's War on Terror* (New York: Free Press, 2004), p. 273.

36. John Bolton, "Should We Take Global Governance Seriously?" *Chicago Journal of International Law* 1, no. 2 (2000); cf. also G. John Ikenberry, "The End of the Neo-Conservative Moment," *Survival* 46, no. 1 (Spring 2004); John Newhouse, *Imperial America: The Bush Assault on the World Order* (New York: Alfred A. Knopf, 2003), pp. 5–34.

37. Pew Research Center for the People and Press, Washington, DC, March 16, 2004, Survey Report: "US Image Still Poor" (News Interest Index).

38. For the decision to reject Kyoto, see the recollections of Treasury Secretary Paul O'Neill in Ron Suskind, *The Price of Loyalty: George W. Bush, the White House, and the Education of Paul O'Neill* (New York: Simon and Schuster, 2004), pp. 99–106, 113–114, 120–128.

39. Ibid., p. 124.

40. Cf. Jack Snyder, "Imperial Temptations," *The National Interest*, no. 71 (Spring 2003). For a propagandist gloss on the intentions of the NSS by one of its contributors, see the companion piece by Philip Zelikow, "The Transformation of National Security: Five Redefinitions."

41. Cf. Walter Russell Mead, "The US-EU Split," address to the New America Foundation, February 13, 2003 (New America Foundation Program Brief). For another reference to the "Roosevelt Corollary" in this context, see Daalder and Lindsay, *America Unbound,* p. 6. For the original corollary, see Samuel Eliot Morison, *Oxford History of the American People*, vol. 3 (New York: Penguin, 1994), p. 149; for its impact on U.S. policy toward Latin America, see Tony Smith, *America's Mission,* pp. 66ff; for its globalization under Franklin Delano Roosevelt and his successors, see Smith, *America's Mission,* pp. 113ff.

42. Cf. Ikenberry, "America's Imperial Ambition"; Snyder, "Imperial Temptations."

43. Joseph S. Nye, *Soft Power: The Means to Success in World Politics* (New York: Public Affairs, 2004).

44. Julien Benda, *The Treason of the Intellectuals,* trans. Richard Aldington (New York: W. W. Norton, 1969), p. 57.

45. I am indebted for this comparison to Dr. David Chambers of the Middle East Institute in Washington.

46. Fouad Ajami, "The Falseness of Anti-Americanism," *Foreign Policy* (September/October 2003).

47. Charles Krauthammer, "To Hell with Sympathy," *Time,* November 17, 2003; or see Dinesh d'Souza, *What's So Great About America* (Washington, DC: Regnery Books, 2002), another American right-wing nationalist intellectual of recent immigrant origins.

48. Schlafly, "Beware of Clinton's 'Web' of Treaties."

50. Brian Klug, "The Collective Jew: Israel and the New Anti-Semitism," *Patterns of Prejudice* 37, no. 2 (2003).

51. J. William Fulbright, *The Arrogance of Power* (New York: Random House, 1966), p. 22.

Chapter One

1. Thomas Mann, *Doctor Faustus: The Life of the German Composer Adrian Leverkuhn as Told By a Friend,* trans. H. T. Lowe-Porter (London: Penguin, 1978), p. 291.

2. The phrase is that of Lipset, *American Exceptionalism*; see also Minxin Pei, "The Paradoxes of American Nationalism," *Foreign Policy* (May-June 2003).

3. Michael Lind, *The Next American Nation: The New Nationalism and the Fourth American Revolution* (New York: Simon and Schuster, 1995), pp. 100–102, 140–161, 215–216, etc.

4. Figures for 1999 from World Values Survey, quoted in Pei, "The Paradoxes of American Nationalism." For the 1985 figures, see Richard Rose, "National Pride in Cross-cultural Perspective," *International Social Science Journal* 37, no. 1 (1985). For the 2003 figures, see Pew Research Center for the People and the Press, *Views of a Changing World 2003,* Washington, DC. See also Lipset, *American Exceptionalism,* p. 51; and Tom W. Smith and Lars Jarkko, *National Pride: A Cross-Cultural Analysis* (Chicago: National Opinion Research Center, 1998). See also Samuel P. Huntington, "Dead Souls: The Denationalization of the American Elite," *National Interest,* no. 75 (Spring 2004).

5. *Washington Post,* June 25, 2003, p. A5.

6. William R. Brock, "Americanism," in *The United States: A Companion to American Studies,* ed. Dennis Welland (London: Methuen, 1974), p. 58.

7. Jim Brosseau, ed., *A Celebration of America: Your Helpful Guide to America's Greatness* (Des Moines, IA: Meredith Publications, 2002).

8. Lynne Cheney, *America: A Patriotic Primer* (New York: Simon and Schuster, 2002); see also George Grant, *The Patriot's Handbook* (Nashville, TN: Cumberland House Publishing, 1996).

9. *Parade* magazine, *Washington Post,* November 9 and December 20, 2003.

10. See Michael Paris, *Warrior Nation: Images of War in British Popular Culture, 1850–2000* (London: Reaktion Books, 2000).

11. See Conrad Cherry, ed., *God's New Israel:* Religious Interpretations of American Destiny (Chapel Hill: University of North Carolina Press, 1998), introduction; Cherry, "American Sacred Ceremonies," in *Social Patterns of Religion in the United States,* ed. Phillip E. Hammond and Benton Johnson, pp. 303–316 (New York: Random House, 1970); W. Lloyd Warner, "An American Sacred Ceremony," in *American Civil Religion,* ed. Russell E. Richey and Donald G. Jones (New York: Harper & Row, 1974).

12. Max Lerner, *American Civilization: Life and Thought in the US Today* (New York: Simon and Schuster, 1957), p. 903.

13. de Tocqueville, *Democracy in America* (first published 1835), vol. 1, pp. 281, 704, 764–766.

14. See Eugen Weber, *Peasants into Frenchmen: The Modernisation of Rural France, 1870–1914* (Stanford, CA: Stanford University Press, 1976), p. 19; see also Theodore Zeldin, *France 1848–1945: Intellect and Pride* (New York: Oxford University Press, 1980), pp. 3ff.

15. For the formation of a British identity and patriotism in the eighteenth century out of the different Protestant nationalities of the British Isles, see Linda Colley, *Britons:*

Forging the Nation, 1707–1837 (London: Yale University Press, 1992). For the ideology of the law as a state-supporting force in eighteenth-century England, see Douglas Hay et al., *Albion's Fatal Tree: Crime and Society in 18th Century England* (New York: Random House, 1975), pp. 32–39.

16. Louis Hartz, *The Liberal Tradition in America* (New York: Harcourt Brace Jovanovich, 1955), pp. 9, 307.

17. Herbert Croly, *The Promise of American Life* (first published 1909) (Boston: Northeastern University Press, 1989), p. 1.

18. Rupert Brooke, "Peace" (1914), in *The War Poets,* ed. Frederick Brereton, p. 53 (London: W. Collins and Co., 1930).

19. William J. Bennett, *Why We Fight: Moral Clarity and the War on Terrorism* (New York: Doubleday, 2002), pp. 132–133.

20. Ernst Glaeser, *Jahrgang 1902* (Berlin 1929), quoted in Gordon Craig, *Germany 1866–1945* (Oxford: Oxford University Press, 1981), p. 340; see also "Days of Victory, August 4 and August 5" (Berlin: Protestant Press Agency, August 1914), quoted in Hartmut Lehmann, "God Our Old Ally: The Chosen Nation Theme in Late 19th and Early 20th Century German Nationalism," in William R. Hutchison and Harmut Lehmann, *Many Are Chosen* (Trinity Press International, 1998), p. 87; see also Heinrich von Treitschke, *The Nature of Politics*, trans. Blanche Dugdale (London: Constable, 1916), extracted in *Nationalism and Realism 1852–1879,* ed. Hans Kohn, pp. 162–166 (Princeton, NJ: D. Van Nostrand, 1958).

21. *"Agir. Ne plus douter de mon pays ni de mes propre forces. Agir. Servir… Ne plus discuter, ne plus m'interroger…"* Georges Ducrocq, *Adrienne.* extracted in *Le Nationalisme Français 1871–1914,* ed. Raoul Girardet, pp. 249–250 (Paris: Arman Colin, 1966).

22. For the successful use of the "patriotic card" by the Republicans in the 2002 congressional elections, see, e.g., "Politics and the Talk of War," *San Francisco Chronicle,* September 26, 2002; Tatsha Robertson, "War Stance Influencing Close Races: Even Veterans Face Queries on Patriotism," *Boston Globe,* November 1, 2002; Joan Vennochi, "Kerry Walks a Fine Line," *Boston Globe,* November 19, 2002; Jim Tharpe, "Cleland, Chambliss Trade Barbs," *Atlanta Journal-Constitution,* July 4, 2002. For a defense of the Bush administration's use of the issue in the 2004 election, see "Is 9/11 an Issue?," *Wall Street Journal,* editorial, March 5, 2004. For books attacking the Bush administration's use of this tactic, see Joe Conason, *Big Lies: The Right-wing Propaganda Campaign and How It Distorts the Truth* (New York: St. Martin's Press, 2003), pp. 52–73; Molly Ivins and Lou Dubose, *Bushwhacked: Life in George Bush's America* (New York: Random House, 2003), pp. 248–275.

23. Quoted by E. J. Dionne, "Finding Answers in Indiana," *Washington Post,* September 27, 2002.

24. Mike Allen, "Address Will Depict Bush as above Politics," *Washington Post,* January 18, 2004; see also Dana Milbank and David S. Broder, "Hopes for Civility in Washington Are Dashed," *Washington Post,* January 18, 2004.

25. As in Thomas Mann, *Betrachtungen eines Unpolitischen* (Observations of an Apolitical Man) (Germany: Fischer Tagenbuch Verlag, 1995).

26. Bacevich, *American Empire,* p. 237; Bill Maher, *When You Drive Alone You Drive with Bin Laden: What the Government Should Be Telling Us to Help Fight the War on Terrorism* (Beverly Hills, CA: New Millennium Press, 2003), introduction.

27. See Joe Galloway, "Thanks to Rumsfeld, Iraq Is Still America's to Lose," www.military.com, December 17, 2003; Max Boot, "Washington Needs a Colonial

Office," *Financial Times* (London), July 3, 2003; Hendrik Hertzberg, "Building Nations," *New Yorker,* June 9, 2003.

28. Polls at www.ropercenter.uconn.edu.
29. "Presidential Debate Clouds Voters' Choice," Pew Research Center for the People and the Press, October 10, 2000, at http://people-press.org/reports.
30. *New York Times,* August 10, 2000.
31. Niall Ferguson, *Empire: The Rise and Demise of the British World Order and the Lessons for Global Power* (New York: Public Affairs, 2003).
32. See Sebastian Balfour, *Deadly Embrace: Morocco and the Road to the Spanish Civil War* (Oxford: Oxford University Press, 2002); for an attempt to place the Russian disaster in Chechnya in this historical perspective, see my *Chechnya: Tombstone of Russian Power* (New Haven, CT: Yale University Press, 1998), pp. 150–151, and passim.
33. Bacevich, *American Empire,* pp. 141–166.
34. See Weber *Peasants into Frenchmen,* pp. 292–302. For the unpopularity of North African service, see the novel "Birih" (1890) by Georges Davien, and the popular 1891 song by Aristide Bruant, *"A Biribi,"* on the CD *Anthologie de la Chanson Francaise: Soldats, Conscrits et Deserteurs* (EPM Musique, 1996).
35. Quoted in Roger Magraw, *France 1815–1914: The Bourgeois Century* (London: Fontana, 1983), p. 261.
36. Douglas Porch, *The Conquest of Morocco* (New York: Alfred A. Knopf, 1983), pp. 187–188, 293–294.
37. Jean-Jacques Becker, *1914* (Paris: Presses de la Fondation Nationale des Sciences Politiques , 1977); Alfred Cobban, *A History of Modern France, 1871–1962* (London: Penguin, 1990), p. 105.
38. See Perry Anderson, "Force and Consent," *New Left Review* (September/October 2002).
39. Transcript of televised debate with Al Gore, Winston Salem, NC, October 11, 2000.
40. See William Pfaff, *Barbarian Sentiments: America in the New Century* (New York: Farrar, Strauss and Giroux, 2000), p. 9.
41. Max Weber, quoted in Clifford Geertz, *The Interpretation of Cultures* (London: Fontana, 1993), p. 5.
42. For works on the history of Wilhelmine Germany which have corrected both the traditional approach based on *Primat der Aussenpolitik* (the dominance of external relations) and simplistic Marxian versions of elite manipulation, see Geoff Eley, "The Wilhelmine Right: How It Changed," in *Society and Politics in Wilhelmine Germany,* ed. Richard J. Evans (London: Croom Helm, 1978), pp. 112–135; Wolfgang J. Mommsen, *Imperial Germany 1867–1918: Politics, Culture and Society in an Authoritarian State,* trans. Richard Deveson (New York: Arnold, 1995), pp. 166ff; David Blackbourn, *The Long 19th Century: A History of Germany 1780–1918* (Oxford: Oxford University Press, 1997), introduction; Klaus Epstein, *The Genesis of German Conservatism* (Princeton, NJ: Princeton University Press, 1966).
43. Sean Hannity, "The Battle over Competing Visions of the Family and Family Values," speech at United Families International Conference, November 21–22, 2003, at www.unitedfamilies.org.
44. See also Robert Bork, *Slouching Towards Gomorrah: Modern Liberalism and American Decline* (New York: Regan Books, 1997); D'Souza, *What's So Great About America,* also raises the question of whether "an open society, where such criticisms are permitted and even encouraged, has the fortitude and will to resist external assault."

45. Richard Rorty, *Achieving Our Country: Leftist Thought in Twentieth Century America* (Cambridge, MA: Harvard University Press, 1998), p. 35.

46. Craig, *Germany 1866–1945*, p. 206.

47. George Kennan, quoted in John Hellmann, *American Myth and the Legacy of Vietnam* (New York: Columbia University Press, 1986), pp. 42–43.

48. Quoted in David Brock, *Blinded by the Right: The Conscience of an Ex-Conservative* (New York: Three Rivers Press, 2002), p. 75.

49. George L. Mosse, *Nationalism and Sexuality: Middle Class Morality and Sexual Norms in Modern Europe* (Madison: University of Wisconsin Press, 1988); see also Fritz Stern, *The Politics of Cultural Despair* (Berkeley: University of California Press, 1974); for an American right-wing nationalist linkage of homosexuality with national weakness and decline, see Norman Podhoretz, "The Culture of Appeasement," *Harper's* (October 1977); for a work linking Clinton's sexual "decadence" with his foreign policy "weakness," see Lieutenant Colonel (ret.) Robert "Buzz" Patterson, *Dereliction of Duty: The Eyewitness Account of How Bill Clinton Compromised America's National Security* (Washington, DC: Regnery Publishing, 2003).

50. Lee Harris, *Civilization and Its Enemies: The Next Stage of History* (New York: Free Press, 2004), pp. 69–84; Robert D. Kaplan, *Warrior Politics: Why Leadership Requires a Pagan Ethos* (New York: Vintage Books, 2003).

51. Timothy Garton Ash, "Anti-Europeanism in America," *New York Review of Books*, February 13, 2003. For a sophisticated neoconservative view of the underlying differences between the United States and Europe, see Robert Kagan, *Of Paradise and Power: America and Europe in the New World* (New York: Alfred A. Knopf, 2002).

52. See *Forfeiting "Enduring Freedom" for "Homeland Security": A Constitutional Analysis of the USA Patriot Act of 2001 and the Justice Department's Anti-Terrorism Measures* (Charlottesville, VA: Rutherford Institute, 2002); *Unpatriotic Acts*, American Civil Liberties Union, July 2003; Muzaffar A. Chishti et al., *America's Challenge: Domestic Security, Civil Liberties and National Unity after September 11* (Washington, DC: Migration Policy Institute, 2003).

53. See Eric Alterman, *What Liberal Media? The Truth About Bias and the News* (New York: Basic Books, 2003), p. 277.

54. "Defending Civilisation: How Our Universities Are Failing America and What Can Be Done About It," American Council of Trustees and Alumni, November 2001.

55. David Frum, "Unpatriotic Conservatives: A War Against America," *National Review*, April 7, 2003.

56. Sean Hannity, *Deliver Us from Evil: Defeating Terrorism, Despotism and Liberalism* (New York: Simon and Schuster, 2004).

57. Saul Padover, ed., *The Complete Jefferson* (New York: Irvington Publishers, 1943), pp. 385–386.

58. See Edward Shils, "Ideology and Civility: On the Politics of the Intellectual," *The Sewanee Review*, no. 66 (1958).

59. Quoted in John Hellmann, *American Myth and the Legacy of Vietnam* (New York: Columbia University Press, 1986), pp. 5–7.

60. Quoted in James H. Moorhead, "The American Israel: Protestant Tribalism and Universal Mission," in Hutchison and Lehmann, *Many Are Chosen*, p. 163; for how this belief was reflected in American textbooks of the 1940s and 1950s, see Frances FitzGerald, *America Revised: What History Textbooks Have Taught Our Children about Their Country, and How and Why Those Textbooks Have Changed in Different Decades* (New York: Vintage Books, 1980), pp. 116–117.

61. Cf Hartz, *The Liberal Tradition in America*, pp. 35–38.

62. See Conor Cruise O'Brien, *God Land: Reflections on Religion and Nationalism* (Cambridge, MA: Harvard University Press, 1987); Lind, *Next American Nation*, pp. 227–234.

63. Paul Johnson, "God and the Americans," *Commentary* (January 1995).

64. Herman Melville, *White-Jacket* (New York: Holt, Rinehart and Winston, 1967), p. 150.

65. Conrad Cherry, in Hutchison and Lehmann, *Many Are Chosen*, p. 111; Walter McDougall, *Promised Land, Crusader State: The American Encounter with the World Since 1776* (New York: Houghton Mifflin, 1997), pp. 204ff.

66. Johann Gottlieb Fichte, "Addresses to the German Nation" (1806), quoted in Lind, *Next American Nation*, 227.

67. Quoted in ibid., p. 230.

68. See Reinhold Niebuhr, *The Irony of American History* (New York: Charles Scribner's Sons, 1952), pp. 68–69.

69. Jules Michelet, quoted in Rogers Brubaker, *Citizenship in France and Germany* (Cambridge, MA: Harvard University Press, 1992), p. 2.

70. For French influence on the American Bill of Rights, see Mark Hulliung, *Citizens and Citoyens: Republicans and Liberals in America and France* (Cambridge, MA: Harvard University Press, 2002), pp. 19ff.

71. *"Il existe un pacte, vingt fois seculaire, entre la grandeur de la France et la liberte du monde."*

72. Reported in the *Financial Times* (London), January 28, 2004.

73. Quoted in Zeldin, *France 1848–1945*, p. 9; see also Jules Michelet, *The People*, trans. John P. McKay (Champlain: University of Illinois Press, 1973), pp. 93–94.

74. Karl Kaiser, quoted in Garton Ash, "Anti-Europeanism in America."

75. See Hulliung, *Citizens and Citoyens*, pp. 162ff.

76. See Brubaker, *Citizenship*, pp. 7–8, 13–14, 35–49.

77. Cf Johannes Willms, "France Unveiled: Making Muslims into Citizens," www.OpenDemocracy.net, February 26, 2004.

78. Hans Rogger and Eugen Weber, *The European Right: A Historical Profile* (Berkeley: University of California Press, 1974), p. 579.

79. Walter Russell Mead, "The Jacksonian Tradition," *The National Interest*, no. 58, Winter 1999/2000.

80. Rogger and Weber, *European Right*, p. 24.

81. See Roger Magraw, *France 1815–1914: The Bourgeois Century* (London: Fontana, 1983), pp. 255–284; Cobban, *A History of Modern France*, pp. 48–57, 86–91, etc.; Anthony D. Smith, *Nationalism: Theory, Idology, History* (Polity Press, 2001), pp. 128–129.

82. *"Je m'ecriais avec Schiller:/ Je suis citoyen du monde .../De mes tendresses detournees/Je me suis enfin repenti./Ces tendresses je les ramene/etroitement sur mon pays/Sur les homes que j'ai trahis/Par amour de l'espece humaine."* Sully Prudhomme, extracted in Girardet, *Le Nationalisme Français*, p. 50.

83. For the strength of such feeling in the Indian diaspora in the West, see the furious attacks on Western historians of India for allegedly "denigrating" Hinduism and the Hindu role in Indian history, reported by Shankar Vedantam, "Wrath over a Hindu God," *Washington Post*, April 10, 2004.

84. For a comparison from the 1950s, see Lerner, *American Civilization*, pp. 934–938.

85. Quoted in Hans Kohn, *American Nationalism: An Interpretative Essay* (New York: Macmillan, 1957), p. 133.

86. McDougall, *Promised Land, Crusader State*, p. 126.

87. Reinhold Niebuhr, "Anglo Saxon Destiny and Responsibility," *Christianity and Crisis,* October 4, 1943, reprinted in Cherry, *God's New Israel,* pp. 296–300; Myrdal, *American Dilemma,* pp. 1018–1024; see also Eric Foner, *Who Owns History? Rethinking the Past in a Changing World* (New York: Farrar, Straus and Giroux, 2002), pp. 65–68.

88. Lind, *Next American Nation,* pp. 105ff; Francis Butler Simkins and Charles Pierce Roland, *A History of the South* (New York: Alfred A. Knopf, 1972), pp. 588 ff.

89. Foner, *Who Owns History,* p. 61

90. See Arthur Cooper, trans. and ed., *Li Po and Tu Fu* (London: Penguin, 1973), pp. 24–26. Like the Russian empire, the Chinese dynasties also possessed ethnic groups of licensed semi-outcastes with strictly defined social roles who were often employed in the entertainment and sex industries: in Russia the Gypsies, in T'ang China the Tanka, a former tribal people of the southern coastal fringes. The Jews in Russia too were assigned particular socioeconomic roles, and attempts were made to repress them when they broke out of those roles and out of the geographical limits to which the state had tried to restrict them.

91. For the difference between the rigid separation and subordination of the American "one drop of blood" system and the relatively more complex and tolerant racial shadings of Brazil, see George M. Fredrickson, "The Strange Death of Segregation," *New York Review of Books,* May 6, 1999.

92. Robert J. Blendon et al., "America's Changing Political and Moral Values," in *What's God Got to Do with the American Experiment,* ed. E. J. Dionne and John J. DiIulio, pp. 26, 29 (Washington, DC: Brookings Institution Press, 2000). Figures for attitudes to interracial "dating" in the public opinion survey "Evenly Divided and Increasingly Polarized: 2004 Political Landscape," The Pew Research Center for the People and the Press, Washington, DC, released November 5, 2003, pp. 45–50. See www.people-press.org.

93. See Adam Clymer, "Divisive Words: GOP's 40 Years of Juggling on Race," *New York Times,* December 13, 2002; David von Drehle and Dan Balz, "For GOP, South's Past Rises in Tangle of Pride, Shame," *Washington Post,* December 15, 2002.

94. For the continuation of racist attitudes in new forms, see David K. Shipler, *A Country of Strangers: Blacks and Whites in America* (New York: Alfred A. Knopf, 1998), especially its discussion of the University of Chicago study of 1990; Orlando Patterson, *The Ordeal of Integration: Progress and Resentment in America's "Racial" Crisis* (New York: Basic Books, 1998); see also George M. Fredrickson, "America's Caste System: Will It Change?" *New York Review of Books,* October 23, 1997.

95. Sara Diamond, *Not by Politics Alone: The Enduring Influence of the Christian Right* (New York: Guilford Press, 1998), pp. 220–228.

96. See Ronald R Stockton, "The Evangelical Phenomenon: A Falwell–Graham Typology," in *Contemporary Political Involvement: An Analysis and Assessment,* ed. Corwin E. Smidt, pp. 45–69 (Lanham, MD: University Press of America, 1989).

97. Peter W. Williams, *America's Religions from Their Origins to the 21st Century* (Chicago: University of Illinois Press, 2002), p. 378.

98. See Howard Elinson, "The Implications of Pentecostalist Religion for Intellectualism, Politics and Race Relations," *American Journal of Sociology* 70, no. 4 (January 1965).

99. See Walter Russell Mead, *Special Providence* (New York: Alfred A. Knopf, 2001), pp. 260–261.

100. See C. Vann Woodward, *The Strange Career of Jim Crow* (New York: Oxford University Press, 2002 [rpt]), pp. 134–139.

101. Lind, *Next American Nation,* pp. 105–106.

102. See Joseph McBride, *Searching for John Ford* (New York: St. Martin's Press, 2001), pp. 452–455, 560–572, 603–611.
103. See Lind, *Next American Nation,* p. 81.
104. See Michelle Cottle, "Color TV: How Soaps Are Integrating America," *The New Republic,* August 27, 2001.
105. See Eastwood's *Unforgiven* (1992), with Morgan Freeman.
106. See *In the Heat of the Night* (1967) and *A Soldier's Story* (1984) directed by Norman Jewison, and *Remember the Titans* (2000), directed by Boaz Yakin, starring Denzel Washington.
107. Clyde Prestowitz, *Rogue Nation: American Unilateralism and the Failure of Good Intentions* (New York: Basic Books, 2003), p. 42.
108. See Loren Baritz, *Backfire: A History of How American Culture Led Us into Vietnam and Made Us Fight the Way We Did* (New York: William Morrow, 1985), p. 40.
109. Lerner, *American Civilization,* p. 921.

Chapter Two

1. Hartz, *Liberal Tradition,* p. 175.
2. Niebuhr, *Irony of American History,* p. 42.
3. See Myrdal, *An American Dilemma,* pp. 1–25. For the original use of the term "American Creed," see G. K. Chesterton, *What I Saw in America* (New York: Dodd, Mead and Co., 1922), quoted in Lipset, *American Exceptionalism,* p. 31.
4. See Lind, *The Next American Nation,* pp. 1–18.
5. David Frum, *Dead Right* (New York: Basic Books, 1994), p. 130.
6. Walt Whitman, *Democratic Vistas,* quoted in Sacvan Berkovitch, *The Puritan Origins of the American Self* (New Haven, CT: Yale University Press, 1975), p. 183.
7. Quoted in Kohn, *American Nationalism,* p. 13.
8. See Michael Hunt, *Ideology and US Foreign Policy,* especially pp. 125–170.
9. See Tocqueville, pp. 544ff and passim. See also the definitions of the Creed in Lipset, *American Exceptionalism,* p. 19; Lind, *The Next American Nation,* pp. 90–91, 219–233; and Herbert McClosky, "Consensus and Ideology in American Politics," *American Political Science Review* 58, no. 2 (June 1964). For "the American Proposition," see *USA: The Permanent Revolution,* by the editors of *Fortune* magazine (1951), quoted in Hartz, *Liberal Tradition,* p. 305.
10. Frances FitzGerald, *Fire in the Lake: The Vietnamese and the Americans in Vietnam* (New York: Vintage Books, 1973), p. 9.
11. Hartz, *Liberal Tradition,* pp. 9, 15, 175, 225–237.
12. Niebuhr, *The Irony of American History,* p. 4.
13. Samuel Huntington, *American Politics: The Promise of Disharmony* (Cambridge, MA: Harvard University Press, 1981), pp. 23, 25.
14. Sacvan Bercovitch, quoted in Lipset, *American Exceptionalism,* p. 291.
15. See Andrei K. Sitov, "America: Back in the USSR?" Tass, Washington, DC, August 4, 2003.
16. Russell Nye, *This Almost Chosen People: Essays in the History of American Ideas,* quoted in William J. Cobb Jr., *The American Foundation Myth in Vietnam: Reigning Paradigms and Raining Bombs* (New York: University Press of America, 1998), p. 4.
17. Samuel P. Huntington, *Political Order in Changing Societies* (New Haven, CT: Yale University Press, 1969), pp. 96–98; see also R. A. Humphreys, "The Rule of Law and the American Revolution," in *The Role of Ideology in the American Revolution,* ed. John R. Howe, pp. 20–27 (New York: Holt, Rinehart and Winston, 1970).

18. Quoted in Lind, *The Next American Nation*, pp. 225ff.
19. Huntington, *Political Order in Changing Societies,* p. 104.
20. Robert N. Bellah, *The Broken Covenant: American Civil Religion in a Time of Trial* (New York: Seabury Press, 1975), pp. 5–8; Cobb, *The American Foundation Myth in Vietnam,* p. 21.
21. Speech in James Melvin Washington, ed., *A Testament of Hope: The Essential Writings of Martin Luther King, Jr.* (New York: Harper & Row, 1986), pp. 217–220.
22. See Lind, *The Next American Nation*, p. 90.
23. Reinhold Niebuhr, *The Irony of American History* (New York: Charles Scribner's Sons, 1952), pp. vii, 133.
24. Ibid., pp. 69ff.
25. See Richard Hughes, *Myths America Lives By* (Urbana: University of Illinois Press, 2003), pp. 6–8, 153–186; Bellah, *The Broken Covenant.*
26. Quoted in "This Is a Different Kind of War," *Los Angeles Times*, October 12, 2001.
27. *The National Security Strategy of the United States of America (NSS)*, September 2002, prologue, at www.whitehouse.gov.
28. Wills, *Reagan's America,* title of Chapter 41, pp. 378–388.
29. See Rabbi Isaac M. Wise, quoted in Bellah, *The Broken Covenant,* pp. 40–41; see also Bellah, pp. 5–8; Cobb, *The American Foundation Myth in Vietnam,* pp. 7–10.
30. Hector St Jean de Crevecoeur, *Letters From an American Farmer* (New York: Dutton, 1926 [rpt]), pp. 40–44; see also Gordon S. Wood, "Republicanism as a Revolutionary Ideology," in Howe, *Role of Ideology,* pp. 83–91.
31. See Randall Bennett Woods, "Dixie's Dove: J. William Fulbright, the Vietnam War and the American South," *Journal of Southern History* 60, no. 3 (August 1994); for Fulbright's condemnation of American messianism, see his *The Arrogance of Power,* passim.
32. Richard Cohen, "Blame, Blindness…," *Washington Post*, February 3, 2004.
33. Conor Cruise O'Brien, "Purely American: Innocent Nation, Wicked World," *Harper's* (April 1980).
34. Fulbright, *Arrogance of Power*, p. 27.
35. Alexis de Tocqueville, *Democracy in America*, trans. Joseph Reeve, intro. Joseph Epstein (New York: Bantam Classics, 2000), p. 305.
36. Robert Bellah et al., *Habits of the Heart: Middle America Observed* (Berkeley: University of California Press, 1985), p. 206.
37. John Higham, "Hanging Together: Divergent Unities in American History," *Journal of American History* 61, no. 1 (June 1974); see also Sidney E. Mead, *The Nation with the Soul of a Church* (Macon, GA: Mercer University Press, 1985), pp. 71–77.
38. Quoted in Sidney Mead, *The Nation with the Soul of a Church,* p. 25.
39. Hughes, *Myths America Lives By*, p. 171.
40. See Will Herberg, "America's Civil Religion: What It Is and Whence It Comes," in *American Civil Religion,* ed. Russell E. Richey and Donald G. Jones (New York: Harper & Row, 1974); Robert N. Bellah, "Civil Religion in America," *Daedalus,* no. 96 (1967); and Bellah, *The Broken Covenant.*
41. Adam Gamoran, "Civil Religion in American Schools," *Sociological Analysis* 51, no. 3 (1990), quoting Fay Adams and Ernest W. Tiegs, *Our People: Tiegs-Adams Our Land and Heritage Series, Level 4* (Lexington, MA: Ginn).
42. Each of Hughes's chapters in *Myths America Lives By* is followed by a coda on the theme he has just explored from a Black point of view; see also Richard Rorty, *Achieving Our Country: Leftist Thought in Twentieth Century America* (Cambridge, MA: Harvard University Press, 1998), pp. 31–32.
43. Hartz, *Liberal Tradition,* pp. 58–59.

44. See Alterman, *What Liberal Media?* pp. 268–292.
45. W. H. Auden, "To Keep the Human Spirit Breathing," speech upon acceptance of the 1967 Medal for Literature, Smithsonian Institution, Washington, DC, November 30, 1967, reprinted in the *Washington Post Book World,* December 24, 1967.
46. Quoted in Cherry, *God's New Israel,* p. 304.
47. Reinhold Niebuhr, "The Children of Light and the Children of Darkness," in *The Essential Reinhold Niebuhr: Selected Essays and Addresses,* ed. Robert McAfee Brown, pp. 160–181 (New Haven, CT: Yale University Press, 1986); for Melville's later disillusionment, see Berkovitch, *Puritan Origins,* pp. 180–181.
48. C. Vann Woodward, *The Burden of Southern History* (Baton Rouge: Louisiana State University Press, 1968), p. 218.
49. For an analysis of *Apocalypse Now,* see Hellmann, *American Myth,* pp. 188–204.
50. Baritz, *Backfire,* pp. 349–350.
51. See Stanley Hoffmann, "The High and the Mighty," *American Prospect,* January 13, 2003.
52. See Richard Slotkin, *Gunfighter Nation: The Myth of the Frontier in Twentieth Century America* (Norman: University of Oklahoma Press, 1998), pp. 643–654.
53. Stanley Hoffmann, "The Great Pretender," *New York Review of Books,* May 28, 1987; see also Hoffmann, "Haig's Revenge," *New York Review of Books,* May 31, 1984.
54. Lou Cannon, *President Reagan: The Role of a Lifetime* (New York: Simon and Schuster, 1991), p. 793.
55. Wills, *Reagan's America,* p. 94.
56. William H. McNeill, "The Care and Repair of Public Myth," in McNeill, *Mythistory and Other Essays* (Chicago: University of Chicago Press, 1986). For a critique of this essay, see Slotkin, *Gunfighter Nation,* pp. 626–628.
57. See Cobb, *The American Foundation Myth in Vietnam,* pp. 196–198.
58. Hellmann, *American Myth,* p. 222.
59. Ibid., pp. 135–136. See also Cobb, *American Foundation Myth,* pp. 151–192.
60. See Baritz, *Backfire,* p. 341.
61. See Slotkin, *Gunfighter Nation,* pp. 632–633.
62. See Eric Foner, *The Story of American Freedom* (New York: W. W. Norton, 1998), p. xxi.
63. FitzGerald, *America Revised,* pp. 100–101, 218.
64. Diane Ravitch, *The Language Police: How Pressure Groups Restrict What Students Learn* (New York: Alfred A. Knopf, 2003), p. 101; for a choice selection of some of the more idiotic words and actions by proponents of political correctness, see David E. Bernstein, *You Can't Say That: The Growing Threat to Civil Liberties from Anti-Discrimination Laws* (Washington, DC: Cato Institute, 2003).
65. Gary B. Nash, Charlotte Crabtree, and Ross E. Dunn, *History on Trial: Culture Wars and the Teaching of the Past* (New York: Alfred A. Knopf, 1997), pp. 124–126, 149–277.
66. Lind, *The Next American Nation,* p. 273.
67. Andrew Gumbel, "What Americans Know," *The Independent* (London), September 8, 2003. The passages quoted are from the original, unpublished draft of the article, kindly supplied by the author.
68. For the continuing sanitization of the American Civil War and the elimination of Blacks and slavery from presentations of the conflict, see Foner, *Who Owns History?* pp. 189–204.
69. National Assessment of Educational Progress, 2001; see also Brian Friel, "Don't Know Much About History," August 2, 2003; Cheryl Wetzstein, "Seniors' History Scores Abysmal," *Washington Times,* June 10, 2002; Georgie Anne Geyer, "What Happened

to Geography—And Just Where Is Iraq?" *Tulsa World,* November 27, 2002; for a comparison to levels of knowledge in the 1940s, see Scott Fornek, "What We Don't Know Hasn't Hurt Us," *Chicago Sun-Times,* July 31, 2003.

70. Lind, *The Next American Nation,* pp. 139-188.

71. Cheney, *America.*

72. Ernest Renan, *What Is a Nation?* (1882), trans. Martin Thom, in *Becoming National: A Reader,* ed. Geoff Eley and Ronald Grigor Suny, p. 45 (New York: Oxford University Press, 1996).

73. Hunt, *Ideology and US Foreign Policy,* p. 189.

74. Henry Kissinger, *Diplomacy* (New York: Simon and Schuster, 1994), p. 833.

75. See Alan Brinkley, "Battle Formation," *Washington Post Book World,* March 14–20, 2004.

76. Henry Kissinger, "The End of NATO as We Know It?" *Washington Post,* August 15, 1999, quoted in Kagan, *Paradise and Power,* p. 127.

77. For the historical background to this belief, see Ernest Lee Tuveson, *Redeemer Nation: The Idea of America's Millennial Role* (Chicago: University of Chicago Press, 1968); Hughes, *Myths America Lives By,* pp. 19–41. For fictional versions of America as liberating and/or modernizing redeemer, see Mark Twain, *A Connecticut Yankee in King Arthur's Court* (1889) (New York: Modern Library, 1917); and the original TV series *Star Trek.* See also Walter A. McDougall, *Promised Land, Crusader State: The American Encounter with the World since 1776* (Boston: Houghton Mifflin, 1997), pp. 81ff; Timothy L. Smith, "Righteousness and Hope: Christian Holiness and the Millennial Vision in America, 1880–1900," *American Quarterly* 31, no. 1 (Spring 1979): 21–45.

78. Hughes, *Myths America Lives By,* p. 1.

79. George Kennan, *American Diplomacy, 1900–1950* (Chicago: University of Chicago Press, 1951), p. 135.

80. See Hughes, *Myths America Lives By,* pp. 106–108.

81. Transcript of second presidential debate, Wake Forest University, Winston-Salem, North Carolina, October 11, 2000, at www.cnn.com/ELECTION/2000/debates.

82. John Quincy Adams, presidential speech on July 4, 1821, quoted in Mead, *Special Providence,* p. 185.

83. Hunt, *Ideology and US Foreign Policy,* pp. 92ff; see Fulbright, *Arrogance of Power,* pp. 21ff.

84. George Kennan, "America and the Russian Future," *Foreign Affairs* 29, no. 3 (April 1951).

85. See Alterman, *What Liberal Media?* p. 270.

86. Bacevich, *American Empire,* pp. 9, 33.

87. For an introduction to the subject, see Jon Elster, ed., *Rational Choice* (New York: New York University Press, 1986).

88. Letter of Professor Michael B. Lehmann, Department of Economics, University of San Francisco, quoted in Chalmers Johnson and E. B. Keehn, "A Disaster in the Making," *National Interest,* no. 36 (Summer 1994).

89. See Hartz, *Liberal Tradition,* pp. 29ff, 284ff; Niebuhr, *Irony of American History,* pp. 60ff; Herbert Bolton quoted in Foner, *Who Owns History?* p. 53.

90. McNeill, "A Defense of World History," in *Mythistory,* pp. 71–95; Herbert Butterfield, *The Whig Interpretation of History* (London: G. Bell and Sons, 1931).

91. Johnson and Keehn, "A Disaster in the Making"; for the quasi-religious nature of American capitalist ideology, see Bellah, *The Broken Covenant,* p. xiii.

92. See Stephen M. Walt, "Rigor or Rigor Mortis? Rational Choice and Security Studies," *International Security* 23, no. 4 (Spring 1999).

93. Edward Shils, "Ideology and Civility: On the Politics of the Intellectual," *The Sewanee Review,* no. 66 (1958).

94. See Anatol Lieven, "Qu'est-ce qu'une nation? Scholarly Debate and the Realities of Eastern Europe," *National Interest,* no. 49 (Fall 1997).

95. See Richard Layard and John Parker, *The Coming Russian Boom: A Guide to the New Markets and Politics* (London: Free Press, 1996).

96. Lind, *The Next American Nation,* p. 99.

97. For the religious nature of the imagery of the "path to democracy and the free market," see Anatol Lieven, *Chechnya: Tombstone of Russian Power* (New Haven, CT: Yale University Press, 1998), pp. 8–11; and Harvey Cox, "The Market as God," *Atlantic Monthly* (March 1999); for a biting critique of these ideological illusions about the world, see also Samuel Huntington, *The Clash of Civilizations and the Remaking of the World Order* (New York: Simon and Schuster, 1996), especially pp. 19–39, 183–206, 301–322.

98. John Ralston Saul, "The Collapse of Globalism and the Rebirth of Nationalism," *Harper's* 308, no. 1846 (March 2004).

99. Bellah, *The Broken Covenant,* p. 36.

100. It should be said that this attitude extends far beyond America. One of the strongest expressions of it was made by British prime minister Tony Blair at the Labour Party Conference of 2002: "Our values aren't Western values. They're human values and anywhere, anytime people are given the chance, they embrace them."

101. William Kristol and Robert Kagan, "Toward a Neo-Reaganite Foreign Policy," *Foreign Affairs* 75, no. 5 (July-August 1996).

102. This phrase is a common misquotation of an original toast, by Commodore Stephen Decatur, which went as as follows: "Our country! In her intercourse with foreign nations, may she always be in the right. But right or wrong, our country."

103. See Adrian Karatnycky, "The 30th Anniversary Freedom House Survey," *Journal of Democracy* 14, no. 1 (January 2003). For Freedom House's "methodology" and mission statement, see www.freedomhouse.org/research/freeworld/2000/methodology. By contrast, for a vivid account of how economic and social change has increased the freedom of one Chinese woman worker, see Peter Hessler, "Boomtown Girl," *The New Yorker,* May 28, 2001.

104. See FitzGerald, *America Revised,* pp. 119ff; Edward S. Herman and Noam Chomsky, *Manufacturing Consent: The Political Economy of the Mass Media* (New York: Pantheon Books, 1988), pp. 26–28, 211–228.

105. Mark Palmer, *Breaking the Real Axis of Evil: How to Oust the World's Last Dictators by 2025* (New York: Rowman and Littlefield, 2003).

106. Jacqueline Newmyer, "Will the Space Race Move East?" *New York Times,* October 20, 2003.

107. See Foner, *Story of American Freedom,* p. 263.

108. Lind, *The Next American Nation,* p. 3.

109. *The National Security Strategy of the United States of America (NSS),* September 2002, prologue, at www.whitehouse.gov.

110. Lipset, *American Exceptionalism,* p. 20; see also Prestowitz, *Rogue Nation,* p. 23; for a comparison with U.S. official language during the Vietnam War, see C. Vann Woodward, *Burden of Southern History,* pp. 219–220.

111. See Max Boot, "George W Bush: The 'W' Stands for Woodrow," *Wall Street Journal,* July 1, 2002; David Ignatius, "Wilsonian Course for War," *Washington Post,* August 30, 2002; William Safire, "Post-Oslo Mideast," *New York Times,* June 27, 2002; "Bush the Crusader," *Christian Science Monitor* editorial, August 30, 2002; for postwar justifications along these lines, see George Melloan, "Protecting Human Rights Is a Valid

Foreign Policy Goal," *Wall Street Journal*, June 10, 2003; Jim Hoagland, "Clarity: The Best Weapon," *Washington Post*, June 1, 2003; Thomas L. Friedman, "Because We Could," *Washington Post*, June 4, 2003.

112. Truman quoted in Hunt, *Ideology and American Foreign Policy*, pp. 157, 163.

113. See Bernard Fall, *The Two Vietnams* (New York: Praeger, 1964).

114. Fulbright, *The Arrogance of Power*, pp. 81, 111–119, 154.

115. For a fuller exposition of the lessons of the Cold War for contemporary policy, see Anatol Lieven, *Fighting Terrorism: Lessons from the Cold War*, Policy Brief no. 7, Carnegie Endowment for International Peace, October 2001.

116. *New York Post* editorial, October 9, 2001.

117. See www.whitehouse.gov/news/releases for September 20, 2001.

118. See the Atlantic Council's report, "The Teaching of Values and the Successor Generation" (Washington, DC: Atlantic Council, 1983).

119. From George Bush's speech, "A Distinctly American Internationalism," delivered at the Reagan Presidential Library, November 19, 1999; quoted in Bacevich, *American Empire*, p. 201; see also James W. Ceaser, "Providence and the President: George W. Bush's Theory of History," *Weekly Standard*, March 10, 2003.

120. www.whitehouse.gov for June 1, 2002.

121. See Smith, *America's Mission*, pp. 6, 189ff, 267ff.

122. Kirkpatrick quoted in ibid., p. 286.

123. Irving Kristol, "'Moral Dilemmas' in Foreign Policy" (1980), reprinted in Kristol, *Reflections of a Neoconservative*, pp. 261–265; for a neoconservative attack on just this line of argument, see James W. Ceasar, "The Great Divide: American Interventionism and Its Oponents," in Robert Kagan and William Kristol, eds., *Present Dangers: Crisis and Opportunity in American Foreign and Defense Policy*, pp. 25–43 (San Francisco: Encounter Books, 2000).

124. Irving Kristol, "The 'Human Rights' Muddle," in Kristol, *Reflections of a Neoconservative*, pp. 266–269; for an almost identical statement by one of the greatest targets of neoconservative abuse, George Kennan, see his "Morality and Foreign Policy," *Foreign Affairs* 64, no. 2 (Winter 1985/86). For the long-standing neoconservative hostility to humanitarian interventionism, see Ehrman, *Neoconservatism*, pp. 50ff.

125. See Joshua Muravchik, *Exporting Democracy: Fulfilling America's Destiny* (Washington, DC: American Enterprise Institute, 1991), pp. 19–38, 64–81; William Kristol and Robert Kagan, "Toward a Neo-Reaganite Foreign Policy," *Foreign Affairs* 75, no. 4 (July-August 1996).

126. See Jeanne J. Kirkpatrick, *Dictatorships and Double Standards* (Washington, DC: American Enterprise Institute, 1982).

127. See Lars-Erik Nelson, "Military-Industrial Man," *New York Review of Books*, December 21, 2000.

128. Michael Tomasky, "Between Cheney and Chomsky," in George Packer et al., *The Fight Is for Democracy: Winning the War of Ideas in America and the World*, pp. 41–42 (New York: HarperCollins, 2003). See also the book by one of Tomasky's fellow authors, Paul Berman, *Terror and Liberalism* (New York: W. W. Norton, 2003).

129. For the PPI's program and ideology, see its website, ppionline.org.

130. Dana Allin, Philip Gordon, and Michael O'Hanlon, "The Democratic Party and Foreign Policy," *World Policy Journal* 20, no. 1 (Spring 2003).

131. *Progressive Internationalism: A Democratic National Security Strategy*, at www.ppionline.org/specials/security_strategy.

132. See "Statement on Post-War Iraq," June 16, 2003, signed by Ronald Asmus, Max Boot, Ivo Daalder, Thomas Donnelly, Peter Galbraith, Robert Kagan and others, on www.brookings.edu/fp/projects/iraq/postwar.htm; Leslie H. Gelb and Justine A.

Rosenthal, "The Rise of Ethics in Foreign Policy," *Foreign Affairs* 82, no. 3 (May/June 2003).

133. Michael McFaul, "The Liberty Doctrine," *Policy Review*, no. 112 (April/May 2002).

134. See Abbas Milani, Larry Diamond, and Michael McFaul, "A Blurred Vision: The U.S. Failure to Articulate a Coherent Policy toward Iran Works against the Goal of Democratic Change," *Los Angeles Times*, July 20, 2003. This article by Democratic intellectuals was virtually identical in its arguments to those on the same subject by neoconservatives: see Reuel Marc Gerecht, "Going Soft on Iran: The Temptation of America's Foreign Policy 'Realists,'" *Weekly Standard*, March 8, 2004.

135. See the magisterial study by Tony Smith, *America's Mission: The United States and the Worldwide Struggle for Democracy in the Twentieth Century* (Princeton, NJ: Princeton University Press, 1994).

136. See Boot, "George W. Bush: The 'W' Stands for Woodrow"; David Ignatius, "Wilsonian Course for War," *Washington Post*, August 30, 2002; Michael Ledeen, "Our Revenge: Turning Tyrannies into Democracies," *New York Sun*, September 12, 2002; Condoleezza Rice, interview with James Harding and Richard Wolfe, *Financial Times*, September 23, 2002; "No Exceptions," *Washington Post* editorial, December 29, 2002.

137. Newt Gingrich, "The Failure of U.S. Diplomacy," *Foreign Policy* (July/August 2003): 42–48. For his speech, "Transforming the State Department," April 22, 2003, see the website of the American Enterprise Institute. In support of Gingrich and against the road map, see also Frank J. Gaffney Jr., "Mideast Road Trap," *Washington Times*, May 6, 2003.

138. See Condoleezza Rice, "Transforming the Middle East," *Washington Post*, August 7, 2003; George Melloan, "Protecting Human Rights Is a Valid Foreign Policy Goal," *Wall Street Journal* (Global View), June 10, 2003; "A Wilsonian Call for Freedom," *Washington Times* editorial, November 7, 2003.

139. For a classic text in this regard, see Charles Krauthammer, "The Poverty of Realism," *New Republic* 194, no. 7 (February 17, 1986).

140. Allin, Gordon, and O'Hanlon, *Democratic Party and Foreign Policy*.

141. William Pfaff, *Barbarian Sentiments*, pp. 270–271.

142. Elie Kedourie, *Nationalism* (London: Hutchinson, 1979), pp. 15–16; see also Girardet, *Le Nationalisme Français*, p. 13.

143. See Kagan and Kristol, *Present Dangers*, introduction; Kagan, *Paradise and Power*, pp. 137–138.

144. Girardet, *Le Nationalisme Français*, p. 13.

145. See Niebuhr, *Irony of American History*, pp. 145ff.

146. C. Vann Woodward, *Burden of Southern History*, pp. 205–207.

147. Alex de Waal, "The Moral Solipsism of Global Ethics, Inc.," *London Review of Books*, August 23, 2001; Michael Edwards, *Future Positive: International Cooperation in the 21st Century* (Earthscan, 2000).

148. Quoted in Foner, *Story of American Freedom*, p. 53.

149. See Mary Kaldor, *Global Civil Society: An Answer to War* (London: Polity, 2002); John Keane, *Global Civil Society?* (Cambridge: Cambridge University Press, 2003).

150. See Anatol Lieven, "The World Is Still Made Out of Nations," *Financial Times* (London), December 19, 2002.

151. For an account of how American nationalism blinds Americans to the national feelings of other nations, see Minxin Pei, "The Paradoxes of American Nationalism," *Foreign Policy* (May-June 2003).

152. See Minxin Pei and Sara Kasper, "Lessons from the Past: The American Record on Nation Building," Carnegie Endowment for International Peace, Policy Brief no. 24, May 2003.

153. See Ray Salvatore Jennings, "After Saddam Hussein: Winning a Peace If It Comes to War," United States Institute of Peace Special Report no. 102, February 2003; Joshua Muravchik, "Bringing Democracy to the Arab World," *Current History* (January 2004). For a counterargument in the same issue, see Barak A. Salmoni, "America's Iraq Strategy: Democratic Chimeras, Regional Realities."

154. See Adam Garfinkle, "The New Missionaries," *Prospect* (London) (April 2003).

155. Martin Jacques, "The Interregnum," *London Review of Books* 26, no. 3 (February 5, 2004); Michael Ignatieff, *Empire Lite: Nation-Building in Bosnia, Kosovo and Afghanistan* (New York: Vintage Books, 2003).

156. See Samuel Pao-San Ho, "Colonialism and Development: Korea, Taiwan and Kwantung," in *The Japanese Colonial Empire, 1895–1945*, ed. Ramon H. Myers and Mark R. Peattie, pp. 347–398 (Princeton, NJ: Princeton University Press, 1984).

157. Henry Kissinger, "Intervention with a Vision," *Washington Post*, April 11, 2004.

158. Joseph Conrad, *Heart of Darkness* (London: Penguin, 1995), p. 18.

159. Fulbright, *Arrogance of Power*, p. 17.

Chapter Three

1. Vachel Lindsay, *Selected Poems*, ed. Mark Harris (New York: Macmillan, 1963), p. 124.

2. Cf. David Blackbourn, *History of Germany, 1780–1918: The Long Nineteenth Century* (Oxford: Blackwell, 2003), pp. 37–68.

3. Cf. Rogger and Weber, *The European Right*.

4. Cf. Klaus Epstein, *The Genesis of German Conservatism* (Princeton, NJ: Princeton University Press, 1966).

5. Daniel Bell, "The Dispossessed," in *The Radical Right*, ed. Bell (New York: Doubleday, 1963), p. 12; see also Richard Hofstadter, "The Pseudo-Conservative Revolt—1955," in the same collection, pp. 64–86.

6. Samuel Huntington, *Who Are We? The Challenge to America's National Identity* (New York: Simon and Schuster, 2004), and "The Hispanic Challenge," *Foreign Policy* (March/April 2004); Huntington, *Clash of Civilizations*, map p. 205; see also his essay, "Dead Souls: The Denationalization of the American Elite," *National Interest*, no. 75 (Spring 2004).

7. Cf. Jean Hardisty, *Mobilizing Resentment: Conservative Resurgence from the John Birch Society to the Promise Keepers* (Boston: Beacon Press, 1999), pp. 30–35.

8. Cf. Joseph Farah, *Taking America Back: A Radical Plan to Revive Freedom, Morality and Justice* (Nashville, TN: Thomas Nelson, 2003).

9. Quoted in Garry Wills, "The Born Again Republicans," *New York Review of Books*, September 24, 1992.

10. Rick Perlstein, *Before the Storm: Barry Goldwater and the Unmaking of the American Consensus* (New York: Farrar, Straus and Giroux, 2001), p. 474.

11. For the immense importance of ethnic and regional origins in shaping different strands of American political culture, see Kevin Phillips, *The Cousins' Wars: Religion, Politics and the Triumph of Anglo-America* (New York: Basic Books, 1999), pp. 117 ff.

12. Cf. Bennett, *Party of Fear*, pp. 27–182; Hofstadter, *Paranoid Style*, pp. 19–23.

13. Hardisty, *Mobilizing Resentment*, p. 32.

14. See John Weiss, *Conservatism in Europe, 1770–1945: Tradition, Reaction and Counter-Revolution* (London: Thames and Hudson, 1977), pp. 71–89. For the role of the small town *Mittelstand* and the effects on later German nationalism of the destruction of

their ancient social and political order by the modern state, see Mack Walker, *German Home Towns: Community, State and General Estate, 1648–1817* (Ithaca, NY: Cornell University Press, 1998), especially pp. 405–431.

15. Cf. Geoff Eley, "The Wilhelmine Right: How It Changed," in *Society and Politics in Wilhelmine Germany,* ed. Richard J. Evans, pp. 112–135 (London: Croom Helm, 1978).

16. Alan Brinkley, *Voices of Protest* (New York: Alfred Knopf, 1982), quoted in Phillips, *Boiling Point,* p. 233.

17. Daniel Bell, *The Cultural Contradictions of Capitalism* (New York: Basic Books, 1976), p. 79; cf. also David H. Bennett, *The Party of Fear: From Nativist Movements to the New Right in American History* (Durham: University of North Carolina Press, 1989); Michael Kazin, "The Right's Unsung Prophets," *The Nation,* February 20, 1989; Richard Hofstadter, *The Age of Reform: From Bryan to F.D.R.* (New York: Alfred A. Knopf, 1956), pp. 135, 175.

18. Quoted by Larry McMurtry, "Separate and Unequal," *New York Review of Books,* March 8, 2001. See also Kohn, *American Nationalism,* pp. 143–144.

19. Cf. Liah Greenfield, *Nationalism: Five Roads to Modernity* (Cambridge, MA: Harvard University Press, 1992); Smith, *Nationalism,* p. 97.

20. David Morris Potter, *The Impending Crisis, 1848–1861* (New York: Perennial, 1976), p. 243; Bennett, *Party of Fear,* pp. 17–20.

21. Reinhold Niebuhr, "A Note on Pluralism," quoted in Sidney Mead, *Nation with the Soul of a Church,* p. 31.

22. A. James Reichley, "Faith in Politics," in Heclo and McClay, *Religion Returns to the Public Square,* p. 175; cf. also Bellah, *The Broken Covenant,* pp. 91ff; Daniel Bell et al., *The Radical Right* (New York: Transaction Publishers, 1963), pp. 1–38.

23. Hofstadter, *The Paranoid Style,* pp. 3–40.

24. Mead, *Special Providence,* p. 241; see also Phillips, *The Emerging Republican Majority,* especially pp. 290–392 (on the Midwest).

25. Nathan Glazer and Daniel P. Moynihan, *Beyond the Melting Pot: The Negroes, Puerto Ricans, Jews, Italians and Irish of New York City* (Cambridge, MA: MIT Press, 1979), p. 222.

26. See Gary Gerstle, *American Crucible: Race and Nation in the Twentieth Century* (Princeton, NJ: Princeton University Press, 2001); and Alan Wolfe, "Strangled by Roots," *The New Republic,* May 28, 2001.

27. For the role of the experience and portrayal of the Frontier in American culture, see the three-part work by Richard Slotkin, *Regeneration Through Violence: The Mythology of the American Frontier, 1600–1800; The Fatal Environment: The Myth of the Frontier in the Age of Industrialisation;* and *Gunfighter Nation: The Myth of the Frontier in Twentieth Century America* (Norman: Oklahoma University Press, 1973, 1985, and 1998 respectively).

28. Quoted in Fischer, *Albion's Seed,* pp. 781–782; for this trait in the Scots Irish, see also James G. Leyburn, *The Scotch-Irish: A Social History* (Chapel Hill: University of North Carolina Press, 1962), especially pp. 68–71, 290–291.

29. Cf. Robert V. Remini, *Andrew Jackson and His Indian Wars* (New York: Penguin, 2001); Morison, Commager, and Leuchtenburg, *The Growth of the American Republic,* pp. 402–404, 419–443. For Jackson's Scots Irish roots and character, see Fischer, *Albion's Seed,* pp. 643–644, 685–688, 755–776.

30. Cf. Remini, *Andrew Jackson,* pp. 254–271. See also John Ehle, *Trail of Tears: The Rise and Fall of the Cherokee Nation* (New York: Anchor Books, 1988), pp. 230–264; and Theda Perdue, "Cherokee Women and the Trail of Tears," in *American Encounters: Natives and Newcomers from European Contact to Indian Removal, 1500–1850,* ed. Peter C. Mancall and James H. Merrell, pp. 526–540 (New York: Routledge, 2000).

31. For some of the history of this tradition, see Kelley, *The Cultural Pattern in American Politics*; and Lee Benson, *The Concept of Jacksonian Democracy: New York as a Test Case* (Princeton, NJ: Princeton University Press, 1961).

32. Hofstadter, *Anti-intellectualism*, p. 57; and Richard Niebuhr, *The Social Sources of Denominationalism* (Cleveland: Meridian Books, 1957), p. 30.

33. For the ideas of Thomas Jefferson as a basis for Jacksonianism, see Lind, *The Next American Nation*, pp. 45–46, 370; Bellah, *Broken Covenant*, pp. 116–119; for the "agrarian myth" as a basis for both Jacksonianism and the later Progressive movement, see Hofstadter, *Age of Reform*, pp. 23–59.

34. Cf. Paul Krugman, "True Blue Americans," *New York Times*, May 7, 2002.

35. Quoted in Phillips, *The Emerging Republican Majority*, p. 65.

36. Hofstadter, *Anti-intellectualism*, pp. 146–151.

37. Morison, *History of the American People*, vol. 2, pp. 76–81.

38. FitzGerald, *America Revised*, pp. 74–75.

39. D'Souza, *What's Great About America*, quoted in Louis Menand, "Faith, Hope and Clarity: September 11th and the American Soul," *The New Yorker*, September 16, 2002.

40. Michael Kazin, *The Populist Persuasion: An American History* (New York: Basic Books, 1995), pp. 19–22; cf. also Robert V. Remini, *The Life of Andrew Jackson* (New York: HarperCollins, 1988), pp. 157–162.

41. Cf. Phillips, *The Emerging Republican Majority*, especially pp. 37–40, 187–289, 315, 407–411, 461–474.

42. Morison, Commager, and Leuchtenburg, *The Growth of the American Republic*, pp. 419–443; Kazin, *Populist Persuasion*, p. 19.

43. Myrdal, *American Dilemma*, p. 459.

44. Michael Lind, *Made in Texas: George Bush and the Southern Takeover of American Politics* (New York: Basic Books, 2003), p. 25.

45. W. J. Cash, *The Mind of the South* (New York: Vintage Books, 1991 [rpt]), pp. 134–141; Woodward, *Burden of Southern History*, pp. 197–203.

46. T. R. Fehrenbach, *Lone Star: A History of Texas and the Texans* (New York: Macmillan, 1968), p. 643.

47. See T. R. Fehrenbach, *Comanches: The Destruction of a People* (New York: Alfred A. Knopf, 1974), pp. 270–271.

48. For contemporary English Protestant portrayals of atrocities and massacres by the native Irish in the 1640s against Protestant settlers (looking forward to similar accounts of atrocities by the Indians), see William Lamont and Sybil Oldfield, *Politics, Religion and Literature in the Seventeenth Century* (London: J. M. Dent and Sons, 1975), pp. 65–69; for the experiences of Jackson's own family at Indian hands, and his later campaigns, see Remini, *Andrew Jackson*; for Frontier warfare in the South, see Armstrong Starkey, *European and Native American Warfare 1675–1815* (London: University of Oklahoma Press and UCL Press, 1998), pp. 90–92, 158–161.

49. Cf. Grady McWhiney, *Cracker Culture: Celtic Ways in the Old South* (Tuscaloosa: University of Alabama Press, 1988).

50. For a vivid picture of the class element in one of the battles over the teaching of Evolution which have taken place over the past generation, see Paul Cowan, *The Tribes of America: Journalistic Discoveries of Our People and their Cultures* (New York: Doubleday, 1979), pp. 77–92.

51. See Paul Boyer, *When Time Shall Be No More: Prophesy Belief in Modern American Culture* (Cambridge, MA: Harvard University Press, 1992), pp. 275, 342 note 9.

52. See Ian Gentles, *The New Model Army in England, Ireland and Scotland, 1645–1653* (Oxford: Blackwell, 1992), pp. 361–367, 371–372; and J. G. Simms, *War and Politics*

in Ireland, 1649–1730 (London: Hambledon Press, 1986), pp. 1–23. For the Irish clearances, see Margaret MacCurtain, *Tudor and Stuart Ireland* (Dublin: Gill and Macmillan, 1972), pp. 51–61, 89–113, 154–166, 188–192. For the history and ideology of the Scots Irish, see Phillips, *The Cousins' Wars*, pp. 177–190.

53. J. T. Cliffe, *The World of the Country House in Seventeenth Century England* (New Haven, CT: Yale University Press, 1999), p. 182; see also Fischer, *Albion's Seed*, pp. 765–771.

54. Lawrence Stone, *The Crisis of the Aristocracy, 1558–1641* (Oxford: Oxford University Press, 1965), p. 223. See also J. A. Sharpe, *Crime in Early Modern England, 1550–1750* (New York: Longman, 1984), pp. 95–99.

55. Bertram Wyatt-Brown, *Honor and Violence in the Old South* (New York: Oxford University Press, 1986); McWhiney, *Cracker Culture*, pp. 146–170; cf. also Joel Williamson, *William Faulkner and Southern History* (New York: Oxford University Press, 1993), pp. 20ff.

56. Warren Leslie, *Dallas, Public and Private: Aspects of an American City* (Dallas: Southern Methodist University Press, 1998), pp. 98–99; see also Lind, *Made in Texas*, pp. 30–31.

57. Wyatt-Brown, *Honor and Violence in the Old South,* pp. 1–15, 187–213, 237–245; John Shelton Reed, *The Enduring South* (Lexington, MA: Lexington Books, 1972), pp. 45–55, and Reed, "Below the Smith and Wesson Line," in *One South*, pp. 143, 146; Edmund S. Morgan, "The Price of Honor," *New York Review of Books,* May 31, 2001.

58. Cash, *The Mind of the South*, p. 43.

59. Cf. Francis Carney, "A State of Catastrophe," *New York Review of Books,* October 7, 1971; Phillips, *Emerging Republican Majority*, pp. 443–452.

60. Caro, *Lyndon Johnson,* vol. 1, pp. 8–32. For wider studies of social violence and vigilantism in the United States beyond the South, see the essays in Hugh Davis Graham and Ted Gurr, eds., *Violence in America: Historical and Comparative Perspectives* (New York: Bantam Books, 1969).

61. Frederick Merk, *History of the Westward Movement* (New York: Alfred A. Knopf, 1978), pp. 474ff; Robert V. Hine and John Mack Faragher, *The American West: A New Interpretive History* (New Haven, CT: Yale University Press, 2000), pp. 337–341.

62. Cf. Thomas Frank, *What's the Matter with Kansas?* (New York: Metropolitan Books, 2004). For a brief portrait of rural defeat in one part of the Midwest, see also Larry McMurtry, "The 35 from Duluth to Oklahoma City," in *Roads: Driving America's Great Highways* (New York: Simon and Schuster, 2000), pp. 24–47.

63. For Populism in the Texas Hill Country and its impact on Lyndon Johnson's family, see Caro, *Lyndon Johnson,* vol. 1, pp. 33–49, 79–85; Lind, *Made in Texas*, pp. 35–36.

64. Ursula K. Le Guin, "Malheur County," in *The Compass Rose* (London: Grafton Books, 1984), p. 230.

65. Christopher Bigsby, notes on Arthur Miller's *The Last Yankee*, quoted in Hutchison and Lehmann, *Many Are Chosen*, p. 10; cf. also Robert K. Merton, *Social Theory and Social Structure* (Glencoe, IL: Free Press, 1957), pp. 167–169; Lipset, *American Exceptionalism*, p. 47; Hartz, *Liberal Tradition*, p. 224.

66. Francis Butler Simkins and Charles Pierce Roland, *History of the South* (New York: Alfred A. Knopf, 1972), p. 11.

67. Cf. Rhodes Cook, "The Solid South Turns Around," *Congressional Quarterly Weekly,* October 2, 1992.

68. July 1, 2002, census figures at www.census.gov. See also Peter Applebome, *Dixie Rising: How the South Is Shaping American Values* (New York: Times Books, 1996), pp. 8–9.

69. Michael Lind, *Up From Conservatism: Why the Right Is Wrong for America* (New York: Simon and Schuster, 1996), pp. 121–137; Lind, *Made in Texas*; cf. also Applebome,

Dixie Rising; Phillips, *American Dynasty*; for the impact of the Southern Baptists on the Republican Party since the 1960s, see Oran P. Smith, *The Rise of Baptist Republicanism* (New York: New York University Press, 1997); Jonathan Knuckey, "Religious Conservatives, the Republican Party, and Evolving Party Coalitions in the United States," *Party Politics* 5, no. 4 (1999); John F. Persinos, "Has the Christian Right Taken over the Republican Party?" *Campaigns and Elections* 15, no. 9 (September 1994).

70. Cf. Zell Miller, *A National Party No More: The Conscience of a Conservative Democrat* (Atlanta, GA: Stroud and Hall, 2003); see also the extracts in the *Washington Times* of November 3, 4, and 5, 2003; for the catastrophic Democratic decline among Southern Whites, see Thomas F. Schaller, "A Route for 2004 that Doesn't Go through Dixie," *Washington Post,* November 16, 2003, and James Taranto, "Why Do Dems Lose in the South? Don't Blame Civil Rights," *Wall Street Journal,* March 8, 2004.

71. For the former Southern grip on Congress, see for example Phillips, *The Emerging Republican Majority,* p. 311, and Caro, *Lyndon Johnson,* vol. 3, *Master of the Senate,* pp. 32, 89–97, 104.

72. See Earl Black and Merle Black, *The Vital South: How Presidents Are Elected* (Cambridge, MA: Harvard University Press, 1992), p. 344.

73. Richard E. Cohen, "How They Measured Up," *National Journal,* no. 9, February 28, 2004; for the impact of conservative religious belief on voting patterns in Congress, see Chris Fastnow, J. Tobin Grant, and Thomas J. Rudolph, "Holy Roll Calls: Religious Tradition and Voting Behavior in the U.S. House," *Social Science Quarterly* 80, no. 4 (December 1999).

74. Cf. Wyatt Brown, *Honor and Violence*; Mead, *Special Providence*, pp. 250–259; Applebome, *Dixie Rising,* p. 10.

75. Peter W. Williams, *America's Religions from Their Origins to the 21st Century* (Chicago: University of Illinois Press, 2002), p. 283.

76. Cf. *Churches and Church Membership in the United States, 2000: An Enumeration by Region, State and County Based on Data for 133 Church Groupings* (Atlanta: Glenmary Research Center, 2002). See especially attached map.

77. Cash, *Mind of the South,* p. xlviii.

78. See John Shelton Reed, *One South: An Ethnic Approach to Regional Culture* (Baton Rouge: Louisiana State University Press, 1982). For a review of Reed's work, see Larry J. Griffin, "The Promise of a Sociology of the South," *Southern Cultures* (Spring 2001).

79. For a classic statement of the argument that modern nationalisms are "invented," see the essays by Eric Hobsbawm in Hobsbawm and Terence Ranger, eds., *The Invention of Tradition* (Cambridge: Cambridge University Press, 1983). For the "constructivist" theory of nationalism, see Ernest Gellner, *Encounters with Nationalism* (Oxford: Blackwell, 1984); for nations as "imagined communities," see the classic work of that name by Benedict Anderson (New York: Verso, 1991); for an overview of the study of nationalism from the point of view of a believer in nations as the product of a combination of modern processes with much older elements (a view generally I share), see Anthony D. Smith, *Nationalism* (Oxford: Blackwell, 2001).

80. Cf. Eugene D. Genovese, *The Southern Tradition: The Achievement and Limitations of an American Conservatism* (Cambridge, MA: Harvard University Press, 1994).

81. Fehrenbach, *Lone Star,* p. 712.

82. For the genesis of this South–North opposition in literature, see William R. Taylor, *Cavalier and Yankee: The Old South and American National Character* (New York: Anchor Books, 1963), especially pp. 72–119; for a reexamination of this issue, see David L. Carlton, "Rethinking Southern History," *Southern Cultures* (Spring 2001).

83. Morison, Commager, and Leuchtenburg, *The Growth of the American Republic,* p. 426.

84. Cf. Slotkin, *Fatal Environment*, p. 303; cf. also Bennett, *Party of Fear*, pp. 163–164, 181–182.

85. Quoted in Slotkin, *Gunfighter Nation*, p. 97.

86. Cf. Leyburn, *The Scotch-Irish*, pp. 108–153; Fischer, *Albion's Seed*, pp. 605–782; Phillips, *The Cousin's Wars*, pp. 177–190.

87. Fischer, *Albion's Seed*, p. 775.

88. For the creation of modern national myths in the Baltic region, see Anatol Lieven, *The Baltic Revolution: Estonia, Latvia, Lithuania and the Path to Independence* (New Haven, CT: Yale University Press, 1983), pp. 118–123; William A. Wilson, *Folklore and Nationalism in Modern Finland* (Bloomington: Indiana University Press, 1990); for the epics themselves, see Elias Lonnrot, *The Kalevala: An Epic Poem after Oral Tradition,* translated with an introduction by Keith Bosley (Oxford: Oxford University Press, 1989); Andrejs Pumpurs, *Lacplesis, A Latvian National Epic* (Riga: Writers Union, 1988).

89. Bernard Quinn et al., *Churches and Church Membership in the United States, 1980: An Enumeration by Region, State and County Based on Data Reported by 111 Church Bodies* (Atlanta: Glenmary Research Center, 1982), p. 32; Dale E. Jones et al., *Churches and Church Membership in the United States, 1980: An Enumeration by Region, State and County Based on Data Reported by 149 Religious Bodies* (Atlanta: Glenmary Research Center, 2000), p. 47.

90. Smith, *Rise of Baptist Fundamentalism,* pp. 17, 43; for a fictional portrait of small-town Texas from the 1950s to the 1990s, reflecting this homogeneity, conservatism, and isolation, see Larry McMurtry's series on the town of "Thalia," *The Last Picture Show* (1966), *Texasville* (1987), *Duane's Depressed* (1999), published by Simon and Schuster.

91. For the thesis that the Black-White split in America as a whole now resembles an "ethnic" division, see Orlando Patterson, *The Ordeal of Integration: Progress and Resentment in America's "Racial" Crisis* (New York: Basic Books, 1998); see also Reed, *Enduring South,* pp. 173–175, 182–183.

92. See for example the *Financial Times'* special report on the region, "Southern Exposure," September 24, 2003.

93. Quoted in Thomas A. Tweed, "Our Lady of Guadeloupe Visits the Confederate Memorial," *Southern Cultures* (Summer 2002).

94. For some aspects of the systematic and murderous oppression and exploitation that formed the background to this migration, see John M. Barry, *Rising Tide: The Great Mississippi Flood of 1927 and How It Changed America* (New York: Simon and Schuster, 1997), especially pp. 308–335. For 1880 census figures, see http://fisher.lib.virginia.edu/census/.

95. Morison, Commager, and Leuchtenburg, *The Growth of the American Republic*, vol. 1, p. 482; Myrdal, *American Dilemma*, p. 1012; cf. also Simkins and Roland, *History of the South*, pp. 161ff.

96. Woodward, *The Burden of Southern History*, pp. 201–202; Cash, *Mind of the South*, 134–135.

97. Cf. Eric Foner, *Reconstruction: America's Unfinished Revolution, 1863–1877* (New York: Harper & Row, 1988), pp. 124–129; Morison, Commager, and Leuchtenburg, *The Growth of the American Republic,* pp. 726–729; Simkins and Roland, *History of the South,* pp. 241–245.

98. Simkins and Roland, *History of the South*, p. 558.

99. See Foner, *Reconstruction;* for an expression of the southern view, see Claude G. Bowers, *The Tragic Era: The Revolution After Lincoln* (New York: Blue Ribbon Books, 1929), especially pp. 45–64, 198–220, 348–371. On the creation of the legend, see

Kenneth M. Stampp, *The Era of Reconstruction, 1865–1877* (New York: Alfred A. Knopf, 1965), especially pp. 3–23.

100. Woodward, *The Strange Career of Jim Crow*, pp. 31–109.
101. Quoted in "Sword of Honor," *The Spectator*.
102. Quoted in Black and Black, *Vital South*, p. 165.
103. Zell Miller, "How Democrats Lost the South," *Washington Times*, November 3, 2003.
104. See Diane Roberts, "Reynolds Rap," *The Oxford American* (Winter 2002): 142–145.
105. As I write this, yet another episode/remake in the *Texas Chainsaw Massacre* film tradition has appeared, featuring deranged and debased small-town Texan rednecks attacking traveling students. This is close to the bottom end of the spectrum in the genre of Hollywood Southern horror, with *Deliverance* and *Easy Rider* at the top.
106. For suppressed religious guilt over the evils of slavery, see Eugene D. Genovese, *A Consuming Fire: The Fall of the Confederacy in the Mind of the White Christian South* (Athens: University of Georgia Press, 1998). For the beginnings of unease over the race question in the post–Civil War literature of the South, see Edmund Wilson, *Patriotic Gore: Studies in the Literature of the American Civil War* (New York: Farrar, Straus and Giroux, 1977), pp. 548–604 (on George Washington Cable).
107. Woodward, *The Burden of Southern History*, pp. 187ff.
108. Cf. FitzGerald, *America Revised*, pp. 83–89.
109. Cf. Foner, *Who Owns History?*, pp. 189–204.
110. See C. Vann Woodward, "A Southern Critique for the Gilded Age," in *The Burden of Southern History*, pp. 109–140; for the classic statement of Southern agrarian conservatism, see the essays by Allen Tate et al., *I'll Take My Stand: The South and the Agrarian Tradition* (New York: Harper, 1930).
111. John Sheldon Reed, "The Banner That Won't Stay Furled," *Southern Cultures* 8, no.1 (Spring 2002). For a Black perspective on the flag question, see Franklin Forts, "Living with Confederate Symbols," in the same issue.
112. One of the finest short portraits of redneck culture has been written by—of all people!—V. S. Naipaul, in *A Turn in the South* (London: Viking, 1989), especially pp. 204–214; for an equally sensitive portrait of the spirit of country music, see pp. 223–233. For the original literary redneck, Sut Lovingood (the creation of George Washington Harris), see Edmund Wilson, *Patriotic Gore*, pp. 507–519.
113. For the enduring prestige of the Confederate soldier even for a Southerner who was bitterly critical of most aspects of his own tradition, see Cash, *Mind of the South*, pp. 44, 428.
114. See for example Reed, *One South*, pp. 166–167.
115. Weber, *The European Right*, pp. 15–16.
116. For example, the dangerous hysteria surrounding General MacArthur's return from Korea after having been dismissed by Truman. See Caro, *Lyndon Johnson*, vol. 3, *Master of the Senate*, pp. 367–382.
117. Hartz, *Liberal Tradition*, pp. 59, 209.
118. Jean-Jacques Rousseau, *The Social Contract*, translated with an introduction by Maurice Cranston (London: Penguin, 1978), pp. 70–83, 149–151, 176–187.
119. J. L. Talmon, *The Origins of Totalitarian Democracy* (New York: Frederick A Praeger, 1960), pp. 40–49; for the debate on this question, see Talmon, ed., *Totalitarian Democracy and After* (New York: Frank Cass and Co., 2002).
120. Ralph Reed, *Separation of Church and State: "Christian Nation" and Other Heresies,* in Cherry, *God's New Israel*, pp. 373–379.
121. Robert Kelley, *The Cultural Pattern in American Politics: The First Century* (New York: Alfred A Knopf, 1979), pp. 39ff.

122. Cf. Walter Russell Mead, "The Jacksonian Tradition," *The National Interest*, no. 58 (Winter 1999/2000); and Mead, *Special Providence*, chapter 7 and passim; Lind, *Made in Texas*; Harris, *Civilization and Its Enemies*, pp. 115–135.

123. Cf. Eric Foner, *The Story of American Freedom* (New York: W. W. Norton, 1999), pp. 307–332.

124. "We don't smoke marijuana in Muskogee;
   We don't take our trips on LSD
   We don't burn our draft cards down on Main Street;
   We like livin' right, and bein' free.

   "I'm proud to be an Okie from Muskogee,
   A place where even squares can have a ball
   We still wave Old Glory down at the courthouse,
   And white lightnin's still the biggest thrill of all."

   —Merle Haggard, "Okie from Muskogee"

125. Cf. Myrdal, *American Dilemma*, pp. 558–569.

126. Helen Lee Turner and James L. Guth, "The Politics of Armageddon: Dispensationalism Among Southern Baptist Ministers," in *Religion and Political Behavior in the United States*, ed. Ted G. Jelen, p. 203 (New York: Praeger, 1989).

127. Mead, *Special Providence*, pp. 236, 245.

128. For an account of the abuses by the journalist who broke the story, see Seymour Hersh, "Torture at Abu Ghraib," *New Yorker*, May 10, 2004, and "The Gray Zone: How a Secret Pentagon Program Came to Abu Ghraib," May 24, 2004; see also Scott Wilson, "An Iraqi Detainee Tells of Anguishing Treatment at Iraq Prison," *Washington Post*, May 5, 2004; Scott Wilson and Sewell Chan, "As Insurgency Grew, So Did Prison Abuse," *Washington Post*, May 9, 2004; Dana Priest and Joe Stephens, "Secret World of U.S. Interrogation," *Washington Post*, May 11, 2004; Ian Fisher, "Iraqi Recounts Hours of Abuse by U.S. Troops," *New York Times*, May 4, 2004; Ian Fisher, "Iraqi Tells of U.S. Abuse," *New York Times*, May 13, 2004. For a discussion of the abuse and the background in Bush administration thinking, see Mark Danner, "Torture and Truth," *New York Review of Books*, June 10, 2004, and "The Logic of Torture," *New York Review of Books*, June 24, 2004.

129. For a recent new account of atrocities by U.S. forces in Vietnam, see the *Toledo Blade*'s series on the killing of civilians by the "Tiger Force" in 1967: Michael D. Sallah and Mitch Weiss, "Rogue GIs Unleashed Wave of Terror in Central Highlands," *Toledo Blade*, October 22, 2003; and Nicholas Turse, "The Doctrine of Atrocity," *Village Voice*, May 11, 2004.

130. Poll by the Roper Center, University of Connecticut, May 27, 2004, at abcnews.go.com/sections/US/Polls/torture.

131. For the Gonzales memo and Powell's dissent, see Michael Isikoff, "Memos Reveal War Crimes Warnings," *Newsweek*, May 18, 2004. For the other memos, see Dana Priest and R. Jeffrey Smith, "Memo Offered Justification for Use of Torture," *Washington Post*, June 8, 2004; and Edward Alden and James Harding, "U.S. Lawyers Said Interrogators Could Violate Torture Laws Abroad," *Financial Times* (London), June 8, 2004, and "Bush Team Accused of Sanctioning Torture," *Financial Times* (London), June 9, 2004.

132. Quoted by Charles Babington, "Senator Critical of Focus on Prisoner Abuse," *Washington Post*, May 12, 2004.

133. Lott quoted in "Media Notes," *Washington Post*, June 4, 2004; see also Zoe Heller, "How Quickly America Forgot Its Outrage," *Daily Telegraph* (London), May 15, 2004; for attempts in the right-wing media to defend what happened at Abu Ghraib or

play down its importance, see, for example, Wesley Pruden, editor in chief, "He Said the Word. Who's Sorry Now?" *Washington Times,* May 7, 2004; James D. Zirin, "The Objective...and a Metaphor Too Far," *Washington Times,* May 17, 2004; Victor Davis Hanson, "Abu Ghraib," *Wall Street Journal,* May 3, 2004; Mark Alexander, "The Abu Ghraib Feeding Frenzy," *The Federalist,* May 7, 2004; Deroy Murdock, "Kinder, Gentler War on Terror: Are We Overreacting?" *National Review Online,* May 17, 2004; Reuel Marc Gerecht, "Who's Afraid of Abu Ghraib," *Weekly Standard,* May 24, 2004.

134. Rush Limbaugh, on May 6, 2004; transcript at http://americanassembler.com/newsblog.

135. Michael Savage, on *Savage Nation* (radio show), May 12, 2004; transcript at http://mediamatters.org.

136. Figures at www.wjno.com/hosts/rush and www.talkradionetwork.com.

137. "Red Double Cross," *Wall Street Journal* editorial, May 14, 2004.

138. John McCain, "In Praise of Do-Gooders: The Red Cross Is Right to Criticize the U.S. Military When It Steps Out of Line," *Wall Street Journal,* June 1, 2004.

Chapter Four

1. *The Hunting of the Foxes...by Five Small Beagles* (Leveller Tract against Cromwell), in Lamont and Oldfield, *Politics, Religion and Literature in the Seventeenth Century,* pp. 154–155.

2. For a suggestion from Britain that it is Europe, and not the United States, that now represents the more successful and civilized version of modernization, see Will Hutton, *The World We're In* (London: Little, Brown, 2002).

3. Lerner, *America as a Civilization.*

4. Quoted in Howard Elinson, "The Implications of Pentecostal Religion for Intellectualism, Politics, and Race Relations," *American Journal of Sociology* 70, no. 4 (January 1965).

5. Samuel Huntington, "Dead Souls: The Denationalization of the American Elite," *National Interest,* no. 75 (Spring 2004); see also Adrian Hastings, *The Construction of Nationhood: Ethnicity, Religion and Nationalism* (New York: Cambridge University Press, 1997).

6. Joel Carpenter, *Revive Us Again: The Reawakening of American Fundamentalism* (New York: Oxford University Press, 1997), pp. 234–235.

7. Cf. Corwin Smidt, "Evangelicals within Contemporary American Politics: Differentiating between Fundamentalist and Non-Fundamentalist Evangelicals," *Western Political Quarterly* 41, no. 3 (September 1988).

8. For individual motivations for new converts to the fundamentalist churches, see Robert R. Monaghan, "Three Faces of the True Believer: Motivations for Attending a Fundamentalist Church," in Hammond and Johnson, eds., *American Mosaic,* pp. 65–79.

9. *Churches and Church Membership in the United States, 2000* (2002). See especially the attached map.

10. Cf. Wald, *Religion and Politics,* p. 49.

11. Simkins and Roland, *History of the South,* pp. 152–175; Genovese, *The Southern Tradition,* p. 27.

12. Cf. Leyburn, *Scotish-Irish,* pp. 71–79, 143ff, 282ff.

13. Cf. Bellah, *Civil Religion,* pp. 113–124.

14. George Grant, quoted in Lipset, *American Exceptionalism,* p. 37; Hofstadter, *Anti-Intellectualism,* p. 238.

15. Cf. Gabriel A. Almond, R. Scott Appleby, and Emmanuel Sivan, *Strong Religion: The Rise of Fundamentalism Around the World* (Chicago: University of Chicago Press, 2003), pp. 106ff.

16. Richard Hofstadter, "The Pseudo-Conservative Revolt-1955," in *The Radical Right*, ed. Bell, pp. 64, 85.

17. Robert Kelley, *The Cultural Pattern in American Politics: The First Century* (New York: Alfred A Knopf, 1979), p. 39.

18. Cf. Kenneth D. Wald, *Religion and Politics in the United States* (New York: Rowman and Littlefield, 2003), pp. 200ff.

19. See Dean M. Kelley, *Why Conservative Churches Are Growing* (Macon, GA: Mercer University Press, 1986), p. 4.

20. Cf Thomas Frank, *What's the Matter with Kansas? How Conservatives Won the Heart of America* (New York: Metropolitan Books, 2004).

21. Cf. the Christian Coalition's "2001 Senate Score Card" and "2001 House Scorecard" at www.cc.org.

22. Howard Fineman, "Bush and God," *Newsweek*, March 10, 2003.

23. Cf. Phillips, *American Dynasty*, p. 233.

24. Matthew xii 30, cited in Henry Ward Beecher's sermon at the start of the Civil War, "The Battle Set in Array," in Cherry, *God's New Israel*, pp. 169–183.

25. David Frum and Richard Perle, *An End to Evil: How to Win the War on Terror* (New York: Random House, 2003); see also the critique of Bush's religion in Kevin Phillips, *American Dynasty: Aristocracy, Fortune and the Politics of Deceit in the House of Bush* (New York: Viking, 2004), pp. 228–244.

26. The provenance of the president's phrase was pointed out by the Reverend Fritz Ritsch in the *Washington Post*, March 2, 2003.

27. Stephen Marshall, quoted in Michael Walzer, *Exodus and Revolution* (New York: Basic Books, 1985), p. 147.

28. Norman Podhoretz, "How to Win World War IV," *Commentary* 113, no. 2 (February 2002).

29. Stephen Mansfield, *The Faith of George W Bush*, p. 174.

30. George W Bush, *A Charge to Keep* (New York: William Morrow and Co., 1999), p. 6; David Gergen quoted in "A President Puts His Faith in Providence," *New York Times* February 9, 2003; see also Elizabeth Bumiller, "Talk of Religion Provokes Amens as well as Anxiety," *New York Times*, April 22, 2002; for Bush's religion and its political uses, see Phillips, *American Dynasty*, pp. 211–244. See also Bob Woodward, *Bush at War* (New York: Simon and Schuster, 2002), p. 75.

31. Woodward, *Bush at War*, p. 67.

32. Mansfield, *The Faith of George W. Bush*, pp. 172–173.

33. Cf. Phillips, *American Dynasty*, pp. 211–244.

34. Cf. Myrdal, *American Dream*, pp. 457, 523–558.

35. James A. Morone, *Hellfire Nation: The Politics of Sin in American History* (New Haven, CT: Yale University Press, 2003).

36. Ibid., pp. 260–273.

37. Ira M. Wasserman, "Prohibition and Ethnocultural Conflict: The Missouri Prohibition Referendum of 1918," *Social Science Quarterly* 70, no. 4 (December 1989).

38. For a reasoned argument in favor of prohibition and its partial success, see Norman H. Clark, *Deliver Us From Evil: An Interpretation of American Prohibition* (New York: W. W. Norton, 1976), especially pp. 145–153.

39. Morone, *Hellfire Nation*, p. 304.

40. Cf. Bennett, *Party of Fear*, pp. 208–237.

41. Lind, *The Next American Nation*, p. 88.

42. Quoted in Cherry, *God's New Israel*, p. 269.

43. Stanley Coben, "A Study in Nativism: The Red Scare of 1919–20," *Political Science Quarterly* 79, no. 1 (March 1964). For a description of the two scares, see Bennett, *Party of Fear,* pp. 183–198; Samuel Eliot Morison, *Oxford History of the American People*, vol. 3 (New York: Penguin, 1994), pp. 206–219. For the World War I hysteria in Texas, see Fehrenbach, *Lone Star*, pp. 643–648; Caro, *The Years of Lyndon Johnson*, vol. 1, pp. 80–81. For pressure on the (traditionally pro-German) Yiddish press during World War I, see Irving Howe, *World of Our Fathers: The Journey of the East European Jews to America and the Life They Found and Made* (New York: Harcourt Brace Jovanovich, 1976), pp. 538–540.

44. Cf. George Marsden, "The Religious Right: A Historical Overview," in *No Longer Exiles: The Religious New Right and American Politics,* ed. Michael Cromartie (Washington, DC: Ethics and Public Policy Center, 1993), p. 1; Marty, *Pilgrims*, p. 410.

45. Bell, *Radical Right,* p. 79.

46. Cf. Seymour Martin Lipset and Earl Raab, *The Politics of Unreason: Right Wing Extremism in America, 1790–1970* (New York: Harper & Row, 1970), pp. 209–247.

47. Kazin, *Populism*, pp. 109–133; Bennett, *Party of Fear*, pp. 253–266.

48. This argument for the sources of McCarthyism is set out in the essays by Richard Hofstadter, Peter Viereck, and others in *The Radical Right*, ed. Bell; see also Bennett, *Party of Fear,* pp. 310–315.

49. See Hofstadter, *Anti-intellectualism*, p. 55.

50. For the mid-nineteenth century, see Noel Ignatiev, *How the Irish Became White* (New York: Routledge, 1995).

51. Glazer and Moynihan, *Beyond the Melting Pot*, p. 270.

52. See David Schoenbaum, *Hitler's Social Revolution: Class and Status in Nazi Germany, 1933–1939* (New York: W. W. Norton, 1980).

53. Ann Coulter, *Treason: Liberal Treachery from the Cold War to the War Against Terrorism* (New York: Crown Forum, 2003), p. 69.

54. Cf. Dorothy Doren, *Nationalism and Catholic Americanism* (New York: Sheed and Ward, 1967); Glazer and Moynihan, *Beyond the Melting Pot,* pp. 230–231, 247–250.

55. Glazer and Moynihan, *Beyond the Melting Pot,* pp. 262, 270–274.

56. Cf. Lerner, *American Civilization*, p. 904.

57. Quoted in McBride, *John Ford*, p. 6; see also Thomas Flanagan's essays on John Ford, "Western Star," *New York Review of Books,* November 29 and December 20, 2001.

58. Cf. Slatkin, *Gunfighter Nation*, pp. 334–343; McBride, *John Ford,* pp. 446–458.

59. Doren, *Nationalism*, pp. 134–162

60. Including at least one Irish American character who is first soldier and then gangster, the protagonist of the film *The Roaring Twenties*.

61. McWhiney, *Cracker Culture*, pp. xxi–xliii. I should perhaps place on record that I am of German Irish ethnicity myself, with a mother whose maiden name was Monahan; and I have nothing against pugnacity in a good cause.

62. McBride, *John Ford*, p. 698.

63. Glazer and Moynihan, *Beyond the Melting Pot*, p. 271.

64. Sean Hannity, *Let Freedom Ring: Winning the War of Liberty Over Liberalism* (New York: Regan Books, 2002), p. 127.

65. Cf. Eric Alterman, *What Liberal Media?* p. 35; Michael Kinsley, "O'Reilly Among the Snobs," *Washington Post,* March 2, 2001; Noam Scheiber, "Class Act: Chris Mathews and Bill O'Reilly v. The Working Man," *New Republic,* June 25, 2001; for John Ford's assumption of an Irish macho style at odds with aspects of his real nature, see McBride, *John Ford,* p. 298; for Ford on the Vietnam War, see ibid., pp. 691–692.

66. Will Herberg, *Protestant, Catholic, Jew: An Essay in American Religious Sociology* (New York: Doubleday, 1956), pp. 146–147.

67. Cromartie, ed., *No Longer Exiles*; Oscar Handlin, "American Jewry," in *The Jewish World: Revelation, Prophecy and History*, ed. Elie Kedourie, pp. 281–282 (London: Thames and Hudson, 1979); Lerner, *American Civilization*, pp. 703–717.

68. Quoted in Hofstadter, *Anti-intellectualism*, p. 125.

69. Cf. Daniel J. Kevles, "Darwin in Dayton," *New York Review of Books*, November 19, 1998; Liebman and Wuthnow, *The New Christian Right*, p. 1.

70. Almond et al., *Strong Religion*, pp. 26–27.

71. Morison, Commager, and Leuchtenburg, *History*, pp. 435–436; see also Martin Marty, *Pilgrims in Their Own Land: 500 Years of Religion in America* (New York: Penguin, 1985), pp. 380–381.

72. Kazin, *Populism*, p.106.

73. Marty, *Pilgrims*, pp. 410–415; Carpenter, *Revive Us Again*, pp. 211–229.

74. On *The Prairie Home Companion*, National Public Radio, October 26, 2003.

75. Cf. Kenneth Wald et al., "Churches as Political Communities," *American Political Science Review*, no. 82 (1988).

76. Oran P. Smith, *The Rise of Baptist Republicanism* (New York: New York University Press, 1997), pp. 46–67, 98–112, 191–212.

77. Cf. Applebome, *Dixie Rising*, pp. 241ff.

78. Cr. Max Lerner, *American Civilization*, pp. 172–182.

79. Cf. Bellah, *Habits of the Heart*, pp. 196, 204–206, 251, etc.

80. For this recovery, see Herberg, *Protestant, Catholic, Jew*, pp. 59–84.

81. Figures quoted in Sara Diamond, *Not By Politics Alone: The Enduring Influence of the Christian Right* (New York: Guilford Press, 1998), pp. 9–10.

82. Ibid.

83. American National Election Studies (ANES), Center for Political Studies, University of Michigan. Quoted in Wald, *Religion and Politics*, pp. 160–162.

84. For the impact of the Southern Baptists on the Republican Party since the 1960s, see Oran P. Smith, *The Rise of Baptist Republicanism* (New York: New York University Press, 1997).

85. Pew telephone survey commissioned by *Newsweek* and cited in David Gates, "The Pop Populists," *Newsweek*, May 24, 2004.

86. Cited in Lipset, *Exceptionalism*, pp. 268–269.

87. Williams, *America's Religions*, p. 379.

88. See Blendon et al., in *What's God Got To Do with the American Experiment?*, p. 26.

89. Almond et al., *Strong Religion*, p. 227.

90. Cf. Colbert I. King, "Dean's Faith-Based Folly," *Washington Post*, January 10, 2004; Steven Waldman, "When Piety Takes Center Stage," *Washington Post*, January 11, 2004.

91. Ralph Reed, "The Future of the Religious Right," in *Christian Political Activism at the Crossroads*, ed. William R. Stevenson Jr., pp. 81–86 (Lanham, MD: University Press of America, 1994); see also Reed quoted in Wald, *Religion and Politics*, p. 200; for a survey of Christian rightist activism and organization building, see Mark J. Rozell and Clyde Wilcox, "Second Coming: Strategies of the New Christian Right," *Political Science Quarterly* 111, no. 2 (Summer 1996); Kimberley H. Conger and John C. Green, *Campaigns and Elections* (February 2002).

92. Cf. *Washington Post*, October 20, 2003: "Outfitted with Placards and Prayer: Students from Virginia's New Patrick Henry College Planting Political Seeds."

93. Cf. Diamond, *Not by Politics Alone*, pp. 63–66, 131–155; Alan I. Abramowitz, "It's Abortion, Stupid: Policy Voting in the 1992 Presidential Election," *Journal of Politics* 57, no. 1 (February 1995); Hughes, *Myths America Lives By*, pp. 85–89.

94. Cf. Phillips, *Emerging Republican Majority*, pp. 25, 33, 37.

95. Cf. Bellah, *The Broken Covenant*, pp. 105–106.

96. Cf. Tracy L. Scott, "Gay Characters Gaining TV Popularity," *Washington Post TV Week*, November 30–December 6, 2003.

97. Maurice Isserman and Michael Kazin, *America Divided: The Civil War of the 1960s* (New York: Oxford University Press, 2000), pp. 205–220.

98. For the correlation between relative poverty and lack of education and fundamentalist belief, see Corwin Smidt, "Born Again Politics," in *Religion and Politics in the South: Mass and Elite Perspectives*, ed. Tod A. Baker et al. (New York: Praeger, 1983), pp. 27–56.

99. This spirit breathes, for example, from Newt Gingrich's book *To Renew America* (New York: HarperCollins, 1995).

100. For the correlation between evangelical belief and opposition to nuclear reduction treaties, see Smidt, ed., *Contemporary Evangelical Political Involvement*, pp. 85–96.

101. Robert C. Liebman, "Mobilizing the Moral Majority," in Liebman and Wuthnow, eds., *The New Christian Right*, p. 69; Almond et al., *Strong Religion*, pp. 45ff; Bennett, *Party of Fear*, pp. 375–377, 396–398.

102. Cf. an early call for the war against terrorism to be extended from Afghanistan to Iraq and elsewhere, Robert L. Maginnis, "Hunting Down Backers of Terrorism," *LA Daily Journal*, October 22, 2001, reproduced on the website of the Family Research Council at www.frc.org. The link in the minds of this conservative religious group between their pro-family, antiabortion beliefs and a hard-line strategy in the fight against terrorism may not be intellectually apparent, but is entirely culturally coherent.

103. Robert D. Novak, "Bush's Gay Marriage Test," *Washington Post*, December 1, 2003.

104. Speech at the Islamic Center of Washington, DC, September 17, 2001, at www.whitehouse.gov.

105. Mansfield, *Faith of George W. Bush*, pp. 139–142.

106. Hal Lindsey, *The Everlasting Hatred: The Roots of Jihad* (Murrietta, GA: Oracle House Publishing, 2002), especially pp. 58–124.

107. Cf. Phillips, *American Dynasty*, p. 235; see also the attack on these figures by Fareed Zakaria, "Time to Take On America's Haters," *Newsweek*, October 21, 2002.

108. Larry McMurtry, *In a Shallow Grave: Essays on Texas* (New York: Touchstone Books, 2001), p. 155; and Leslie, *Dallas*, pp. 89, 95, 167.

109. For a sketch of millenarian beliefs, see Carpenter, *Revive Us Again*, pp. 247–249; Boyer, *When Time Shall Be No More*, pp. 21–45; for the seventeenth-century-England origins of American beliefs, see Niebuhr, *Social Sources of Denominationalism*, pp. 46–49.

110. Turner and Guth, *Politics of Armageddon*, pp. 187–190. For a useful chart of the relationship between the different schools of millenialism, see Timothy P. Weber, *Living in the Shadow of the Second Coming: American Premillennialism, 1875–1925* (New York: Oxford University Press, 1979), p. 10.

111. See Boyer, *When Time Shall Be No More*, pp. 1–7.

112. Hal Lindsey, *The Late Great Planet Earth* (Murrietta, GA: Oracle House, 2002 [rpt]); Tim LaHaye and Jerry B. Jenkins, *Left Behind: A Novel of the Earth's Last Days* (Wheaton, IL: Tyndale House Publishers, 1995).

113. Pat Robertson, *The End of the Age* (Dallas: Word Publishing, 1996). This sketch is from Diamond, *Not by Politics Alone*, p. 198.

114. LaHaye and Jenkins, *Left Behind*, pp. 25–76.

115. Cf. the passages by Jerry Falwell, Hal Lindsey, and others quoted in Grace Halsell, *Prophecy and Politics: Militant Evangelists on the Road to Nuclear War* (Westport, CT: Lawrence Hill and Co., 1986), pp. 28–35.

116. Boyer, *When Time Shall Be No More*, p. 303 note 29.

117. Cf. Bennett, *Party of Fear*, pp. 409–475.

118. Cf. Gerald Flurry, "Continue to Watch Stoiber," *Philadelphia Trumpet* (November 2002), www.thetrumpet.com; Boyer, *When Time Shall Be No More*, pp. 111, 121, 148, 277.

119. Mike Davis, *Ecology of Fear: Los Angeles and the Imagination of Disaster* (New York: Metropolitan Books, 1998), p. 355.

120. Boyer, *When Time Shall Be No More*, p. 10.

121. Ibid., pp. 257–260. For the racial element in American apocalyptic fears, see Davis, *Ecology of Fear*, pp. 281–300, 325–344; for Lindsey's new anti-Muslim hysteria, see Lindsey, *The Everlasting Hatred*.

122. Norman Cohn, *The Pursuit of the Millennium: Revolutionary Millenarians and Mystical Anarchists of the Middle Ages* (New York: Oxford University Press, 1990), pp. 58–74, 309–310; cf. also Edward Shils, "Ideology and Civility: On the Politics of the Intellectual," *Sewanee Review*, no. 66 (1958).

123. Turner and Guth, *Politics of Armageddon*, pp. 191–192, 208.

124. See R. Laurence Moore, *Religious Outsiders and the Making of Americans* (New York: Oxford University Press, 1986).

125. Richard Niebuhr, *Social Sources*, pp. 30–31.

126. Quoted in Carpenter, *Revive Us Again*, p. 224; for class resentment in the attitudes and works of Tim LaHaye, see Gates, "The Pop Prophets."

127. Billy Graham, quoted in Boyer, *When Time Shall Be No More*, p. 320.

128. Quoted by Molly Ivins, in the *Fort Worth Star-Telegram*, September 14, 1993.

129. See *Washington Post*, October 21, 2003.

130. Cf. Kings I, 18: 20–40. I am indebted for this reference to Professor Charles King of Georgetown University.

131. See Michelle Cottle, "Bible Brigade," *New Republic*, April 21 and 28, 2003; Alan Cooperman, "Bush's Remark about God Assailed," *Washington Post*, November 22, 2003.

132. Peter Beinart, "Bad Faith," *New Republic*, March 25, 2002; for more such statements, see *The Religious Right: The Assault on Tolerance and Pluralism in America* (New York: Anti-Defamation League, 1994), p. 5.

133. Cf. Molly Ivins, "Cheney's Card: The Empire Writes Back," *Washington Post*, December 30, 2003.

134. Hofstadter, *Paranoid Style*, p. 31.

Chapter Five

1. Quoted in Leslie, *Dallas*, p. 222.

2. James Mann, *Rise of the Vulcans: The History of Bush's War Cabinet* (New York: Viking, 2004), p. 293.

3. Ibid., p. 246.

4. Cf. Joshua Micah Marshall, "Vice Grip," *Washington Monthly* (January/February 2003); and Nicholas Lemann, "The Quiet Man" (profile of Dick Cheney), *The New Yorker*, May 7, 2001; for the importance of the Cold War as a moral and political paradigm among the radical Right, see Bennett, *Party of Fear*, pp. 469–470.

5. David Hume Kennerly, quoted in Phillips, *American Dynasty*, p. 93; See also Derek Leebaert, *The Fifty Year Wound: How America's Cold War Victory Shapes Our World* (New York: Little, Brown and Co., 2002); Chalmers Johnson, *Blowback: The Costs and Consequences of American Empire* (New York: Owl Books, 2003).

6. Cf. Joshua Micah Marshall, "Remaking the World: Bush and the Neoconservatives," *Foreign Affairs* (November/December 2003).

7. Cf. Lars-Erik Nelson, "Military-Industrial Man," *New York Review of Books,* December 21, 2000.

8. Cf. Lind, *Up from Conservatism,* p. 69.

9. Quoted in Ehrman, *Neoconservatism,* p. 42.

10. Ibid., pp. 45–46.

11. Huntington, *Clash of Civilizations,* pp. 301–321.

12. Jacob Weisberg, "The Family Way: How Irving Kristol, Gertrude Himelfarb, and Bill Kristol Became the Family that Liberals Love to Hate," *The New Yorker,* October 21 and 28, 1996.

13. Plato, *The Republic,* translated by Desmond Lee (London: Penguin, 1976), pp. 181–182, 316–325.

14. Holmes, *Anti-Liberalism,* pp. 61–87.

15. Bacevich, *American Empire,* p. 167; Hunt, *Ideology and U.S. Foreign Policy,* pp. 29–45.

16. In the words of a U.S. senator (from the Democratic Party) to me in January 2002.

17. See David Stockman, *The Triumph of Politics: Why the Reagan Revolution Failed* (New York: HarperCollins, 1986); David Brock, *Blinded by the Right: The Conscience of an Ex-Conservative* (New York: Three Rivers Press, 2002), p. 71; cf. also "Zealous Norquist Plans Conservative Golden Era," *Washington Post,* January 12, 2004.

18. Mark Almond, "Your Tyrant or Ours?" *The New Statesman* (London), November 17, 2003.

19. Irving Kristol, "My Cold War," *The National Interest* (Spring 1993).

20. Daniel Bell, "The Dispossessed–1962," in Bell, ed., *The Radical Right,* pp. 8–12.

21. Cobban, *France,* p. 48.

22. Coulter, *Treason.*

23. Bainbridge, *The Super-Americans,* p. 237.

24. Cf. Lemann, "The Quiet Man," p. 69.

25. C. Wright Mills, *The Power Elite* (New York: Oxford University Press, 1959), p. 184.

26. Quoted in Morison, *History of the American People,* p. 417.

27. Cf. Michael T. Klare, "America's Military Revolution: Cold War Government with No War to Fight," *Le Monde Diplomatique* (English edition), July 2001.

28. Cf. Johnson, *The Sorrows of Empire,* pp. 44–45.

29. Cf. Craig, *Germany 1866–1945,* pp. 288, 293–296, 307–308; Eckart Kehr, *Economic Interest, Militarism and Foreign Policy* (Berkeley: University of California Press, 1977), pp. 75ff.; Richard Owen, "Military Industrial Relations: Krupp and the Imperial Navy Office," in Evans, *Society and Politics in Imperial Germany;* V. R. Berghahn, *Germany and the Approach of War in 1914* (New York: St. Martin's Press, 1993), pp. 136–143.

30. Leebaert, *Fifty Year Wound,* pp. 230–231, 243–246.

31. Cf. Caro, *The Years of Lyndon Johnson,* vol. 3, *Master of the Senate,* pp. 306–334.

32. Cf. Anatol Lieven, "The (Not So) Great Game," *The National Interest* (Winter 1999/2000). For the later stages of the debate on the Russian threat to India and British responses, see Max Beloff, *Imperial Sunset,* vol. 1, *Britain's Liberal Empire, 1897–1921* (New York: Alfred A. Knopf, 1970), pp. 20–25, 31–39; Aaron Friedberg, *The Weary Titan: Britain and the Experience of Relative Decline, 1895–1905* (Princeton, NJ: Princeton University Press, 1988), pp. 212–280; and David Gillard, *The Struggle for Asia, 1828–1914* (London: Methuen, 1977). For the mid-nineteenth-century origins of the particular British fear and dislike of Russia, see John Howes Gleason, *The Genesis of Russophobia in Great Britain: A Study of the Interaction of Policy and Opinion* (Cambridge, MA: Harvard University Press, 1950).

33. Quoted in Paris, *Warrior Nation,* pp. 88–89.

34. Cf. the premise of John Milius's 1984 film of heroic American resistance to a Soviet-Cuban-Nicaraguan occupation, *Red Dawn*.
35. Cf. Hofstadter, *Paranoid Style*.
36. Norman Podhoretz, *Present Danger: Do We Have the Will to Reverse the Decline of American Power?* (New York: Simon and Schuster, 1980), quoted in Lind, *Up From Conservatism*, p. 61 note; cf. also Ehrman, *Neoconservatism*, pp. 108–109.
37. Podhoretz, "How to Win World War IV."
38. Cf. Craig, *Germany*, pp. 104–113; Berghahn, *Germany and the Approach of War in 1914*.
39. For another classic piece of later anti-Soviet paranoia, see Raymond Sleeper, ed., *Mesmerized by the Bear: The Soviet Strategy of Deception* (New York: Dodd, Mead and Co., 1987), with contributions by Jack Kemp and Paul Nitze.
40. Cf. the recommendations for the struggle against terrorism set out by Clarke in *Against All Enemies*, pp. 247–287.
41. Zbigniew Brzezinski, *The Grand Chessboard: American Primacy and Its Geostrategic Imperatives* (New York: Basic Books, 1998).
42. Owen Harries, "The Dangers of Expansive Realism," *The National Interest* (Winter 1997/98).
43. Kurt M. Campbell (former deputy assistant secretary of Defense for East Asian and Pacific affairs), "China Watchers Fighting a Turf War of Their Own," *New York Times*, May 20, 2000. Quoted in Johnson, *Blowback*, p. 62.
44. Cf. Bob Woodward's book *Plan of Attack*, excerpts from which were serialized in the *Washington Post* in April 2004.
45. Mead, *Special Providence*, p. 303.
46. Robin Wright, "Top Focus Before 9/11 Wasn't on Terrorism," *Washington Post*, April 1, 2004.
47. Suskind, *Price of Loyalty*, p. 81.
48. Cf. "Still Within Reach of the Russian Bear," *Washington Post*, January 5, 1997.
49. George Will, "Eastward-Ho—and Soon," *Washington Post*, June 13, 1996.
50. Peter Rodman, "Four More for NATO," *Washington Post*, December 13, 1994.
51. Hugh Gratton Donnelly, *The Stricken Nation* (U.S. 1890), quoted in Paris, *Warrior Nation*, p.102.
52. For an account of the link between Russian military defeat and the condition of Russian culture and society, see my *Chechnya*.
53. See, for example, William E. Odom and Robert Dujarric, *Commonwealth or Empire: Russia, Central Asia or the Caucasus* (New York: Hudson Institute, 1996); William E. Odom, "Realism About Russia," *The National Interest* (Fall 2001); George Will, "Back in the USSR," *Washington Post*, September 3, 2000; William Safire, "Dangerous Consequences," *New York Times*, November 4, 1999; Bill Gertz, "Defense Official Says U.S. Still Needs Nukes; Threat Remains from Russia, Others," *Washington Times*, February 13, 1997; Ariel Cohen et al., "Making the World Safe for America," *Issues 96: The Candidates' Briefing Book* (Washington, DC: Heritage Foundation, 1996); Richard Pipes, "Russia's Past, Russia's Future," *Commentary* (June 1996). For a challenge to such views, see Stephen Sestanovich, "Geotherapy: Russia's Neuroses, and Ours," *The National Interest*, no. 45 (Fall 1996). For a discussion of these views, see my *Chechnya: Tombstone of Russian Power*, introduction.
54. For the role of institutional vested interests in perpetuating hatred and fear of Russia in the 1990s, see Harries, "The Dangers of Expansive Realism."
55. Cf. Condoleezza Rice, "Promoting the National Interest," *Foreign Affairs* 79, no. 1 (January/February 2000); press conference by President Bush, February 22, 2001, at www.whitehouse.gov.

56. Cf. Maryann Bird, "A Poisonous Plot," *Time* (Europe), January 20, 2003.

57. Rice, "Promoting the National Interest."

58. Cf. James Lilley and Carl Ford, "China's Military: A Second Opinion," *The National Interest*, no. 57 (Fall 1999). This essay formed part of an exchange with Bates Gill and Michael O'Hanlon, who in "China's Hollow Military" had taken a much more sober and realistic view of Chinese power. *The National Interest*, no. 56 (Summer 1999). See also "China Viewed Narrowly," *New York Times*, June 10, 2000; for an extreme anti-Chinese view, see Bill Gertz, *The China Threat: How the People's Republic Targets America* (Washington, DC: Regnery Publishing, 2000). See also Tom Donnelly's review essay, "Peking Won't Duck," *The Weekly Standard*, December 4, 2000. For the campaign to adopt a strategy of "containment" against China, see Robert G. Kaiser and Steven Mufson, "Blue Team Draws a Hard Line on Beijing; Action on Hill Reflects Informal Group's Clout," *Washington Post*, February 22, 2000; Jay Branegan, "A 'Blue Team' Blocks Beijing," *Time*, April 16, 2000; Johnson, *Blowback*, pp. 82–88.

59. www.house.gov/coxreport; for critiques of the Cox Report, see Walter Pincus, "Hill Report on Chinese Spying Faulted; Five Experts Cite Errors, 'Unwarranted' Conclusions by Cox Panel," *Washington Post*, December 15, 1999. See also the critique by Jack Kemp and Gordon Prather quoted by John McCaslin, "Kemp and Cox," *Washington Times*, July 15, 1999; Tom Plate, *LA Times*, July 21, 1999; "Lessons of the Cox Report," *Christian Science Monitor* editorial, May 28, 1999.

60. Quoted in Cal Thomas, "Damage Assessments . . . and Duplicity," *Washington Times*, May 28, 1999.

61. Ibid.

62. Juliet Eilperin, "DeLay Assails China, Urges Taiwan Trade Talks," *Washington Post*, June 3, 2003. For the views of conservative Republican colleagues, see for example Representative Dick Armey, "Saying No to China," *Washington Times*, October 30, 1997; and Senator Trent Lott, "Ten Ways to Engage China," *Washington Times*, June 24, 1998.

63. Cf. John Bolton, "Democracy Makes All the Difference," *The Weekly Standard*, April 3, 2000; "Beijing's WTO Double-cross," *The Weekly Standard*, August 14, 2000. See also Bush's remarks on China in the South Carolina Republican primary debate, February 15, 2000, shown on *Larry King Live*.

64. Nancy Gibbs et al., "Saving Face," *Time*, April 16, 2001.

65. Ibid.

66. Joshua Cooper Ramo, *Time*, March 12, 2001; Johanna McGeary, "Dubya Talks the Talk," *Time*, April 2, 2001.

67. Kagan and Kristol, *Present Dangers*.

68. Jonathan Clarke, "The Guns of 17th Street," *The National Interest*, no. 63 (Spring 2001).

69. Charles Krauthammer, "The Bush Doctrine," *Time*, March 5, 2001.

70. Frum and Perle, *An End to Evil*, chapter 8, "Friends and Foes," pp. 235–273.

71. Cf. Lerner, *American Civilization*, pp. 907ff.

72. Niall Ferguson, "American Terminator," *Newsweek, Issues 2004* (January 2004). See also Michael Ignatieff, November 20, 2003, quoted on www.theglobalist.com.

73. Cf. Max Boot, "American Imperialism? No Need to Run Away from Label," *U.S.A. Today*, May 6, 2003.

74. Irving Kristol, in L. Gordon Crovitz, ed., *The Fettered Presidency: Legal Constraints on the Executive Branch* (Washington, DC: AEI Press, 1989), quoted in Michael Lind, "A Tragedy of Errors," *The Nation*, February 23, 2004.

75. Tom DeLay, "Power and Principle," *Washington Times*, May 26, 1999.

76. Cf. Phillips, *American Dynasty,* p. 236; Meyrav Wurmser, "No More Excuses: Anti-American Leaders Stand to Be Accused," *Washington Times,* September 17, 2001; Zev Chafets, "Arab Americans Have to Choose," *Daily News* (New York), September 16, 2001.

77. Quoted in *Arab American Issues* 5, no. 6 (February 13, 2004).

78. Quoted in Ivins and Dubose, *Bushwhacked,* p. 268.

79. A. M. Rosenthal, "Winning the War on Terror," *Washington Times,* September 17, 2001; and "War Lessons," *Washington Times,* September 24, 2001.

80. Charles Krauthammer, "This War Is Different and Must Be Won," *Washington Post,* October 30, 2001; see also William Kristol, "The Wrong Strategy," *Washington Post,* October 30, 2001.

81. *The O'Reilly Factor,* Fox News, March 26, 2003, quoted in Peter Hart (with Fairness and Accuracy in Reporting), *The Oh Really Factor: Unspinning Fox News Channel's Bill O'Reilly* (New York: Seven Stories Press, 2003), p. 148.

82. Cf. Senator Trent Lott, "New World, New Friends," official press statement, March 21, 2003, at lott.senate.gov; Helle Dale, "The World according to Chirac," *Washington Times,* June 4, 2003; "Thanks, but No Thanks, France," *Washington Times* editorial, March 19, 2003; Paul Johnson, "Au Revoir, Petite France," *Wall Street Journal,* March 18, 2003; Holman Jenkins, "A War for France's Oil," *Wall Street Journal,* March 19, 2003.

83. Cf. the extraordinarily bitter and mendacious attack on France by Frum and Perle in *An End to Evil,* pp. 238–253; and "David Frum's Diary," *National Review Online,* February 19 and March 11, 2003. For French reporting of these charges, see for example Denis Lacorne, "*Les dessous de la francophobie,*" *Le Nouvel Observateur* (Paris), February 27– March 5, 2003.

84. Thomas L. Friedman, "Our War with France," *New York Times,* September 18, 2003; Justin Vaisse, "Bringing Out the Animal in Us," *Financial Times,* March 15, 2003. For a rare acknowledgment of the rationality of French objections to the Iraq War and their roots in the disastrous French experience in Algeria, see Paul Starobin, "The French Were Right," *National Journal,* November 7, 2003.

85. Stanley Hoffmann, "France, the United States and Iraq," *The Nation,* February 16, 2004.

86. For the weapons charge, see William Safire, *New York Times,* March 13, 2003; Bill Gertz, *Washington Times,* March 7, 2003; *Newsweek,* April 21, 2003. For the biological weapons charge, see "Four Nations Thought to Possess Smallpox," *Washington Post,* November 5, 2002. For the Ba'ath fugitive charge, see *Washington Times,* May 6, 2003. For an official French rebuttal of all these accusations, see the fact sheet issued by the French embassy in Washington on May 14, 2003, and published in the *Washington Post.*

87. Stanley Hoffmann, "The Great Pretender," *New York Review of Books,* May 28, 1987; see also "Haig's Revenge," *New York Review of Books,* May 31, 1984, by the same author.

88. Cf. Reuters: "Experts: U.S. Military Overstretched, Morale at Risk," *New York Times* on the Web, January 9, 2004; Lee Hockstader, "Army Stops Soldiers from Quitting: Orders Extend Enlistments to Curtail Troop Shortages," *Washington Post,* December 29, 2003.

89. Mark Thomson et al., "Four Key Lessons," *Time,* April 23, 2001. Cf. also Daalder and Lindsay, *America Unbound,* pp. 67–71.

90. Cf. Johann McGeary, "A Salesman on the Road," *Time,* July 30, 2001.

91. Evan Thomas and Roy Gutman, "See George. See George Learn Foreign Policy," *Newsweek,* June 18, 2001.

92. President Bush and Premier Wen Jiabao, Remarks to the Press, on www.whitehouse.gov, December 9, 2003.

93. John Ikenberry, "The End of the Neoconservative Moment," *Survival* 46, no. 1 (Spring 2004). See also Martin Walker, "And Now, the End of U.S. Unilateralism," *The Globalist*, March 5, 2004 (*www.theglobalist.com*).

94. Cf. Ikenberry, "America's Imperial Ambition."

95. Cf. David Frum and Richard Perle, "Beware the Soft-Line Ideologues," *Wall Street Journal*, January 12, 2004; for an early radical nationalist reaction to the change of official wind, see Michael Ledeen, "Grim Anniversary," *National Review Online*, September 11, 2003.

96. Cf. Leebaert, *Fifty Year Wound*, pp. 614–616, Johnson, *The Sorrows of Empire*, p. 57.

97. Ian Williams, "A Faithful Servant," *The Nation*, February 23, 2004.

98. NSS, 2002, p. 15.

99. Johnson, *The Sorrows of Empire*, p. 34.

100. "X" (George Kennan), "The Sources of Soviet Conduct," *Foreign Affairs*, no. 25 (July 1947).

101. Cf. the presidential speech on February 5, 2004, declaring that the United States had to go to war because it could not "take the word of a madman."

102. John J. Mearscheimer and Stephen M. Walt, "Iraq: An Unnecessary War," *Foreign Affairs* (January/February 2003).

103. Cf. Colonel H. R. McMaster, *Dereliction of Duty: Johnson, McNamara, the Joint Chiefs of Staff and the Lies that Led to Vietnam* (New York: HarperCollins, 1997).

104. For Shinseki's views, see Thom Shanker, "Retiring Army Chief Warns against Arrogance," *New York Times*, June 12, 2003. For the attacks on Shinseki, see Rowan Scarborough, "Wolfowitz Criticizes 'Suspect' Estimate of Occupation Force," *Washington Times*, February 28, 2003; Michael O'Hanlon, "History Will Get the Last Word: Rumsfeld and Shinseki's Tough Relationship," *Washington Times*, June 20, 2003.

105. Cf. Michael T. Klare, "America's Military Revolution: Cold War Government with No War to Fight," *Le Monde Diplomatique* (English edition), July 2001.

106. Cf. David M. Lampton and Kenneth Lieberthal, "Heading off the Next War," *Washington Post*, April 12, 2004.

Chapter Six

1. Amos Oz, addressing Israeli Zionist and fundamentalist extremists, in *In the Land of Israel*, trans. Maurie Goldberg-Bartura (New York: Harcourt Brace and Co., 1983), p. 139.

2. For the texts of the UN General Assembly resolutions and summaries of the debates, see www.un.org/News/Press/docs/2003.

3. Texts of the U.S. Senate and House resolutions of May 6, 2002, on the website of Democracy for the Middle East (DFME) at: http://www.broadscapeventures.com/weblog/dfme.

4. Zbigniew Brzezinski, speech on October 28, 2003, at the Conference on New American Strategies for Security and Peace, Washington, DC. See also his essay "Hegemonic Quicksand," *The National Interest* (Winter 2003/2004). For the history of such repeated U.S. votes on behalf of Israel in the face of overwhelming UN majorities, see Stephen Zunes, "Israel, the United States and the United Nations," *Tikkun* 18, no. 3 (May/June 2003).

5. Cf. Elizabeth Bumiller, "In Major Shift, Bush Endorses Sharon Plan," *New York Times*, April 15, 2004; for the European reaction, see Judy Dempsey, "EU Condemns Bush

Over Israel Stance," *Financial Times*, April 16, 2004, and the lead article in the same issue. For the background to the Bush decision, see Peter Slevin, "Delicate Maneuvers Led to U.S.-Israeli Stance," *Washington Post*, April 16, 2004.

6. Kerry quoted in Dan Balz, "Kerry Calls Bush's Iraq Policy Ineffective," *Washington Post*, April 19, 2004.

7. Cf. the editorials in the *New York Times* and *Washington Post* on April 16, 2004, and David Ignatius, "A Handshake That Doesn't Help Israel," *Washington Post*, April 16, 2004. For the Bush administration's calculation that the move would help Bush win Jewish American support in the elections, see Howard LaFranchi and Ben Lynfield, *Christian Science Monitor*, April 16, 2004, and Michael Tackett, "Political Gain from Bush Shift on Israel Seen as Questionable," *Chicago Tribune*, April 16, 2004.

8. Cf. the Zogby International Poll of Winter/Spring, 2002, cited in Daniel Brumberg, "Arab Public Opinion and U.S. Foreign Policy: A Complex Encounter," testimony to the Committee on Government Reform, Subcommittee on National Security, U.S. House of Representatives, October 8, 2002; the Pew Research Center for the People and the Press, Global Attitudes: 44-Nation Major Survey (2002); Report of the Advisory Group on Public Diplomacy for the Arab and Muslim World, chaired by Edward P. Djerejian, "Changing Minds, Winning Peace," submitted to the U.S. Congress, October 1, 2003; see also the Saudi polls of 2002 and 2003 cited by Shibley Telhami, "Polling and Politics in Riyadh," *New York Times*, March 3, 2002; and "Those Awkward Hearts and Minds," *The Economist*, April 1, 2003.

9. Quoted in James Blitz, "U.S.-Europe Splits 'Misguided and Dangerous,'" *Financial Times*, March 19, 2003; see also Blair's speech to the U.S. Congress, July 17, 2003. For a similar U.S. view, see Brzezinski, "Hegemonic Quicksand."

10. Issued by the European Council, December 2003; quoted in Ambassador Marc Otte (EU representative for the Middle East peace process), "Towards an EU Strategy for the Middle East," speech in London, March 1, 2004, published by World Security Network, www.worldsecuritynetwork.com, March 12, 2004.

11. Timothy Garton Ash, "Anti-Europeanism in America," *New York Review of Books*, February 13, 2003.

12. "President Bush Discusses Freedom in Iraq and Middle East," speech at National Endowment for Democracy, November 6, 2003, on www.whitehouse.gov; and the remarks by Vice President Dick Cheney to the World Economic Forum in Davos, January 24, 2004, on the same site.

13. Cf. Elisabeth Bumiller, "A Partner in Shaping an Assertive Foreign Policy," *New York Times*, January 7, 2004; Robert Kaiser, *Washington Post*, February 9, 2003.

14. M. J. Rosenberg, "The Full Court Pander," *Israel Policy Forum*, no. 163, January 9, 2004, at www.israelpolicyforum.org.

15. Robert D. Novak, "Politics vs. the Road Map," *Washington Post*, May 26, 2003; for Newt Gingrich's views, see his "Rogue State Department," *Foreign Policy* (July-August, 2003); see also Robert Kaiser, "Bush and Sharon Nearly Identical on Mideast Policy," *Washington Post*, February 9, 2003. Thomas Neumann, director of the Jewish Institute for National Security Affairs, quoted in the same article. Suskind, *Price of Loyalty*, pp. 70–76, 288–290; Philip H. Gordon, "Bush's Middle East Vision," *Survival* 45, no. 1 (Spring 2003); Elisabeth Bumiller, "A Partner in Shaping an Assertive Foreign Policy," *New York Times*, January 7, 2004.

16. Joseph C. Harsch, "Politics and Race," *Christian Science Monitor*, October 27, 1988.

17. Cf. "2003 Annual Survey of American Jewish Opinion," American Jewish Committee, November 25–December 11, 2003; Jewish Virtual Library for voting figures in presidential elections (www.us-isreal.org).

18. Roberta Feuerlicht, *The Fate of the Jews: A People Torn Between Israeli Power and Jewish Ethics* (New York: New York Times Book Co., 1983), p. 166. For worries in the Israeli lobby concerning the domestic U.S. agenda of the Christian fundamentalists and their partly anti-Semitic tradition, see Abraham Foxman, *Never Again? The Threat of the New Anti-Semitism* (San Francisco: HarperCollins, 2003), pp. 133–159; cf. also the study by the Anti-Defamation League, *The Religious Right: The Assault on Tolerance and Pluralism in America* (New York: ADL, 1994).

19. Cf. Joel Benin, "Tel Aviv's Influence on American Institutions," *Le Monde Diplomatique*, July 2003.

20. Richard Perle, Douglas Feith, et al., "A Clean Break: A New Strategy for Securing the Realm," report of 1996 prepared by the Institute for Advanced Strategic and Political Studies' Study Group on a New Israeli Strategy Toward 2000.

21. Elliott Abrams, "Israel and the 'Peace Process,'" in Kristol and Kagan, *Present Dangers*, pp. 219–240.

22. Cf. "The Olive Branch and the Gun," *The Nation* editorial, November 30, 1974; see also "UN: Shadow of a Gunman," *Newsweek*, November 25, 1974. For the recognition in the United States after 1991 of the Palestinians' existence as a people, see Kathleen Christison, *Perceptions of Palestine* (Berkeley: University of California Press, 2000), pp. 268ff.

23. New York Times/ABC poll of April 1978, cited in William J. Lanouette, "The Many Faces of the Jewish Lobby in America," *National Journal*, May 13, 1978.

24. Cf. the remarks by Irving Kristol on America's ideological duty to support Israel as a democratic state in "The Neoconservative Persuasion," *The Weekly Standard*, August 25, 2003.

25. Meron Benvenisti, "The Turning Point in Israel," *New York Review of Books*, October 13, 1983.

26. Mathew Engel, "Senior Republican Calls on Israel to Expel West Bank Arabs," *The Guardian* (London), May 4, 2002.

27. Tom DeLay, "Be Not Afraid," speech to Israeli Knesset, July 30, 2003, on www.nationalreview.com; for a similar statement by Senator Sam Brownback (R-Kansas), see "Brownback Meets with Israeli Prime Minister Sharon," July 31, 2003, at www.brownback.senate.gov. See the criticism of DeLay's words by Congressman Chris Bell, *Houston Chronicle*, August 1, 2003, quoted in IPFFriday, August 1, 2003, at www.isrealpolicyforum.org.

28. Cf. Hughes, *Myths America Lives By*, pp. 30–33, 110–123.

29. Fehrenbach, *Lone Star*, p. 712.

30. John Wayne, interview with *Playboy* magazine (May 1971), quoted in McBride, *John Ford*, p. 296; for the treatment of the Indians over the centuries in American school textbooks, see FitzGerald, *America Revised*, pp. 90–93.

31. Holmes, *Antiliberalism*, pp. 66–67.

32. Cf. Christison, *Perceptions of Palestine*, pp. 16–25, 103–104, and passim.

33. Senator James Inhofe, Senate Floor Statement, March 4, 2002; see also Chris Mitchell, "The Mountains of Israel," Christian World News, January 1, 2003, at www.cbn.com. Strikingly enough, the Jewish American liberal feminist Phyllis Chesler—a figure as utterly different from Senator Inhofe in other ways as can well be imagined—repeats exactly the same bases for Israel's claim to the land of Israel in her *The New Anti-Semitism: The Current Crisis and What We Must Do About It* (San Francisco: Jossey-Bass, 2003), p. 237.

34. Cf. Pat Robertson, "Why Evangelical Christians Support Israel," speech in Israel on December 17, 2003, on www.patrobertson.com.

35. Cf. the survey by Asher Arian, "Israeli Public Opinion on National Security, 2003," Tel Aviv University; Daniel Pipes, "Does Israel Need a Plan?" *Commentary* (February 2003); for support for the idea of "transfer" on the Right in Israel, see Ehud Sprinzak, *The Ascendance of Israel's Radical Right* (New York: Oxford University Press, 1991), pp. 172–176, 293–298; Ian Lustick, *For the Land and the Lord: Jewish Fundamentalism in Israel* (New York: Council on Foreign Relations, 1988), pp. 178–180.

36. Morris, "Survival of the Fittest." For a liberal Israeli attack on Morris's latest views, see Professor Adi Ophir, "Genocide Hides Behind Expulsion," *Counterpunch,* January 16, 2004 (originally published in *Ha'aretz*).

37. Lustick, *For the Land and the Lord,* p. vii.

38. Sprinzak, *The Ascendance of Israel's Radical Right,* p. 13; see also Bernard Avishai, *The Tragedy of Zionism: How Its Revolutionary Past Haunts Israeli Democracy* (New York: Helios Press, 2002), pp. 278–294; Almond et al., *Strong Religion.* For the background to these movements in Israeli society and political culture, see the vignettes in Oz, *In the Land of Israel.*

39. *Moral Majority Report,* March 14, 1980.

40. Sidney Blumenthal, "The Righteous Empire," *The New Republic,* October 22, 1984.

41. Lindsey, *The Everlasting Hatred,* pp. 59, 127–129; quote from the Book of Job 39: 5–8; Joan Peters, *From Time Immemorial* (New York: Harper & Row, 1984), quoted in Lindsey, pp. 127, 135–140, 149–158. For the immense audience for fundamentalist and millenarian TV shows, see Grace Halsell, *Prophecy and Politics: Militant Evangelists on the Road to Nuclear War* (Westport, CT: Lawrence Hill and Co., 1986), pp. 11–14.

42. Cf. www.hvk.org/articles/0203.

43. Mansfield, *Faith of George W. Bush,* p. 126. For the growing relationship between American evangelical fundamentalism and Israeli fundamentalism, see also Gershom Gorenberg, *The End of Days: Fundamentalism and the Struggle for the Temple Mount* (New York: The Free Press, 2000); Hassan Haddad and Donald Wagner, eds., *All in the Name of the Bible: Selected Essays on Israel and American Christian Fundamentalism* (Brattleborough, VT: Amana Books, 1986); Donald Wagner, "Short Fuse to Apocalypse?" *Sojourners* magazine (July–August 2003); Paul Boyer, *When Time Shall Be No More,* pp. 183–191, 203–08. For the historical origins of American evangelical support for Zionism, see Peter Grose, *Israel in the Mind of America* (New York: Alfred A. Knopf, 1984), pp. 4–15.

44. Colin Shindler, "Likud and the Christian Dispensationalists," *Israel Studies* 5, no. 1; Halsell, *Prophecy and Politics,* pp. 145–160; Gorenberg, *The End of Days,* pp. 238–240.

45. Julia Duin, "Israeli Pits U.S. Politics Against Road Map," *Washington Times,* August 18, 2003.

46. Rick Perlstein, "The Jesus Landing Pad," *Village Voice,* May 18, 2004; see also Donald E. Wagner, "The Alliance Between Fundamentalist Christians and the Pro-Israel Lobby," *Holy Land Studies* 2, no. 2 (March 2004).

47. Cf. Pew Center poll, *A Year After the Iraq War,* March 16, 2004; Bill Schneider, "Mideast 101: Evolution of U.S. Feelings Towards Israel," CNN, April 17, 2002.

48. For limitations on debate in the United States, see Paul Findley, *They Dare to Speak Out: People and Institutions Confront Israel's Lobby* (Westport, CT: Lawrence Hill and Co., 1985). For self-censorship in the Jewish community in the United States, see the remarks of General Mattiyahu Peled and Irving Howe, quoted in Feuerlicht, *Fate of the Jews,* pp. 280, 278–283.

49. Cf. I. F. Stone, "Confessions of a Jewish Dissident," in *Underground to Palestine and Reflections Thirty Years Later* (New York: Pantheon Books, 1978), pp. 229–240.

50. Quoted by Molly Moore, "Ex-Security Chiefs Turn on Sharon," *Washington Post*, November 15, 2003.

51. Avraham Burg, "A Failed Israeli Society is Collapsing: The End of Zionism?" *International Herald Tribune*, September 6, 2003. For moderate Palestinian and Arab views of this alternative, see Marwan Bishara, *Palestine/Israel: Peace or Apartheid* (New York: Zed Books, 2001), and Shibley Telhami, *The Stakes: America and the Middle East* (Boulder, CO: Westview Press, 2002); for an argument along similar lines by a British Jewish journalist who has always been in her words, "an ardent supporter of Israel," see Melanie Phillips, "Can Israel Disengage?" *Prospect* magazine (London), (February 2004).

52. Cf. the advice to the Israeli government and lobby from the public relations firm Wexner Analysis, "Israeli Communications Priorities, 2003"; the report is available from www.motherjones.com.

53. For a suggestion that Israeli settlement policy has in fact already wrecked the possibility of a two-state solution and that the only possible and just solution that remains is a unitary binational state, see Tony Judt, "Israel: The Alternative," *New York Review of Books*, October 23, 2003; for a rejoinder from a liberal partisan of Israel, see Leon Wieseltier, "What Is Not to Be Done," *New Republic*, October 27, 2003.

54. Cf. Stephen Zunes, *Tinderbox: U.S. Middle East Policy and the Roots of Terrorism* (Monroe, ME: Common Courage Press,, 2003), pp. 109–111; Shawn Twing, "A Comprehensive Guide to U.S. Aid to Israel," *Middle East Report* (May–August 1996); Dan Ackman, "Iraq Aid Will Dwarf U.S. Foreign Aid Budget," Forbes.com, August 9, 2003.

55. Cf. "Middle East Partnership Initiative: Arab Press Wary," Department of State, International Information Program, Foreign Media Reaction, December 20, 2002; see also Augustus Richard Norton, "America's Approach to the Middle East: Legacies, Questions and Possibilities," *Current History* 101, no. 651 (January 2002).

56. Contrast, for example, the discussion of this issue by Quentin Peel, "A Big Idea that Europe Won't Buy," *Financial Times*, February 5, 2004, with that of David Ignatius, "The Allies' Mindless Bickering," *Washington Post*, February 10, 2004.

57. I. L. Kenen, former chairman of the American Israel Public Affairs Committee (AIPAC), links both these assertions in his autobiographical profile of the Israeli lobby and its battles, *Israel's Defense Line: Her Friends and Foes in Washington* (Buffalo, NY: Prometheus Books, 1981), pp. 332 and passim.

58. Donald Rumsfeld, remarks on *Face the Nation*, CBS, September 23, 2001; for a populist media version of this, see editorial "An Alliance to Fit the Task," *New York Post*, September 23, 2001.

59. Correlli Barnett, *Engage the Enemy More Closely: The Royal Navy in the World War II* (London: W. W. Norton, 1991), pp. 378–389.

60. Cf. D. C. B. Lieven, *Russia and the Origins of the First World War* (London: Macmillan, 1983), pp. 40–43, 139–151.

61. Hoffmann, "The High and the Mighty."

62. Quoted in Joyce R. Starr, *Kissing Through Glass: The Invisible Shield Between Americans and Israelis* (Chicago: Contemporary Books, 1990), p. 225.

63. Conrad Cherry, ed., *God's New Israel: Religious Interpretations of American Destiny* (Chapel Hill: University of North Carolina Press, 1998), epigraph. See also Samuel Langdon, "The Republic of the Israelites an Example to the American States," ibid., pp. 93–105.

64. For the combination of religious, cultural and ideological sympathy in the United States for the Zionist movement, see Grose, *Israel in the Mind of America*; for the representative views of Justice Oliver Wendell Holmes, see Edmund Wilson, *Patriotic Gore*, pp. 784–785.

65. Quoted in Halsell, *Prophecy and Politics*, pp. 113–114.

66. Secretary Rumsfeld town hall meeting, August 6, 2002, at www.defenselink.mil.

67. Cf. David Weisburg with Vered Vinitzky, "Vigilantism as Rational Social Control: The Case of the Gush Emunim Settlers," in Myron J. Aronoff, ed., *Cross Currents in Israeli Culture and Politics* (New Brunswick: Transaction Books, 1984), pp. 69–88.

68. Amos Elon, *The Israelis: Founders and Sons* (New York: Penguin, 1983), pp. 232–235; David Hirst, *The Gun and the Olive Branch: The Roots of Violence in the Middle East* (London: Faber and Faber, 1977), pp. 183–184; for a portrait of a similar (unnamed) figure and his views concerning Israeli policy toward the Palestinians and Arabs, see Amos Oz, "The Tender Among You, and Very Delicate," in *In the Land of Israel*, pp. 85–100. For the comparison with "Indian fighters," see also Uri Avnery, *Israel Without Zionism* (New York: Collier Books, 1971). For the tradition of freelance and vigilante violence on the American frontier, see Joe B. Franz, "The Frontier Tradition: An Invitation to Violence," in Hugh Davis Graham and Ted Gurr, eds., *Violence in America: Historical and Comparative Perspectives* (New York: Bantam Books, 1969), pp. 127–153; H. Jon Rosenbaum and Peter C. Sederberg, "Vigilantism: An Analysis of Establishment Violence," *Comparative Politics* 6, no. 4 (July 1974).

69. Meron Benvenisti, "The Turning Point in Israel," *New York Review of Books*, October 13, 1983.

70. Leon Uris, *Exodus* (New York: Bantam Books, 1959). The conflation of images of the American and Israeli settler in American iconography is rather amusingly illustrated by the cover, showing the Star of David and the ship *Exodus* flanked by two blond, blue-eyed, square-jawed supposed Jewish fighters in Palestine—the very image of American pioneers from a Hollywood B-movie. See also Christison, *Perceptions of Palestine*, pp. 103–104.

71. Cf. Tony Smith, *Foreign Attachments: The Power of Ethnic Groups in the Making of American Foreign Policy* (Cambridge, MA: Harvard University Press, 2000), pp. 16ff; Mitchell Geoffrey Bard, *The Water's Edge and Beyond: Defining the Limits to Domestic Influence on U.S. Middle East Policy* (New Brunswick, NJ: Transaction Publishers, 1991).

72. Cf. Lind, "The Israel Lobby."

73. For the philosophy and views of Ahad Ha'am, see Shlomo Avineri, *The Making of Modern Zionism: The Intellectual Origins of the Jewish State* (New York: Basic Books, 1981), pp. 112–124; for Ha'am's views on Jewish treatment of the Arab population of Palestine, see Feuerlicht, *Fate of the Jews*, pp. 225–226.

74. Nahum Goldmann, *Autobiography: Sixty Years of Jewish Life*, trans. Helen Sebba (New York: Holt, Rinehart and Winston, 1969), pp. 332–333.

75. For the centrality of the divine presence and his worship to the Jewish diaspora communities and traditions, see Rabbi Jonathan Sacks, *A Letter in the Scroll: Understanding our Jewish Identity and Exploring the Legacy of the World's Oldest Religion* (New York: Simon and Schuster, 2000), pp. 122–180; Howe, *World of Our Fathers*, pp. 11–14.

76. *Jewish Observer and Middle East Review*, June 10, 1977. Quoted in Feuerlicht, *Fate of the Jews*, p. 170; Howe, *World of Our Fathers*, p. 628; Cf. also Goldmann, *Autobiography*, p. 315.

77. Marty, *Pilgrims*, pp. 462–463; see also Wald, *Religion and Politics in the United States*, p. 153.

78. Cf. Carlton J. H. Hayes, *Nationalism: A Religion* (New York: Macmillan, 1960); Hans Kohn, *The Idea of Nationalism* (New York: Macmillan, 1945), pp. 574ff.

79. Cf. Oz, *In the Land of Israel*.

80. Concerning Israel's overall achievements as a state and society—and, like him, leaving aside for the moment Israel's record in the occupied territories—I would endorse the glowing assessment by Professor Amnon Rubenstein quoted in Alan

Dershowitz, *The Case for Israel* (Hoboken, NJ: John Wiley & Sons, 2003), p. 225; and indeed expressed, albeit in more wry and ambiguous terms, in Amos Elon's portrait of Israel.

81. Goldmann, *Autobiography*, pp. 299–300.

82. Amos Oz, "From Jerusalem to Cairo: Escaping from the Shadow of the Past," in *Israel, Palestine and Peace: Essays* (New York: Harcourt, Brace and Co., 1994), pp. 36–37.

83. Hannah Arendt, "Zionism Reconsidered," *Menorah Journal* 33, no. 2 (Autumn 1945): 213–214.

84. Abba Eban, *Personal Witness: Israel Through My Eyes* (New York: Putnam, 1992), pp. 49–50.

85. Fehrenbach, *Lone Star*, p. 529.

86. Cf. *New York Times*, June 21, 1979; Feuerlicht, *Fate of the Jews*, p. 174.

87. Saul Bellow, *To Jerusalem and Back: A Personal Account* (New York: Viking, 1976), pp. 158, 160–163.

88. Dershowitz, *Case for Israel*, p. 60; for the amalgamation of the Palestinians and Nazis in Israeli and Israeli lobby rhetoric, see Christison, *Perceptions of Palestine*, pp. 119ff. Concerning the terrible results of such assumptions of collective guilt, see, for example, Tom Friedman on how the common Israeli elision of the words "Palestinian" and "terrorist" led to indifference to the Sabra and Shatila massacres, in *From Beirut to Jerusalem* (New York: Farrar Straus Giroux, 1989), p. 163. For a warning of this risk in the American war on terrorism, cf. William Pfaff, "As Captor, the United States Risks Dehumanizing Itself," *International Herald Tribune*, January 30, 2002.

89. Quoted in Nahum Goldmann, *The Jewish Paradox* (New York: Grosset and Dunlap, 1978), p. 99.

90. Cf. Dershowitz, *Case for Israel*, pp. 78–90.

91. Benny Morris, *The Birth of the Palestinian Refugee Problem, 1947–49* (New York: Cambridge University Press, 1989), and the account of the 1948 conflict in his *Righteous Victims: A History of the Zionist-Arab Conflict, 1881–2001* (New York: Random House, 1999), pp. 191–258. For a discussion of his work and this issue by Israeli and Palestinian scholars, see the essays in Eugene L. Rogan and Avi Shlaim, eds., *The War for Palestine: Rewriting the History of 1948* (Cambridge: Cambridge University Press, 2001). For earlier descriptions of this issue, see the Israeli reports and eyewitness accounts of the expulsions and the terrorization and oppression of the Palestinian population quoted in David Hirst, *The Gun and the Olive Branch: The Roots of Violence in the Middle East* (London: Faber and Faber, 1977), pp. 136–43; Uri Avnery, *Israel Without Zionism* (New York: Collier Books, 1971), p. 223 ff; Feuerlicht, *Fate of the Jews*, pp. 242–267; and Edward Said, *The Question of Palestine* (New York: Times Books, 1979), pp. xxxvii, 83-114.

92. Benny Morris interviewed by Ari Shavit, "Survival of the Fittest," *Ha'aretz*, January 9, 2004.

93. Cf. Anatol Lieven, "Divide and Survive," *Prospect* magazine (London), (May 1999).

94. Cf. Anatol Lieven, "Peace Cannot Be Fudged," *Financial Times* (London), September 10, 2003.

95. For a recent denial of the expulsions coupled with an accusation that talking about this had weakened the national will of Israeli liberal intellectuals and contributed to their futile search for peace in the 1990s, see Efraim Karsh, "Revisiting Israel's 'Original Sin': The Strange Case of Benny Morris," *Commentary* 116 no. 2 (September 2003).

96. *Sunday Times*, June 15, 1969; quoted in Hirst, *Gun and the Olive Branch*, p. 264. The important point is not, however, whether there was a fully self-conscious Palestinian nationality in 1948—which is indeed a highly debatable question. The point is that in 1948 there were a majority of people in Palestine who were well aware that they

were different from and threatened by the Jews. By 1969 it was already obviously wrong to deny that the Palestinians had developed a clear national identity. In 2004 this would be madness. Whatever they were in 1948, today the Palestinians are undeniably a nation.

97. Quoted in Lanouette, "The Many Faces of the Jewish Lobby in America," *National Journal*, May 13, 1978.

98. For example, Shlomo Avineri's magisterial study of the intellectual bases of Zionism (*Making of Modern Zionism*) contains no reference to "Palestinians." The index entry for Arabs under "Palestine" reads: "Palestine: Arab problem in."

99. Said, *Question of Palestine*, p. 51.

100. Croly, *Promise of American Life*, p. 75; for a kind of distillation of the Israeli lobby's presentation of the Israeli-Palestinian conflict—with no mention either of the expulsions of 1948 or of any Israeli atrocity—see Phyllis Chesler, "A Brief History of Arab Attacks Against Israel, 1908–1970s," in her *New Anti-Semitism*, pp. 44–52.

101. Cf. Michael Lind, "The Israel Lobby," *Prospect* magazine (London), April 2002.

102. Arnaud de Bochgrave, "Democracy in the Middle East," *Washington Times*, March 5, 2004.

103. Cf. Thomas L. Friedman, "An Intriguing Signal from the Saudi Crown Prince," *New York Times*, February 17, 2002; editorial, "A Peace Impulse Worth Pursuing," *New York Times*, February 21, 2002; editorial, "Support for the Saudi Initiative," *New York Times*, February 28, 2002.

104. Cf. "Israel and the Occupied Territories: Country Report on Human Rights Practices—2003," released by the Bureau of Democracy, Human Rights and Labor, U.S. Department of State, February 25, 2004, at www.state.gov.

105. For the establishment of the settlements and their role in preventing full diplomatic exploitation of the Sadat initiative, see Avishai, *Tragedy of Zionism*, pp. 272–296; see also Meron Benvenisti, *Intimate Enemies: Jews and Arabs in a Shared Land* (Berkeley: University of California Press, 1995), pp. 30–37, 52–71; Bernard Wasserstein, *Israel and Palestine: Why They Fight and Can They Stop?* (London: Profile, 2003).

106. Cf. William Safire, "Post-Oslo Mideast," *New York Times*, June 27, 2002; editorial, "Those Arab Peacemakers," *Washington Times*, May 20, 2002; Victor Davis Hanson, "Our Enemies, the Saudis," *Commentary* (July-August 2002); for liberal Jewish American responses in favor of the Saudi offer, see Richard Cohen, "Kristol's Unwelcome Message," *Washington Post*, June 11, 2002; Henry Siegman, "Will Israel Take a Chance?" *New York Times*, February 21, 2002.

107. Daniel Pipes, "Does Israel Need a Plan?," *Commentary*, 115 no. 2 (February 2003); Yaacov Lozowick, *Right to Exist: A Moral Defense of Israel's Wars* (New York: Doubleday, 2003); Cf. also Daniel Ayalon (Israeli ambassador to the United States), "Israel's Right to be Israel," *Washington Post*, August 24, 2003.

108. Henry Siegman, "Israel: The Threat from Within," *New York Review of Books*, February 26, 2004; cf. also Oz, "Whose Holy Land?" in *Israel, Palestine and Peace*, p. 91.

109. Elon, *Founders and Sons*, p. xiii.

110. Cf. Benvenisti, "Turning Point."

111. For the background to the failure of the negotiations in 2000 and 2001, see the debate in the *New York Review of Books* between various participants in the talks: Robert Malley and Hussein Agha, "Camp David: the Tragedy of Errors," August 9, 2001; the exchange of letters with Dennis Ross and Gidi Grinstein in the same issue; Benny Morris's interview with Ehud Barak, *New York Review of Books*, June 13, 2002; Malley and Agha's reply in the same issue, and the further exchange on June 27, 2002. For the role of settlement expansion in the 1990s in undermining Palestinian faith in the peace process, see Christison, *Perceptions of Palestine*, pp. 300ff. See also Deborah

Sontag, "Quest for Middle East Peace: How and Why It Failed," *New York Times*, July 26, 2001.

112. Manfred Gerstenfeld, "Anti-Semitism: Integral to European Culture," in the series "Post Holocaust and Anti-Semitism," no. 19, April 1, 2004, published by the Jerusalem Center for Public Affairs; cf. also Nidra Poller, "Betrayed by Europe: An Expatriate's Lament," *Commentary* (March 2004); Marc Strauss, "The New Face of Anti-Semitism," *Foreign Policy* (November/December 2003).

113. Quoted in Dershowitz, *Case for Israel*, p. 232.

114. Pew Research Center public opinion survey of March 2003, cited in Foxman, *Never Again?* p. 36.

115. Foxman, *Never Again?* p. 4.

116. Chesler, *New Anti-Semitism*, p. 3

117. Cf. George Thomas, "Does Hate Against Jews Threaten Us All?" *Christian World News*, August 2, 2002, at www.cbn.com; and Marney Blom, "Christians and Jews, Arm-in-Arm Against Hate and Violence," June 28, 2002, at the same site.

118. Gabriel Schoenfeld, "Israel and the Anti-Semites," *Commentary* 113, no. 6 (June 2002); see also Paul Berman, *Terror and Liberalism* (New York: W. W. Norton, 2003), pp. 166ff, 186–189; Hillel Halkin, "The Return of Anti-Semitism," *Commentary* 113, no. 2 (February 2002); Robert S. Wistrich, "The Old-New Anti-Semitism," *National Interest*, no. 72 (Summer 2003); Edgar Bronfman and Cobi Benatoff, "Is Darkness Falling on Europe Again?" *Financial Times*, February 19, 2004; Ruth R. Wisse, "Israel on Campus," *Wall Street Journal*, December 13, 2002.

119. Lipset, *American Exceptionalism*, p. 172.

120. Howe, *World of Our Fathers*, pp. 630–632; see also Roberta Feuerlicht's depressing account of how the Holocaust surfaced as a reason given for Jewish fears of Blacks during discussions with Blacks in New York in the 1970s, to the stupefaction and fury of moderate Black representatives: Feuerlicht, *Fate of the Jews*, pp. 206–215.

121. Irving Kristol, "The Political Dilemma of American Jews," *Commentary* (July 1984); see also Lind, *Up From Conservatism*, pp. 99–120; Bennett, *Party of Fear*, pp. 423–425.

122. Nathan Perlmutter, *The Real Anti-Semitism in America*, quoted in Halsell, *Prophecy and Politics*, pp. 154–155; Cf. also Shindler, *Likud and the Christian Fundamentalists*; and David Frum, *Dead Right*, pp. 159–173.

123. Cf. the booklet issued by the America Israel Public Affairs Committee (AIPAC): Jonathan S. Kessler and Jeff Schwaber, *The AIPAC College Guide: Exposing the Anti-Israel Campaign on Campus*, AIPAC Papers on U.S.-Israel Relations, no. 7, 1984.

124. For an excoriating and often justified critique of left-wing attacks on Israel during the Cold War, see Conor Cruise O'Brien, *The Siege: The Saga of Israel and Zionism* (New York: Touchstone Books, 1987).

125. Cf. David Corn, "The Banning of Rabbi Lerner," at thenation.com, February 10, 2003; Michael Lerner, "The Antiwar Anti-Semites," *Wall Street Journal*, February 12, 2003; David Friedman, "Democracy and the Peace Movement; see also the response by Joel Kovel, "Anti-Semitism on the Left and the Special Status of Israel," *Tikkun* 18, no. 3 (May/June 2003).

126. Cf. Joshua Micah Marshall, "The Orwell Temptation: Are Intellectuals Overthinking the Middle East?" *Washington Monthly* (May 2003).

127. For the use of "straw men" by propagandists for the Israel lobby, see Dershowitz, *The Case for Israel*. This book is structured around a variety of propositions, some of them apparently carefully selected for the ease with which they can be refuted (i.e., "Did Israel Start the Six-Day War?" and "Is Israel the Prime Human Rights Violator in the World?"). Of these propositions, twelve are by Edward Said and eight by Noam Chomsky. One is by Leonid Brezhnev—not, as far as I am aware, one of the leading

voices today in the debate over Israel and Palestine. Apart from four by the Israeli peace activist Ilan Pappe, none is by an Israeli. Nowhere do the names of Amos Oz, Meron Benvenisti, or any of the other centrist liberal critics of the Israeli occupation of the West Bank and Gaza Strip appear. Although one proposition is given to Rabbi Michael Lerner, none is given to other leading American liberal critics of unconditional U.S. support for Israel, as represented in the *New York Review of Books,* for example—people who, like Oz in Israel, are strong supporters of Israel's right to exist and defend itself within the borders of 1967. The question of Palestinian rejection of the Barak-Clinton peace proposals is put in stark black-and-white terms ("Was Arafat right in turning down the Barak-Clinton peace proposal?") and the question given to Chomsky, not to Ambassador Robert Malley or the other U.S. and Israeli moderates who have sought to elucidate this question. The overall effect is, of course, to create an impression of hysterical malignance toward Israel, unqualified by support or sympathy. This is the approach of a ruthless advocate in a court; whether it is appropriate behavior for a professor of law at one of America's leading universities is another matter.

128. Akiva Eldar, "From Refuge for Jews to Danger for Jews," *Ha'aretz,* November 3, 2003. See also M. J. Rosenberg, "Confusing Criticism with Anti-Semitism," *Israel Policy Forum,* February 6, 2004; Judith Butler, "No, It's Not Anti-Semitic," *London Review of Books,* August 21, 2003; Henry Siegman, "If Israel's Policies Are Unjust, We Should Say So," *Financial Times,* February 10, 2004.

129. Cf. Romano Prodi (president of the EU Commission) in the *Financial Times,* February 19, 2004.

130. Brian Klug, "The Collective Jew: Israel and the New Antisemitism," *Patterns of Prejudice* 37, no. 2 (June 2003); and "The Myth of the New Anti-Semitism," *The Nation,* February 2, 2004.

131. Cf. Chesler, *New Anti-Semitism,* p. 33; see also Jerome Chanes, *A Dark Side of History: Anti-Semitism Through the Ages* (New York: Anti-Defamation League, 2000).

132. The notion of an eternal, essentially unchanging anti-Semitism has been called fundamental to much of the philosophy of Zionism and long predates the latest Israeli-Palestinian conflict and its repercussions; cf. Arendt, "Zionism Reconsidered," p. 225; Howe, *World of Our Fathers,* p. 25; Halsell, *Prophecy and Politics,* pp. 131ff.

133. For balanced overviews of the debate on democratization and the war against terrorism, see Thomas Carothers, "Democracy: Terrorism's Uncertain Antidote," *Current History* (December 2003); and Carothers, "Is Gradualism Possible? Choosing a Strategy for Promoting Democracy in the Middle East," Working Paper no. 39 (June 2003), Carnegie Endowment for International Peace.

134. Cf. Gerard Baker on John Kerry's foreign policy ideas, *Financial Times* (London), March 12, 2004.

135. Philip Gordon, while adopting a tone of reasonable skepticism concerning Bush administration rhetoric, also declares that something does indeed have to change: "Bush's Middle East Vision," *Survival* 45, no. 1 (Spring 2003).

136. Cf. Michael Ledeen, "War on Terror Won't End in Baghdad," *Wall Street Journal,* September 4, 2002.

137. Paul Berman, *Terror and Liberalism* (New York: W. W. Norton, 2002), pp. 128–132, 189; for a similar omission, see Cheryl Benard, "Civil Democratic Islam: Partners, Resources and Strategies," RAND National Security Research Division, 2003.

138. Cf. Boot, "George W. Bush: The 'W' Stands for Woodrow"; David Ignatius, "Wilsonian Course for War," *Washington Post,* August 30, 2002; Michael Ledeen, "Our Revenge: Turning Tyrannies into Democracies," *New York Sun,* September 12, 2002; editorial, "No Exceptions," *Washington Post,* December 29, 2002; Fouad Ajami, "If Not Now, When?" and Kenneth Pollack and Daniel Byman, "Democracy as Realism," *Prospect* magazine (London), (April 2003); Condoleezza Rice, interview with James Harding

and Richard Wolfe, *Financial Times*, September 23, 2002, and "Transforming the Middle East," *Washington Post*, August 7, 2003; George Melloan, "Protecting Human Rights Is a Valid Foreign Policy Goal," *Wall Street Journal* (Global View), June 10, 2003; "A Wilsonian Call for Freedom," *Washington Times* editorial, November 7, 2003.

139. Marina Ottaway, "Promoting Democracy in the Middle East: The Problem of U.S. Credibility," Working Paper no. 35 (March 2003), Carnegie Endowment for International Peace. See also Bruce Stokes and Mary McIntosh, "How They See Us," *National Journal*, December 21, 2002; and "The United States Image in the Islamic World," transcript of a discussion at Georgetown University, Washington, DC, February 19, 2002, at cf.dev.georgetown.edu/sfs/programs/isd/research_Islamic.

140. Cf. Anatol Lieven, "Islam and America," *Prospect* magazine (London), October, 2001.

141. Cf. Liah Greenfeld, *The Spirit of Capitalism: Nationalism and Economic Growth* (Cambridge, MA: Harvard University Press, 2003).

142. Cf. Anatol Lieven, "Lessons for Bush's Mideast Vision," *Financial Times*, March 1, 2004.

143. For a sketch of the attempts by Pipes, Berman, and others to create this parallel, see John Lloyd, "Radical Islam Sees Itself Just as Communism Did—in a Battle with a Hostile World," *Financial Times*, January 11, 2003; and Joshua Micah Marshall, "The Orwell Temptation: Are Intellectuals Overthinking the Middle East?" *Washington Monthly* (May 2003).

144. For a critique of the Eisenhower administration's failure to understand the importance of nationalism, see Robert J. McMahon, "Eisenhower and Third World Nationalism: A Critique of the Revisionists," *Political Science Quarterly* 101, no. 3 (1986).

145. Cf. Noah Feldman, *After Jihad: America and the Struggle for Islamic Democracy* (New York: Farrar, Straus and Giroux, 2003).

146. Cf. Charles Glass, *Tribes with Flags: A Dangerous Passage Through the Chaos of the Middle East* (Boston: Atlantic Monthly Press, 1991).

147. Ottaway, *Promoting Democracy*; see also "Middle East Partnership Initiative: Arab Press Wary," Department of State, International Information Program, Foreign Media Reaction, December 20, 2002.

148. The phrase is from "A Joint Plan to Help the Greater Middle East," by a U.S.-European group including Urban Ahlin and Ronald Asmus.

149. Cf. Feith et al., "A Clean Break"; and an analysis of this approach by Arnaud de Borchgrave, "Democracy in the Middle East," *Washington Times*, March 5, 2004.

150. Frank Gaffney, address to the 57th Annual Conference of the Middle East Institute, Washington, DC, on October 23, 2003; for a version of the same argument, see Michael Ledeen, "Polling the Palestinians," *Jerusalem Post*, August 23, 2002.

151. Cf. Hersh, "The Gray Zone"; Mark Danner, "The Logic of Torture," *New York Review of Books*, June 24, 2004; for the original analysis, see Raphael Patai, *The Arab Mind*, rev. ed. (New York: Hatherleigh Press, 2002), especially pp. 126–151. For an earlier article on this subject, see my "A Second Chance to Learn the Lesson of Vietnam," *Financial Times* (London), June 8, 2004.

152. L. B. Namier, *1848: The Revolution of the Intellectuals* (London: British Academy, 1944).

Conclusion

1. Figures in *Economic Report of the President*, Council of Economic Advisers, cited in Jeff Madrick, "How New Is the New Economy?" *New York Review of Books*, September 23, 1999.

2. Frank Levy, *The New Dollars and Dreams: American Incomes and Economic Change* (New York: Russell Sage Foundation Publications, 1999), cited in Madrick, "New Economy."

3. Cf. "The Wal-Martization of America," *New York Times* (editorial), November 15, 2003.

4. Cf. Alan Ryan, "Call Me Mister," *New York Review of Books,* February 27, 2003.

5. Cf. Clair Brown, *American Standards of Living, 1918–1988* (New York: Blackwell, 2002); Kevin Phillips, *Boiling Point: Democrats, Republicans and the Decline of Middle Class Prosperity* (New York: HarperCollins, 1994); Madrick, "How New Is the New Economy?; Michael Head, "The New, Ruthless Economy," *New York Review of Books,* February 29, 1996.

6. Cf. Stephanine Strom, "For Middle Class, Health Care Becomes a Luxury," *New York Times,* November 16, 2003.

7. Hans Fallada, *Kleiner Mann—was nun?* (Hamburg: Rowohlt Verlag, 1976 [rpt]).

8. Frank, *What's the Matter with Kansas? How Conservatives Won the Heart of America* (New York: Metropolitan Books, 2004).

9. Cf. Bellah, *Broken Covenant,* p. xv.

Index